D0359972

The Hidden
History of
America at War

## Also by Kenneth C. Davis

# The Hidden History of America at War

## Untold Tales from Yorktown to Fallujah

&rarr;&gt;–&lt;–

## Kenneth C. Davis

hachette
BOOKS
*New York*

Copyright © 2015 Kenneth C. Davis

All rights reserved. In accordance with the U.S. Copyright Act of 1976, the scanning, upload-ing, and electronic sharing of any part of this book without the permission of the publisher constitutes unlawful piracy and theft of the author's intellectual property. If you would like to use material from the book (other than for review purposes), prior written permission must be obtained by contacting the publisher at permissions@hbgusa.com. Thank you for your support of the author's rights.

Hachette Books
Hachette Book Group
1290 Avenue of the Americas
New York, NY 10104

www.HachetteBookGroup.com

Printed in the United States of America

RRD-C

First Edition: May 2015

10 9 8 7 6 5 4 3 2 1

Hachette Books is a division of Hachette Book Group, Inc.

The publisher is not responsible for websites (or their content) that are not owned by the publisher.

Library of Congress Cataloging-in-Publication Data

Davis, Kenneth C.
   The hidden history of America at war: untold tales from Yorktown to Fallujah / Kenneth C. Davis. — First edition.
      pages cm
   Includes bibliographical references and index.
   ISBN 978-1-4013-2410-0 (hardcover) — ISBN 978-1-4789-0376-5 (audio download) — ISBN 978-1-4013-3078-1 (ebook)  1. United States—History, Military.  2. Battles—United States—History.  3. Soldiers—United States—History.  4. Civilians in war—United States—History.  5 Civil-military relations—United States—History.  6. War and society—United States—History.  7. Social change—United States—History.  8. United States—Social conditions.  9. United States—Military policy.  I. Title.
   E181.D26 2015
   355.020973—dc23
                                                                                    2014024942

We are met on a great battlefield of that war. We have come to dedicate a portion of that field, as a final resting place for those who gave their lives that the nation might live. It is altogether fitting and proper that we should do this.

But, in a larger sense, we cannot dedicate—we cannot consecrate—we cannot hallow—this ground. The brave men, living and dead, who struggled here have consecrated it far above our poor power to add or detract.

—*Abraham Lincoln (November 19, 1863)*

*Dedicated to those who*
*"gave the last full measure of devotion"*

# Contents

# Introduction

"It is sweet and honorable to die for one's country."
(*Dulce et decorum est pro patria mori.*)
—*Horace,* Odes *(23 BC)*

"There never was a good war or a bad peace."
—*Benjamin Franklin (September 11, 1783)*

"War is not merely a political act, but also a political instrument, a continuation of political relations, a carrying out of the same by other means."[1]
—*Karl von Clausewitz (1833)*

"War is an ugly thing, but not the ugliest of things: the decayed and degraded state of moral and patriotic feeling which thinks that nothing is worth a war, is much worse."
—*John Stuart Mill (February 1862)*

"War is barbarism. . . . It is only for those who have neither fired a shot nor heard the shrieks and groans of the wounded who cry aloud for blood, more vengeance, more desolation. War is hell."
—*William Tecumseh Sherman (June 19, 1879)*

War stories. We have been telling them for a very long time. You can start with Bible tales of Egyptians drowning in their chariots in the sea or a shepherd boy with a slingshot killing a giant, or the epic siege of Troy in Homer's *Iliad*. Move on to the American classics—from James Fenimore Cooper to *The Red Badge of Courage*, Hemingway, *The Killer Angels*, and *The Things They Carried*. Then watch all the way through Hollywood's long love affair with wartime, from *The Birth of a Nation* to *Saving Private Ryan*, *Apocalypse Now*, *Glory*, and *The Hurt Locker*. Tales of men in combat are at the heart of our literature, culture, history, and mythology.

Unfortunately, many war stories have been told and retold so many times—repackaged and often heavily embellished along the way—that the truth behind them has been whitewashed and airbrushed, buried under a thick gloss of romanticism, lyricism, patriotic fervor, and propaganda. As Walt Whitman, mournful observer of America's Civil War, once wrote, "The real war will never get in the books."[2]

My first taste of war and battle came in the backyard of my boyhood suburban home. The lawn and woods behind my house in Mount Vernon, New York, filled in for the Alamo, Gettysburg, and Normandy. Weighted down by a small armory's worth of toy weaponry, my friends and I did regular battle with Santa Anna's Mexicans, the Johnny Rebs, and the Nazis. Then we went up the street to the playground and played some stickball.

This was the late fifties and early sixties. John Wayne, Audie Murphy, and Charlton Heston were comfortably fixed in the pantheon of America's war gods. War, as we knew it, was glorious, exciting, fun, and harmless. And soldiers were revered as tough guys with soft hearts.

My late father was one of them. He had served in North Africa and Italy during World War II and, along with several of my uncles, was one of those "Greatest Generation" veterans. These were the men, we had learned growing up, who had been willing to sacrifice everything for their country and each other. Ordinary "citizen soldiers," they were the noble, patriotic, average Joes who had whipped the Nazis and the Japanese.

My father rarely spoke of his wartime experiences—a silence I now greatly regret. I had never really asked, "What did you do in the war, Daddy?" But I could tell from the mention of a glorious sunrise glimpsed in North Africa or the few choice words in Italian, as well as the mean meatball recipe he had brought home, that his wartime experiences had mattered deeply to him. I still believe that his army years were among his happiest. I never knew for sure.

Instead, we went to movies like *The Guns of Navarone* and *The Longest Day*, sat together to watch television shows like *Combat* and *The Rat Patrol*, and went camping with army surplus sleeping bags and tents to places like Fort Ticonderoga in upstate New York, or Gettysburg, Pennsylvania. I still have my souvenir of that latter visit—a wooden toy revolver stamped with the dates of the battle: July 1–3, 1863. I also possess a powerful recollection of standing on that battlefield—Lincoln's "hallowed ground"—and feeling that something extraordinary had happened there.

But then a switch was thrown. Within a few years, my playlist had a new sound. The folk songs and antiwar anthems of Bob Dylan and Richie Havens spoke to me far more convincingly than the "Fighting soldiers from the skies" elegized in Barry Sadler's 1966 hit song "Ballad of the Green Berets."

By 1968, the answer blowing in the wind meant that John Wayne's jingoistic bravado was no longer box-office boffo. *The Green Berets*, the movie inspired by Sadler's tune, was described by a *New York Times* critic as "so unspeakable, so stupid, so rotten and false in every detail that it passes through being fun, through being funny, through being camp, through everything and becomes an invitation to grieve."[3]

My reading list had changed, too. *Johnny Tremain*—the book that brought the American Revolution alive for me—was replaced by *Johnny Got His Gun*, Dalton Trumbo's bleak story of a quadriplegic victim of World War I. This was more than shifting literary tastes. Radical changes were reshaping mass media and the political landscape. Late in February 1968, when legendary television newsman Walter Cronkite, fresh from a reporting trip to Vietnam, told the country, "We are mired in stalemate," there was no longer any doubt that America had undergone a seismic shift. The times, they were a-changing.

The subsequent withdrawal of President Lyndon B. Johnson from the 1968 presidential campaign, followed by the assassinations of Martin Luther King Jr. and Robert F. Kennedy, continued the violent tremors that were reshaping American attitudes during Vietnam. Racial unrest was turning bloodier, and the antiwar movement and the response to it were growing more violent, culminating at the Democratic National Convention in Chicago as protestors, journalists, and even some delegates were bludgeoned by Chicago cops in what was later called a "police riot." In that fateful summer of 1968, I had also begun to contemplate the reality of going to war.

I turned fourteen in that watershed year. And I had come to see that war was no longer fun and games in the backyard or sixty minutes of excitement on network television. And it was certainly not a gallant but doomed charge across a Pennsylvania wheat field in the summer sun. After the killings of antiwar protestors by National Guard troops at both Kent State University in Ohio and Jackson State in Mississippi in May 1970, a broad sense of an unraveling America only deepened.

When the government announced an end to most draft deferments and a shift to a lottery system beginning with the draft class of 1970, I soon got as close as I would ever come to military service. As high school graduation neared, with my eighteenth birthday and Selective Service registration upon me, I took an air force pre-enlistment exam. Thinking that the air force was a palatable alternative to a low lottery draft number, I was attempting to exercise a small piece of control over my fate.

Many of my bell-bottom-wearing, peace activist friends were aghast that I would consider enlisting in the detested military. But conscientious objector status or heading off to Canada were not options on my table. Then I lucked out with a high lottery number and dodged both the proverbial and real bullets. Uncle Sam may have wanted me, but the feeling was not mutual.

In spite of my aversion toward the war in Vietnam, I had not lost my admiration for the people who serve—or the literature and history of war. I had always been fascinated by such books as Harrison Salisbury's *The 900 Days*, an account of the fight for Leningrad, one of the most brutal battles in World War II, in which people were reduced to cannibalism. Or *Goodbye, Darkness*, historian William Manchester's riveting memoir of returning to the scene of his World War II experiences in the Pacific. Gritty, real, and disturbing, these books painted a picture of war completely at odds with the tidy version served up by schoolbooks and Hollywood.

When I wrote *Don't Know Much About History*, first published in 1990, one of my goals was to make war real, to show how wars had been central events in shaping American history, and shouldn't be reduced to a bullet-pointed list of dates, battles, and stock, simplistic causes. I wanted to tell real stories of real people as a counterpoint to the mythmaking. And the tedium of most textbooks. I continued the effort in a number of other books, including, in particular, *Don't Know Much About the Civil War*, *America's Hidden History*, and *A Nation Rising*.

But many people still know far too little about America's wars and the role the military has played in the nation's history. We may show an obligatory but fleeting sense of reverence for our war dead on Memorial Day. We kick off the Super Bowl festivities with a stirring salute to the troops—a "feel-good" moment that soon passes. We may mark Veterans Day with paper poppies and by thanking some of the service people we pass in the airport. But we are sometimes blinded by an image of a noble and unflinching America at war.

That is an understandable, even valid notion. Part of conveying a national identity comes from creating a war narrative highlighting glory, idealism, and sacrifice. It forms a central piece of the "foundation legend," the story of a nation's birth meant to inspire and rally a people—not only in America but in many countries. But that is not history. The underside of the story—the dark tales of what men do in war and the grim toll exacted on civilians—is often swept under the carpet as schoolbooks quickly jump from an overview of the Revolution to the Civil War, and then briefly through two "world wars." Some wars are ignored entirely, while others simply get sucked into the black hole of American history. We don't do a very good job of teaching some of our most important history. A few years ago, Colonel Cole C. Kingseed, a history instructor at the United States Military Academy at West Point, told the *New York Times,* "I might as well be teaching the Peloponnesian Wars." He was talking about the perspective of the class of incoming cadets in 2000 on the Vietnam War.[4]

Which brings me to the reason for this book. Let me start by saying that this is *not* an encyclopedic history of the country's handful of congressionally declared wars, which can actually be counted on one hand, as there have been only five: 1812, Mexico, Spain, World War I, and World War II. In fact, the tally is larger if you separately count the declaration of war against Austria-Hungary in 1917 and the multiple declarations of war in 1941 and 1942, bringing the total to eleven. America's declared wars were with: Great Britain (1812); Mexico (1846); Spain (1898); Germany (1917); Austria-Hungary (1917); Japan, Germany, and Italy (1941); and Bulgaria, Hungary, and Romania (1942).

Nor does this book detail the hundreds of conflicts or other military deployments, whether authorized by Congress or not. Since the United States shifted to an all-volunteer army in 1973, there have been more than 140 such deployments, compared with only nineteen in the twenty-seven years after World War II.[5]

*The Hidden History of America at War* is also *not* military history in the traditional sense. There is an old, cherished literary and historical school of writing that details maneuvering regiments and sweeping battles, told in breathless, excited tones more appropriate to sports coverage. That style of military history was once used by war correspondents and a generation of writers, some of whom treated war as Arthurian legend or one of the romances of Sir Walter Scott. As Mark Twain famously put it in *Life on the Mississippi*, "Sir Walter had so large a hand in making Southern character, as it existed before the war, that he is in great measure responsible for the [Civil] war."

Instead this book spans America-at-arms from the Revolution to the war in Iraq, using six emblematic battles as a lens through which to explore how America has gone to war; who has fought its battles since the Revolution; how each of America's wars has transformed the American military establishment; and how the country's uneasy relationship with its armed services has shifted over more than 235 years.

Some of these battles may seem to tread on familiar ground, especially for seasoned readers of traditional military history—but even they will find some surprises here. Others may be more obscure or completely new territory. But in all six narratives, this book explores some "hidden history," an idea addressed in my earlier books *America's*

*Hidden History* and *A Nation Rising.* The goal is simple: to fill some of the gaping holes in our knowledge—whether the gap is the result of ignorance, incomplete information, widely held misconception, or, at worst, a legendary fabrication. And to tell the stories that the schoolbooks leave out.

The tale of each battle explores a few fundamental concepts:

- Why these battles were significant at the time.
- Who fought in them; I highlight the role of the average people who actually served and the civilians often caught up in the conflict, rather than focusing on the generals and politicians making the decisions.
- How each of these battles changed the nature and development of America's military institutions and fighting capabilities.
- How each battle had a lasting impact on American history well beyond its immediate effect.

These six battles were chosen not because they were necessarily the decisive turning points that altered the course of the wars in which they took place. Each is surely a distinctive, landmark battle—yes. But I selected them because they speak to something much larger than casualty counts and a simple assessment of winners and losers.

## Yorktown, Virginia (1781)

The schoolbooks may have told you that this was the decisive victory in the war that made America free and was one of the hallmark examples of George Washington's military genius. You probably did *not* learn that it was a deadly siege preceded by a crucial naval battle in which no American vessels took part. Not only did this battle depend entirely upon America's French allies to secure the victory over England, but it also held many lessons about what kind of military force a fledgling America would need to survive in a world fraught with dangers.

The hidden history of this battle also includes the story of people who deserve wider recognition—black soldiers who fought there; the black patriots who played a role during the American Revolution; and the thousands of black Americans, trying to escape their bondage, who were the unwitting victims of that battle. Yes, it was Washington's supreme moment, but it was also a battle that highlights all of the contradictions of a man fighting for liberty while keeping slaves.

## Petersburg, Virginia (1864)

Unlike the fierce battle for Atlanta, which inspired novelist Margaret Mitchell, the fight for Petersburg did not yield a *Gone with the Wind*. That is too bad, in a sense, even though popular fiction is not the best way to learn history. The longest siege of an American city in U.S. history, the story of Petersburg is not typical textbook material, but it should be. More battles were fought and more lives lost in Petersburg's defense than in many of the battles around other more famous Civil War sites.[6] The story of this once-proud town brought low speaks to the impact of the Civil War on civilians, as well as the overlooked role of African Americans—both those fighting in the war and those trapped by it—and the tragic consequences of poor leadership and indecisiveness in war. The story of Petersburg also carries the seeds of bitterness sown in the Confederate defeat that would last long after the siege guns were silenced.

## Balangiga, Philippines (1901)

Mass media has made our world more accustomed to the grim face of modern war. We would like to think that it was once different—that war was perhaps more honorable and chivalrous in an earlier time. But the story of the Spanish-American War underscores how past is prologue. A guerrilla war in a far-off Asian jungle. A long, protracted conflict against Islamist fighters. Controversies over torture and atrocities with reverberations reaching directly into the White House. All of these issues—which remain current in recent history and could easily come from today's headlines—emerged during a largely forgotten and overlooked part of the conflict at the turn of the twentieth century begun when the American effort to drive Spain from its colony in Cuba led to the Spanish-American War.

When that conflict expanded with almost no planning or foresight to another Spanish colony, the Philippines, an archipelago in Southeast Asia that few Americans—including their president—could locate on a map, it made America a global power overnight. The fact that the fighting in the Philippines continued long after the war "ended" and peace was made with Spain and that the war's politics threatened a president is part of the history that is largely forgotten or overlooked. Its lessons are more valuable than ever.

## Berlin, Germany (1945)

Many Americans are familiar with the epic World War II battles of Normandy and Iwo Jima; those battles and their heroes live on in monuments and movies. But the Battle of Berlin and the dramatic downfall of the Third Reich was not a celebrated piece of America's "Good War" narrative.

The reason is simple: The Soviet Red Army took the city, and soon afterward, the role of the Soviet Union as America's wartime ally was largely wiped away by Cold War animosities. The anticommunist propaganda of the Cold War era left little room for stories that credited the Red Army's central and extremely costly contribution to the victory over the Nazis. But the story of the German capital's fall is one of the war's most compelling. The brutality directed at civilians, especially the countless numbers of women reportedly raped after Berlin fell, is rarely discussed in American World War II accounts. Why Stalin was so eager to take Berlin, General Dwight D. Eisenhower's decision to leave Berlin to the Red Army, the ghastly battle itself, the role of American airpower in Germany's final days, and finally the postwar occupation and division of Berlin, are all part of a hidden history that set the stage for a half century of superpower conflict.

## Hué, South Vietnam (1968)

The 1968 Tet or Lunar New Year offensive by the North Vietnamese and Vietcong forces has been among the most analyzed and controversial episodes in the long American experience in Vietnam. It is considered a turning point in America's attitudes toward that war, and the stunning attack on the U.S. embassy in Saigon is usually highlighted as the defining event during the Tet Offensive.

But the battle for Vietnam's third-largest city—Hué—was the longest engagement during Tet and one of the longest and bloodiest in the entire Vietnam War. The story of Hué was partly about the failure of American intelligence, the mistaken assumptions that were part of the entire American experience in Vietnam, and the lies foisted on an American public and media. It is about what it meant when Americans got to see and hear the hard truth of a hellish war delivered nightly to their living rooms instead of the official version served up by the government and military and too often blithely accepted by the media and public. In other words, it is a story in which what the reporters did is as significant as what the troops did. And finally, it is yet another story of a dreadful massacre suffered by a civilian population, which remains the subject of controversy largely unknown to many Americans then and now.

*Introduction*

## Fallujah, Iraq (2004)

A hardscrabble industrial center in western Iraq, Fallujah briefly resurfaced in American headlines in late 2013 when the city fell to forces associated with Al Qaeda as part of Iraq's ongoing civil strife. But largely forgotten are the events that once placed Fallujah on the front pages.

On March 31, 2004, an American-led truck convoy was attacked in the city, about forty miles west of Baghdad. The world saw graphic pictures of four Americans who were brutally murdered by an Iraqi mob. They were not soldiers but civilians, working for a large company that provided security contractors to the Defense Department. To Americans who had been told that the war in Iraq was a "mission accomplished," the ensuing battle for Fallujah was a wake-up call about soldiers fighting as they have for centuries. But it was also about faulty political judgments matched by poor military judgment and the role of America's domestic politics in fighting its war. Perhaps most significantly, it is the story of how "Handsome Johnny"—the legendary, iconic American soldier—is being replaced in a dawning age of "privatized" war in which America's fighting is outsourced to for-profit contractors.

---

In addition to detailing these six battles, each of these episodes includes a timeline of major events in the conflicts, and an Aftermath section highlighting the fates of some of the major players in each chapter, including a broad overview of significant events in American military history between each of these battles. In this, the book will provide a brief, telescopic overview of the transformation of American military power, how America has gone to war, and a history of how Americans have changed their views of war and the military. Finally, an Afterword offers a glimpse at what America's military is becoming in the early decades of the twenty-first century at a very definite new stage in its military and global history.

That history is part of a larger theme—who fights and how America goes to war. For a long time, Americans have been offered a comfortable and inspiring narrative of the nation at war that has portrayed everyday citizens dutifully answering the call to arms. It is part of what might be called the "Minuteman Myth"—the cherished idea that Americans faced by threats have always reached for their handy muskets and stood shoulder-to-shoulder to face the enemy, just as those famed patriots did in 1775 at Lexington, Concord, and Bunker Hill.

But the truth is always far more complicated.

At the dawn of the nation's history, many of America's political leaders feared and mistrusted a professional standing army, in spite of the patriotic talk about honor, duty, and sacrifice that follows most wars. Before the American Revolution, male colonists were expected to train and serve in local militias as a reserve force. If attacked, they defended their towns, never straying too far from home. While we like to think of the sharpshooting American pioneer like Cooper's hawkeyed Natty Bumppo of *Deerslayer* and *Pathfinder* fame, efficiently dispatching invaders and Indians, the ranks of the colonial militia were filled with merchants, shopkeepers, and farmers who barely touched a gun. They were compelled to train and serve in preparation for fighting Indians, putting down riots, and maintaining political order. In all thirteen colonies, but particularly in the South, the militia had a special role in suppressing slave rebellions and capturing runaways.

To colonial Americans, militia service was often an unwelcome duty, which some managed to avoid or evade. But relying on the militia was better than the alternative. Professional standing armies were viewed as a dangerous threat to individual freedom. What is more, to tight-fisted Americans, they were expensive to keep at taxpayers' expense—one reason for those taxes on stamps and sugar you learned about—and Americans were sometimes forced to quarter soldiers in their own homes. (Now you know the reason behind the Third Amendment: "No Soldier shall, in time of peace be quartered in any house, without the consent of the Owner, nor in time of war, but in a manner to be prescribed by law.")

It was not until the Revolution had begun that the Continental Congress—before independence was even declared—adopted the militiamen of New England as the nation's first standing army. They eventually became George Washington's Continental Army, an army largely made up of recent immigrants and ethnic minorities, out-of-work young men, and African Americans—the people usually left out of the patriotic paintings and traditional textbooks. Each state still maintained its own militia force, whose use was often jealously guarded by state governors and legislatures, creating serious problems of command, coordination, and training throughout the war for independence.

The deeply ingrained American fear of the power of a standing army loomed behind the early American republic's reliance on "citizen soldiers." Once the Revolution was over, the army as we think of it today was largely dismantled. The future fate of a standing peacetime army was hotly debated as the Constitution was being improvised in Philadelphia in the summer of 1787. James Madison, Father of the Constitution and generally a proponent of a strong national government, had said, "A standing military force with an overgrown executive will not long be safe companions to liberty."[7]

Elbridge Gerry of Massachusetts spoke for many of the Framers who fretted over the cost of keeping an army but worried even more about the potential for mischief when he mockingly compared a standing army to an erect penis: "An excellent assurance of domestic tranquility, but a dangerous temptation to foreign adventure."[8] They probably didn't tell you that story in Civics 101 when discussing the Constitution.*

Although once adopted, the Constitution called for Congress "to raise and support Armies" and "to provide and maintain a Navy," the regular standing army was largely dismantled and the few ships of the Continental Navy sold off shortly after the Revolution. A skeleton force adopted by Congress in September 1789—which went by various names, such as the Legion of the United States—stood in for a professional regular army, with sometimes disastrous results, especially in the Indian wars of the 1790s. In theory, American men were expected to own a weapon, train with it regularly, and muster if called to answer threats. This was a crucial underpinning of the Second Amendment, which says, "A well regulated Militia, being necessary to the security of a free State, the right of the people to keep and bear Arms, shall not be infringed."[9]

As George Washington made clear in his first presidential message to Congress, "A free people ought not only to be armed, but disciplined."[10] When Washington called for troops to suppress the Whiskey Rebellion in 1794, they were composed of militiamen from New Jersey, Pennsylvania, Maryland, and Virginia, functioning as a national army. Most experienced soldiers and their leaders—including George Washington—dismissed militia forces as untrained and unreliable amateurs. But the idea of the "citizen-soldier" acquired an almost mythical quality as America's foundation legend was created.

In 1796, Congress abolished the Legion and reorganized the army. At about the same time, the Naval Act of 1794 called for the establishment of a small U.S. Navy. The young nation was confronting the realities of getting caught up in Europe's wars as the nineteenth

---

* Gerry (pronounced with a hard G like *Gary*) was one of three delegates who refused to sign the Constitution, along with Virginia's George Mason and Edmund Randolph, also outspoken opponents of a standing army.

century opened, erasing the reluctance of most Americans to build and maintain a meaningful national military force.

But the question of who fought our wars and how we fought them is a complex and important one. Apart from hearing about the occasional large-scale campaign, such as the "shock and awe" attack on Iraq that began in March 2003, or the Navy SEALs mission that killed Osama bin Laden in May 2011, many Americans are divorced from the realities of military service. That detachment has only grown as combat in the twenty-first century increasingly relies upon remote-control fighting with high-tech drones and cyberwarfare, which attacks the computers that provide modern-day command and control.

Also critical to the conversation is how we treat those who serve. Despite all the lip service paid to honoring our warriors—that is, taking care of the men, and increasingly, women, who serve—America has had a spotty record of treating its soldiers and veterans adequately. The Constitutional Convention of 1787 was largely forced by an uprising of farmers in western Massachusetts, many of them veterans of the Revolution, who had seen the independence they fought for being taken from them by unjust taxes, debtors' prison, and bars to voting. The word *shoddy* came into wide use during the Civil War to describe the cheap cloth used for army uniforms. After World War I, one of the greatest scandals in presidential history involved corruption and kickbacks in the newly created Veterans Department during the Harding administration. In 2007, the care of wounded troops in Walter Reed Army Medical Center became another national scandal. In 2014, another scandal over the treatment of veterans by Veterans Affairs hospitals led to the resignation of the head of the department, former general Eric Shinseki. And today, the rates of suicide, unemployment, and homelessness among veterans remain shockingly high.

It is that side of the story that our schoolbooks and Memorial Day observances tend to overlook while extolling the "sacrifice of the troops and their families" in often perfunctory fashion.

Late in 2013, the country was in the midst of another of its periodic soul searches about the use of American military power as the nation and the world debated America's response to the purported use of chemical weapons by Syrian forces loyal to the regime of Bashar Assad. A few weeks later, a pair of commando raids was launched against targets in Libya and Somalia. In Tripoli, a wanted terrorist leader was seized from his home. And in the other raid, the SEAL team that killed Osama bin Laden assaulted a villa in an unsuccessful attempt to capture another wanted terrorist. These events, coming as the United States was in a political crisis that had shut down the government in October 2013, were followed in 2014 by a trade of five prisoners—accused "enemy combatants" held by the U.S. government at Guantanamo in Cuba—for an American soldier held in Afghanistan for five years and a resurgence of the sectarian war in Iraq.

By the summer of 2014, the situation in Syria and Iraq had worsened gravely, as forces of ISIS, the Islamic State of Iraq and Syria, a fundamentalist Islamic group known for its ruthless tactics against civilians and opposing armies alike, took large sections of territory in Iraq, threatening the dysfunctional Iraqi government and military that the United States had helped create. At the same time, America and its allies were trying to counter Russia's "interference" in Ukraine—leaving the president with limited options to cope with two serious military crises.

All of these developments raised some key issues:

- The president's power to use military force or make other military decisions without congressional approval;
- The role of the United States military as "international policeman";
- The nation's apparent exhaustion over a decade of war in Afghanistan and Iraq, as well as with the global war on terror that commenced in the wake of 9/11.

These issues, along with the revelations of widespread domestic surveillance by the National Security Agency (NSA), the controversy over the use of drones at home and abroad, and cyberwarfare are all part of a necessary conversation about the proper role of military power in a democracy. It is a debate that Americans have had since the days of the Revolution. These discussions go along with other major changes to America's military forces—the end of the policy of "Don't Ask, Don't Tell" and the ban on homosexuals serving openly in the military; the role of women in combat forces; and the ongoing crisis of sexual assault in the American military.

This history also raises questions about something more fundamental—but largely lost on generations of leaders. It is a truth that bears repeating: that it is always easier to get into a war than to get out of one. And most wars—even the so-called good and just ones—are usually unnecessary or avoidable, the frequent outcome of what historian Barbara Tuchman described in *The March of Folly*. "Wooden-headedness, the source of self-deception, is a factor that plays a remarkably large role in government," wrote Tuchman about the follies of governments throughout human history. "It consists in assessing a situation in terms of preconceived fixed notions while ignoring or rejecting any contrary signs. It is acting according to wish while not allowing oneself to be deflected by the facts."[11]

The chief intent of *The Hidden History of America at War* is to underscore the importance of the courage and sacrifice of the men and women who have fought our wars for centuries. I especially sought to give voice to those most often left out of the story, including the civilians euphemistically defined as "collateral damage." But I am also intrigued by a very fundamental question. When he wrote, "There never was a good war or a bad peace," was Benjamin Franklin right?

This is a point underscored as the United States marked the Civil War's 150th anniversary between April 2011 and April 2015. Some historians honestly question whether the Civil War and the astonishing loss of as many as 800,000 American lives—some 2 percent of the population at the time—was "worth it," in the sense that some political compromise might have ended slavery and preserved the Union without the loss of so many lives. To that proposition, writer Ta-Nehisi Coates replied, "American slavery was a system of perpetual existential violence. The idea that it could have been—or should have been—ended, after two and a half centuries of practice, with a handshake and an ice-cream social strikes me as really wrong."[12]

Who is right—Mr. Franklin or Mr. Coates? Are there "good wars"? And are they "worth it"? Are all wars best avoided? Or was the Roman poet Horace correct about dying for one's country being "sweet and honorable"?

All hard questions and not easily answered.

War, unfortunately, is often the greatest folly and its consequences are usually greatest for the people who have least say in the matter— the soldiers who serve, the civilians who are caught in the war zone.

And that is the real point of this book. We cannot answer these tough questions if we don't replace the myths with an honest accounting of the real war—the one that Walt Whitman said would never get in the books. To those who have never fought, it is nearly a moral imperative to understand war. Every battle in every war produces stories that demonstrate the capacity for cruelty, deceit, dishonor, and the foolhardy waste of precious lives. But they must also be weighed against the tales of sacrifice, courage, loyalty, duty, and honor—to do what Lincoln at Gettysburg reminded Americans to do 150 years ago:

> That from these honored dead we take increased devotion to that cause for which they gave the last full measure of devotion; that we here highly resolve that these dead shall not have died in vain.

# Chapter One

→-◄-

# Washington's Men

*Yorktown, Virginia—October 1781*

"The time is now near at hand which must probably determine
whether Americans are to be freemen or slaves.... The fate of
unborn millions will now depend, under God, on the courage
and conduct of this army. Our cruel and unrelenting enemy
leaves us only the choice of brave resistance or the most abject
submission. We have therefore to resolve to conquer or die."

—*General George Washington (August 27, 1776)*

"I cannot insist too strongly on how I was surprised by the
American army. It is truly incredible that troops almost naked,
poorly paid, and composed of old men and children and
Negroes should behave so well on the march and under fire."

—*Count de Bourg, a French officer (July 1781)*

"We this night [October 6, 1781] completed laying out the works.
The troops of the line were there ready with the entrenching
tools and begun to entrench, after General Washington
had struck a few blows with a pickaxe, a mere ceremony,

that it might be said, 'Gen. Washington with his own hands first broke the ground at the siege of Yorktown.'"[1]

—*Sergeant Joseph Plumb Martin (October 1781)*

"We remained in Little York [Yorktown] a few more days until General Washington brought all of Master Jefferson's folks and about 20 of Thomas Mann Randolph's Tuckahoe folks back to Richmond."[2]

—*Isaac Granger (1846)*

## Milestones in the American Revolution

### 1775

**April 19** The first battles of the Revolution are fought at Lexington and Concord, Massachusetts.

**June 14** Congress authorizes enlistment of riflemen to serve the United Colonies for one year; this is considered the birth date of the U.S. Army.

**October 13** The Continental Congress votes to outfit two sailing vessels; this is considered the birth date of the U.S. Navy.

**November 10** Two battalions of marines, or naval infantry, are formed by Congress; this is considered the birth date of the U.S. Marine Corps.

### 1776

**July 4** Congress formally adopts the Declaration of Independence.

**October 11** Following disastrous defeats in New York, George Washington and the Continental Army retreat from Manhattan.

**December 25–26** Washington successfully attacks the British garrison at Trenton, New Jersey. He follows that victory with another at Princeton, New Jersey, on January 3, 1777.

### 1777

**October 17** In the wake of two defeats at Saratoga, New York, British general John Burgoyne surrenders his force of 7,500.

**December 17** Following the American victories at Saratoga, France officially recognizes the independence of the American colonies.

## 1778

**July 10** France declares war against Great Britain.

## 1780

**September** The plot to betray America by Benedict Arnold is revealed. Arnold joins the British army.

## 1781

**January 17** The Battle of Cowpens (South Carolina) is a crucial American victory.

**March 15** After suffering heavy casualties at the Battle of Guilford Courthouse (North Carolina), the British forces depart the Carolinas for Virginia.

**August 2** Led by Charles Lord Cornwallis, the British occupy Yorktown, Virginia.

**September 5–8** The French navy drives off the British fleet in the Battle of the Virginia Capes.

**September 28** Sixteen thousand American and French troops begin to dig fortifications and trenches around Yorktown.

**October 19** The British surrender at Yorktown; it is the end of British hopes for victory in America.

*Yorktown, Virginia*
*October 14, 1781*

It would be "cold steel." George Washington wanted stealth and speed. The young officers passed along the order to their men—leave muskets unloaded and fix bayonets.

It was a foggy evening in Yorktown as Colonel Alexander Hamilton and Lieutenant Colonel John Laurens stood anxiously waiting to lead four hundred American soldiers into the darkness. Nearby, their comrade, the Marquis de Lafayette, a Continental Army general with overall command of this combined French and American mission, also readied four hundred French veterans. There would be no flags flying or regimental drummers or screams to "Charge." At a signal, the troops would move out in a coordinated strike against a badly battered but determined British enemy in a pair of fortified British outposts just outside this small Virginian tobacco port.

The three young officers—all in their mid-twenties—understood the stakes. So did many of the men in the massed French and American army surrounding Yorktown. A single, swift blow on this October night could end this siege and perhaps the British will to continue the war. Failure meant delay. And delay meant the threat of British reinforcements arriving to turn the tide once more against the patriot cause.

The plan was simple. The French and Americans would cross a quarter mile of fields pitted by days of relentless cannon fire to assault the two small but well-protected British outposts. Bristling with sharpened wooden stakes, each of these two redoubts—temporary, small defensive positions, usually made of earthworks reinforced by timbers and surrounded by a moat and sharpened stakes—was manned by about one hundred British regulars and Hessians, German mercenaries. For five days, these British outposts and the small riverside port of Yorktown had been pounded relentlessly by American and French artillery. The two redoubts were the last line of defense for a devastated Yorktown, which had become a hellish trap for thousands of British soldiers and thousands more civilians.

It was a moment of truth that the three young officers had dreamed of for years. Meeting early in the Revolution, they had all joined George Washington's "military family," a small circle of aides and advisers, in 1777. Alexander Hamilton, born in the Caribbean, was the bastard child of an adulterous liaison who had been dispatched to school in New York, where he caught patriot fever. A fabulously wealthy French aristocrat, Lafayette enlisted in Washington's army at nineteen, the most loyal and idealistic of the Europeans drawn to the American cause. And John Laurens, brilliant scion of prominent South Carolina slaveholders, had been schooled in some of Europe's finest academies and nurtured quixotic dreams of independence and abolition.

The three young men, from widely different worlds, were ambitious, brave, and held in varying degrees of affection by their commander. Serving Washington together, they had quickly become devoted friends, sharing a passion for the rebel cause, romantic dreams of glory, and boundless courage that bordered on the reckless. All of them had been under fire—both Lafayette and Laurens had the wounds to prove it—and they had survived the worst days of war and winter camps, witness to the many defeats, disappointments, and dashed hopes since the fighting for independence began in April 1775.

Now, more than six years after those first shots were fired in Concord and Lexington, they were poised to strike a blow in Virginia that could reverse all of the war's darkest days. The capture of these two redoubts was essential. Once these British positions were taken, Washington could tighten his grip on the already devastated British forces in Yorktown. Any delay in finishing off the enemy army trapped there, Washington feared, would allow time for a British fleet, thought to be sailing from New York, to reach Yorktown and rescue the British army.

Hamilton's men were seasoned Continentals, the professional troops and officers who had followed Washington and suffered through disaster and defeat. They had emerged out of the ragtag band of militiamen that Washington had inherited outside Boston in the summer of 1775 and which eventually evolved to become a sorely tested but professional, national army. They had spent the day sleeping and smoking, feeling that age-old mixture of boredom and nervous excitement that precedes a battle. As they waited in the muddy trenches, their forty-nine-year-old commander in chief—"Old Hoss," as some called General Washington—had spoken to the ranks, urging them to "act the part of firm and brave soldiers."

"I thought that His Excellency's knees rather shook," Captain Stephen Olney, a veteran from Rhode Island, recalled of Washington's pre-battle "harangue," as he called it. "But I have since doubted whether it was not mine."[3]

In the French trenches, Lieutenant General Jean-Baptiste Donatien de Vimeur, Comte de Rochambeau,* the grizzled, veteran commander in chief of the French army, delivered an impassioned plea to the regiment he had once personally commanded. "My children, I have great need of you tonight. I trust you will not forget that we have served together in the Regiment of the Auvergne—*Auvergne sans tache*, the spotless." One of the young French infantrymen answered: "We will fight like lions…until the last man is killed."[4]

---

* The Marquis de Lafayette was at this time an American general in command of both the French and American troops in this attack at Yorktown; Comte de Rochambeau was in overall command of the French expeditionary force fighting alongside Washington's Continental Army.

All stood ready; the battlefield had been prepared. Earlier that day, George Washington had brought the combined firepower of the massed French and American guns to bear on the two small earthworks, each protected by a high wooden fence, or palisade. After hours of pounding, the redoubts appeared to be vulnerable and Washington ordered the final assault, the cold steel, now-or-never moment.

As night fell on October 14, the four hundred American light infantrymen waited for Alexander Hamilton's word with bayonets fixed. At 6:30 p.m., a battery of French guns commenced a diversionary bombardment, and thirty minutes later, six mortar rounds signaled the beginning of the assault. Hamilton sent his closest friend, John "Jack" Laurens, with a company of eighty men to circle to the rear of the redoubts and cut off any British escape. Then he curtly ordered his troops, "Follow me."

As the men quietly stepped out of the trenches, a party of sappers and miners*—the men who dug the trenches and were the predecessors of the Army Corps of Engineers—advanced first, carrying axes and picks. Joseph Plumb Martin was among those leading the way. A twenty-two-year-old veteran of five years of the marching, fighting, hunger, and deprivation that had been the constant realities for the Continental Army's enlisted men, Martin recalled the night. "Our watchword was 'Rochambeau,' the commander of the French forces, a good watchword, for being pronounced Ro-sham-bow, it sounded when pronounced quick, like rush-on-boys.... The word up, up, was then reiterated through the detachment."[5]

As he left the trench, Martin knew his task. "The Sappers and Miners were...to proceed in front and cut a passage for the troops

---

* "Sappers," also known to the French as "pioneers," or later as "combat engineers," have routinely performed a variety of jobs in all wars, such as digging fortifications, building bridges, and laying or clearing minefields. The word comes from the French word *saper*, meaning to undermine.

through the abatis, which are composed of the tops of trees, the small branches cut off…sharp as spikes," Martin later wrote. "These trees are then laid out a small distance from the trench or ditch, pointing outwards.…—it is almost impossible to get through them."

The two columns moved stealthily out into the moonlit night. Before they left the trenches, Captain Stephen Olney, the veteran Rhode Islander who had enlisted in 1776 and weathered the Valley Forge winter and numerous major battles, spoke bluntly to his men: "I know you'll be brave men, come what will," said Olney. "If you lose your gun—take the gun of the first man killed."[6]

Among Olney's Rhode Islanders were some of the best-drilled, best-equipped, and most smartly uniformed men in Washington's often-ragtag army. They were the more than 140 African Americans from the tiny state, slaves who had been promised emancipation in return for enlisting. The First Rhode Island Regiment, known as the "Black Regiment," had marched behind Washington, who had begrudgingly accepted them into his ranks when he was desperate for fighting men. Merged with another white Rhode Island regiment at Yorktown, they were now in the vanguard to fight for their own freedom as well as America's.

As Joseph Martin and his fellow axmen neared the redoubt, a British sentry heard some noise and fired a shot. The sappers began to hack away furiously at the abatis with their axes and picks, and the first squad of soldiers hustled into the shallow moat surrounding the outpost. As Martin watched men fall around him, he thought they had been shot. Then he realized that they were stumbling in the craters that had been carved out by the days of intense shelling.

Close behind the sappers came Hamilton's infantrymen, including Olney and his Rhode Islanders. Springing into the ditch that surrounded the redoubt, Hamilton ordered his men to hoist him to the top of the wall, where the future first Treasury secretary dueled sword-to-bayonet with the cursing British. So much American history might have changed if a single British ball or bayonet had found its mark. For a frenzied moment, Hamilton fought for his life until his men joined him and drove the redcoats from the wall.[7]

As Hamilton mounted the redoubt's walls, Captain Olney found a gap in the palisade and shouted, "Olney's men form here!" Leading his First Rhode Islanders through, Olney confronted half a dozen enemy soldiers with bayonets and fought them off desperately with his espontoon—a long pike, the sort of weapon carried by infantrymen since medieval days. One enemy bayonet sliced his fingers, another pierced his thigh, and a third slashed his stomach. The element of surprise was clearly over. Two of Olney's men, free to fire, took aim at the knot of British attackers and drove them off. Holding his exposed intestines with his hands, Olney thought he was done for. But, later removed to a Williamsburg hospital, he lived to see another fifty years.[8]

After they had hacked through the abatis, the sappers had been ordered to hold back, but, exposed to enemy fire in the heat of the assault and unwilling to be denied a chance to fight, Martin and his war-hungry comrades pressed forward, armed only with their tools. Better to fight than chance dying as a spectator holding an ax. "I forced a passage at a place where I saw our shot had cut away some of the abatis," said Martin. "While passing, a man at my side received a ball in the head and fell under my feet, crying out bitterly."[9]

In ten minutes, it was over. The British and Hessians in Redoubt No. 10 were overwhelmed. Lieutenant Colonel Jack Laurens and his eighty men captured the British trying to escape. Nine Americans had died in the lightning attack and another twenty-five were wounded. The British lost eight soldiers killed or wounded.

About a hundred yards away, Lafayette led the four hundred Frenchmen, bayonets fixed, on the second British outpost, Redoubt No. 9, held by about 120 British and German soldiers.* The French advance over the field was silent until another alert sentry opened fire on the attackers, still eighty yards from the British works. Ignoring the order for stealth, some of the French infantrymen stopped, loaded muskets, and returned fire. Others continued in their rush on the redoubt, as the French sappers began hacking away at the abatis. Frenchmen began climbing over the wooden palisade and the thick tangle of deadly, sharpened stakes using ladders and fascines, round bundles of sticks tied together and used to reinforce the trenches. After the first French officer to the top of the wall was shot in the legs and another was mortally wounded, brutal hand-to-hand, close combat followed—even fiercer than what Hamilton and his men encountered. But here, too, the attack was over soon, lasting under thirty minutes. With the element of surprise and outnumbering the British by four to one, the French had overwhelmed the English soldiers and Hessian mercenaries.

While the assault was under way, Washington and several of his officers waited anxiously nearby, unable to see what was happening. When the sound of firing grew more intense, Colonel David Cobb, Washington's aide-de-camp, cautioned Washington: "Sir, you're much too exposed here. Hadn't you better step back a little?"

In typical fashion, Washington simply returned the suggestion. "Colonel Cobb, if you are afraid, you have the liberty to step back."[10]

Washington soon had the word he longed for; his cold steel assault had won the day. After the brief action, Lafayette reported to his commander in chief, "Colonel Hamilton's well known talents and gallantry were on this occasion most conspicuous and serviceable. Our obligations to him, to Colonel Gimat [a French commander], to

---

* German troops also fought with the French at Yorktown. According to *America Goes to War*, by Charles Patrick Neimeyer, one-third of Rochambeau's troops at Yorktown were German or Austrian, so the battle featured a polyglot collection of men, all shouting in different languages as they fought.

Colonel Laurens, and to each and all the officers, are above expression. . . . It adds greatly to the character of the troops, that, under the fire of the enemy, they displayed and took their ranks with perfect silence and order. Not one gun was fired . . . and owing to the conduct of the Commanders and bravery of the men, the redoubt was stormed with uncommon rapidity."[11] Lafayette's gallant and glowing report humbly ignored his own participation. But he must have also meant that no guns were fired in the initial American approach, because many shots eventually rang out in both brief firefights.

"The works we have carried are of vast importance," a relieved and confident-sounding General Washington wrote to the Congress in Philadelphia. "From there we shall be able to enfilade [to direct gunfire along the length of an enemy battle line] the enemy's whole line."[12]

Wasting no time, the miners had begun to dig new trenches before the British prisoners could even be removed. Linking the captured redoubts to the American and French lines, the French and American gun crews moved in more artillery. Besieged Yorktown was now in near point-blank range for the allied artillerymen. George Washington knew it was only a matter of time before the British yielded. But the end could not come soon enough. He still feared the arrival of the British fleet.

Tempered by long experience of disasters and defeats—the catastrophic loss of New York in 1776, the long winter in Valley Forge, a series of devastating setbacks in the South—Washington's fear was understandable, but on this occasion it was unfounded. What Washington did not know was that on the next morning, his British adversary, General Cornwallis, had written to the British commander in chief for North America, General Sir Henry Clinton, in New York: "My situation now becomes very critical; we dare not show a gun to their old batteries, and I expect that their new ones will open tomorrow morning. . . . The safety of the place is therefore so precarious that I cannot recommend that the fleet and army should run great risque in endeavouring to save us."[13]

Although Washington still worried about the large British forces still in America and the possibility that London would replace Cornwallis's lost army, the Marquis de Lafayette was more optimistic. He wrote to the French first minister, Comte de Maurepas, and other French royal officials: "The play is over, Monsieur le Comte, the fifth act has just come to an end."14

———

For Washington and many of the men around him, the siege at Yorktown was a moment they had dreamed of—a moment in which they finally had the men and firepower to convincingly defeat a British army in battle. But it was a dream long deferred. And along the way, there had been too many nightmarish moments and reversals to count.

After the first, fleeting triumphs in Massachusetts in 1775, where the fighting began around Boston, George Washington had taken command of the ragged, undisciplined, ill-trained, and poorly out-fitted Continental Army. It was composed mostly of New England militiamen—the amateur "citizen-soldiers" who took up arms against the British in 1775. Some of these men Washington would lead had been converted into the first United States Army by an act of the Continental Congress on June 14, 1775. Full of patriot zeal but lacking organization and professional leadership, they had still scored stunning early victories. But after the British evacuated Boston in March 1776, the American Revolution had largely been a series of dreadful setbacks and disasters for Washington and his men.

Washington's genius seemed to be for escaping battles he had lost, rather than actually winning any. Strapped with a penny-pinching Congress and jealous rivals for command, he had managed to hold together his often pitifully underfed, ill-equipped, and initially amateurish Continental Army with the military equivalent of spit and baling wire—an achievement that must be counted among his greatest. But he had few victories to show.

By early 1781, the American Revolution had limped ingloriously into its seventh year. Most of Washington's Continental soldiers, reduced to some six thousand men—many shoeless, hungry, and unpaid—were camped along the Hudson River north of New York City. In the midst of another harsh winter, unrest had boiled over into mutiny when 1,300 troops of the Pennsylvania Line had rebelled near Morristown, New Jersey, and killed two officers on New Year's Day 1781. Usually an unrelenting disciplinarian who had never shown hesitation in lashing soldiers for petty crimes and threatening to string up deserters, Washington allowed a mediated settlement with these men. But the next group of mutineers was not so lucky. When two hundred soldiers in the New Jersey Line, fired up by rum and the inspiration of the Pennsylvanians, also mutinied, Washington dispatched five hundred men under General Robert Howe to restore order. On January 27, two of the mutiny's ringleaders were executed by a firing squad that included some of the mutineers.[15]

With his army short on rations and nearly out of ammunition, and with little hard cash to pay his disgruntled troops, General Washington recorded that he felt "bewildered and gloomy." In April 1781, he wrote, "We are at the end of our tether....Now or never our deliverance must come."[16]

Yet even in the bleakest days of early 1781, Washington envisioned another battle for New York, the scene of one of his greatest disasters in August 1776. There, in a series of battles fought on Long Island, Brooklyn, and Manhattan, a vastly larger British army, supported by the Royal Navy, had routed the Americans, nearly destroying Washington's Continental Army and forcing a desperate retreat into New Jersey and Pennsylvania.

Five years after that debacle, New York remained the headquarters of some sixteen thousand British troops under General Clinton.

Ringed by Royal Navy ships, the island of Manhattan was a nearly impregnable fortress. It was also a stronghold of American loyalists, who preferred the rule of King George III to George Washington.

Washington's best hope for "deliverance" rested with his recently arrived friends. Numbering 5,500 well-equipped, battle-tested veterans, America's French allies had landed in Newport, Rhode Island, in July 1780 but had stayed there, hoping for reinforcements from France. Their commander, Comte de Rochambeau, was glumly pessimistic. "Send us troops, ships and money," he had written home to France in near desperation and skepticism about the Americans. "But do not count on these people, nor on their resources. They have neither money nor credit; their forces only exist momentarily, and when they are about to be attacked in their own homes they assemble during the time of personal danger to defend themselves."[17]

Clearly frustrated that a year had nearly passed without French action, Washington met with Rochambeau in May 1781 to devise a plan to attack the British. A French fleet capable of challenging the British navy and carrying needed reinforcements was expected to arrive in New York later that summer. Washington hoped to coordinate the French fleet's arrival with an attack on General Clinton in New York, using an army strengthened by the French veterans under Rochambeau.

But "Papa Rochambeau," as he called himself, had other ideas. A grizzled survivor of some forty years of fighting in the near-constant wars of eighteenth-century continental Europe, the stout, fifty-six-year-old Rochambeau argued against attacking the imposing British defenses in New York. Nonetheless, he listened politely to Washington for the moment, and diplomatically ceded the decision to the American leader. While agreeing to march his troops to join Washington outside New York, Rochambeau and his aides secretly prepared for a very different campaign.

Their opportunity arrived after Rochambeau's French army joined forces with Washington's troops outside New York City in

July 1781, only to learn that a French fleet was sailing not to New York but to the lower Chesapeake Bay. Under Admiral François Joseph Paul, Comte de Grasse, twenty-nine French ships carrying thousands of French troops were coming to America. A second smaller French fleet, carrying siege guns and more French troops, would sail from Newport to join de Grasse's ships, creating a powerful naval force large enough to challenge the British fleet in America.

The target of the French navy and the combined French and American armies would shift to the British force occupying the small port of Yorktown, Virginia, where General Lord Charles Cornwallis had encamped with more than eight thousand British troops, many of them sick and wounded. Surrounded on three sides by water, Cornwallis had allowed himself to be put at the mercy of a naval blockade from the sea.

Washington and his French allies knew that if they could take Cornwallis's army off the chessboard that was America, it would be a crushing blow to British hopes for victory in America.

To accomplish that, Washington needed to trick the British high command. In what would be Washington's most dazzling sleight-of-hand performance, he and Rochambeau convinced Clinton that they planned to attack New York, while instead stealing a march south to trap Cornwallis and his army in Virginia. Washington pulled off the ruse by ordering his men to build large camps and huge brick bread ovens visible from New York to give the appearance of preparations for a campaign against the British there.

This golden opportunity for Washington and the French to strike in Virginia had been created after Clinton had divided his armies, committing a large force to a campaign in the Southern states. Appointed British commander in chief in North America in February 1778, Clinton had turned his focus to the South in 1779 after abandoning hopes of conquering the fiercely combative Northern states. With little American resistance, Clinton's armies had swept through Georgia and South Carolina in a series of smashing victories, with the key ports of Savannah and Charleston in British hands. In 1780, Clinton had returned to New York with the bulk of his army and the Royal Navy, leaving eight thousand men under Cornwallis to continue the plan of severing the Southern states from the American rebellion.

---

In a war that had been largely devoid of cruelty and atrocities—excepting perhaps the treatment of American prisoners of war, who died in large numbers aboard notorious prison ships—the British campaign in the South was surprising for its savage turn, particularly toward civilians. The civility and honorable warfare were abandoned as British raiders freely pillaged and plundered their way through the Southern states with a ruthlessness that had generally not characterized the earlier fighting in the North. Most notorious among the British commanders was Lieutenant Colonel Banastre Tarleton, who led a unit of mixed British cavalry and Pennsylvania loyalists. At one battle in which Tarleton's men routed an American unit, a French officer serving with the Americans asked "for quarter," meaning an honorable surrender. Instead he was mangled and killed by British sabers. At Fair-Lawn, the South Carolina plantation of Sir John Colleton, Tarleton's men sexually assaulted several women, even though one of them, Sir John's widow, Lady Jane Colleton, was a prominent loyalist. She was slashed with a sword as she successfully fought off a rapist.[18] Some of the attackers were later arrested but went unpunished and Fair-Lawn was burned by the retreating British.[19]

In May, Tarleton had led another infamous attack after which surrendering and wounded Americans were bayoneted to death. This massacre in the Waxhaws region on the border of North and South Carolina was notable in part because local people, including Elizabeth Jackson and her two sons, Robert and Andrew, helped treat the American survivors. Just thirteen years old, future president Andrew

Jackson later joined South Carolina's partisan fighters, many of them Scots-Irish settlers of the Carolinas backcountry with no love for the British. "The phrase, 'Tarleton's quarter,' wrote a nineteenth-century Presbyterian clergyman, 'became a proverb for wholesale cruelty.' "[20]

At Camden, South Carolina, in August 1780, General Cornwallis had crushed another American army, inflicting heavy losses and a humiliating defeat for some of the American generals.

Adding to the patriot woes, the turncoat Benedict Arnold, now a British general, had launched a series of scorched-earth raids in Virginia. Once a successful and trusted patriot leader who had distinguished himself at Fort Ticonderoga, the battle of Valcour Island on Lake Champlain, and the pivotal battles of Saratoga in 1777, Arnold had grown bitter when passed over for promotions. Given command of the crucial fortress of West Point on the Hudson River (site of the future military academy), Arnold had schemed to turn the fort over to the British. His plot was discovered in September 1780 and Arnold had narrowly escaped, later to join the British army as a brigadier general. By the end of the first week of 1781, Arnold's forces—mixed British troops and American loyalists—had looted and burned parts of Richmond, Virginia, and scattered the state legislature.

With an American price on his own head, Arnold set out to arrest Thomas Jefferson, then Virginia's governor, who was forced into hiding. In Richmond, Arnold's men captured some of the enslaved people from Jefferson's household. And at Monticello, four more of Jefferson's enslaved people willingly joined another British raiding party, believing that the British promised them freedom. A Royal Navy ship also carried off seventeen enslaved blacks, who willingly left George Washington's Mount Vernon plantation in hopes of escaping bondage.

To counter Arnold and his raids, Washington dispatched Lafayette, with orders to execute Arnold "in the most summary way" if the patriot hero turned British general should fall into his hands.

In spite of this otherwise bleak scenario, a few faint flickers of hope were lit for the patriot cause. The supremely confident Cornwallis had been shocked by a string of sharp blows delivered by American forces. In October 1780, a British loss at Kings Mountain, South Carolina, near the North Carolina border, was the first reversal. A change in American commanders brought Nathanael Greene, a Rhode Island–born Quaker who proved a remarkably adept soldier, to the scene. Aided by partisan militia fighters alongside his regular Continental troops, Greene turned the American fortunes at Cowpens, South Carolina, and produced another "Bunker Hill" moment at Guilford Courthouse in North Carolina, where the British suffered heavy losses in an otherwise empty victory.

Bickering with Sir Henry Clinton over tactics and strategy, General Cornwallis had moved his army, now bloodied in these setbacks and severely weakened by epidemic, out of the Carolinas and into Virginia. He hoped to combine his forces with those of Benedict Arnold and defeat Lafayette. But with Cornwallis in Virginia, Arnold returned to New York to consult with Clinton and pressed for an attack on Philadelphia, a strategy rejected by the cautious Clinton, who still feared that Washington was going to strike at New York.

Infuriated by Cornwallis's decisions, an exasperated Henry Clinton concluded an exchange of increasingly irritated letters by ordering his subordinate in July 1781 to establish a naval base somewhere on the lower Chesapeake Bay, the new "seat of war." Clinton remained in New York, as the smoke from Washington's bread ovens and other "disinformation" had convinced him that the French and Americans planned to strike there. For his part, Cornwallis "had obeyed with the least possible grace," historian Thomas Fleming noted, "refusing to ship surplus men to Sir Henry and erecting fortifications at Yorktown that presumed an attacking enemy would have only light field artillery."[21]

A small port with about sixty homes, Yorktown was chosen as a deepwater harbor on the York River. After arriving in July 1781, the British spent the summer fortifying the port and Gloucester Point on the opposite riverbank, where the hated Banastre Tarleton—minus two fingers lost at Guilford Courthouse—was based.

At roughly the same time, Washington and Rochambeau had learned that the large French fleet commanded by Admiral de Grasse was sailing not for New York but for the Chesapeake. The fortunes of war had created a perfect opportunity for the American cause. The French fleet from the Caribbean, carrying more troops and gold to pay the armies, would join with the combined American-French land forces in Virginia. The smaller French fleet from Newport carried more men and siege guns.

At Yorktown, the trap would be sprung around Cornwallis's army, which had been weakened by two powerful forces often overlooked by many battle accounts: an epidemic of smallpox, typhus, and other deadly "camp diseases"—contagious diseases that spread rapidly in the crowded confines of army camps with poor sanitation and which were ravaging the British troops; and thousands of escaped slaves who had flocked to the British, clinging to a desperate hope of winning freedom from their American masters in what has been called the "greatest slave rebellion in American history."[22] While Cornwallis had put many of these African-American refugees to work, they had become a burden—slowing his movements, drawing on limited food and medical supplies, and by their mere presence worsening the spread of deadly contagion through Yorktown.

———

Washington's deceptions had worked. Lafayette's adroit leadership had penned Cornwallis inside Yorktown, and the French fleets— more than thirty ships—were under sail. Leaving behind a small force to disguise their moves, Washington and Rochambeau set out for Yorktown in mid-August. It was not easy to move thousands of infantrymen, with cannons, oxen, and supplies, without raising British suspicions. But the American and French armies, taking separate routes south and staggering their marches, did just that.

By early September they were parading before the Continental Congress in Philadelphia, and in mid-September 1781 they arrived in Williamsburg, thirteen miles west of Yorktown. By then, de Grasse's French fleet had entered the lower Chesapeake Bay and disembarked another three thousand French troops to wait for Washington and Rochambeau in Williamsburg. He sent ships to collect some of the army to move them more quickly to Yorktown. The second French fleet had arrived from Newport, carrying siege guns and more troops.

But more significantly, on September 5, the French navy, numbering twenty-four ships, encountered a smaller British fleet of nineteen ships in a crucial engagement known as the Battle of the Virginia Capes. In a battle lasting about two hours, the British were forced to abandon the damaged HMS *Terrible*, and five other British ships were all disabled. When the second French fleet arrived on September 11, the British commanders agreed the next day to sail for New York. The British fleet limped back to its home port in New York for repairs. When the normally stoic and reserved Washington arrived in Virginia and saw the anchored French fleet in control of the lower Chesapeake and blockading Clinton's army, he actually jumped for joy, excitedly waving his hat at de Grasse from the shore.

With no navy, no cash with which to pay his troops, and precious little powder and ammunition, Washington had been leading a young nation in what seemed a hopeless cause in the eyes of observers in America and abroad. Trying to fight the most powerful army and navy on earth, confounded by congressional critics who sniped at his every failure, dismayed by state leaders who kept their troops from the fray, and bedeviled by rivals who wanted his command, Washington had worked miracles to have merely survived this long. The arrival of the French fleet changed everything.

Not only had de Grasse driven off the British navy, but his ships had also delivered hard cash—gold and silver with which to pay both American and French troops. Much of it had been collected from the people of Havana, Cuba. This was another often overlooked piece of the Yorktown and American Revolutionary narratives—the crucial support of foreign nations, without which the Revolution may have been doomed.[23]

The French and Spanish kings had both been secretly supporting the American cause, even before independence was declared. Louis XVI, the French king, had given arms and supplies to the Americans through a fictitious firm. Charles III of Spain matched these donations. This was not from the goodness of their regal hearts and it was certainly no symptom of liberal zeal; it was global power politics, pure and simple. As historian Barbara A. Mitchell put it, "The two Catholic Bourbon monarchs on the French and Spanish thrones continued to assist the American Revolution, more to divert British resources than from a desire to aid the revolutionary cause."[24]

Other French allies were also secretly arming, bankrolling, and supporting the American cause. The Dutch Republic—the Netherlands*— had provided financial support for the Revolution.

The French went a step further when they sent veteran professional troops to America in 1780. The French navy was later committed to the conflict. And when Rochambeau pleaded with de Grasse for money as well as ships, de Grasse met with the Spanish minister on the island of Santo Domingo and the two devised a plan to deliver to the French commander one million pesos, which came from the output of Spain's profitable gold and silver mines in South and Central America, minted into coins, most of which flowed through the Spanish city of Havana.

---

* Henry Laurens, father of John Laurens, was captured by the British while on a mission to the Netherlands to raise funds; the younger Laurens had successfully completed that mission, winning Dutch loans, before returning to fight at Yorktown.

Spain and some of its American colonies played a crucial role in particular in "bankrolling the Battle of Yorktown," as Barbara Mitchell described it.[25]

Meeting with the wealthy plantation owners and merchants of Santo Domingo, de Grasse offered his own plantation in Haiti as collateral for a loan. When the Spanish people of Puerto Rico and Santo Domingo were unable to raise the necessary funds, de Grasse turned to Cuba. On August 16, after making an announcement of his needs for the French fleet, de Grasse and his men were able to collect the sufficient funds from the enthusiastic people of Havana in only six hours. The ladies of Spanish Cuba even gave their diamonds to aid the cause.[26] With cash in hand, de Grasse set sail for America and his fateful encounter with the British fleet.[27]

Despite his bouts of apparent madness, King George III understood the stakes. One year earlier, the British monarch had confidently predicted that America and its French and Spanish allies were in such poor financial shape that "[t]his war, like the last, will prove one of credit." The Americans and their allies, the king believed, simply could not afford to keep up the fight. But after the French naval victory at the Virginia Capes in early September 1781, the king told his friend the Earl of Sandwich, "I nearly think the empire ruined... this cruel event is too recent for me to be as yet able to say more."

---

By the end of September, approximately 17,600 American and French soldiers were gathered in Williamsburg, more than double the 8,300 British and Hessian soldiers occupying Yorktown. The American and French contingents left Williamsburg on the morning of September 28. By late afternoon, they had begun to arrive on the outskirts of Yorktown, a once-thriving river port whose economy had been damaged by the war. The armies outdistanced their supply wagons and Washington was forced to spend the first night outside Yorktown without his customary field tents, sleeping under a mulberry tree instead.

Soldiers like young Joseph Martin, a sergeant from Massachusetts who had trudged behind Washington for more than five years, were delighted to find that the woods nearby were full of hogs.

"Here again we encountered our old associate, hunger," Martin recounted. "We were, therefore, compelled to try our hands at foraging again.... There was plenty of shoats [young, weaned pigs] all about this wood, fat and plump, weighing, generally from fifty to a hundred pounds apiece. We soon found some of them, and as no owner appeared to be at hand, and the hogs not understanding our enquiries (if we made any) sufficiently to inform us to who they belonged, we made free with some of them to satisfy the calls of nature till we could be better supplied, if better we could be."[28]

Washington's men were also met by scores of British deserters seeking to escape the deadly trap being set around Yorktown. Lord Cornwallis had already pulled back most of his troops within the town itself, recognizing the noose that was being tightened around his army's throat. Cornwallis again wrote Clinton, desperately asking for rescue, and Clinton promised that a British fleet with five thousand men would sail from New York on October 5. Relieved, Cornwallis could not know that the sailing would be delayed a week due to political backstabbing and bickering between Clinton and the Royal Navy commanders.

Taking over the extensive earthworks that the British had abandoned, the Americans and French soon began digging new trenches that would extend these lines, allowing them to move their artillery closer and closer to the British garrison.

"A third part of our Sappers and Miners were ordered out this night to assist the Engineers in laying out the works," as Joseph Martin described the labor. "It was a very dark and rainy night. However, we repaired to the place and began by following the Engineers and laying laths of pine wood end to end upon a line marked by the officers, for the trenches." In a short time, Martin recalled, they were told to stop work, as a stranger walked by and engaged some of the officers in conversation. After a while, the stranger spoke with Martin and his fellow soldiers, advising them, as Martin recalled, "in case we should be taken prisoners, not to discover to the enemy what troops we were. We were obliged to thank him for his kind advice." Only later did Martin learn that he had been speaking with George Washington on that dark, rainy night.

Soaking rains halted the first night's digging, but the men returned the next night to complete laying out the works. Washington also returned, struck a few symbolic blows with a pickaxe, and the digging of trenches began in earnest. Two or three days later, the trenches were done. The bombardment of Yorktown could begin. By October 9, the allies began the deadly work of shelling, which would continue without mercy. By the end of that first day, more than one hundred French and American guns were at work—3,600 cannonballs fell on Yorktown and the harbor in the first twenty-four hours alone.

And it would continue without relief. The allied guns rained cannon fire down on the beleaguered port town and the thousands of soldiers—and thousands more civilians—now cowering in caves and demolished buildings in the small Virginia town that had become hell on earth for its starving inhabitants, many of them sick and dying. Pressed against the York River, the British troops, the remaining townspeople of Yorktown, and the thousands of African Americans who had followed the British army there were caught in the deadly waves of shot and shell that were reducing the town to rubble.

The shelling was "like the shocks of an earthquake," one British soldier said later. "One saw men lying everywhere who were mortally wounded and whose heads, arms and legs had been shot off...."[29]

With the capture of Redoubts 9 and 10 on the night of October 14, George Washington moved up his guns and continued to hurl shot at the British from three directions. On the fifteenth of October, a perfunctory and almost desperate British counterattack—made to preserve a sense of honor rather than any true military purpose—was launched on a battery held by one hundred Virginia militiamen. The British overran the Virginians at the gun battery, damaging some guns, until a detachment of French regulars countered and drove the British off. Informed of the raid, Washington thought that the incident was "small and ineffective and of little consequence to either party." Seventeen Americans had been killed and wounded; the British had lost six when the French repulsed them.[30]

By the morning of October 16, more guns were brought up to the firing line.

That evening, General Cornwallis attempted to remove some of his wounded and sick troops by boat across the narrow channel to Gloucester Point on the opposite side of the river, where a smaller British detachment was also pinned in by American troops, but a violent squall ruined the effort. The allied firing on Yorktown grew more intense. By day's end, Cornwallis and his officers agreed that their situation was hopeless and that reinforcements expected from New York would not arrive in time, if at all.

On the morning of October 17, Washington's guns again opened up at sunrise. Then, at about nine o'clock in the morning, a drummer boy appeared, followed by an officer waving a white handkerchief. The bombardment ceased and negotiations between the besieged British and the French-American allies began. Colonel John Laurens led the American negotiating team.

On October 19, the articles of capitulation were signed. At 2 p.m., the remnants of Cornwallis's army that could walk limped out of Yorktown, past the mile-long columns of French and American soldiers and civilian spectators who had flocked to the scene. Black drummers, a contingent of men who had joined the British in hopes of freedom, beat a muffled march as the defeated British looked to the front, refusing to acknowledge the American colors—a breach of eighteenth-century wartime niceties. Viewing this British behavior as an insult to the victorious American rebels, Lafayette ordered his drum major to strike up "Yankee Doodle Dandy."[31] Once a British song that derided American soldiers and their masculinity, it had become a source of pride for the rebel Americans, and at the sound, the surrendering British troops turned their eyes toward the victorious Americans.

But no British slight could spoil the moment. "It was a noble sight to us," young Joseph Martin later recorded. "And the more so, as it seemed to promise a speedy conclusion to the contest. The British did not make so good an appearance as the German forces; but there was some allowance to be made in their favour; the English felt their honour wounded, the Germans did not greatly care whose hands they were in. The British paid the Americans, seemingly, but little attention as they passed them, but they eyed the French with considerable malice depicted in their countenances."[32]

Brigadier General Charles O'Hara, Cornwallis's second in command, led the column as Cornwallis claimed illness that day. When O'Hara offered his sword in surrender to Rochambeau, the Frenchman declined and pointed to Washington, who indicated that his second in command, Benjamin Lincoln, should receive the honor. A town clerk, magistrate, and farmer from Massachusetts, Lincoln had been humiliated by the treatment he received at British hands when he was captured at Charleston in 1780. He ceremonially took O'Hara's sword, later returning it to the British officer.

In all, nearly 7,500 British and Hessian troops surrendered, along with 840 naval personnel. Their casualties included as many as 300 killed and many more wounded. Combined American and French losses totaled 88 killed in action and another 301 wounded.

In addition, the British handed over 243 pieces of artillery with over 2,000 rounds of ammunition, 7,000 muskets and 266,000 cartridges, thousands of swords, and 100 flags. The Americans—many of them soldiers who had foraged for their meager meals for months—also captured massive British stores of food. The news of this large and unexplained cache of food must have been startling to the British soldiers who had gone hungry during the siege. Cornwallis also had to surrender a personal chest filled with 1,800 British pounds sterling.

Once the ceremony concluded, the rank-and-file British soldiers were marched off to prisons in Virginia and Maryland; the officers were allowed to sail to a British port but, under the terms of capitulation, could take no further part in the war. With a victory of this magnitude and the glint of an end to the war in sight, the usually strict discipline that Washington enforced gave way to a somewhat forgiving mood. He had the army's stockades opened, freeing all prisoners without regard to their offenses. But deserters, men who had once served with Washington, were another matter. Washington hung every American deserter found in Yorktown from gibbets, public gallows meant to be seen by all.[33]

---

After the surrender, the French and British commanders commenced an oddly friendly relationship as they dined together and reminisced about the campaign. Rochambeau even provided a loan to Cornwallis, who complained that he was impoverished, having surrendered his silver chest to the victorious Americans.[34]

Five days later, the British fleet with five thousand fresh troops sent to rescue Cornwallis arrived in Chesapeake Bay. It was too late, and after a few days' tense standoff between the British and French navies, the British fleet returned to New York, reaching the city on November 5. Lord Clinton realized that the battle for America had been lost.

A victorious American army returned to camps on the Hudson River above New York, while the French army remained in Yorktown and Williamsburg for the winter. The loss of Cornwallis's army did not officially end the war. But the fate of the British in America had been sealed.

News of the British defeat sparked celebrations around the United States, although the news brought despair to Tories throughout America. In London, the reaction was complete shock. King George III contemplated abdicating his throne but was counseled against such a radical decision by his prime minister, Lord North, who resigned instead.

The British still had twenty-six thousand troops in North America, but the political will to continue the war was gone. The fighting with the American colonies had been long and costly, and the simultaneous wars with France and Spain continued to drain the royal treasury. While battling the American patriot ruffians, the British were also fighting wars in India, Gibraltar, the West Indies, and Ireland. In March 1782, Parliament passed a resolution saying the British should not continue the war against the United States. Later that year, commissioners of the United States and Great Britain signed provisional articles of peace. In September 1783, the final treaty was signed, which ended the war and acknowledged American independence.

It did not take long before the victory at Yorktown inspired a proud, patriotic narrative that quickly became part of American legend. But as historian Henry Wiencek noted, "Paintings of the Yorktown victory show its undeniable glory and give no hint of the scene of horror beyond the lines of fluttering banners and crisply uniformed officers."[35]

Entering the rubble-strewn town, the victorious Americans discovered "an immense number of Negroes" lying dead from smallpox. Most of them were refugees who had flocked to the British army with the hope of freedom. Having thought they had escaped plantation slavery, they had been forced by Cornwallis to do the hard work of fortifying Yorktown. But smallpox had struck down hundreds of them before the siege even began.

That was only part of the real story. Although Washington's leadership in fashioning the victory at Yorktown quickly and forever cemented his place as America's greatest Revolutionary military hero, the simple truth is that the battle would not have been fought much less won without the French, especially the French fleet that won the naval battle against a British force earlier in September 1781. It is true that Washington clearly agreed that Yorktown was the ripe target and he had conceived the dazzling march from New York to Virginia. But he had signed on to the plan only after stubbornly holding on to his own pet project to attack New York, while the French engineered the Virginia campaign.

The victory at Yorktown was foremost a victory at sea in which no American vessels took part. Instead of playing some role in the campaign, the celebrated American naval war hero John Paul Jones, a Scotsman, was ordered to Portsmouth, New Hampshire, where he was to assume command of a still-unfinished seventy-four-gun ship, the *America*.

Washington could not be faulted for the lack of American ships in the Yorktown campaign. In the wisdom of Congress, Washington had never been permitted to lead the navy—such as it was. As naval historian George C. Daughan summarized America's paltry seagoing fighting effort at the time, "Most [in the Continental Congress] just shrugged their shoulders and assumed the Royal Navy was just too strong. Starting from scratch in the midst of a war, the United States could not hope to compete against it."[36] In a history of the U.S. Navy, Ian W. Toll added, "Of the thirteen American frigates built during the Revolution, seven were captured and taken by the Royal Navy, and another four were destroyed either by the British or their own crews."[37]

In the aftermath of Yorktown, one of the greatest pieces of Revolutionary legend would emerge over the role of the American militia in the military struggle for independence. From the time of their arrival in what would become the United States of America, colonists had relied for their defense on groups of men who trained regularly and were compelled by law to maintain their own weapons and ammunition. These militia forces grew more important as the colonial population exploded and conflicts with Native Americans, such as King Philip's War, fought in colonial New England between 1675 and 1678, actually threatened the colonies' existence.

As James Kirby Martin and Mark Edward Lender described the colonial-era defense forces: "Although early militia, especially those in New England, had been essential in defense against hostile Native Americans, militia units during the 1730s and 1740s in the South played a large part in guarding the white populace against individual slave depredations and group uprisings. Over time, the militia became the exclusive province of free, white, adult, propertied males....Indians, free blacks, indentured servants, apprentices, and indigents came to be excluded from militia service. A primary function of the militia thus turned out to be protecting the propertied and privileged in colonial society from the unpropertied and unprivileged."[38]

During the French and Indian War—fought in America from 1754 to 1760—Anglo-American colonists were expected to contribute men and finances to this British war with France. In his twenties, young George Washington gained his first military experience commanding Virginia militiamen in this war. And when that fighting ended, the colonial militias were still expected to train regularly to be prepared for any invasion, put down riots, and suppress slave insurrections and capture runaways.

It is a comforting piece of the American narrative that everyone was ready, willing, and able to take up arms. But in pre-Revolutionary America, the urge to avoid militia duty was already powerful. Conscription—forced enlistment or a draft by another name—was needed to fill out militia quotas, and the ability to pay for a substitute soon became an essential part of America's militia tradition.

There is no question that in 1775, militiamen who had trained for the moment fired the first shots of the Revolution. But the idea that the American militia—poorly trained, ill-equipped, underfinanced, and reluctant to stray far from their home states—was the only force that the new American republic would rely upon to defeat the largest, best-trained professional army in the world was ludicrous. George Washington knew that from the beginning. He understood that a standing, professional, paid army—disciplined and led by an experienced officers corps—was the only way Americans could hope to fight and defeat the British. Although militia forces often served admirably and contributed to some significant victories in the Revolution, their role in the fighting was largely negligible. At Yorktown, the Virginia militia on hand had essentially served a support role, and in one instance—the British counterattack on a gun emplacement—they had been completely overrun, rescued by a last-minute French intervention.

Washington's Continentals were part of the very sort of regular standing army that many of the Founding Fathers distrusted. To a large number of the American Revolutionary generation, armies had existed throughout history as the weapon of kings and popes—with their lower ranks usually drawn from the most brutish dregs of society. Officers with titles were often honorary, and skepticism of an aristocratic officer class only added to the mistrust. And truly professional soldiers were often viewed as mercenaries, willing to sell a sword to the highest bidder.

"As Americans tried to define their army, they clung to the conviction that a professional soldier was dangerous, vicious, and damned," historian Charles Royster explained. "He killed for money. He made war a trade and preferred long, easygoing wars that yielded him the largest gains for the smallest inconvenience. These gains came at the expense of both taxpayers and the civil government."[39]

Early in 1776, Boston rebel leader Samuel Adams had written to fellow patriot James Warren, "A standing Army, however necessary it may be at some times, is always dangerous to the Liberties of the People. Soldiers are apt to consider themselves as a Body distinct from the rest of the Citizens."[40]

In spite of the fears of men like Samuel Adams and Thomas Jefferson—another critic of standing armies—the nation's birth *demanded* a regular army. Washington himself had once written to the president of Congress, "To place any dependence upon militia, is, assuredly, resting upon a broken staff."

The question of who fought and triumphed—Continentals or militia—became more intense as the early-nineteenth-century version of Revolutionary history began to cloud the picture. "These descendants of 1776 debated about who had won the war—the Continental Army or the far more numerous part-time soldiers known as militia, who turned out only during emergencies," historian Thomas Fleming commented. "Politicians, quick to flatter a majority of the voters, had long since opted for the militia, beginning an American tendency to denigrate professional soldiers. Even in the Congress of the Revolution, there had been a party of populists who sneeringly called the Continental Army's officers 'gentlemen of the blade.'"[41]

Thomas Jefferson also voiced the ambivalence or antagonism toward soldiers, which even finds voice in the Declaration, where Jefferson's complaints about King George included this charge: "He has kept among us, in times of peace, Standing Armies without the Consent of our legislatures."

As Virginia's governor during the Revolution, Jefferson found it difficult to meet the state's required recruitment quotas, offering bounties and reluctantly forcing a conscript act—in other words, a draft. "The requirement that Virginia should have no standing army meant that the state had to rely on a system ill-prepared to respond to major invasion," wrote Michael Kranish, a former fellow at the International Center for Jefferson Studies at Monticello. "Jefferson and many other Virginians worried that a standing army would abuse its power and act tyrannically."[42]

Yet never having served in the military himself and later accused of cowardice in his flight from Benedict Arnold's attack, Jefferson would continue to resist a professional army as a danger to the republic. In *Notes on Virginia*, written in 1781, Jefferson stated his belief that most wars should be avoided and a European enemy be met on the sea. "A land army would be useless for offence, and not the best nor safest instrument for defence. For either of these purposes, the sea is the field on which we should meet a European enemy." But, the future third president continued, such a navy would be an onerous expense. "To aim at such a navy as the greater nations of Europe possess, would be a foolish and wicked waste of the energies of our countrymen…that load of military expense which makes the European laborer go supperless to bed, and moistens his bread with the sweat of his brow."[43]

He was among those who claimed that the "citizen soldier" had won the Revolution. Yet, ironically, it was during his presidency, in 1802, that the United States Military Academy was founded at West Point to turn out a class of professional U.S. Army officers especially trained in engineering, mathematics, and the sciences—subjects largely overlooked by other colleges of the time, which focused on a classical education. The idea could be traced back to Henry Knox. During the war, he recommended to John Adams that America create a school that would produce a "respectable army," instead of a force that Knox described in 1776 as "merely a receptacle for ragamuffins."[44]

So, who fought the American Revolution? Washington's Continental Army was not composed simply of patriotic farmers who left their plows, but young men who were out of work and often desperate to earn a living. After all, the farmers had to go back to their fields, leading pamphleteer Thomas Paine to famously deride them as "Summer Soldiers" in *The Crisis*.

"Contrary to popular lore and some modern commentators, the well-to-do and 'yeoman farmers' seemed to prefer staying at home rather than rushing to the front lines after the *rage militaire* of the first campaign had worn off," writes Charles Patrick Neimeyer. "Seizing on the idea that an army of citizen-soldiers represented true republican virtue, later generations skewed the history of the Continental army, ascribing the characteristics of the first year to the whole war."[45]

Regular soldier Joseph Martin, who joined up at fifteen simply because most of his friends were enlisting, wrote derisively of the militiamen, underscoring this distinction: "The militia did good and great service...on particular occasions, I well know....But I insist that they would not have answered the end so well as regular troops....They would not have endured the sufferings the army did; they would have considered themselves...free citizens, not bound by any cords that were not of their own manufacturing, and when the hardships of fatigue, starvation, cold and nakedness...[had] begun to seize upon them in such awful array as they did on us, they would have instantly quitted."[46]

Martin was apparently correct. During the course of the war, according to historian Ray Raphael's account of the common people who fought the Revolution, an estimated one-half of all the men who served in the militias deserted at least once.[47]

Certainly there were farmers among the proud patriots enrolled in Washington's ranks. But many of them were also immigrants—Irish and German in particular—who were accustomed to fighting in Europe's wars. They were the "rabble" often dismissed by haughty Americans. But they were the men who typically filled the ranks of America's Revolutionary army. And it was this armed and sometimes angry underclass that frightened many of the founding generation.

There remains another significant aspect of the American militia's history that has been consistently ignored by the heroic image bestowed on these forces. In Virginia, men were exempt from militia duty if they owned property or more than three slaves. "In other words," Michael Kranish wrote, "those least able to afford service were required to serve, while the wealthier could avoid it."[48]

When confronted by outside threats, American militiamen were often more concerned with another danger at home. When Benedict Arnold launched an onslaught on Virginia in early 1781, the men of the state—where Patrick Henry had proudly proclaimed, "Give me liberty or give me death" a few years earlier—did not rally to the flag. With Arnold's raiders raging across Virginia, the militia turnout was "abysmal," historian Gary B. Nash reported. "One of the reasons...was that too many officers, and some of the enlisted men, were fearful of leaving farms and plantations in the hands of slaves who were flocking to the British whenever the redcoated army appeared.... Protecting slave property had trumped the common defense of Virginia."[49]

This uncomfortable fact accounts for the other crucial missing piece of the typical Yorktown military history—the large part played by people usually invisible in the traditional narratives and the patriotic paintings that celebrated the victory. Thousands of African Americans fought and lived through or died on both sides of the siege of Yorktown. Black soldiers in the Continental Army were "the Forgotten Fifth," as Nash called them, but by some estimates they may have actually counted for as many as one-quarter of American Revolutionary soldiers.

Complicating this picture was the other side of the battle lines, where thousands of black "Followers of Army and Flag" had flocked to the British in the hopes of promised emancipation. Some actually were given uniforms and weapons—or musical instruments—and fought as British soldiers. But the vast majority of blacks who fled to the British forces in hopes of being freed found instead a new form of slavery as a British wartime workforce, which suffered starvation, disease, and death in large numbers.

"It was in Virginia that the plight of African American refugees took its most tragic turn," Elizabeth A. Fenn stated in her history of smallpox in Revolutionary America. "Pursuing the British eastward from Richmond in the summer of 1781, American soldiers observed the bodies of black loyalists strewn along the roadside. 'Within these days past, I have marched by 18 or 20 Negroes that lay dead by the way-side. Putrefying with the small-pox,' wrote a Connecticut soldier named Josiah Atkins on June 24, 1781. 'These poor creatures, having no care taken of them, many crawl'd into the bushes about & died, where they lie infecting the air around with intolerable stench and great danger.' The epidemic had exploded and so sickly were the black loyalists that despite their great numbers, Cornwallis desperately sought more. As workers, he wrote in July, they were 'constantly wanted' for a 'variety of fatiguing Services' which soldiers were not willing to perform."[30]

But as they suffered the same bombardment, starvation, and disease that were cutting down the British defenders of Yorktown, these African Americans feared something worse than defeat. If Yorktown fell, they would be slaves once more. During the siege, Cornwallis had forced thousands of sick and diseased blacks from his camp, unable to feed them and fearful that they would add to the contagion among his troops, many of them already suffering from typhus, malaria, and smallpox. No doubt Cornwallis also hoped that if they reached the American lines, they might spread illness to the patriot and French side as well.

A German soldier serving under Cornwallis later recorded, "We had used them to great advantage and set them free, and now with fear and trembling, they had to face the reward of their cruel masters."[31]

"During the siege," young Joseph Martin recounted, "we saw in the woods herds of Negroes which lord Cornwallis (after he had inveigled them from their proprietors), in love and pity to them, had turned adrift, with no other recompense for their confidence in his humanity, than the small pox for their bounty and starvation and death for their wages. They might have been seen scattered in every direction, dead and dying, with pieces of ears of burnt corn in their hands and mouths, even of those that were dead."[52]

Within days of the British surrender at Yorktown, Virginians arrived in search of their surviving slaves. Martin described how plantation owners offered rewards to soldiers for helping to recover what they considered lost property. Martin was given a dollar in "paper money" for his assistance, money he later used to purchase a "single quart of rum: to such a miserable state had all the paper stuff, called—money—depreciated."[53]

Among those blacks recaptured after the British surrender were two refugees who had once been the legal property of George Washington. According to Henry Wiencek, "Washington was able to recover the two at Yorktown and return them to slavery at Mount Vernon because of a clause Washington demanded in the articles of surrender permitting the repatriation of captured slaves."[54] In his biography of Washington, Ron Chernow noted, "Yorktown had struck a blow for American liberty with one exception; those slaves who had flocked to the British side to win their freedom were now restored to the thrall of their owners." Washington, recorded Chernow, recovered two and was "determined to recover the remaining fifteen slaves he had lost."[55]

Washington was not the only Founding Father who was able to recover lost "property" at Yorktown. A number of people who had been taken earlier in the year from Jefferson's homes by Benedict Arnold's forces were with the British. One of them was a young boy named Isaac, who would later recount his experiences during the siege. "The smell was awful," Isaac later reported. "You could smell the fear in all of us. Blood and death was everywhere. The birds would come and pick at the dead. They would take the eyes first."[56]

Describing his "rescue," Isaac said, "When the battle was over, we rejoiced at being together and alive. We remained in Little York [Yorktown] a few more days until General Washington brought all of Master Jefferson's folks and about 20 of Thomas Mann Randolph's Tuckahoe folks back to Richmond with him and sent word to Jefferson to send to Richmond for his servants."[57]

Isaac and the other enslaved people Washington recaptured would return to the Monticello home of the author of the Declaration of Independence, who Isaac later said was "mightily pleased to see his people come back safe and sound."[58] *

Another former slave in Yorktown was James Armistead, a black man who had volunteered to join Lafayette's network of spies within Cornwallis's camp. As a courier and source of information, Armistead had supplied valuable intelligence to Lafayette in the weeks that led up to the battle. But his master reclaimed him after the war. Lafayette learned of this and later interceded. In January 1787, Armistead was freed by the Virginia legislature and took the name Lafayette.[59]

It is the largely untold tale of these people—blacks who served in the Continental Army or tried to escape to their liberty with the British—that is revealed through the unique roles played by three of Washington's men: Hamilton, Lafayette, and Laurens.

United by their belief in the American cause and admiration for Washington, the three men also shared a view about the role of African Americans in the army and the future of slavery in America that separated them from their commander in chief. For all three men, Laurens in particular, the success of that evening's assault at Yorktown held special meaning. The capture of the redoubts had clearly proven the truth of what all three men had been arguing for years: If

---

* Isaac continued to work at Monticello, eventually gaining his freedom and working as a blacksmith in Petersburg, Virginia, where his recollections of life as a Monticello slave were recorded in 1847.

permitted to fight for the United States, black men—both freemen and emancipated slaves—could serve the nation well and could possibly tip the balance of war with England.

"The bravery exhibited by the attacking troops was emulous and praiseworthy," Washington later noted in his journal. "Few cases have exhibited stronger proofs of intrepidity, coolness, and firmness than were shown upon this occasion."[60]

Unacknowledged by Washington in these words—and in many traditional Yorktown narratives—is that part of Hamilton's handpicked vanguard included the First Rhode Island Regiment, about three-quarters of them African-American soldiers, many of them former slaves who had been promised freedom in return for their service—and whose masters had been compensated for their emancipation.

The significance of the Rhode Island Regiment at Yorktown is closely connected with the story of John Laurens, the son of slaveholders who had been advocating for emancipation of blacks to aid the Revolutionary cause for years. Laurens, who was also directly responsible for negotiating a loan from the Netherlands and returning to America with those funds in time to pay the army that fought at Yorktown, had been born into one of South Carolina's wealthiest and most influential families. During the Revolution, he had become an outspoken voice of reform, a dreamer who thought that American independence must also bring liberty to nearly half a million slaves.

The son of Eleanor Ball and Henry Laurens, he was born in Charleston, South Carolina, in 1754 and enjoyed a life among the most privileged of Americans in the mid-eighteenth century. His father had made a fortune in the slave trade, was later active in politics during the American Revolution, and would go on to serve as both a member and president of the Continental Congress. As "President of the United States in Congress Assembled," Laurens belongs to a select group of men. Congressional officials who presided over meetings of the Continental Congress were called "presidents," but this was prior to ratification of the U.S. Constitution, the creation of the executive branch, and election of George Washington as the first president of the United States. After his wife's death, Henry Laurens had taken John and his three brothers to Switzerland to continue their education, and John later moved to England to study law.

But John Laurens was less interested in law than in the growing political tensions between the American colonies and England. He had been converted in London to the abolitionist cause and possessed the zeal of a true believer. But the handsome and dashing young American had also met a young English woman, Martha Manning, whose father was a close associate of Henry Laurens. When she became pregnant, John Laurens dutifully married her, and Martha gave birth to a daughter. Shortly after, Laurens boarded a ship bound for Charleston, leaving wife and daughter behind as he went off to join the patriot cause.

Inspired by *Common Sense*—Thomas Paine's pamphlet that made a persuasive case for American independence and was published anonymously in January 1776—John (Jack to his close friends) Laurens left England to join the Continental Army. Elegant in uniform, blue-eyed, bookish yet bold, Laurens believed that it was worthy to die in a glorious cause; in his case there were two—independence and abolition. He saw combat at the Battle of Brandywine and came to the attention of Washington, who chose the twenty-two-year-old Laurens to serve as an aide.

Fluent in French, Laurens became an invaluable asset to Washington, who would cryptically later note that the young officer was given confidential missions "which neither time nor propriety would suffer me to commit to paper."[61] It was Laurens who translated for Washington when Baron von Steuben arrived in Valley Forge. A Prussian mercenary, von Steuben was credited with whipping the Continental Army into fighting shape. Laurens, Alexander Hamilton, and

Lafayette formed an almost inseparable trio, whose affections for each other prompted later historical speculation that two of the men might have been lovers.*

Despite his family's wealth from slavery, Laurens was outspoken about his belief that Americans fighting for republican principles were hypocritical if they continued to utilize slave labor. His idealism formed part of his rapport with Hamilton, also an abolitionist when that was far from a popular stance.

From the time he joined Washington's inner circle, Laurens campaigned for a plan to free slaves and allow them to fight in the Continental Army. He had first witnessed the fighting spirit and courage of African-American troops at the Battle of Newport in 1778, where he fought alongside the First Rhode Island Regiment. Like other states in the early years of the Revolution, Rhode Island was struggling to meet its quota of regiments, which were thinned by disease, absenteeism, and desertion. Contrary to the patriotic image of the Minutemen, Americans did not always flock to the rebel banners.

Reversing his own earlier orders, Washington had instructed Rhode Island's governor to fill quota shortfalls for Continental Army enlistments with blacks. "White Rhode Islanders," writes Gary B. Nash, "now rebuilt what some called 'the ragged lousey naked regiment' with slaves liberated by their masters, who were promised compensation from the public coffers for their loss of labor."[62]

---

* A homosexual relationship between Hamilton and Laurens or Hamilton and Lafayette has been suggested. Hamilton's biographer Ron Chernow writes: "Because the style of eighteenth century letters could be quite florid, even between men, one must tread gingerly in approaching the matter, especially since Laurens's letters to Hamilton were warm but proper....If Hamilton and Laurens did become lovers...they would have taken extraordinary precautions. At the very least, we can say that Hamilton developed something like an adolescent crush on his friend" (*Alexander Hamilton*, p. 95). As for Lafayette, Chernow adds, "As with John Laurens, we will never know. But the breathless tone of the letters that Hamilton exchanged with Laurens and Lafayette is unlike anything in his later letters. This may simply have been a by-product of youth and wartime camaraderie" (ibid., p. 97).

Black troops had participated in every engagement of the war since the fighting began in Massachusetts in 1775. And, as Nash points out, "Early in the war, black Americans had to fight for the right to fight. New Englanders at first were glad to have men of color fighting alongside them.... But pressure from white southern leaders led General Washington to purge the army of African Americans with an order issued on November 12, 1775, just five days after Virginia's royal governor offered freedom to slaves who reached his encampment."[63]

The significance of the offer made by Virginia's governor, Lord Dunmore, to liberate any slaves that joined his ranks was a landmark in the war for independence that was long unrecognized in the traditional version of patriots fighting for "Life, Liberty and the Pursuit of Happiness." In *Rough Crossings*, his landmark history of the role of slavery in the American Revolution, Simon Schama wrote:

> The strategy backfired, as it did throughout the South. Instead of being cowed by the threat of a British armed liberation of the blacks, the slaveholding population mobilized to resist. Innumerable whites, especially in the habitually loyal backcountry of Virginia, had been hitherto skeptical of the more hot-headed of their Patriot leaders. But the news that British troops would liberate their blacks, then give them weapons and their blessing to use them on their masters, persuaded many to think that perhaps the militant Patriots were right and that the British government, in tearing up the "bonds of civil society" (as Washington had put it), might be capable of any iniquity. It is not too much, then, to say that in the summer and autumn of 1775, the revolution in the South crystallized around this one immense, terrifying issue.... Theirs was a revolution, first and foremost, mobilized to protect slavery.[64]

First in 1776 and again when the British began the Southern campaign in 1779, when Henry Clinton repeated Dunmore's promise, thousands of slaves were willing to risk the chance for freedom offered by the British. Dunmore's offer was part of the larger British plan to break off the Southern states from the independence movement. The British promise was not made out of sincere abolitionist sentiment, but in the belief that luring slaves from plantations would wreak havoc on the American economy, force slaveholders to focus on defending their plantations instead of fighting the British, and generally inspire fear among the white Southern populace. In addition, the British made it clear that the offer of freedom *did not* extend to those slaves of loyalist Tories in the American South.

After witnessing black soldiers fight in Rhode Island in 1778, John Laurens believed that the argument for freeing slaves to fight for the American cause had both a moral and a strategic value. At the time, he wrote his father, Henry, asking him to free his slaves "instead of leaving me a Fortune." Said Laurens, "We Americans, at least in the Southern Colonies, cannot contend with a good Grace, for Liberty, until we shall have enfranchised our Slaves."

As the British stepped up operations in the South, Laurens promoted the idea of arming slaves and granting them freedom in return for their service. He had an ally in Hamilton and others in Washington's military circle. Eventually even Laurens's father supported the idea as the only way the South could defend itself against British attack.[65]

In March 1779, a Congress desperate for manpower approved the concept, commissioned John Laurens as lieutenant colonel, and sent him south to recruit a regiment of three thousand black soldiers. Still in uniform, Laurens won election to the South Carolina House of Representatives, where he introduced his black regiment plan in 1779 and 1780, only to be met with overwhelming rejection each time.

Commanding an infantry regiment during the battle for Charleston, Laurens was taken prisoner in May 1780 after the city was taken in a calamitous defeat that included the capture of 5,400 American soldiers. The Continental Army suffered another disaster at Camden, South Carolina, where nine hundred Americans were killed or wounded and a thousand were taken captive.

A British prisoner, Laurens was shipped to Philadelphia. Under the terms of his parole, he was able to see his father before the elder Laurens set off for the Netherlands in the hope of securing loans for the American cause. The British seized the ship carrying Laurens's father and he was imprisoned for treason in the Tower of London, the only American held in the Tower during the Revolution.

Meanwhile, Congress had appointed the twenty-five-year-old Laurens, also freed in a prisoner exchange, as a special minister to France in December 1780. Accompanied by *Common Sense* pamphleteer Thomas Paine, Laurens went to Paris to join Benjamin Franklin in the effort to win French assurances that their navy would support American operations by May 1781. He also arranged loans and supplies from the Netherlands before returning to America in May, arriving in time to join Hamilton and Lafayette in Yorktown.

Although Laurens and Hamilton shared much in personality, ambition, and philosophy, they did not share much in the way of biography or bloodlines. Hamilton was an illegitimate child born in the West Indies island of Nevis and raised on St. Croix. Studious, intellectually advanced, with a knack for capturing the confidence of older men, he wrote an essay in a local journal. Recognizing his obvious intelligence and writing talent, some local merchants underwrote a trip to America, where young Hamilton excelled at King's College in New York (the future Columbia University).

As a student at King's College, Hamilton wrote a 1775 pamphlet arguing for American freedom. Among those who read it was Boston bookseller Henry Knox. A Quaker with patriot zeal and ambitions of military adventure, Henry Knox would emerge as one of the heroes of Washington's Boston campaign when he carted cannons captured at Fort Ticonderoga across Massachusetts by ox-drawn wagons; that artillery eventually helped drive the British from Boston in March

1776. When the twenty-six-year-old Knox arrived in New York in April 1776 to establish Washington's artillery, he met Hamilton, a young captain in a New York artillery company, and, recognizing him as the author of the pamphlet, quickly offered him a place in his command. Soon after that, Hamilton came to the attention of General Washington, who invited him to join his staff in January 1777 as one of his chief aides-de-camp.

It was a stunning arrival, as biographer Ron Chernow noted: "In fewer than five years, the twenty-two-year-old Alexander Hamilton had risen from despondent clerk in St. Croix to one of the aides of America's most eminent man." The decision to join Washington set Hamilton on a path that would make him one of America's most influential Founders.[66]

But Hamilton craved the battlefield and balked at the idea of a desk job. Passed over for promotions, a prideful and ambitious Hamilton was rankled by Washington's reluctance to give him a shot at combat. Time after time, Hamilton's pleas for command and the chance at glory and honor on the battlefield fell on deaf ears—Washington did not want to risk such a valued aide to a British ball or bayonet. The commander's well-intended caution did not mollify the mercurial Hamilton. Shortly after his marriage in December 1780 to the daughter of Philip Schuyler, a prominent, wealthy New Yorker and friend of Washington, the headstrong young officer risked career suicide by storming out of Washington's tent, threatening to resign. Cooling down, Hamilton returned to the fold early in 1781.

And finally, at Yorktown, Washington relented by giving Hamilton a command of his own and then allowing him the honor of leading the October 14 assault. Two days before the attack, with typical bravado, Hamilton had written to his bride, Eliza, now five months pregnant, "You shall engage shortly to present me with *a boy*. You will ask me if a girl will not answer the purpose. By no means. I fear, with all the mother's charms, she may inherit the caprices of her father, and then she will enslave, tantalize and plague one half [the] sex."⁶⁷

———————

By the fall of 1781, Lafayette was well on his way to becoming an American legend. The wealthy young French aristocrat—an orphan by the time he turned thirteen and whose marriage at fourteen to a young aristocratic woman secured his status as one of France's wealthiest men—had joined the patriot cause out of a passionate zeal for independence.

Not long after April 1775, when the first shots were fired at Lexington and Concord, Lafayette had joined a French Masonic military lodge and embraced the secret fraternity's radical new philosophy. As biographer Harlow Giles Unger wrote, "Nowhere in the political and intellectual darkness of Europe's aristocratic monarchies did the Age of Enlightenment shine brighter than in France's Masonic lodge, where the American Revolution represented a struggle by Freemasons like Washington and Franklin for Masonic principles and man's right to life, liberty, and property." ⁶⁸

With the blessings and endorsement of Benjamin Franklin, who was serving as American emissary at the Court of Versailles, Lafayette had sailed for America at the age of nineteen. Arriving in July 1777, he had agreed to serve in the American army without pay, bought a ship outfitted at his own expense, and spent freely to arm the patriot troops. He was also one of America's best friends at the French court when French aid was essential to America's survival. Stylish, dashing, and absolutely committed to the cause of independence, he had an electric effect on all those who encountered him. As historian Burke Davis explained, "The French boy had charmed a hostile Congress... and had been made a major general—an honorary one, congressmen thought."[69] But the boy would prove his mettle on the battlefield and earn his rank, charming Washington as well, who would watch the young man's skill. That was why it was Lafayette who was assigned to hunt down Benedict Arnold and then harass Cornwallis in 1781.

When the two met at Williamsburg on Washington's arrival on September 14, 1781, Washington threw his bridle on his horse's neck, opened both arms, and caught Lafayette in a great hug, kissing him from ear to ear.

But as much as Washington may have admired, respected, and perhaps even loved these three—Lafayette, Laurens, and Hamilton—"His Excellency" resisted their abolitionist ambitions. As Gary B. Nash wrote, "It can only be a matter of speculation whether Washington's enormous prestige might have convinced slave owners of the Lower South that it would be better to free some of their slaves to fight *against* the British invaders than to see them flee *to* the British."[70]

Washington's unwillingness to embrace the abolitionist sentiment, and even his reluctant acceptance of emancipating some slaves to fight, is one of the tragic what-ifs of American history. What is clear is that after Yorktown, the Mount Vernon slaves who had either run away or been captured by the British were quickly collected and returned to bondage.

The number of slaves who fled their masters during the Revolution has been debated for centuries. A figure of 100,000 has been suggested—an astonishing number given that the total slave population was around 400,000. Thomas Jefferson thought Virginia alone lost 30,000 slaves, but recent research suggests that number is inflated. Modern historians of the period suggest that South Carolina lost as many as 25,000 and Georgia 75 to 85 percent of its slaves. Their fates are largely unknown, although many certainly died of disease and starvation. A handful took the offer of British emigration only to end up as slaves once more in the West Indies. Another 3,000 moved to Nova Scotia, having been promised land there. But they were given only wretched hovels and slavelike work until British abolitionists raised funds to relocate some of them to West Africa. Here British abolitionists sponsored a settlement in Sierra Leone, where, as Simon Schama wrote, "American blacks experienced for the first time (and all too ephemerally) a meaningful degree of local law and self-government."[71] A small band of black soldiers who had fought in a British brigade continued to fight in South Carolina after the Revolution was over until a Southern militia force wiped them out.

Rather predictably, black veterans who had served in the Continental Army had trouble acquiring their promised freedom after the war. Or, as many white soldiers also did, in receiving their pensions. After the war, a future governor of Massachusetts, William Eustis, who had served as an American army surgeon since 1775, would write of these black patriots: "The war over, and peace restored these men returned to the Respective states; and who could have said to them, on their return to civil life, after having shed their blood in common with whites in the defense of liberties of the country: 'You are not to participate in the rights secured by the struggle or in the liberty for which you have been fighting.'"[72]

Who could have said such a thing? The Framers of the Constitution, for starters.


## AFTERMATH

A relieved and victorious George Washington had one difficult personal obligation remaining after the cheering was over—a visit to a gravely ill family member, twenty-six-year-old John Parke Custis. Born in 1754, Jackie, as he was known, was the son of Martha Washington and her first husband, wealthy planter Daniel Parke Custis.

Following his father's death in 1757, Jackie Custis was due to inherit almost eighteen thousand acres of land and some three hundred slaves. In January 1759, when he was five, his mother married

George Washington and the Washingtons raised him, along with his younger sister Patsy, at Mount Vernon.

In 1774, at age eighteen, he came into his full inheritance and suddenly married. Viewed as lazy and disinterested in school, he took up the life of a Virginia planter-squire, with a brief, desultory stint in Virginia's legislature. But at every step he failed to impress his stepfather. In fact, while young men like Laurens, Hamilton, and Lafayette possessed all of the gentleman's qualities that Washington prized, his stepson seemed to have none. Like many sons of America's elite, Jackie Custis had, in historian Thomas Fleming's cutting view, "sat out the war on his various plantations in Maryland and Virginia, letting other men his age do the fighting and dying."[73]

At Yorktown, traveling as Washington's aide-de-camp—in title only—Jackie Custis had nothing to do with the siege or the battle. Critics complained that he had merely come to bask in the reflected glory without having "paid his dues." While there, Custis contracted "camp fever," most likely typhus spread by lice and fleas. He observed the British surrender from a carriage on the battlefield and was later transported to the home of his uncle, Burwell Bassett (Martha Washington's brother-in-law), about thirty miles away.

Setting out for his Mount Vernon estate, Washington stopped at the Bassett plantation on November 5, moments after Jackie Custis died, three weeks before his twenty-seventh birthday. Martha Washington was crushed by the loss of her son. Washington outwardly expressed little grief over the loss of his stepson, an accidental casualty of Yorktown.

As for Washington's other men, the aftermath of Yorktown was a mixture of the triumphal, bittersweet, and tragic.

Alexander Hamilton returned to Albany, New York, and began a life in New York State politics that would eventually take him to Congress, which was still operating under the Articles of Confederation, the agreement that established the United States as a loose collection of thirteen sovereign states and served as the nation's first constitution. Plagued by weaknesses under the constraints of the Articles, the national government was woefully inadequate—lacking the ability to tax, print currency, or maintain a defense force. Fully recognizing these flaws, Hamilton would play a key role as delegate in the Constitutional Convention of 1787, and as one of the authors of *The Federalist Papers*, which argued for ratification of the U.S. Constitution. A key founder of what would become the Federalist Party, he reached the pinnacle of his achievements as Washington's first secretary of the Treasury, when he became architect of America's economic structure.

One of Hamilton's early champions, Henry Knox, the Boston bookseller who had become one of Washington's most trusted aides, remained with the Continental Army—then an army mostly in name only. With news of a preliminary peace settlement in April 1783, Congress had begun to demobilize the American troops, and Washington gave Knox day-to-day command of what remained.

But first Washington and Knox were forced to confront a serious crisis within the ranks. Still operating under the Articles of Confederation, Congress had not made good on a plan for paying soldiers or providing them with pensions. Early in 1783, there were widespread rumors of outright revolt building within the ranks over the question of compensation. With America lacking a national government capable of raising taxes to pay its debts or soldiers, this issue had been festering, and the fundamental distrust of the standing army added to the tension. As Mark Puls, a biographer of Henry Knox, put it, "Many American political leaders—including Virginia's Thomas Jefferson, Patrick Henry and Richard Henry Lee, and Massachusetts' John Hancock and Samuel Adams—viewed the states as more important than the national government, which was seen as little more than the skeletal framework that loosely held the alliance of states together.... The national army only brought fears of a growing national government and bureaucracy."[74]

When an anonymous letter critical of Congress and complaining of unpaid wages began to circulate and called for a meeting of officers to air their grievances, Washington saw it as "little short of outright mutiny," according to biographer Ron Chernow. A second letter, stoking the sense of injustice and boldness, coursed through the officers' ranks. "Change the milk and water style of your last memorial—assume a bolder tone," this missive urged. Both letters are now widely attributed to Major John Armstrong Jr., an aide to General Horatio Gates, Washington's chief wartime rival. Armstrong later served as war secretary during the War of 1812. Considering Washington, D.C., insignificant as a military target, he chose not to protect it, and the British burned parts of the capital and the White House in August 1814. He was removed as secretary shortly afterward.

But when the second letter appeared, Washington was alarmed. "That only made it more threatening," wrote Chernow, "for it aroused the prospect of a military putsch."[75]

Washington called a meeting of officers on March 15, 1783, but did not announce his own attendance. With America as close as it ever might be to an outright military coup—now known as the Newburgh Conspiracy—Washington arrived at the army's main camp in Newburgh, New York, on March 15, 1783, to make an unexpected and emotional address in response to the pair of letters. To the surprise of the officers, Washington entered unannounced. The meeting was convened in a building known as the Temple of Virtue, completed a month earlier and constructed to provide a place for Sunday services, dances, and Masonic meetings. Using eyeglasses recently given to him, and which his men had never seen, Washington said, "Gentlemen, you will permit me to put on my spectacles, for I have not only grown gray, but almost blind, in the service of my country."

He continued with a plea that the officers assembled reject any attempt at an uprising:

And let me conjure you, in the name of our common country, as you value your own sacred honor, as you respect the rights of humanity, and as you regard the military and national character of America, to express your utmost horror and detestation of the man, who wishes, under any specious pretences, to overturn the liberties of our country; and who wickedly attempts to open the flood-gates of civil discord, and deluge our rising empire in blood.[76]

Washington's appeal nipped any possibility of a budding coup, and he lobbied Congress for the officers' cause. Alexander Hamilton brought the question to Congress, which voted to grant officers five years of pay plus 6 percent interest instead of half pay for life. There has been considerable debate over how serious this threat was and what motivated it. The crisis was averted mostly due to Washington, whom most historians credit with not only resisting the temptation to join but also squashing the so-called conspiracy. "The man who had pulled off the exemplary feat of humbling the most powerful military on earth had not been corrupted by fame," concluded Ron Chernow of the Newburgh Conspiracy. "Though quietly elated and relieved, he was neither intoxicated by power nor puffed up with a sense of his own genius."[77]

During this time, Knox also contributed to suspicions many Americans held about the military when he organized the Society of the Cincinnati, a hereditary fraternity of Washington's officers. Allowing membership to pass from father to son, it raised eyebrows in a new nation that feared and hated aristocracy, hereditary titles, and a professional military. With the Newburgh crisis still fresh, many Americans distrusted the Society as the source of a potential military cabal.

When the British withdrew the last of their troops from New York on November 21, 1783, Knox was at the head of the American forces that took over. He stood beside Washington during the commander in chief's teary farewell address to his officers on December 4, 1783, at Fraunces Tavern in lower Manhattan and became the senior officer of the army. He later became the war secretary under the Articles of Confederation. By the end of 1783, however, the size of the United States military had dropped to seven hundred men, thinly spread from Massachusetts to New York and west to Pittsburgh. The remnants of the rather pitiful Continental Navy were also sold off and by 1785 the United States had no vessels under its control. The Continental Marines, without funds, also simply petered out of existence.

Curiously—and more than ironically—Knox again crossed paths with one of the soldiers who dug his artillery trenches, Joseph Plumb Martin. After the war Martin became a schoolteacher and eventually settled in what is now Maine (then part of Massachusetts). In 1794, he became involved in a bitter land dispute with Knox, who claimed that he owned Martin's hundred-acre farm, as well as the surrounding six hundred thousand acres in an area now known as Waldo County. Martin argued that he owned the land and had the right to farm it. In 1797, Knox's claim was upheld in court, and Martin was ordered to pay $170 in rent. He could not raise the money and begged Knox to allow him to keep the land. Knox denied the request. With his own business ventures failing, Knox died in 1806 after a chicken bone lodged in his throat.

Knox's creditors continued to pursue Martin. By 1811, the size of Martin's farmland was cut by half, and by 1818, when he appeared in court to claim a war pension with other Revolutionary veterans, he owned nothing. In 1818, Martin's war pension was approved and he received ninety-six dollars a year for the rest of his life. Still, other war veterans were fighting for what they were properly owed. In an effort to further the cause of these veterans, Martin published his memoirs anonymously as *Private Yankee Doodle* in 1830. Although not considered a success, Martin's poignant and often humorous memoir of life in Washington's army became a source of Revolutionary history from the "grunt's eye view."

———

Once one of Washington's most trusted men, Benedict Arnold had returned to New York before the Yorktown debacle. Advising Clinton to aggressively attack Philadelphia, he was instead sent to assault New London on the Connecticut coast, not far from his birthplace of Norwich. Once again, his men burned and pillaged an American town, and the attack on September 6, 1781—six weeks before Yorktown surrendered—resulted in the deaths of 148 Americans at Fort Griswold, some of them massacred after surrendering. The Fort Griswold Massacre sealed Arnold's fate as the most despised figure in American history. Arnold eventually sailed to England aboard the same ship that carried Cornwallis to London, where Arnold—who lived for a time in Canada—died in 1801.

———

The wily Rochambeau, whose strategy helped lead to the American victory, returned to France in January 1783. When the French Revolution broke out, he supported the republic, but he was accused of treason in April 1794 and imprisoned under the Reign of Terror and threatened with the guillotine. In the end, Rochambeau was only set free by invoking his service with General Washington. As he explained to prison officials, "I cannot believe in this era of equality a former aristocrat has no rights except to march to the scaffold before anybody else, and to be the last man to prove his innocence. Those are not the principles I learned from Washington, my colleague and my friend, when we were fighting side by side for American independence." Rochambeau was released in October 1794 and died in 1807.[78]

Lafayette and Washington remained close friends and the Frenchman named his only son George Washington Lafayette. In the closing days of the American Revolution, Lafayette wrote a letter to Washington, suggesting an experiment. Lafayette would purchase land where Washington's slaves would work as free tenants. He believed that Washington's participation in the project would help to "render it a general practice"; if the idea succeeded in America with the blessing of George Washington, it might then spread into the West Indies.

Responding warmly to the idea, Washington said he preferred to discuss the details in person, explaining: "The scheme…which you propose as a precedent, to encourage the emancipation of the black people of this Country from that state of Bondage in wch. they are held, is a striking evidence of the benevolence of your Heart. I shall be happy to join you in so laudable a work; but will defer going into a detail of the business, 'till I have the pleasure of seeing you."

Lafayette had purchased a cinnamon and clove plantation, La Belle Gabrielle, in Cayenne, part of French Guiana, then a French colony on the north coast of South America. In June 1785, he began the experiment by emancipating the plantation slaves, educating them, and paying them wages.[79]

But Washington never took action. As Henry Wiencek noted, "Despite his desire to be 'rid of' his slaves, Washington was not yet ready to take steps to liberate them."[80] In fact, he would keep his slaves for the rest of his life, bringing some of them to New York and Philadelphia as America's first president, finally emancipating some of his personal slaves in his will. Wiencek added, "During the Revolution, Washington had witnessed the heroism and patriotism of the black troops, yet this had not been enough to persuade him to begin freeing his slaves. There was no evidence in the following decade of a sudden and massive improvement in the character of the slaves that would have convinced Washington that they were 'ready.'…Washington's stated reason for wishing to free his slaves in 1794, was not a sudden belief in their readiness for freedom or the urgency of it, but his conviction that slavery was 'repugnant.' "[81]

In July 1789, shortly after the start of the French Revolution, Lafayette was named commander of the French National Guard. One of his first acts was to raze the Bastille, a symbol of the French monarchy's excesses. After doing so, he sent Washington one of the keys to the notorious French prison; that key still hangs in the hallway at the Mount Vernon mansion.

Like Rochambeau, Lafayette became a victim of the French Revolution as it began to eat its own. Warring factions turned the Revolution into the Reign of Terror and the guillotine became its symbol. Like Rochambeau, Lafayette was branded a traitor to the Revolution, and fled France in August 1792, only to be taken prisoner by the Austrians, who were then at war with France. Held for five years in an Austrian prison until the French general Napoleon defeated Austria, Lafayette returned to France in 1797, promising Napoleon that he would stay out of politics after Napoleon seized power. Lafayette, who might have taken power in France if he had chosen to do so, was broken and even had his French citizenship revoked.*

As French-American relations deteriorated in what would later be called the "Quasi-War" of 1798–1800, Lafayette hoped to return to America and become an American citizen. With tensions between America and France running high, now former president Washington rejected Lafayette's request for aid as politically impossible, but they remained close friends and corresponded regularly until Washington's death in 1799. Lafayette was not invited to participate in France's memorial to Washington, a ceremony held in Paris. In his will,

---

* While Lafayette was imprisoned in 1792, his Cayenne property was confiscated and the Cayenne blacks resold as slaves. France's Convention of the First Republic abolished slavery in February 1794, but French slavery was reinstituted under Napoleon in 1802. In 1848, slavery was definitively abolished throughout France.

Washington bequeathed to Lafayette a pair of steel pistols captured from the British during the Revolution.[82]

After the French monarchy was restored in 1815, Lafayette was elected to the country's legislature, and to mark the celebration of the fiftieth anniversary of American independence, he returned to America for what amounted to a hero's tour of the country in 1824 and 1825. Visiting all twenty-four of the states, he was cheered by crowds that reached one hundred thousand in some places.[83] He went to a celebration on the anniversary of the Yorktown victory in October 1824, where he paid tribute to his "father," Washington, and his "brothers" Laurens and Hamilton, the latter of whom had been killed in a duel with Aaron Burr in 1804. During that visit, Lafayette reportedly told the feeble, sick, eighty-one-year-old Thomas Jefferson, who would die on the fiftieth anniversary of the Declaration of Independence in 1826, that he still believed in the abolition of slavery and had devoted his life to the cause of freedom.

When word of Lafayette's death from pneumonia reached America in 1834, he was mourned across the nation as a great American hero.

Hamilton and Lafayette are well-remembered names, memorialized in money and monuments, but the name of John Laurens soon faded from public memory and the history books. And that is unfortunate. Laurens was idealistic, incredibly courageous, and might have ably served the young nation. Like Lafayette, Laurens was also a voice of conscience on the question of slavery. But throughout his military career, contemporaries viewed him as reckless, and he had been injured in nearly every battle in which he fought.

After Yorktown, Laurens returned to South Carolina and served under Nathanael Greene, coordinating a network of spies that tracked British operations in and around Charleston. He had not surrendered his abolitionist views and continued to plan for enlisting black troops while the war was still being fought. He had even designed a uniform for African-American soldiers. But as Thomas Fleming noted, "His dream of black emancipation was receding into the mists of the impossible."[84]

In mid-August 1782, Hamilton, then in Congress, had written to him: "Quit your sword my friend put on the *toga*, come to Congress, We know each others' sentiments, our views are the same. We have fought side by side to make America free. Let us hand in hand struggle to make her happy."[85]

Whether Laurens saw Hamilton's note is unknown. Late in August 1782, he learned of a British movement to gather supplies near Charleston and left his post to intercept them, against orders. Laurens ordered a bayonet charge and led the fifty-man column. But the British forces ambushed his party. Washington had once said that Laurens had one serious fault: "intrepidity bordering on rashness."

Laurens was gravely wounded in the neck. He died in an otherwise meaningless battle long after the guns had fallen silent at Yorktown.

"Poor Laurens," Hamilton wrote to Lafayette. "He has fallen sacrifice to his ardor in a trifling skirmish.... You know how truly I loved him and how much I regret him."[86]

———

By the spring of 1783, Alexander Hamilton, the hero of Yorktown, now twenty-eight and at the center of national affairs in Philadelphia, was still "in his toga," as he might have said, in Congress.

Weak and ineffective, still operating under the Articles of Confederation, Congress was dithering about how to raise money. As chair of a committee that was trying to form a peacetime army, Alexander Hamilton feared that there was no way to pay for an army.

Shortly after the Newburgh Conspiracy had been aborted, Hamilton's worst fears were realized when rebellious troops in Pennsylvania petitioned Congress for their back wages. Coming so soon after the Newburgh affair, this confirmed some of the worst fears held by Americans about the dangers of a standing army. Word soon came that eighty armed soldiers were marching toward Philadelphia to claim the pay owed them. On June 20, the disgruntled troops entered the City of Brotherly Love and were joined by more discontented soldiers from the Philadelphia barracks. Growing to a force of about four hundred men, they seized several arsenals in the city.

As a special session of Congress was called, the mutinous soldiers surrounded the State House. "The symbolism was especially troubling," Ron Chernow wrote of the scene. "A mob of drunken soldiers had besieged the people's delegates in the building where the Declaration of Independence had been signed."[87]

It was not the first time that angry American soldiers had marched on Philadelphia. In 1779, in the midst of the Revolution, a mob of soldiers, also unpaid and hungry, had descended on the home of James Wilson and threatened him, financier Robert Morris, and other signers of the Declaration. Morris, along with other members of Philadelphia's wealthiest and merchant classes, had been accused of hoarding supplies to force up prices.

These scenes of angry American soldiers rebelling against the Founding Fathers are usually missing from the more idyllic, genteel depiction of Philadelphia as scene of the Continental Congress that adopted the Declaration, and later, in 1787, the convention that created the Constitution.

In May 1783, Congress finally departed the State House, jeered by the soldiers who had been liberally served by local "tippling houses," as taverns or pubs were once called. Remnants of the Revolutionary army that had won the war for America had become a mob now threatening America's feeble government.

In short order, Congress fled from Philadelphia, setting up a new temporary capital in Princeton, New Jersey. Among the delegates was a young Virginian and former Princeton student named James Madison. The Congress would remain there for months until Pennsylvania finally called up a reserve of five hundred militiamen. The mutineers eventually laid down their arms and most went back to their base in Lancaster.

Two lessons emerged from the Philadelphia mutiny. The government should be situated in a federal district that did not have to rely upon state governments for protection. And Alexander Hamilton became more convinced that the Articles of Confederation had to be strengthened.

A few months later, on November 25, 1783, the British finally departed Manhattan on what became known as Evacuation Day. A triumphant George Washington rode into the city as a conquering hero and a few days later gave his farewell address to his tearful officers at Fraunces Tavern.

At the same time, Washington recommended to Knox and Hamilton his plan for the future of America's military: He proposed a small army to "awe the Indians" and garrison the west; a militia that would be "respectable and well established," meaning it should be organized with uniformity of arms, organization, and training—but under strict national, not state control; a navy and coastal fortifications; arsenals and manufacturing of weapons to support the armies; and military academies to foster the study of military science, much lacking among his Continental troops. Hamilton's report to the Congress followed these recommendations, but Congress largely rejected it in 1784, when the army was reduced to *"eighty men* and a few officers" (emphasis added).[88]

"As soon as the war ended," wrote Stephen E. Ambrose, "Congress indicated its feelings by declaring that 'standing armies in time of peace are inconsistent with the principles of republican government, and generally converted into destructive engines for establishing despotism.'"[89]

The young republic continued to limp along for the next few

years as Hamilton, Madison, and Washington—among others—pressed for a more effective federal government. Chief among the problems confronting the United States were finances, as both national and state governments were groaning beneath mountainous debts incurred during the Revolution. Paying for a regular army (still deemed undesirable to a good many Americans) or outfitting a respectable navy were impossibilities when there was no money to pay for them.

The crisis boiled to a head once more in 1787 as a group of farmers and tradesmen in western Massachusetts, many of them veterans of the Continental Army, rose up against the state government seated in Boston. The uprising would be known as Shays's Rebellion, after one of its leaders. Daniel Shays was a farmer from western Massachusetts who had served at Bunker Hill and later in the Continental Army and been rewarded for his service by the Marquis de Lafayette with a golden-hilted sword.

The drama in Springfield, Massachusetts, played out until a militia force, paid for with private funds and commanded by Benjamin Lincoln—George Washington's second in command at Yorktown—faced down the "Shaysites," or insurgents, as they were called, outside the federal arsenal in Springfield. A few canisters of grapeshot were fired, killing four of the rebels and scattering the disorganized rebellion. But Shays's Rebellion was not the only insurgency of its kind. Severe economic turmoil was bubbling up into angry resistance in other states and feeding popular uprisings throughout the young nation.

Stung by these popular rebellions, the Congress authorized a convention to amend the Articles of Confederation. Instead the group that gathered in secret behind locked doors and shuttered windows in Philadelphia in the summer of 1787 wrote a whole new plan of government. It was approved by the delegates on September 17, 1787, and ratified by the ninth state on June 21, 1788.

Before that landmark was achieved, the question of a federal army and navy became part of the ratification debate, particularly in Virginia, influential for obvious reasons of wealth and the fame of its leading citizens, such as Washington, Jefferson, and Madison. But Virginians like Patrick Henry feared a national government backed by a national military that could threaten the rights of its citizens— including the right to own slaves. Henry feared that Congress would be powerful enough to abolish slavery and if engaged in war could liberate slaves to fight. Henry pointed to the history of the Revolution: "We were not so hard pushed, as to make emancipation general. But acts of Assembly passed that every slave who would go to the army should be free." Like other slaveholders, Henry claimed he wanted to free the slaves. Just not right away. "Manumission," he warned, "is incompatible with the felicity of the country."[90]

The Constitution set out to create a delicate balance in which the central government could provide for the "common defense" and "insure domestic tranquility." But the states would retain the power over their militias, subject to the Congress calling upon them. The Congress and the executive who was named commander in chief would share power over the military—another dance that has been playing out for more than 225 years. But Congress had the power to pay for the army and declare war.

When the Framers authorized Congress to "provide and maintain a navy" and "raise and support armies," there was still little stomach for a standing army. But in September 1789, Congress adopted the soldiers and artillery unit that had put down Shays's Rebellion and authorized additional recruitments six months later, bringing the nascent army to 1,216 men.[91] The realities of threats from Indians and foreign nations eventually led to passage of the Militia Act of May 1792, which read, in part, "An ACT more effectually to provide for the National Defence, by establishing an Uniform Militia throughout the United States," the first attempt to codify the role of

the military in the new republic. Spurred in part by a series of disastrous defeats of American armies by Indians in what is now Indiana,
Washington and Knox won congressional approval to increase the
size of the army.

The law created the concept of universal military service, and
while it contained an exemption list, the Militia Act required all *white*
males between eighteen and forty-five to arm and equip themselves.
While its impact would be felt for more than a century, the act had
severe shortcomings, as historians Allan Millett and Peter Maslowski
point out: "It did not provide for a select corps in each state or for
federal control over officership and training, and it imposed no
penalties on either the states or individuals for noncompliance, thus
representing little more than a recommendation to the states. The
government virtually abdicated responsibility over the militia.... The
Uniform Militia Act killed the nationalized militia concept by failing to establish uniform, interchangeable units, a prerequisite for a
national reserve force. What little vitality the militia retained reposed
in volunteer units forming a de facto elite corps; this was far from
what Washington visualized...."[92]

Almost haltingly and always under the thumb of partisan politics,
the United States slowly began to build a very small and circum-
scribed military force. After the Confederation sold the last Continental Navy ship in 1785, the country had no navy until passage of
the Naval Act of 1794, which authorized the construction of a rather
insignificant six ships. The navy was under the control of the War
Department until 1798, when Congress established the Navy Department and a revived corps of marines, who were employed as specially
trained infantrymen aboard navy ships to provide protection, board
enemy ships, conduct amphibious operations, and suppress any muti-
nies. Then in 1802, under President Thomas Jefferson, the Military
Peace Establishment Act led to the foundation of West Point as the

nation's first military academy for the training of officers, primarily as engineers.

--------

But throughout the nineteenth century, America would respond to military emergencies under the general concept that standing armies and fleets of ships were expensive and dangerous. Only when required would military force be called upon. In 1803, the Barbary Wars, fought over the seizure of American ships by North African pirates, required President Jefferson to send navy gunboats to challenge the Barbary States on North Africa's Mediterranean coast. In 1805, American marines captured the city of Tripoli (inspiring the well-known lyric from the Marine hymn). At the time, they wore a leather collar to protect against sword slashes, inspiring the Marine nickname "leatherneck."

These were all small steps and America was highly unprepared for the War of 1812. Attempting to stay neutral as England and France fought, the United States was drawn into its first congressionally declared war over British attacks on American ships and the forcible "impressment" of American sailors into the British Royal Navy (as many as nine thousand Americans were forced into service on British ships before the war). Fought with little enthusiasm by either side, it included, notably, the invasion of Canada by the United States and the burning of Washington, D.C., and the White House in August 1814. The major land victory in the war, the Battle of New Orleans, came after the war was officially over but made a hero of Andrew Jackson, who rode his larger-than-life-war-hero fame as "Old Hickory" into politics, eventually becoming the seventh president.

When the Mexican-American War (1846–48) was fought largely to expand American continental holdings, this conflict concluded fairly easily as the United States invaded Mexico and eventually captured the national capital in 1847. The peace terms included the purchase of the area from California to New Mexico and the annexation of Texas. When Congress declared war, the army had about 8,600 men, most of whom had been fighting the long, costly war against the Seminoles in Florida. In May 1846, Congress had to call for 50,000 volunteers. But states were given the option of deciding whether these call-ups were for one year or the duration of the war. Most states chose the one-year option. With high rates of desertion, the "volunteer army" of the Mexican War also was notorious for its behavior. "The mass infusion of volunteers led to traditional problems associated with citizen-soldiers," write Millett and Maslowski. "Ill-disciplined, they murdered, robbed, rioted and raped with such abandon that Mexicans considered them 'Vandals vomited from Hell.'"[93]

What the war with Mexico did accomplish, however, was to give a whole generation of American officers—among them Robert E. Lee, Thomas "Stonewall" Jackson, James Longstreet, George Meade, and Ulysses S. Grant—real battleground experience, which many of them would put to use against each other when the Civil War broke out in 1861.

*Chapter Two*

+>-<+

# The Battle of the Old Men and the Young Boys

*Petersburg, Virginia—June 1864*

"The art of war is simple enough. Find out where your enemy is. Get at him as soon as you can. Strike him as hard as you can, and keep moving."[1]

—*General Ulysses S. Grant (1862)*

"It was not war, it was murder."

—*Confederate general Evander Law (June 1864)*

"All the soldiers of the Twenty-ninth Regiment, although dark-skinned, felt the full responsibility of their mission. They were in the South, to do, to dare, to die...."[2]

—*Alexander H. Newton (1910)*

"Future years will never know the seething hell and the black infernal background of countless minor scenes and interiors... of the Secession war; and it is best they should not—the real war will never get in the books. . . . I have at night watch'd by the side of a sick man in the hospital, one who could not live many hours. I have seen his eyes flash and burn as he raised himself and recurr'd to the cruelties of his surrender'd brother, and mutilations of the corpse afterwards."

—*Walt Whitman* (1892)

"If I were to speak of war, it would not be to show you the glories of conquering armies but the mischief and misery they strew in their tracks. . . . While they march on . . . some one must follow closely in their steps, crouching to the earth, toiling in the rain and darkness, shelterless like themselves, with no thought of pride or glory, fame or praise, or reward; hearts breaking with pity, faces bathed in tears and hands in blood. This is the side which history never shows."[3]

—*Clara Barton* (1915)

# Milestones in the Civil War

## 1861

**April 12** South Carolina militia forces commanded by General Pierre G. T. Beauregard bombard Fort Sumter, the federal garrison in the harbor at Charleston, South Carolina.

**April 15** Declaring a state of "insurrection," President Abraham Lincoln calls for 75,000 volunteers for three months of service. Lincoln rejects the suggestion that black volunteers be accepted.

**April 17** Virginia secedes from the Union, the eighth and most influential state to do so.

**August 5** After the humbling defeat at Bull Run (First Manassas), the Union realizes that this conflict will not be a ninety-day war. To pay for the war, Congress passes the first income tax and enlistment periods are increased from three months to two years.

## 1862

**April 6–7** At the Battle of Shiloh (Pittsburg Landing, Tennessee), losses on both sides in two days of fighting are staggering: 20,000 Union and Confederate soldiers are killed or wounded.

**May 4–14** In Virginia, a Union army takes Yorktown and Williamsburg, moving within twenty miles of Richmond, the Confederate capital.

**June 25–July 2** In the Seven Days' Battles, Robert E. Lee, in command of the Army of Northern Virginia, drives the Union forces from Richmond.

**July 17** Congress passes a second Confiscation Act, which frees the slaves of all rebels and authorizes the acceptance of blacks for nonmilitary army service.

**September 17** In the Battle of Antietam (Sharpsburg, Maryland), the single bloodiest day of the war, some 23,000 men are killed, wounded, or left missing. With Lee's offensive against the Union halted, the possibility of European recognition of the Confederacy is greatly reduced.

## 1863

**January 1** The Emancipation Proclamation is formally issued. It frees only those slaves in rebel states, with the exception of some counties and parishes already under Union control.

**March 3** Lincoln signs the first Conscription Act. It requires enrollment of males between the ages of twenty and forty-five; substitutes can be hired or payments of three hundred dollars can purchase a draft exemption.

**May 22** The U.S. War Department establishes the Bureau of Colored Troops to supervise recruitment and enlistment of black soldiers.

**July 1–3** At the Battle of Gettysburg, the Union army turns back repeated Confederate assaults. Confederate losses reach 28,000 killed, wounded, or missing, a third of the army's effective strength, to the Union's 23,000. Lee retreats to Virginia.

**July 4** General Grant's siege of Vicksburg, Mississippi, ends with the city's surrender; the Union now controls the length of the Mississippi River.

## 1864

**March 12** Ulysses S. Grant is named commander of the Union armies.

**May 4** Grant begins an assault on Virginia with more than 100,000 soldiers.

**May 5–6** In the bloody Battle of the Wilderness (Virginia), many of the wounded on both sides die when trapped by brushfires ignited by gunfire in the dense woods of the battleground.

**May 8–12** After five days of inconclusive fighting at the Battle of Spotsylvania (Virginia), Grant's plan is clear: a war of attrition aiming to wear down and destroy Lee's outnumbered, poorly fed, and ill-clothed forces.

**June 3** At Cold Harbor, outside Richmond, Union forces are devastated following a frontal assault on Lee's defenses.

**June 9** The first Battle of Petersburg, Virginia, is fought.

**June 15** After a second Battle of Petersburg, Grant begins the siege of the city.

## 1865

**April 2** Lee withdraws from Petersburg, ending the siege begun the previous June. He advises Confederate president Jefferson Davis to leave Richmond. A day later, Union troops enter Petersburg and Richmond. Two days after that, Lincoln tours the fallen Confederate capital and sits in President Davis's chair.

**April 9** Surrounded, and with dwindling forces facing starvation, Lee surrenders to Grant at Appomattox Court House in Virginia.

*Petersburg, Virginia*
*June 9, 1864*

The clanging of the tocsin was loud and fierce. Breaking the stillness of the June morning, the city's alarm bell could mean only one thing. The war had come to Petersburg.

Before dawn on June 9, 1864, two separate columns of Union infantry, thousands of Federal soldiers, including 1,300 United States Colored Troops (USCT), emerged from the darkened woods to the north and east and began to approach the "Cockade City." By seven in the morning, they were advancing on the Confederate picket lines—groups of soldiers or troops placed in forward positions to warn against an enemy advance—guarding the eastern approach to the sleeping city.

For three years, Petersburg had been spared the worst ravages of the fighting that had raged across much of Virginia during the Civil War, but the city's turn had arrived at last. The worst nightmare of many a Virginian was coming to pass: Armed black men, some of them former slaves, were marching on their homes. For Virginians who still shook at the recollection of the murderous slave rebellions led by Nat Turner and Gabriel a few decades earlier, the prospect brought terror.

Waking to the sound of the alarm bells and the clamor of approaching battle, Petersburger Fanny Waddell said the noise "[b]roke upon our ears, which palsied our very hearts.... It was the sullen roar of cannon and musketry along our lines, and the tolling of the City Hall bell, the signal which summoned grandsires and boys to the defence of their homes."[4]

On this spring morning, the Virginia air redolent with the scent of honey locusts, roses, and magnolia, the city bells demanded that Petersburg's men come out to fight. For some of them, the bells were a death knell.

By this point in the "War of Northern Aggression"—a little more than three years after Virginia left the Union on April 17, 1861—most of Petersburg's men of fighting age were gone. "The Petersburg Rifles, the Petersburg Grays, Graham's Battery... were just some of the seventeen separate units that disappeared into the maw of the war," wrote historian Noah Andre Trudeau.[5]

Most of Petersburg's men of fighting age who had survived this long were now with Robert E. Lee's dwindling army. Approximately sixty thousand Confederate soldiers were charged with defending Richmond, twenty miles to the north of Petersburg. Many of those fighting with Lee had lived through three years of brutal combat and starvation, against overwhelming odds. Now they were dug in around Richmond, desperately trying to keep alive the last hopes of the Confederacy by fending off more than one hundred thousand Yankees knocking at the gates of the Confederate capital.

Once more, Robert E. Lee cajoled and encouraged his troops—outmanned, outgunned, tattered, and hungry—to hurl back another blue-coated onslaught by a well-provisioned, well-equipped, but war-weary Federal army. Other Union generals had threatened Richmond before. Each time, fierce Confederate resistance had turned them away. But the relentless General Ulysses S. Grant now commanded those Yankee armies.

Ulysses S. Grant was not like Lincoln's other generals.

Appointed by Lincoln to lead all of the Union armies in March 1864, Grant had by early June made his name infamous with a series of deadly frontal assaults. At battles in the Wilderness, Spotsylvania, and Cold Harbor, the carnage on both sides had been unspeakable. In barely a month's time, Grant had suffered more than 39,000 casualties—dead, wounded, and missing—a number approaching the size of Lee's entire army. Estimates of Lee's losses for the same period were 25,000, according to Grant biographer Jean Edward Smith.[6] Union reinforcements continued to pour in despite the outcry that Grant was a "butcher."

But as Lee and his vastly outnumbered troops confronted Grant's combined armies outside Richmond, Petersburg lay exposed and vulnerable. It was guarded by fewer than two thousand Confederate troops and dependent upon the militiamen who were now being summoned from their beds by the peals of the alarm bells.

The remnants of Petersburg's men were either too old or too young for regular service. They included a motley assortment of teenagers and older men, several of them veterans, some having served in the Mexican War nearly two decades earlier. There were also dentists, druggists, business owners, bankers, and a few men who had been exempt from military service because of infirmity or age—the youngest was only fourteen. Anthony Keiley, a young lawyer, was exempted as a Virginia legislator. Few had uniforms and some did not even possess a working rifle.[7]

By 9 a.m., the general alarm had gone up across Petersburg—"all the available bell metal in the corporation broke into chorus with so vigorous a peal and clangor…as to suggest to the uninitiated a general conflagration," one of the city's residents later recalled. "The enemy are now right upon us," the men were told.[8] "Men who had been going about their normal routines dropped everything, grabbed the antique firearms they had been issued, and hurried over crossroads and paths to rally."[9]

The women and children they left behind could only fret. Consigned to a sickbed at home, Fanny Waddell remembered, "I could hear the roar and the din of the fierce conflict going on at our very doors nearly; sometimes the firing would be so near our hearts would stand still expecting every minute to see the enemy rush in."[10]

Commanding the piecemeal force that would have to hold Virginia's second-largest city was attorney Fletcher H. Archer. A forty-seven-year-old veteran of the Mexican War who had also served as a Confederate officer earlier in the Civil War, Archer had retired from the army in 1862 to return to his Petersburg law practice. But when Grant's armies moved into Virginia for the spring offensive in 1864, Archer offered his service and military experience to Virginia once more. On May 4 of that year, Archer was commissioned as a major and given command of Archer's Battalion of the Virginia Reserves. Composed of men who were supposed to be between sixteen and eighteen and older than forty-five, these reserves had received a few weeks of cursory training and drill.

If called upon, they were meant to support the small number of Confederate regular troops who were then stretched thinly along the northeastern ramparts of Petersburg's defensive fortifications, a ten-mile-long earthen breastwork with about fifty pieces of artillery, called the Dimmock Line. But when the alarm sounded, Archer's company of militiamen was not going to support the city's defenders—they were going to *be* its principal defenders.

The men were ordered to take up a line facing south across the Jerusalem Plank Road, a roadway covered in wooden boards that ran south from Petersburg and was roughly parallel to one of the rail lines coming into the city. Archer had assembled his men at Batteries 27 and 28 on the Jerusalem Plank Road.[11]

The unit included about 125 militiamen and five regular soldiers, some of them armed with cast-off weapons and a single light field-piece. Archer had been left with this company of inadequately armed men, still in their civilian clothes, including those "with head silvered o'er with the frosts of advancing years," like William C. Banister, a sixty-one-year-old bank manager, and others who "could scarcely boast of the down upon the cheek."[12] They would come down in Virginia history and lore as "the Old Men and the Young Boys." Among them were three members of the city council and a mill manager who had been up all night guarding prisoners.[13]

What this small band—hastily assembled, ill-trained, and poorly equipped—did not know was that they were about to confront a vastly larger and much better armed Union cavalry force, numbering about 1,300 horsemen, who were planning to sweep into Petersburg.

With a little more than 18,000 residents, Petersburg was then Virginia's second-largest city and the seventh largest in the Confederacy. About half of its residents were black, including more than 3,100 free blacks.[14] After the American Revolution, some Virginians had emancipated their slaves in a burst of post-independence fervor. Over time, a vibrant free black community had grown up in and around Petersburg. Founded in the 1630s by English colonists, and known as Peter's Post after Peter Wood, an early settler, the city had first flourished as a tobacco trading post.

By the early nineteenth century, Petersburg had grown from a small farming community to a thriving cotton, tobacco, and manufacturing center and an important port on the Appomattox River, which linked the city to the nearby James River, Chesapeake Bay, and the Atlantic Ocean. In the War of 1812, the city's men had fought wearing a rosette, or cockade, on their caps. President James Madison, a Virginian, had admiringly nicknamed Petersburg the "Cockade City," and a monument to the town's dead of that war stood in the town's Blandford Cemetery.

With the arrival of the railroad, Petersburg's affluence and importance had grown considerably. By 1864, five different rail lines converged on Petersburg from points west and south, all connecting north to Richmond. But the Union blockade of Confederate ports had severely damaged Petersburg's economy. Tobacco and cotton exports, once the city's lifeblood, had been brought to a near standstill. Once a proud and prosperous city of brick sidewalks, with streets paved with granite and lit by gas lamps, Petersburg was now crippled by food shortages, with flour selling at the inflated price of two hundred dollars per barrel—if it could even be found.

Whatever beans, butter, and other supplies passed over Petersburg's rail lines did not stay long. The railroads were Robert E. Lee's last lifeline and the only means of moving available food supplies, ammunition, and reinforcements to his battered and hungry army. Those railroads also made the city an inviting target for the Union army.

On June 9, as 5,300 Union infantrymen moved in from the woods east of Petersburg, 1,300 Union cavalrymen led by Brigadier General August V. Kautz,* a German-born infantry officer turned cavalry commander, were going to attempt to sweep into the city from the south and destroy the railroad bridge over the Appomattox River. The mission was clear. Take the lightly defended city and sever the rail lines to Richmond that were keeping Robert E. Lee's army in the field: Starve Lee of food, reinforcements, and ammunition and the war would end. A little after midnight on June 9, the infantrymen, including the 1,300 United States Colored Troops, began their march. Under Kautz, the cavalrymen also galloped off into darkness.

But from the outset, the Union's well-laid plan for a coordinated attack misfired badly. If not so ultimately tragic, it might have all passed for a comedy of errors. The infantry columns, poorly led, had gotten off to a slow start after midnight and then became lost in the woods at night. General Quincy Gillmore, a West Point–trained engineer who was first in his class of 1849, commanded them. Despite his engineering expertise, Gillmore lacked combat experience—and possibly a stiff resolve. On this night and during the following day, both his inexperience and hesitation showed.

Designed to draw out Petersburg's defenders, Gillmore's advance

---

* Kautz's Civil War service was largely unremarkable, but he did serve on the military commission that tried the conspirators in the Lincoln assassination.

began in fits and starts and was then slowed by the muddy Virginia woods. Facing the Confederate defenses in the light of day, Gillmore was extremely reluctant to chance taking heavy casualties. In spite of considerable intelligence that the Confederate defenses were weak, thinly manned, and could be overwhelmed at little cost, Gillmore feared making a direct assault on the Confederate breastworks, even though the U.S. Colored Troops assigned to him had already demonstrated their considerable willingness to take such risks. The maneuver was doomed. Gillmore refused to press his men against the Dimmock Line.

While Gillmore dithered, Kautz's cavalry had been expected to make its attack by about 9 a.m. But Gillmore heard nothing about the cavalry force, a silence that only increased his caution. Sometime around noon, Gillmore issued orders for his entire infantry force to withdraw. His total casualties were sixteen men. For all intents, the fighting northeast and east of the town was over by midday.

Meanwhile, Kautz's Union cavalry had moved into Petersburg from the south. But they had also been delayed, and by the time Kautz and his men had reached the first defensive breastworks, the Old Men and the Young Boys of Archer's Battalion were ready. With a wagon overturned across the road and a hastily built rail fence, Archer's men had created a barricade that confronted the first Union assault. A squadron of the Eleventh Pennsylvania, sabers drawn, made the first charge up the road. "Amid the clatter of hoofs against the planks, the horse soldiers, riding boot-to-spur, surged forward in column by twos," National Park Service historian Edwin Bearss recorded. "A crashing volley delivered by Archer's battalion sent the Pennsylvanians recoiling."[15]

At that moment, General Raleigh Colston, a regular Confederate officer who had been ordered to hold the Jerusalem Plank Road at all costs, joined Archer, bringing with him a few more men and another small artillery piece. Archer and Colston clearly knew they were not going to be able to hold off 1,300 Federal cavalrymen with 125 men and two light field guns. They needed help and Archer called for a courier. "Eighteen-year-old Lt. Wales Hart of the Junior Reserves stepped forward," recounted Edwin Bearss. "Hart mounted Colston's horse and thundered off. Bullets kicked up dust around him and under his horse's hoofs."[16]

Attempting to avoid another frontal assault on the Confederate line, Kautz maneuvered some of his troops to the sides and rear of the Confederate position. Some of his cavalrymen dismounted and slowly advanced, securing a position behind Archer's militia. But every minute that the Virginians stood their ground increased the chance that more Confederate reinforcements might appear. With the Union soldiers now threatening to surround them, Archer and Colston agreed to fall back. As they began to withdraw, a second concentrated Union advance pushed Archer and his dwindling force back into the city. The Union horse soldiers had taken the Confederate position but were still outside of the town. A little after one in the afternoon, Kautz ordered the Eleventh Pennsylvania to advance into town.

But the delay created by Archer's militiamen had been all that Henry Wise, the former governor of Virginia who was commanding Petersburg's defenses, had needed. Wise pulled men from the lines that Gillmore was supposed to have attacked and sent them racing to Archer's position.

Thinking that the resistance had collapsed and that Gillmore's Union infantry was engaging the Confederates on the other side of town, Kautz and his Union cavalrymen were in for a shock. Just as the first Union horse soldiers reached the edge of Petersburg, the Fourth North Carolina Cavalry and the four cannons of the Petersburg Artillery arrived on the scene. A second Union column, moving along the Jerusalem Plank Road, was also near one of Petersburg's churches when they were met by what became known as the Patients and Penitents, a collection of the walking wounded rousted from the city's military hospitals and some prisoners from the city jails, bolstered by the companies of reinforcements pulled from Petersburg's outer defenses to counter the Union offensive.

The sudden arrival of Confederate cavalry and artillery, which had been freed by Gillmore's withdrawal, blunted any further Union movement. Near the city reservoir, another small force of Confederate regulars, the Virginia Battery, made another last-ditch stand against the much larger Union forces, keeping the blue-coated cavalry out of Petersburg.

As one survivor of the militia stand recalled, "They were almost in Petersburg—could see its spires and steeples and many of the houses on our suburban limits—but...the city was saved from the tread of the ruthless invader.... The missiles of death coming so unexpectedly to the foe, he at first seemed overwhelmed with surprise, and halted neither advancing nor retreating."[17]

Unaware of Gillmore's failure and facing the unexpected and growing Confederate resistance, Kautz feared disaster. A foolhardy advance might lead to the loss of his entire command. On his own and outnumbered inside the Confederate lines, having pressed to Petersburg's doorstep, Kautz withdrew his cavalrymen out of an abundance of caution.

The Old Men and the Young Boys had held, keeping the Union army out of the city. But Archer's Petersburg militia paid a heavy price in slowing the Union raid: fifteen dead, including William C. Banister, the elderly bank manager, and George Jones, the town's respected druggist. Another eighteen men were wounded and forty-two had been captured and taken to Federal prison camps, including Anthony Keiley.[18]

Anne Banister, the dead banker's daughter, was standing on the family porch with her mother and sister when her father's body was returned. "My uncle...drove up in a wagon with my father's lifeless body shot through the head, his gray hair dabbled in blood," she remembered. In a few seconds, she recalled, her mother was "kneeling by my father in such grief as I had never seen before."[19]

Petersburg had been saved almost miraculously. But its defense had demanded, in the words of one survivor, "[a]n extraordinary sacrifice of life and blood."[20] Like Lexington, Concord, and Bunker Hill during the American Revolution, the Battle of the Old Men and the Young Boys would go down in Confederate lore.

---

The plan to attack Petersburg on this June morning had been conceived by General Benjamin Butler, one of Lincoln's so-called "political generals," men whose appointments had depended upon their political power rather than their battlefield expertise.

An ambitious Massachusetts politician, Butler had become one of the Civil War's most controversial characters. As a Democrat before the war, he had actually nominated Jefferson Davis—the future president of the Confederacy—for president of the United States at the party's 1860 convention. Once the war began, however, Butler was loyal to the Union and Lincoln gave him one of the political generalships that were awarded to pro-war Democrats. "These appointments," wrote historian James McPherson, "made political sense but sometimes produced military calamity.... 'Political general' became almost a synonym for incompetency, especially in the North." But, added McPherson, "The appointment of political generals, like the election of company officers, was an essential part of the process by which a highly politicized society mobilized for war."[21]

Despite the numerous controversies that dogged him during the war, Butler had retained that political currency and was also influential with the Radical Republicans—the powerful Senate faction that vocally opposed slavery and often clashed with Lincoln over war policy. As a Democrat with these Republican friends, Butler was approached by Lincoln about becoming his running mate in the upcoming 1864 election. Butler demurred because he wanted to remain in the army and he was still in command of a large Union force.[22]

Since Richmond was supplied by the railroads that ran through Petersburg, Butler knew that taking Petersburg would cripple Lee's supply lines. He was also aware that Confederate troops had been moving north to reinforce Lee, leaving Petersburg's defenses even more vulnerable. Butler knew his Union forces had a clear numerical advantage.

Late on the night of June 8, when the Federal troops had begun moving, there had been delays and confusion from the start. It was 3 a.m. before they were finally across the Appomattox River. But the infantry had drawn almost all of the Petersburg defenders to the eastern side of the Dimmock Line, leaving the southern approach more exposed. Butler's tactic actually seemed to be working.

Butler's opposite was Confederate general Pierre G. T. Beauregard, in charge of the defenses of Richmond and Petersburg as commander of the Department of North Carolina and Southern Virginia. Appointed superintendent of the military academy at West Point, Beauregard had served five days before losing his position after his home state of Louisiana seceded from the Union in January 1861. Resigning from the U.S. Army, Beauregard returned south to join the Confederate forces.

It was Beauregard who had commanded the troops in Charleston Harbor that fired on Fort Sumter on April 12, 1861. He had also won the first convincing Confederate victory at Manassas, Virginia, also called the First Battle of Bull Run, in the summer of 1861. But Beauregard and Confederate president Jefferson had a stormy relationship and came to loggerheads. When he had fallen sick in June 1862, Davis accused Beauregard of abandoning his post and dismissed him. Now in 1864, the Louisianan had been ordered back to Virginia by Davis to aid Robert E. Lee in the defense of Richmond and Petersburg.

Beauregard and Butler had locked horns a few weeks earlier. In May, Butler's army had advanced toward Richmond but been halted at Drewry's Bluff, a high point above the James River. There, Beauregard's guns and defenders had prevented Butler from moving Union gunboats up the river so his army could join Grant in the attack on Richmond. Forced to withdraw and frustrated in his attempts to strike Richmond from the south, Butler was waiting for his opportunity at redemption. On May 25, when Grant detached sixteen thousand of Butler's men to join the Army of the Potomac for an assault at Cold Harbor outside Richmond, Butler's forces were greatly diminished. He remained almost entirely on the defensive, with barely enough troops to hold his lines.

But he believed that he still had enough men to launch a raid on Petersburg. Initially, he planned to have the expedition led by Brigadier General Edward W. Hinks. A Massachusetts politician and ally of Butler, he is best remembered in Civil War history for commanding the Hinks Division, U.S. Colored Troops, Army of the James, an all-black unit, in a major action. (He had changed his surname, Hincks, after he entered the army, dropping the *c*.)

First recruited in 1863, the African-American men of the U.S. Colored Troops made up approximately one-tenth of the Union army by the end of the Civil War. Permitted to enlist after the Emancipation Proclamation was issued in January 1863, African Americans had eagerly stepped forward to fight for their freedom. Among them was Alexander H. Newton, born in slavery in New Bern, North Carolina. Newton had escaped, fled north, and, after witnessing New York's 1863 Draft Riots, in which hundreds of African Americans were killed by mostly Irish white mobs, joined an all-black regiment from Connecticut.

"All the soldiers of the Twenty-ninth Regiment, although dark-skinned, felt the full responsibility of their mission," Newton related after the war. "They were in the South, to do, to dare, to die....And I am proud to say that the history of the colored man in warfare has been an enviable one. He has always showed his patriotism, by action, by deeds of sacrifice, by death itself. We had the same muscle, the same strength, the same heart, the same conscience, the same cause, the same right, the same liberty as the white man."[23]

On the subject of blacks serving the Union, Benjamin Butler had become a lightning rod and a leading advocate for African Americans. He had first created complications for Lincoln in May 1861, a month into the war, when three slaves who had been working on Confederate fortifications escaped and entered Butler's Union camp. When the owner of the escaped men appeared under a flag of truce, Butler refused to return the men. Instead, Butler declared that the slaves were "contraband" and put them to work in his own camp. Northern newspapers picked up the phrase, and from then on, slaves who escaped and made their way to Union lines but were still the legal property of their Confederate owners were known as contrabands. Shortly afterward, Congress passed the first Confiscation Act, which allowed seizure of Confederate "property," including slaves, as a war measure.

A year later, Butler made his name hated throughout the South when he was given military command of New Orleans after its capture. There he issued an infamous order that any woman who persisted in the practice of insulting Northern soldiers "shall be regarded and held liable to be treated as a woman of the town plying her avocation"— in other words, viewed as a prostitute. For this he had been anointed "Beast Butler" and depicted in illustrated weeklies as "lobster-eyed," fat, and ugly. The rumor that he was pilfering silver from the Southern homes in which he stayed added to his notoriety, and he was derisively known across the Confederacy as "Spoons Butler."

A loyal Democrat at a time when many Northerners in the Democratic Party were violently opposed to the war, Butler was also a favorite of many Republicans, especially the staunchly abolitionist wing of the party known as the Radical Republicans. Unfortunately, as a military leader he did not cover himself in glory. His failed attempt to march against Lee in Richmond pushed him to instead consider the attack on the more lightly defended Petersburg.

The operation was well in motion when Butler agreed at the eleventh hour to switch command of the attacks from his initial choice of Edward W. Hinks. The switch had come at the request of General Gillmore, who believed the overall command of the attack should be his. Butler, however, personally disliked Gillmore and thought his previous battlefield failures were serious. Nearly a year before, Gillmore had led the failed July 1863 assault of the all-black Fifty-Fourth Massachusetts on Fort Wagner, South Carolina (made famous in the film *Glory*).

Butler had also blamed Gillmore for the recent failure at nearby Drewry's Bluff earlier in May 1864, when Butler had been forced to pull his forces back. After that incident Butler wrote to a member of the Senate Committee of Military Affairs, "Gen. Gillmore may be a very good engineer but he is wholly inept in the treatment of troops. He has been behind in every movement."[24]

But some of the troops to be used in the Petersburg expedition were drawn from Gillmore's command. To his eventual regret, Butler begrudgingly agreed to the change.

The failure of Gillmore and Butler's other commanders in the first Battle of Petersburg on June 9 was more costly than mere casualty reports and accounts by family members could possibly suggest. The losses on both sides were relatively small, considering the carnage that had become typical in the Civil War's pitched battles. But so much more was at stake and had been lost to indecision, poor communications, and a lack of command resolve.

Ulysses S. Grant had famously said, "The art of war is simple enough. Find out where your enemy is. Get at him as soon as you can. Strike him as hard as you can, and keep moving."

A swift, bold Union strike on that day would have put victory near at hand, given the weakness of Petersburg's defenses. It might very well have succeeded beyond Benjamin Butler's grandest hopes. By cutting Robert E. Lee off from supplies, a victory on that day in early June could have forced the Confederacy to its knees. Surrender in June 1864 could have shortened the war and the dreadful suffering that was to follow for soldiers and civilians alike.

Butler had envisioned a "quick, decisive push" into the city and told Quincy Gillmore that losing 1,000 casualties would not be too high a price for victory; total Federal casualties were actually 52. When an infuriated Butler relieved Gillmore of his command on June 17, General Grant took a different view, overruling Butler's decision. "As far as Grant was concerned," historian Stephen B. Oates commented, "Butler was to blame for the 'ill-advised' attack against Petersburg, which had gone forth without Grant's approval."[25]

But this failed strike was only the beginning of Petersburg's agony. Confederate generals Lee and Beauregard must have known they had whistled past the proverbial graveyard. Realizing that they had been fortunate that the Union effort was so lackluster, if not inept, they quickly shifted more Confederate troops to Petersburg. When the Federals next moved on the city, there would be many more men defending the city, almost all of them experienced veterans, behind newly strengthened defensive lines. What Lee and Beauregard did not realize yet was that Petersburg would have to face the full fury of Ulysses S. Grant in what would become the longest siege in the history of an American city.

---

When the Civil War began in April 1861, President Abraham Lincoln initially called for seventy-five thousand volunteers to enlist for just three months, and he rejected proposals that would allow black volunteers to serve. By August of that year, after the first humiliating defeats of the Union army at Confederate hands, the enlistment period was increased to two years. But black troops were still not welcomed in "Mr. Lincoln's Army."

As the war dragged on through another year with embarrassing defeats for the failed Union generals and staggering losses on both sides, Lincoln sought more troops and better leadership. And after formally making the Emancipation Proclamation in January 1863, Lincoln reversed his thinking about black troops. With the creation of the Bureau of Colored Troops in 1863, free blacks in the Union as well as contrabands were eligible to enlist.

But by early 1864, three long years of dreadful war and once-unthinkable losses had stretched into a fourth. And there seemed to be little end in sight as Lincoln prepared to run for a second term; that was when he finally found his general. On March 12, 1864, Ulysses S. Grant was appointed general in chief of all the Union armies. His successes in the western theater of war had convinced Lincoln that this man would do the job that needed to be done.

Grant had a plan that was simple in theory yet daunting in its scope: a concerted assault on a Confederacy weakened by an economic blockade that had closed most of its ports to trade with Europe. He would use the Union's vastly greater manpower and manufacturing capabilities to hammer at every strongpoint in the Confederacy, from Virginia, south to the Gulf Coast, and up the Mississippi, which was now fully in Union control.

The strategy had five key components. William Tecumseh Sherman was assigned to capture Atlanta, Georgia, and eliminate both the Confederate armies in that region and their ability to keep fighting by destroying farms, factories, and railroads. Thirty thousand men under Nathaniel P. Banks—another political appointee who had risen from the cotton mills of Massachusetts to become U.S. congressman and the state's governor—would target Mobile, Alabama, one of the Confederacy's last remaining open ports. But Virginia was the key. Led by the victor at Gettysburg, General George Gordon Meade, the 115,000 men of the main Army of the Potomac would trail Robert E. Lee and his Army of Northern Virginia, hoping to draw them out into a decisive battle. Also, in western Virginia, another 26,000 men, initially led by Franz Sigel,* would seize control of the Shenandoah Valley, known as the "breadbasket of the Confederacy," in a further attempt to starve the rebel armies. And finally, Benjamin Butler would bring another army of 35,000 men in a thrust up the Virginia peninsula on the south side of the James River toward Richmond, to press the Confederate capital from its southern approach.

But God—or the devil—is always in the details, and Grant's grand strategy did not proceed precisely as planned. From the Union perspective, Sherman's devastating Georgia campaign was a stunning success. But after forcing Atlanta's civilians out of the city and burning it in September 1864, and then cutting a destructive swath through the Southern interior on his "March to the Sea," the Union general had changed the face of war. Sherman would become more reviled than "Beast" Butler, and his scorched-earth approach stoked greater hatred and defiant resistance toward the Union. Some of the other Union commanders, on the other hand, tried the patience of both Grant and Lincoln with their overcaution or inadequacy. But Grant persisted. Unlike some of his predecessors, who had been simply incompetent or egotistic prima donnas outmatched by Lee, Grant was an inexorable force who personally accompanied the Army of the Potomac in its relentless pursuit of Lee's army, now reduced to

---

* In addition to such political generals as Butler, Lincoln had appointed foreign-born generals to garner support among different immigrant groups in the North, and Sigel, a German, was one of these, although he did have military experience before coming to America. Sigel was later removed and replaced in the Shenandoah Valley by General Philip Sheridan.

some 60,000 men who had limped back to Virginia after the crushing defeat at Gettysburg, Pennsylvania, in July 1863.

Now, nearly a year later, in early May 1864, the Army of the Potomac and General Robert E. Lee's Army of Northern Virginia began engaging in some of the fiercest and most deadly fighting of the entire war. It was a series of battles for which Grant would be branded a "butcher" as he threw vast numbers of Union troops into deadly frontal assaults with horrifying casualties. The two armies met for two days in early May in a large area known as the Wilderness, in central Virginia, not far from the site of the bloody 1863 Battle of Chancellorsville. At the Wilderness, the wounded men of both sides were left to die on a battlefield consumed by burning brush. Later in the month another gruesome bloodletting followed not far away at the Spotsylvania Court House, a protracted battle fought in rain and muddy fields. Afterwards Grant famously reported to Washington, "I propose to fight it out on this line if it takes all summer."[26]

And finally, in what may have been the worst carnage, Cold Harbor on the outskirts of Richmond, 59,000 Confederates faced off against 109,000 Federal soldiers.

The Battle of Cold Harbor,* begun on May 31, climaxed on June 3 but continued fitfully until June 12. It was an epic Union disaster in which thousands of men were lost in an ill-conceived and hopeless frontal assault on well-defended Confederate positions; Union forces suffered an estimated 7,000 casualties in one day.[27] Later, Grant would note in his memoir, "I have always regretted that the last assault at Cold Harbor was ever made....At Cold Harbor no advantage whatever was gained to compensate for the heavy loss we sustained."[28]

Back in Washington, Secretary of the Navy Gideon Welles read the casualty reports and commented, "The immense slaughter of our brave men chills and sickens us all."[29]

---

* Named for a crossroads tavern that did not serve hot meals.

In a little over six weeks' time, from May to mid-June, some 65,000 Northern boys and men were killed, wounded, or missing, James M. McPherson recorded, adding, "The figure amounted to three-fifths of the total number of combat casualties suffered by the Army of the Potomac during the *previous three years.* No army could take such punishment and retain its fighting edge. 'For thirty days it has been one funeral procession past me,' cried General Gouverneur K. Warren... 'and it has been too much'" (emphasis added). And the wife of Benjamin Butler probably spoke for many when she asked her husband, "What is all this struggling and fighting for? The ruin and death to thousands of families.... What advancement of mankind to compensate for the present horrible calamities?"[30]

Lee's forces suffered 33,000 casualties—dead, wounded, missing[31]—but when Cold Harbor was over, Richmond, seat of the Confederacy, was still in Confederate hands. Unwavering in his support of Grant, Lincoln was also absorbing relentless criticism. Within his own Republican Party, there was a search for a replacement candidate for the upcoming 1864 election. Yet right after Cold Harbor, he was nominated to run for a second term—although Lincoln himself gravely doubted his chances for reelection.

Abruptly altering his plans for Richmond, Grant ordered the army to make a lightning move south, across the James River, to a position outside Petersburg. Like Butler, Grant believed that he could capture Petersburg, cut the railroads linking Richmond with the rest of the Confederacy, and force the capitulation of Lee and the Confederate government. In a stunning maneuver and extraordinary feat of engineering, Grant was able to move the entire Army of the Potomac south across the James River with the help of a pontoon bridge built by 450 men, most of them New York engineers, in less than a day. Eleven feet wide and constructed of wooden pontoons that were lashed to schooners that kept them in place against the tide and river currents, the bridge was ready on the morning of June 15.

"When finished," noted historian Ron Field, "it was 2,100 feet long, making it the longest floating bridge in military history."[32] With it Grant was able to quietly withdraw more than 100,000 soldiers along with cannons, ambulances, baggage wagons, and 3,500 beef cattle that fed the army, negotiate miles of swampy ground, and then cross a half-mile-wide tidal river. His army completely disappeared from the camps near Cold Harbor.

Grant's army seemed to have vanished overnight in the Virginia mists. The Union commander's masterful stroke completely fooled Robert E. Lee, who still expected that Grant was going to move on Richmond and did not even learn of Grant's whereabouts until June 18. (Grant had even kept the secret of his maneuver from President Lincoln, and when Lincoln later learned of the operation, he wrote to Grant, "I begin to see it all. You will succeed. God bless you all.")[33]

Grant established a new base of operations at City Point, at the tip of the peninsula formed between the James and Appomattox rivers. Within a short time, it would become one of the busiest ports in the world. New rail lines carrying supplies and troops were soon added, making City Point a bustling, crowded wartime center, with seven wharves servicing as many as two hundred ships a day, and a bakery that produced one hundred thousand loaves of bread daily for Grant's vast army. "There were slaughterhouses, army repair and blacksmith shops, a post office, coffin shops and parlors for embalming," described historian Stephen B. Oates. "The U.S. Military Railroad Construction Corps rebuilt the City Point railroad track, and whistling military trains came right up to the wharves so that the army's black workers could load supplies on boxcars and flatcars for the troops at the front line. In time twenty-five locomotives pulling 275 cars would run back and forth on the military railroad."[34]

When Lee finally realized what had happened, he quickly began to reinforce Petersburg's defenses, but by then Grant was already hitting the city. Before getting his army fully established at City Point, Ulysses S. Grant ordered another attack on Petersburg on June 15. This time, Major General William F. "Baldy" Smith was given command of a force of approximately 15,500 men facing the few thousand Confederates dug in around the city.

It was another David-versus-Goliath moment, and the odds again clearly favored Goliath. But the second Union assault on Petersburg turned into another poorly led attack that was undone by Smith's timidity. Union troops made several advances and the U.S. Colored Troops who captured a Confederate battery were singled out for praise. One white officer said, "I am now prepared to say that...I never saw troops fight better, more bravely, and with more determination."[35]

But the day also brought one of the recorded instances of U.S. Colored Troops killing surrendering Confederate soldiers, in retribution for the widely reported massacre of surrendering black troops by Confederate forces at Tennessee's Fort Pillow in April 1864. As Henry Turner, a chaplain with the USCT, recorded, "They and the rebels were both crying out—'Fort Pillow!' This seems to be the battle-cry on both sides....The next place we saw the rebels, was going out the rear of the forts with their coat-tails sticking straight out behind. Some few held up their hands and pleaded for mercy, but our boys thought that over Jordan would be the best place for them, and sent them there, with a very few exceptions."[36]

Black soldiers didn't need to be told about the Fort Pillow massacre, which actually solidified Northern support for the USCT and the attitudes of black fighting men. "At times they fought under the black flag, which warned the Confederates that they would neither take prisoners nor ask for any mercy for themselves," wrote Joseph T. Glatthaar in a history of black soldiers and white officers.[37] He added, "During the extended siege of Petersburg, thousands of Confederates deserted to Federal lines, but very few came to the black units for fear of mistreatment. When they did accidentally surrender to commands in the USCT, both white officers and their black men enjoyed observing the 'terrified' look once 'they found out they had thrown themselves into the hands of the avenging negro.' "[38]

The reality of this fear of black troops was recognized by a white officer with the USCT who wrote that "our men unfortunately, owing to the irregular feature of the ground took no prisoners.... This I am *morally persuaded of.* I know that the enemy won't fight us if he can help it.... The real fact is, the rebels will not stand against our colored soldiers when there is any chance of their being taken prisoner" (emphasis in original).[39]

Despite the advances made by his forces, Smith pulled back his troops even as Petersburg seemed within the Union's grasp. Suffering from dysentery, Smith hesitated, as did other Union generals. Confusion over orders and poor communication worsened the problems of balky commanders, and when the Federal troops failed to press the attack, Beauregard's defenses were reinforced and the war again prolonged.

On June 17, Grant was still trying to get his army to aggressively attack the Confederate defenses. By the morning of June 18, Lee's army began to arrive, bolstering Beauregard along the Dimmock Line around Petersburg. And that day, Lee himself arrived in the beleaguered city.

Hampered by poor communications, the Union armies never made the coordinated push that Grant expected. In fact, some of the attacks they *did* make ended in disaster. In one of the final assaults on June 18, nine hundred men from a Maine unit charged across an open field only to be raked by Confederate artillery and rifle fire. Thirty minutes later, 632 men had been killed or wounded—the heaviest single battle loss by any regiment during the Civil War.[40]

Beauregard knew the city had dodged another disaster. "Petersburg at that hour was clearly at the mercy of the Federal commander," he later admitted.[41]

Ulysses S. Grant would later agree, writing in his memoir, "If General Hancock's orders of the 15th had been communicated to him, that officer,* with his usual promptness, would undoubtedly have been upon the ground around Petersburg as early as four o'clock in the afternoon of the 15th....I don't think there is any doubt that Petersburg itself could have been carried without much loss."[42]

But the assault had been turned back. Days of close-quarters combat and assaults repulsed by artillery batteries had cost the Federals another ten thousand casualties. And Beauregard had bought Lee some more time. As Lee continued to rush more reinforcements into Petersburg, Grant knew that the city would become the stage where he would settle his duel with Grant.

The twin failures of Butler's assault on June 9 and the one ordered on June 15 by Grant can be attributed, many historians contend, to two words: Cold Harbor. There, on the morning of June 3, 60,000 blue-coated soldiers hit Confederate trenches just outside Richmond. Perhaps 7,000 of them were shot down in the first thirty minutes on this infamous killing ground.[43]

The fearsome losses at Cold Harbor and at other recent battles between Grant and Lee had clearly had an effect on Union commanders, Baldy Smith among them. Some of Grant's generals were now gun-shy, unwilling to risk committing troops in a way they feared might mean certain death. As historian Ernest B. Furgurson wrote, "A Cold Harbor syndrome, a reluctance to charge enemy breastworks,

---

* General Winfield Scott Hancock had been one of the Union heroes at Gettysburg a year earlier, where he was severely wounded when a bullet hit his saddle pommel, driving a nail and the bullet into his inner thigh. He removed the nail himself as a tourniquet was applied. In 1880, running as a Democrat, Hancock lost a close presidential election to another Civil War general, Ohio Republican James A. Garfield. Hancock was then elected president of the National Rifle Association in 1881.

a memory of comrades left dying in the sun, hung over Grant's soldiers, and especially his generals. It held them back when they could have easily overrun the puny Confederate force at Petersburg. Meade himself said that the effort failed 'principally owing to the moral condition of the army.' [44] Smith was relieved of his command after some sniping between him and Benjamin Butler. Smith did not command in combat again.*

After the Battle of the Old Men and the Young Boys at Petersburg on June 9 and the repeated failure of the assaults Grant had ordered on June 15, the Union commander announced on June 18 that he would settle in for a siege of Petersburg. Lincoln was disappointed by the news but remained sure that Grant "would hold on with a bull-dog grip and chew and choke as much as possible." [45] Perhaps not even Lincoln realized that all the chewing and choking would take another nine hard months.

Grant had used similar tactics a year earlier in his successful campaign against Vicksburg, a fortress city occupying a high bluff above the Mississippi River. That siege had lasted about six weeks, beginning on May 25 and ending on July 4, 1863, and had begun when two major assaults against the Confederate fortifications were repulsed with heavy casualties. With no possible reinforcements, supplies nearly gone, and after holding out for more than forty days, the garrison finally surrendered on July 4.

The news of Vicksburg's surrender had been a moment of jubilation for Lincoln and the Union, coming a day after the Union victory

---

* After his dismissal, Smith wrote to his Vermont senator Solomon Foot, accusing Grant of drunkenness, a charge that had dogged Grant's career. Benjamin Butler, a witness to the drinking in Smith's account and no friend of Smith, later came to Grant's defense when the charge was made public. "There was never any such happening as Smith relates," Butler wrote in a memoir. "I never saw General Grant drink a glass of spirituous liquor in my life" (H. W. Brands, *The Man Who Saved the Union*, p. 316).

at Gettysburg. But for the residents of Vicksburg, the siege had been the stuff of nightmares. The constant bombardment of the city by Union gunboats drove the people of Vicksburg and the Confederate garrison into man-made caves. As weeks went by and the city could not be resupplied, soldiers were reduced to quarter rations. As James McPherson recorded, "Skinned rats appeared beside the mule meat in the markets. Dogs and cats disappeared mysteriously. The tensions of living under the siege drove people to the edge of madness."[46]

The war against Petersburg's civilians began in earnest on June 16, when a Union battery threw the first shells into the city. Women and children soon began to flee the city for the safety of houses in the countryside around Petersburg as the battle began. As the summer came, it brought deadly heat and humid Virginia air thick with flies, lice, and ticks. Troops on both sides were confined in a maze of winding trenches, similar to those that would be used in the European fighting of World War I, open to rain and exposed to constant artillery fire. On the Union side, U.S. Colored Troops were usually placed in the most forward trenches, shallow dugouts called "bombproofs" where they were expected to warn against incoming shot and enemy movements.

Often tasked with the most unpleasant jobs of digging trenches and latrine duty, the U.S. Colored Troops were also usually assigned the task of recovering the dead and burying them. In one instance, white Union troops made an unsuccessful assault on some Confederate works at Petersburg. "After their dead bodies baked in the hot June sun for ten days, military authorities called in a black regiment to serve as the burial detail," recorded McPherson. "Because they had to perform within range of the Confederate guns, they had to do the work at night, groping around for their bloated comrades in blue amid the stench of decomposition and burying them quietly."[47]

By June 23, twenty-seven-year-old Colonel Washington Roebling* of the New York Artillery noted, "The demand down here for killing purposes is far ahead of the supply. Thank God, however, for the consolation that when the last man is killed, the war will be over. This war...differs from all previous wars in having no object to fight for; it can't be finished until all the men on either one side or the other are killed; both sides are trying to do that as fast as they can because it would be a pity to spin this affair out for two or three years longer."[48]

In Petersburg, there was initially a devil-may-care attitude, perhaps a calculated sense of false bravado as the Union shells fell on the small port town. A Confederate officer wrote, "The enemy throw a number of shells daily into Petersburg but they do little damage.... The women and the children seem not to mind them at all—on one street yesterday where such a number of shells burst that I would have considered it a warm place in the [battle]field, women were passing about with little concern, dodging around a corner when they heard a shell coming or putting their heads out of the windows to see what damage they had done."[49]

Late in June, the Union would again attempt to break down the Confederate defenses in what became one of the most tragic incidents of the war, known as the Battle of the Crater. Outside Petersburg, General Ambrose Burnside was approached with the idea of blowing a hole—literally—in the Confederate defenses. Colonel Henry Pleasants, a coal-mining engineer who led a regiment from Pennsylvania coal country, brought the concept to Burnside.

The Pennsylvania men worked for a month, digging a tunnel four feet wide at the bottom, two feet wide at the top, and five feet high,

---

* Washington Roebling was the son of John A. Roebling, the first designer of the Brooklyn Bridge. An engineer himself, the younger Roebling enlisted in 1861 and fought in many of the Civil War's major engagements. After the war, he joined his father on construction of the famed bridge and became its chief engineer after his father's death in 1869.

that would reach beneath the Confederate lines of defense. The mine would require ventilation, and Pleasants had rigged up an ingenious smokestack system that drew fresh oxygen into the tunnel as his men dug. As a fire burned and smoke went up the chimney to the ground above, the burning fire inside the tunnel created a draft, pulling in fresh air for the miners.

At 3:30 a.m. on July 30, Colonel Pleasants lit the ninety-eight-foot fuse and sprinted out of the tunnel. When the fuse sputtered out, two volunteers went in and relit it. This might sound like a sweaty-palm scene from a Hollywood action thriller. But it was no fiction. If Petersburg had been a series of miscalculations and lost opportunities, the worst was yet to come. And it would result in a horror worse than most disaster movies.

In minutes, 8,000 pounds of gunpowder in 320 kegs was detonated, and a 170-foot section of the Confederate defensive line erupted in a huge blast, throwing tons of dirt and the timbers used to shore up the mineshaft into the air. Men later told of feeling the earth shake from the blast for miles. The massive explosion left a hole in the ground nearly 300 feet long, 60 feet wide, and 30 feet deep. The initial blast had instantly killed or wounded more than three hundred Confederate soldiers.[50]

Under the original plan of attack, the breach was supposed to be taken by a unit of U.S. Colored Troops who had been training for the task for weeks. They were supposed to break through the Confederate lines opened by the explosion and seize a ridge overlooking Petersburg, a mere 533 yards away. "If all went as planned," Kevin M. Levin wrote in an account of the crater explosion, "black soldiers stood a chance of being the first Union soldiers to enter the city of Petersburg.... The presence of African American soldiers signaled a dramatic shift in the overall policy of the Lincoln administration, which had hoped to save the Union through military means without risking popular support by redrawing deeply entrenched racial boundaries."[51]

But General Meade, unsure of the reliability of the black soldiers, abruptly changed plans at the last minute. Meade was also afraid of a potential public relations disaster if something went wrong. "Meade worried that the public might accuse the army of needlessly sacrificing black men if the assault failed," noted Levin. "The evidence suggests that he simply did not believe that inexperienced [black] troops had a better chance of succeeding than veteran units."[52]

The abrupt alteration in the plan of attack meant that men who were unprepared for this assault were pressed into the job as one of their commanders, General James H. Ledlie, was drinking rum in a nearby bomb shelter.[53] Astonished by the imposing sight of the crater before them and the carnage wrought by the explosion, these Union troops, perhaps disoriented by the explosion, ran directly into the gaping crater instead of circling its perimeter, as the U.S. Colored Troops had been prepared to do.

By the time the black soldiers were sent in, it was too late. The Battle of the Crater had become yet another of the Union's great disasters. As the Confederate troops recovered from the initial shock of the explosion, they began to fire at the Union troops caught in the crater and unable to climb up the earth walls. Bodies had literally been blown into the air and the ground was littered with the dead and wounded, many of them maimed and missing limbs. Blood mixing with mud, the crater soon became the scene of brutal hand-to-hand fighting and many of the black soldiers who had been ordered into the hole by ill-prepared officers were butchered without mercy as Confederate soldiers shouted, "Take the white man! Kill the nigger!"[54]

Instead of being taken prisoner, as white soldiers were, surrendering black troops were bayoneted, shot, or clubbed to death. "It had the same effect upon our men that a red flag has upon a mad bull," one South Carolina soldier said. "They were the first we had seen and the sight of a nigger in a blue uniform and with a gun was more than 'Johnnie Reb' could stand. Fury had taken possession."[55]

On the Confederate side of the crater stood a hero of the Confederate cause, General William "Little Billy" Mahone, though his name has largely faded from American history, unlike such legendary generals as Lee and Stonewall Jackson. On the day that Union soldiers detonated those eight thousand pounds of powder, Mahone was the man who led the counterattack. A native of Petersburg, he was a civil engineer, teacher, and railroad executive (and later a member of the U.S. Congress). His story is one of the more complicated tales of how the war divided the country and would continue to sow division for decades afterward.

Born to innkeepers, he went on to the prestigious Virginia Military Institute, where he learned engineering and took an interest in railroading. He had become the chief engineer of several railroads and on the eve of Virginia's secession was the president of the Norfolk & Petersburg Railroad.[56]

When Virginia seceded in April 1861, Mahone immediately joined the Confederate army and rose through the ranks. A wispy five foot five, Mahone barely weighed one hundred pounds. When he was wounded at the Second Battle of Bull Run, his wife had been told it was only a "flesh wound." But she exclaimed to the governor of Virginia that his wound had to be serious because "[t]he general hasn't any flesh."[57] He was promoted after fighting at Spotsylvania and Cold Harbor and returned to his hometown of Petersburg to aid in its defense. As an engineer who had laid some of the rail lines around Petersburg, Mahone knew the surrounding terrain better than anyone with a mere map, and he put his knowledge to work in successfully defending Petersburg against the initial Union attacks.

When the powder blast obliterated the huge section of the Confederate lines, Mahone was a mile away. Rushing to the scene with reinforcements, he quickly organized a counterattack, rallying the dazed remaining Confederate troops nearby. Turning back the Union assault, Mahone ordered fixed bayonets and then led his men in the deadly hand-to-hand fighting that turned the crater into a slaughter-house. Mahone's Confederates gradually gained control of the crater. The official report identified 3,826 Union casualties out of the 16,722 engaged, with 504 killed or mortally wounded. Another 1,441 were missing, presumably taken prisoner.

Making matters worse, Robert E. Lee refused a truce that day, according to historian Stephen B. Oates. "The wounded lay under the blazing sun without food, water, or medical aid."[58] Famed battle-field nurse Clara Barton, whose cousin in a Massachusetts unit was wounded at the crater, went to the scene the next day. As Oates recorded, "Burial parties were still at work, and she saw a great many corpses in the crater. They were infested with flies and maggots—the stench was overpowering—and so blackened and bloated that Negroes and whites could be distinguished only by their hair."[59]

In the aftermath of the Battle of the Crater, roughly 1,500 black and white Union prisoners were marched into the town of Petersburg. "As the prisoners marched and countermarched through the streets, they were subjected to taunts and verbal abuses from spectators at the street level and on the verandas," wrote Levin:

> The cries of "See the white and nigger equality soldiers" and "Yanks and niggers sleep in the same bed." ... The order to march both black and white Union prisoners through Petersburg served to remind soldiers and civilians alike of just what was at stake as the American Civil War entered its fourth summer. The torrents of abuse hurled that early Sunday morning were directed first and foremost at the black Union soldiers (now stripped of their uniforms), some of whom were once property of Virginia slave owners. Their presence on the battlefield reinforced horrific fears of miscegenation, the raping of white Southern women, and black political control that had surfaced at various times throughout antebellum period and that many had come to believe would ensue if victory were not secured.[60]

But the momentary jubilation that might have been felt as those Union troops were humiliated in the streets of Petersburg would fade quickly, replaced by the long, harsh reality of life in a besieged city. With the Union failure at the crater, the siege of Petersburg dragged on over the next long, deadly months.

For the citizens of the Cockade City, life had become almost as dangerous and difficult as it was for the troops. At the Second Presbyterian Church, the Reverend John Miller ascended the pulpit one Sunday in June 1864 and began to lead the congregation in prayer. "'Almighty Father we are assembled to worship Thee in the presence of our enemies' had just passed his lips when a Federal shell crashed through the wall of the sanctuary," recounts historian Heidi Campbell-Shoaf. "Life for the reverend and his flock had changed forever."[61]

For most of the nineteenth century, Petersburg had been a prosperous, even cosmopolitan city that was, if anything, more sophisticated than its neighbor Richmond, a few miles to the north. It boasted a municipal water system supplied by a large reservoir, two daily newspapers, 159 grocers, several banks, numerous tobacco companies, flour and textile mills, and a customs house—where duties on imports and exports were processed. The town's chief industry and employer were the railroad lines, which also required machine shops, another chief source of employment.

A city of some eighteen thousand, in which about half the population was black, Petersburg included a flourishing community of more than three thousand free African Americans. Most were freedmen who had been able to purchase their freedom.

A large number of the city's free blacks worked for the railroads, which also employed many of Petersburg's enslaved blacks—their wages were paid to the owners who hired them out. Petersburg was also home to auction houses, where many slaves were sold, some to be shipped away by rail. Some of the city's six thousand slaves who remained either worked alongside free laborers or in the prosperous white households.[62] And it was slave labor that had largely built Petersburg's defenses.

Once the siege was established, Grant brought in heavy artillery to pound the Confederate trenches around the city. Union shells reached the town as well. One of the Union weapons was a huge field gun, a 13-inch, 8.5-ton mortar known as "the Dictator"; transported on a railroad flatcar, it was capable of hurling two-hundred-pound missiles at the enemy. When Grant received word that General William T. Sherman had captured Atlanta in September 1864, he "celebrated" by ordering a one-hundred-gun salute in Sherman's honor fired at the Confederate lines in front of Petersburg.

"To escape the terrifying missiles, some people dug bomb shelters, known as bomb proofs, in their back yards," recorded Campbell-Shoaf. "Others fortified their basements with sandbags and bales of cotton. Eventually, the shelling became just another hardship the citizens had to endure and try to ignore. The Confederate artillery commander, Brigadier General William Nelson Pendleton, wrote, 'The people of the place, ladies and all, bear this outrage upon their pleasant homes with great fortitude and dignity.' "[63]

For the Union armies, November 1864 would bring a pleasant surprise when the Union League, a charitable organization first formed in New York by wealthy men like Theodore Roosevelt's father, Theodore Sr., organized a Thanksgiving feast for the Federal troops. A year before, Abraham Lincoln had issued the first official Thanksgiving proclamation, and in 1864 a massive fund-raising and food collection effort was undertaken. Four steamers left New York for Grant's City Point headquarters carrying 400,000 boxes and barrels. Cooked turkeys, boiled hams, canned peaches, apples, and cakes were delivered to troops around Petersburg as well as to other Union camps around the country.

In *Starving the South*, his history of the Union effort to cripple resistance by cutting off food supplies to both civilians and troops, Andrew F. Smith wrote, "The Thanksgiving dinner in the North was a visible manifestation of civilian support for the Union military. In addition to private mailings of food and other treats, Northern civilians gave 70 million dollars for the welfare of their fighting men.... While the food itself was just a token, Union soldiers and sailors believed that this gesture showed that the North was behind them, and their spirits soared."[64]

A similar Confederate effort was bravely proposed and failed in the face of the severe shortages throughout the Confederacy. But the winter of 1864–65 was unusually cold and life inside Petersburg worsened as the months dragged on. The crime rate in the city exploded as people began to steal what they could not buy. "Shops were broken into regularly, and farm wagons entering Petersburg via the western corridor were waylaid with alarming frequency," wrote Noah Andre Trudeau.[65]

Basics like firewood became precious commodities. As the shelling continued, the soldiers and civilians chopped down and stripped every tree, and people began dismantling Petersburg's bridges for firewood. The food situation grew even worse and locals reported the disappearance of the usual flocks of pigeons, and the meat pies being sold on the streets gave new meaning to the term "mystery meat." As one local noted, it was common knowledge that people were eating rat, mouse, and mule meat.[66]

But a gritty sense of fatalistic determination was also part of Petersburg's public life. As Petersburg's Dr. Herbert Claiborne wrote, "There were parties, starvation parties, as they were called, on account of the absence of refreshments impossible to be obtained; ball followed ball, and the soldier met and danced with his lady at night, and on the morrow danced the dance of death in the deadly trenches out on the line...."[67]

The war was not so courtly. In early December, Grant sent a

large infantry force south to cut another of the rail lines coming into Petersburg. This maneuver, according to Trudeau, led to a series of atrocities committed by both sides.

As they marched, the Union troops were soon joined by thousands of black people fleeing the plantations and flocking to the Federal wagons. One group of escaped blacks reported that they had seen a number of Union stragglers caught by Confederate guerrillas and massacred. When a Union detachment went to investigate, a general reported finding the bodies: "The throats cut, the head crushed in by blows of an axe, and the breast pierced by a knife." Another Union commander wrote to his wife, "From appearances they had been stripped of all their clothing and, when in the act of kneeling in a circle, they were shot in the head."

In revenge, the Union men vented their anger by burning barns and buildings to the ground as they returned toward Petersburg. Driven from her home, a Virginia woman watched as it burned and screamed at the Yankee troops: "Is this what you call subjugating the South?" A Confederate soldier later wrote, "We cannot believe Americans can do these things."[68]

For Lee's troops, life grew even harder. By January 1865, as the Union effort to blockade and starve the South, physically and financially, took its deadly toll, the Army of Northern Virginia was on one-quarter rations, and "some days the troops had no food at all," Andrew F. Smith noted.[69]

And then it was over.

In late February, there was a last failed attempt at a negotiated peace. Lincoln was inaugurated in March 1865 for a second term, and he was staying near Grant's City Point camp aboard his steamer *River Queen* as Grant continued to pound away at Lee. On April 1, there was still heavy fighting all around Petersburg, and by dawn the next morning, hundreds of guns had opened up along the ten miles of Union front lines. "For a time," as Stephen Oates described, "Lincoln stood out in the trenches and watched the battle, then he manned the City Point headquarters where he relayed messages on to Washington as rapidly as they came in from Grant. The next morning came the news Lincoln had been waiting for. Lee had evacuated Petersburg."[70]

After a series of defeats in skirmishes and battles on the outskirts of Petersburg, Robert E. Lee knew the end was near and decided to leave the city behind. On April 3, a Union officer accepted the surrender of Petersburg.

Lincoln was overjoyed at the victory, biographer Oates writes, and "rode into a smoldering Petersburg and pumped Grant's hand for this glorious victory."[71] A former resident of Petersburg, Elizabeth Keckley, later accompanied President and Mrs. Lincoln into the fallen town. Mary Todd Lincoln's confidante and dressmaker, Keckley had been born into slavery in the Petersburg area, serving a local family by the time she was four. As a young girl, she had been raped and given birth to a son. After being taken to St. Louis, Elizabeth was able to earn enough to purchase her own freedom and that of her son. She had been away many years but knew the city well when she returned in April 1865—as a free woman—with President and Mrs. Lincoln.

The rest of Petersburg's African-American people were as astonished as Keckley must have been by the new realities. "For the most part, the white population remained out of sight as the Union army marched through town," Heidi Campbell-Shoaf notes. "But the black community was overjoyed, particularly the slaves. A soldier from New England wrote, 'The colored portion of the people were wild with singing, praysing [sic] God for sending the Yankee hosts to free them, claping [sic] hands…, singing hymns, shaking hands, pushing one another with joy. The most boisterous outpouring of joy was reserved for the passing of the U.S. Colored Troops, who displayed even more than usual of their famed soldierly discipline and decorum in front of the grateful throng.' "[72]

Lincoln would soon travel to Richmond, which Lee and the Confederate cabinet had abandoned. A few days later, on April 9, Lee and Grant would meet and arrange the surrender of Lee's army. Lincoln would playfully sit at Jefferson Davis's desk in the Confederate capital. But then, on April 14, he was dead.

## AFTERMATH

The Civil War fighting that took place in and around Petersburg, Virginia, lasted nearly a year and culminated in the surrender of Robert E. Lee and the end of the war in April 1865. This campaign is more appropriately referred to as the Siege rather than the Battle of Petersburg. Whichever term is used, these long months of fighting were among the most deadly and horrific in the war, and the period of combat between June 15, 1864, and April 2, 1865, would go down as the longest attack on an American city in the nation's history.

The battles and the siege produced 60,000 casualties among the more than 180,000 soldiers involved on both sides. The fighting in and around the city was shocking in its brutality in a war that had already sorely tested American sensibilities about the staggering losses that the Civil War had meant to both sides.

But the fight for Petersburg also exposed the raw edges of the deep racial animosities that had helped lead to the Civil War and would continue for decades in its wake. Whatever slim hopes had ever existed for a biracial, united America were crushed in the hatred and anger spawned by the war.

That reality was best illustrated in the life of William Mahone, the celebrated hero of the Battle of the Crater. Coming from the world of the killing fields, men like Mahone had to grapple with creating a viable government in the defeated South. After the war, Mahone remained involved in Confederate veteran activities while expanding his railroading business. He also went into politics and formed the Readjuster Party, the chief aim of which was to solve the problem of paying off Virginia's huge wartime debts.

What was unusual about Mahone's Readjusters was that they won a majority vote after the war with black support. With his party in control, Mahone set out to build schools that aided poor white and African-American communities in Virginia. He made sure that African Americans got a share of government jobs. "The visibility of African Americans in the state government constituted a radical change in the distribution of political power and was seen as a threat to white political rule in Virginia," wrote Kevin M. Levin. "Readjusters also changed the make-up of the public schools. Their reforms increased the number of black teachers and students, and the establishment of the Virginia Normal and Collegiate Institute opened up new avenues of upward mobility."[73]

Not surprisingly, this did not sit well with the conservative white powers in the state. Among the men who fought hardest against the Readjuster movement was attorney Fletcher Archer, who had led the Old Men and the Young Boys on that June day in 1864. When Mahone later left the Readjusters and joined the despised Republican Party, he was castigated as a Benedict Arnold of the Confederate cause. Although he had a long career in politics, including as a senator from Virginia, Mahone was pilloried and attacked by whites who saw him as a traitor to the Lost Cause of the Confederacy. Many who now opposed him had served under him. His conciliatory racial policies could have created a template that if followed elsewhere in the South might have changed the arc of history.

The siege of Petersburg also deserves recognition for its role in another piece of iconic American history—it can stake a legitimate claim as the birthplace of Memorial Day. In May 1866, the ladies of Petersburg formed a Ladies' Memorial Association, whose purpose was to "devise means to perpetuate their gratitude and admiration for those who died defending homes and loved ones."

At their May 30, 1866, meeting the ladies discussed celebrating June 9 as the anniversary of the city's "noble defense," and by a unanimous vote it was decided to make this day a Memorial Day. On June 9, 1866, one of the ladies, a teacher, took her students to the city's Blandford Cemetery and decorated the graves of both Union and Confederate soldiers with flowers and flags, beginning an annual tradition.

While visiting Petersburg in 1868, Mary Logan learned how the city's women decorated the soldiers' graves and wrote about the practice to her husband, John Logan. An attorney and politician before the Civil War, General John Logan was a veteran of both the Mexican and Civil wars. He had served under Grant and returned to politics after the war, becoming a representative—later senator—from Illinois, and managed the impeachment of Lincoln's successor, Andrew Johnson. Logan also placed the name of Ulysses S. Grant into nomination for the presidency by the Republican Party in 1868. (Grant won election easily.) Logan also led a powerful fraternal veterans' organization called the Grand Army of the Republic (GAR).

In May 1868, as commander in chief of the group, Logan issued the GAR's "General Order Number 11," which called for a nationwide day to decorate the graves of fallen soldiers with fresh flowers. Logan's order read, in part:

> Their soldier lives were the reveille of freedom to a race in chains, and their deaths the tattoo of rebellious tyranny in arms. We should guard their graves with sacred vigilance. All that the consecrated wealth and taste of the nation can add to their adornment and security is but a fitting tribute to the memory of her slain defenders. Let no wanton foot tread rudely on such hallowed grounds. Let pleasant paths invite the coming and going of reverent visitors and fond mourners. Let no vandalism of avarice or neglect, no ravages of time

testify to the present or to the coming generations that we have for-gotten as a people the cost of a free and undivided republic.[74]

Although Logan's "Decoration Day"—as it was initially known when marked at Arlington National Cemetery for the first time in 1868—was seen as a Northern holiday, it was the beginning of a national Decoration Day. Later to be called Memorial Day, it was eventually established as a federal holiday honoring America's war dead. While other American towns and cities have staked a claim as the birthplace of Decoration, or Memorial, Day, the specific link between Mary Logan's visit to Petersburg and the establishment of the holiday connect the day to June 9 and the Battle of the Old Men and the Young Boys, a convinc-ing case for it to be recognized as the birthplace of the holiday.*

On May 23, 1865, the Civil War over, Washington, D.C., celebrated with a parade, actually a two-day affair. The 150,000 men of the Union armies marched down the capital's Pennsylvania Avenue in a grand review, past a reviewing stand in which Ulysses S. Grant and President Andrew Johnson, Lincoln's successor, were seated. On the first day, the cavalry units of General Meade's Army of the Potomac alone reportedly stretched for seven miles. The march was orderly and precise until the horse of a young general named George Armstrong Custer broke from the ranks, even though Custer was an expert horseman. "With his buckskin breeches, trademark red scarf, and

---

* Many people, including Professor David Blight, contend that Charleston, South Caro-lina, deserves the honor because of a ceremony on May 1, 1865, in which freedmen of the city reburied Union dead who had been held in a racetrack-turned-prison, and newly emancipated children decorated the soldiers' graves. This and other similar dedication ceremonies were widespread after the war, but the connection of Mrs. Logan to Peters-burg gives that city its distinctive claim.

mane of yellow hair flapping in the wind," Jay Winik wrote, "Custer galloped madly past the reviewing stand—as the crowd gasped—and then with a kick, he wheeled his horse gracefully around and returned to the head of his column."[75]

Day two belonged to Sherman's men, the so-called Bummers who had swept through Atlanta and left a swath of destruction on the March to the Sea. Mostly Western men whose appearance was more rugged and ragged than the men of the Potomac, they marched with less formality but perhaps more swagger. Their formations included goats, sheep, cattle, chickens, wagons, and carts—all the equipage carried by the Bummers on their hard campaign through the South.

It was a last hurrah. Within days of the grand review, the Union military forces began to demobilize. By November 1866, only 11,043 of the more than one million volunteers who had served in the Union army were still in uniform.[76] Congress authorized an increase in the size of the peacetime army to a little more than 54,000 men. But a decade later, by 1876, the army's overall size was reduced to a little more than 27,000 men. The navy was also downsized (to borrow a modern term), going from 700 ships at the peak of the war down to 52, many of them obsolete wooden sailing vessels. In America's postwar navy, officers continued to serve more of a diplomatic role, supporting the nation's commercial interests rather than military adventures.[77]

But the four years of the Civil War had changed warfare; in many ways it was the first modern war. The Civil War had put to use all the new tools of the Industrial Age—technology, factory production, mechanization, innovation, and invention. It was the first war in which troops moved by railroad. The "Iron Horse" would ultimately replace the horse-drawn wagon and eventually the mounted horse soldiers of the cavalry—although the cavalry tradition would continue in mechanized armor and eventually the Air Cavalry. (Think Robert Duvall donning his cavalry hat in *Apocalypse Now.*) The telegraph had transformed communications. And battlefield innovations had brought about rapid transformations in weaponry. Muzzle-loaded muskets and paper cartridges were replaced by repeating rifles. The Gatling gun, patented in 1862, was the forerunner of the modern machine gun. (Richard Gatling,* its inventor, hoped his device would actually save lives because, as he wrote, it would "supersede the necessity of large armies.")[78] And battlefront reporting and engraved illustrations published by the nation's booming newspapers, combined with the advent of photography, had begun to transform the way civilians saw the war. In October 1862, Mathew Brady brought an exhibit of photographic images from the Antietam battlefield to New York. According to a report in the *New York Times*:

> Mr. BRADY has done something to bring home to us the terrible reality and earnestness of war. If he has not brought bodies and laid them in our dooryards and along the streets, he has done something very like it. At the door of his gallery hangs a little placard, "The Dead of Antietam." Crowds of people are constantly going up the stairs; follow them, and you find them bending over photographic views of that fearful battle-field, taken immediately after the action. Of all objects of horror one would think the battle-field should stand preeminent, that it should bear away the palm of repulsiveness. But, on the contrary, there is a terrible fascination about it that draws one near these pictures, and makes him loth to leave them. You will see hushed, reverend groups standing around these weird copies of carnage, bending down to look in the pale faces of the dead, chained by the strange spell that dwells in dead men's eyes. It seems somewhat singular that the same sun that looked down on the faces of the slain, blistering them, blotting out from the bodies all semblance to humanity, and hastening corruption, should have thus caught their features upon canvas, and given them perpetuity for ever. But so it is.[79]

---

* Besides the famous gun, Gatling's name also lives on in the slang term *gat* for gun.

War had changed with the times. So had America and its attitudes toward combat. As the large armies demobilized, it would take generations for many Americans to forget the terrible Civil War years. Eventually, time and patriotic fervor replaced some of the nation's divisions and deep wounds with a gauze of romantic, reverential nostalgia for the war. Eventually veterans' gatherings at places like Gettysburg would include men—white men, that is—from both sides.

But the country had had enough of fighting. Protected from conflicts in Europe and Asia by two wide oceans, Americans settled in to the late-nineteenth-century effort to construct an industrial and agricultural powerhouse. "Geography and European balance of power considerations," historians Allan Millett and Peter Maslowski wrote, "gave the United States virtually total security. Moreover, through the 1880s, a foreign policy with limited goals required little mobilized military power."[80]

In fact, the only real warfare that continued through this era was taking place in the American West and Great Plains against the Indian tribes. Even during the Civil War, Lincoln had dispatched troops to put down a Sioux uprising in Minnesota that ended with the hanging of thirty-eight Indians, still the largest mass execution in American history. Among the worst incidents was the battle at Sand Creek, Colorado, where as many as 160 Cheyenne under Chief Black Kettle— many of them women and children—were massacred in 1864.*

Despite a series of peace treaties signed after the Civil War, Indians were under constant pressure. The Homestead Act, which opened up vast Western territories to settlers; a series of gold strikes on Indian lands; and the completion of the transcontinental railroad brought more white settlers into confrontation with the Indians.

The ongoing conflicts with a numerically smaller and nomadic

---

* Sand Creek Massacre National Historic Site marks the scene of this tragedy and is now operated by the National Park Service.

enemy still armed mostly with bows against repeating rifles and artillery was nonetheless a daunting challenge for the U.S. government. Of the more than 950 recorded engagements between the years 1866 and 1890, the most famous was the disastrous defeat of George A. Custer's Seventh Cavalry at Little Big Horn, Montana, in June 1876. In the following year, the pursuit of the Nez Percé in the Northwest concluded with the surrender of Chief Joseph. Ten years later, Geronimo, the leader of the Apache in Mexico and what is now New Mexico, Arizona, and western Texas, was captured and sent to a series of prison camps. (Later reduced to selling his autographed photos, Geronimo would live to ride in Theodore Roosevelt's 1905 inaugural parade; he was never allowed to return to his home.)

The Indian wars created another legendary group. Born out of the U.S. Colored Troops created during the Civil War were four black infantry regiments (later reduced to two) and two black cavalry regiments—all led, of course, by white officers. These were the men who would become known as the Buffalo Soldiers by the Indians they were sent to fight in the West.

They had been given their memorable name following an 1867 battle in which eight hundred Cheyenne fought ninety black troopers near Fort Leavenworth, Kansas. The scalps of the black soldiers became highly prized by the Cheyenne. "Comparing them to an animal they considered sacred," Gail Buckley writes, "Cheyenne called the 10th Cavalry troopers buffalo soldiers. The term would come to apply to all the black western units. While Indians continued to scalp whites, it was said that they later refrained from scalping blacks, and in fact, did not relish fighting them."[81]

---

The army's other chief task in the postwar era was securing the defeated South and bringing the former Confederate states back into the Union. Before his death, Lincoln had begun this process by appointing military governors for the occupied states of the former Confederacy. The army worked with the Freedmen's Bureau to protect blacks in the Old Confederacy and build schools and labor programs during the Reconstruction era.

The federal troops in the South numbered some seventeen thousand men in 1868. But the army presence was a bitter pill for white Southerners who resented the federal role and its support of the growing political power of emancipated blacks. The resistance to federal troops protecting free blacks boiled over in the growing violence of the Ku Klux Klan. Formed as a social fraternity by six Confederate veterans in Pulaski, Tennessee, in May 1865, the KKK* had emerged as a powerful paramilitary force that terrorized blacks with a campaign of whippings, rape, and murder. The KKK also struck at members of a benevolent social organization called the Union Club, representatives of the Freedmen's Bureau, and at Republican politicians in general. By 1876, a presidential year, white Democrats had regained control of the former Confederate states.

The role of the army in Reconstruction essentially ended with the contested presidential election of 1876. Democrat Samuel Tilden, governor of New York, had won the popular vote over Republican Rutherford B. Hayes, an Ohio Civil War veteran. But Tilden lacked sufficient electoral votes due to some contested states. To settle the dispute, a bipartisan federal electoral commission was formed to judge the contested vote counts. Republican Hayes essentially guaranteed to the Democrats on the election commission, most of them from the South, that he would remove the federal troops from the Southern states. He won their votes in one of the most tainted presi-

---

* According to Susan Campbell Bartoletti's *They Called Themselves the K.K.K.*, "Most likely, the men were influenced by Kuklos Adelphon, a popular Southern college fraternity that had disbanded during the war."

dential elections in history. Once Hayes—who would be known as "Rutherfraud" B. Hayes—was in the White House, the army's role in Reconstruction was over and oppressive Jim Crow racial policies were allowed to take hold.

———

A third crucial role for America's peacetime army emerged during the great social upheavals of the Industrial Age. Hit hard by recurring booms and busts, the largely immigrant labor force of factory workers, miners, and other working people in America began to unionize in the late nineteenth century. Several presidents of this era responded to the requests of American businessmen to suppress these unions and labor actions by using the army as strikebreakers. After Grover Cleveland sent federal troops to help put down the Pullman Strike in 1894, he later signed a federal Labor Day holiday law hoping—unsuccessfully, it turned out—to win workers' votes.

As the last decade of the nineteenth century opened, a professor at the Naval War College—founded in 1884 in Newport, Rhode Island, as an adjunct to the Naval Academy, which had moved to Newport during the Civil War—published his lectures in book form. Hardly a page-turner for the average reader, the book was titled *The Influence of Sea Power upon History, 1660–1783* (1890). The author, Captain Alfred Thayer Mahan, soon became the world's foremost naval historian. Pointing to the history of England and other seagoing empires, Mahan argued that a nation's greatness, prosperity, and commercial strength were all linked to a powerful navy that could control the seas. His "gospel of armed aggressiveness" found an audience in America, Europe, and Asia. Following Mahan's guidance, Great Britain, Germany, and Japan all began to build powerful navies based on his philosophy.[82] The U.S. Navy also paid attention and by 1898 had embarked on construction of a modernized fleet with battleships and cruisers.

Also paying attention to Mahan was another naval historian, a wealthy New Yorker by birth who attended Harvard and had turned his student research work into a much-admired naval history of the War of 1812. He also became an enthusiastic supporter of Mahan's ideas. His name was Theodore Roosevelt.

## Chapter Three

-+->-<+-

# The Water Cure

*Balangiga, Philippines—September 1901*

"In the interests of our commerce and our fullest
development, we should build the Nicaraguan canal, and
for the protection of that canal and for the sake of our
commercial supremacy in the Pacific we should control the
Hawaiian Islands and maintain our influence in Samoa....
Commerce follows the flag, and we should build up a navy
strong enough to give protection to Americans in every
quarter of the globe."[1]
—*Senator Henry Cabot Lodge (March 1895)*

*"Remember the* Maine! *To hell with Spain!"*
—New York Journal *(February 16, 1898)*

"The boys are getting sick of fighting these heathens, and all
say we volunteered to fight Spain, not heathens. Their patriotism is wearing off....If I ever get out of this army I will never
get into another. They will be fighting four hundred years, and

then never whip these people, for there are not enough of us to follow them up."[2]

—*Tom Crandall, Nebraska Regiment (1899 letter)*

"I want no prisoners. I wish you to kill and burn. The more you kill and burn, the better you will please me."[3]

—*General Jacob Smith (October 23, 1901)*

"You have wasted 600 millions of treasure. You have sacrificed nearly 10,000 American lives—the flower of our youth. You have devastated provinces. You have slain uncounted thousands of the people you desire to benefit. Your practical statesmanship has succeeded in converting a people who three years ago were ready to kiss the hem of the garment of the American and to welcome him as liberator...into sullen and irreconcilable enemies, possessed of a hatred which centuries cannot eradicate."

—*Senator George Frisbie Hoar (May 1902)*

## Milestones in the Spanish-American War

### 1898

**February 15** The USS *Maine* mysteriously explodes while anchored in Havana Harbor, resulting in the deaths of 266 crewmembers.

**April 22** Congress passes the Volunteer Army Act, which calls for organization of a First Volunteer Cavalry—a "cowboy cavalry" that the press will christen "Rough Riders." Resigning his post as assistant secretary of the navy, Theodore Roosevelt takes a commission as lieutenant colonel of the brigade. He joins his friend Leonard Wood—physician to President McKinley—who commands the unit.

**April 23** President McKinley calls for 125,000 recruits.

**April 24** Spain declares war on the United States.

**April 25** The United States declares that a state of war exists as of April 21, the day Spain broke off diplomatic relations.

**May 1** The United States launches a surprise naval attack on the Spanish navy in Manila Bay in the Philippines, a Spanish colony, even though Cuba has been the focal point of the conflict.

**June 10** A force of 647 marines lands at Guantanamo Bay, beginning the invasion of Cuba.

**June 24** Led by Joseph Wheeler, a onetime general in the Confederate cavalry, and Leonard Wood, one thousand regular army troops and Rough Riders, accompanied by several war correspondents, win the first land battle of the war at Las Guásimas, Cuba.

**July 1** The battles of El Caney and San Juan Hill are hard-fought American victories in Cuba.

**July 17** In Santiago, Cuba, the Spanish garrison surrenders to American forces and the U.S. flag is raised over the government building.

**July 26** Through the French ambassador, Spain requests peace terms. The "splendid little war" ends after three months of fighting. McKinley announces terms: Independence is granted to Cuba; the United States takes control of Puerto Rico; and the United States will occupy Manila pending further negotiations.

**August 13** The Spanish in Manila surrender to Admiral George Dewey and General Wesley Merritt.

**November 8** Theodore Roosevelt, the "hero of San Juan Hill," is elected governor of New York.

## 1899

**February 6** The Senate ratifies the Treaty of Paris with Spain.

**March 2** Congress authorizes the addition of 65,000 men to the regular army and asks for 35,000 volunteers to suppress a Filipino rebellion led by Emilio Aguinaldo.

**June 20** While fighting continues in the Philippines, the United States also sends troops to China as part of an international "relief force" to quell the anti-Western Boxer Rebellion.

**November 6** President McKinley wins reelection; his new vice president is Theodore Roosevelt.

## 1901

**March 23** Emilio Aguinaldo, the key leader of the Philippine rebellion against the United States, is captured by American troops.

**September 14** President McKinley dies after being shot on September 6. Forty-two-year-old Vice President Theodore Roosevelt takes the oath of office.

**September 28** A company of American soldiers is attacked and massacred in the Philippine town of Balangiga.

### 1902

**July 1** Congress passes the Philippine Government Act, authorizing a commission selected by the president with the advice and consent of Congress to govern the Philippines; it states that the inhabitants of the islands are not U.S. citizens.

**July 4** President Roosevelt declares a successful end to the conflict in the Philippines.

*Balangiga, Philippines*
*September 28, 1901*

It was early Sunday morning and most of the seventy-four men of Company C were in their mess tents, settling down to breakfast. Cook Melvin Walls was dishing out his popular corned beef hash. The men had left their weapons racked in the barracks. The company dog, an adopted stray, hungrily sniffed the air. As they ate, the men talked about the news. The president was dead.

It had taken almost two weeks for word of President William McKinley's death to reach them, half a world away from home on the Philippine island of Samar. After mess, the officers and men of Company C would pay their respects to America's third assassinated president at a memorial mass. Company C's commander, Captain Thomas Connell, a twenty-eight-year-old West Pointer and Roman Catholic from New York, was preparing to lead the service inside the town's Catholic church.

The shocking reports of President McKinley's death on September 14, 1901, had arrived two days before, just as an uneasy tension had fallen over the Philippine port of Balangiga (pronounced bal-un-JEE-guh), about four hundred miles southeast of Manila. Each morning, large groups of Filipinos were pressed to work clearing away garbage and sewage from the streets of the fishing town. Since arriving and establishing this outpost about a month earlier, Captain Connell had forced about eighty local men to live in two small, squalid, overcrowded tents, forced to perform the daily cleanup detail, clearing the streets and cutting back the encroaching jungle. Antagonism toward the occupying American troops had begun to bubble over.

Townspeople had reported stealing and at least one rape commit-ted by the soldiers.[4] For their part, the Americans typically dispar-aged the Filipino natives as "niggers" or "goo-goos" (precursor to the Vietnam-era term *gook*).

For days, the American soldiers had watched an unusual number of women hurrying to the nearby Franciscan church, carrying small coffins. One woman had caught the attention of an American sentry. Heavily clothed—unusual for the season in the tropics—she too car-ried a small coffin. But when the suspicious soldier stopped her and opened the coffin lid with his bayonet, he saw the body of a child. The panicked woman shouted, "Cólera," the Spanish word for cholera.

There had been no reports of a cholera outbreak in the region, but the American soldier was taking no chances. An epidemic would explain the large number of dead children whose coffins were being brought to the church for funerals. It might even explain the sudden disappearance of the parish priest. The soldier resealed the lid and allowed the woman to pass on to the church.

At about six thirty on the morning of September 28, as the Amer-icans settled in with their chow and talked about the McKinley news, Balangiga's police chief, Valerian Abanador, lined up the disgruntled native laborers to start their daily cleanup detail. It was part of Cap-tain Connell's attempt to enforce order and a clear sense of American control over the town.

In the town square, four soldiers were posted on sentry duty as the Filipino laborers began clearing away brush from the nearby jungle, removing garbage that lay in the streets, and clearing out raw sewage that collected in ditches. The men set to work with picks, axes, and bolos, the long, machete-like knives used by many Filipinos.

As his men ate and the Filipino workmen began the day's cleanup detail, Captain Connell was in the nearby convent, where he had taken rooms for himself and the company's two other officers. Seated at a writing desk, Connell was finishing up the remarks he planned to deliver in McKinley's honor.

Connell could not see as Police Chief Abanador approached twenty-one-year-old Private Adolph Gamlin, one of the sentries on duty. Gamlin, from Iowa, was pacing the square from mess tent to church in his two-hours-on, two-hours-off guard routine. Without warning, the policeman grabbed Gamlin's rifle and smashed the butt down on the soldier's head. The farm boy turned soldier crumpled to the ground as Abanador fired the rifle and shouted something in the local dialect. Suddenly the church's three bells began to peal. The tolling of the bells was soon mixed with the sound of conch shell whistles coming from the edge of the jungle.

With the violence of a Philippine volcano erupting, the doors of the church burst open and dozens of "mourners" streamed out. Some tore off their dresses—about one-third of the "women" carrying small coffins into the church had been men in disguise. Hidden inside the wooden boxes were dozens of concealed bolos, which the fighters had attached to their wrists with leather cords.

The Filipinos fell on the sentries and the unsuspecting men of Company C at their breakfast tables and were joined in the rampage by some of the workers in the plaza, who attacked the mostly unarmed soldiers with their picks, shovels, and bolos. In an instant, hundreds more bolo-wielding Filipinos rushed out of the surrounding jungle and joined the blood-spilling spree in the town square.

In the mess tent, the Filipino guerrillas slashed at the Americans in a furious onslaught. Caught without their weapons, the soldiers began fighting back with chairs and kitchen utensils. Cook Melvin Walls threw boiling water and cans of beans at the attackers. The tent ropes were slashed, bringing the tent down on the struggling Americans. The Filipinos continued to hack away at the men trapped beneath the canvas.

Caught completely off guard and heavily outnumbered, the soldiers of Company C were largely helpless as the onslaught took a shocking toll. First Sergeant James Randles had his skull split open by an ax. A bolo swing severed the head of another American soldier.[5] In the nearby convent, the bolo men found the officers and hacked two of them to death. At the sound of the mayhem, Captain Connell jumped from a second-story window before he was run down and butchered by the bolo-wielding attackers.

In just a few minutes, Company C was nearly wiped out. Led by a surviving sergeant, a handful of the soldiers were able to reach their weapons and began to fight back. By 7:30 a.m., about an hour after the massacre had begun, the few American survivors were able to finally drive the attackers from town. But the Filipinos had captured 100 rifles, 25,000 rounds of ammunition, and a large quantity of food, medicine, and equipment.[6] Although some of the Americans would later report killing hundreds of Filipinos, the Americans had actually killed twenty-eight of the locals and wounded another twenty-two.[7]

Whatever the precise numbers, the carnage left a devastating scene. The bodies of dozens of Americans littered the town square. The handfuls of American survivors, including some who were seriously wounded, made their way to five outrigger canoes in an attempt to escape, but some of these men were also caught and butchered before they could get their boats to open water. One American was caught on the beach while attempting to return to the camp to take down the American flag. A few survivors managed to reach the American garrison in Basey, about forty miles up the coast of Samar, after twenty harrowing hours spent in the canoes. Nine of the wounded had died along the way.[8]

In all, forty-eight of Company C's seventy-four officers and men died in the attack or during the escape.[9]

When a fresh American detachment reached Balangiga, they reported finding only death and mutilation. "Disemboweled bodies had been stuffed with molasses and jam to attract ants," historian Stanley Karnow recorded. "The sergeant killed while washing his mess kit was still upended in the water barrel, his feet chopped off. A bag of flour had been poured into the slit stomach of an unidentified corpse. Even the company dog had been slain....Captain Connell's head was found in a fire, far from its torso, his West Point ring missing, along with the finger."[10]*

The self-appointed leader of the Filipinos fighting the American occupation on Samar, General Vicente Lukban, later called the massacre "a manifestation of God's 'justice.' "[11]

Shocked, angry Americans had a different view. They had been told that U.S. troops were sent to the Philippines to bring peace, order, and "Christian" civilization to the islands. The official response of the military was clear. There was going to be no "mollycoddling of the treacherous natives," as the American commander in the Philippines put it.[12]

Like Pearl Harbor in 1941 or the events of September 11, 2001, the Massacre in Balangiga, or the Balangiga Incident, sent shock waves across America when the news reached the States. And, as with those events, the public outrage soon led to demands for a sharp, decisive punitive military response, as it had in 1835, when the massacre of a detachment of U.S. soldiers in Florida had set off a bloody phase of the decades-long Seminole Wars.† Or in 1876, when 268 American cavalry troopers had been wiped out by the Sioux at what became

---

* The question of how the remains of the dead Americans were treated remains controversial. In a recent account of the war in the Philippines, Brian McAllister Linn notes that there is much mythology about this incident on both sides. He specifically notes that one organizer of the attack "[s]trongly denied that his partisans had mutilated the dead; not only was this a cultural taboo, but 'there was no time to lose for such acts.' "

† The history of the December 1835 massacre of Colonel Francis Dade's regiment, and the long Seminole War that followed, is recounted in my book *A Nation Rising*.

known as Custer's Last Stand—a memory that was still fresh enough to draw comparisons to the Balangiga incident in 1901.

The task of doling out revenge fell to McKinley's successor. Just a few weeks in office and America's youngest president at forty-two years old, Theodore Roosevelt was eager to avoid a controversial military catastrophe that would threaten his legitimacy as president. Never one to shrink from using force—the "big stick," in his oft-quoted phrase—President Roosevelt ordered his commanders to crush the Philippine resistance.[13] This was no time to "speak softly."

The assignment fell to General Adna Romanza Chaffee, America's military governor in the Philippines. An Ohioan who had enlisted in 1861, he had fought at Antietam and outside Gettysburg, and was with Philip Sheridan's cavalry at Dinwiddie Court House near Petersburg, Virginia, in March 1865. Chaffee spent the next thirty years fighting Indians in the Central Plains and Southwest before becoming an instructor at Fort Leavenworth and then serving as brigadier general of volunteers in Cuba. In the summer of 1900, he led the American contingent that joined an Allied expedition sent to China to rescue Westerners in the diplomatic quarter of Peking (now Beijing) who were threatened by the Boxer Rebellion, a violent anticolonial, anti-Christian uprising supported by the imperial Chinese government. Following a swift and decisive Western victory over the Boxers and Chinese imperial troops, Chaffee had been assigned in 1901 to the Philippines post.

Chaffee welcomed the orders to exact revenge after Balangiga, according to historian Gregg Jones. "Orders went out to punish every hostile act 'quickly and severely' and instill a 'wholesome fear' of the Army. He reassured Washington that the men he had dispatched to Samar would 'start a few cemeteries for *hombres*' and get the savage island under control."[14]

Chaffee in turn passed along the assignment of putting down the resistance in Samar to General Jacob H. Smith, "one of the most colorful scoundrels ever to wear the uniform," Jones noted.[15] Another Ohioan with Civil War experience, Smith had been severely wounded at Shiloh by a ball in his hip. He had also survived a military record marred by controversy and charges of black marketeering.

Smith's selection, historian Brian McAllister Linn argues, "must go down as one of the gravest blunders of the entire [Philippine] war. Smith's career had given ample evidence of his muddy ethics, his limited military skills, and his intemperate character.... [H]is temper tantrums and lack of judgment led to his being court-martialed twice for insubordination and once for operating an illegal saloon."[16]

Smith had amassed a fortune during the Civil War as an army recruiter who specialized in providing freed slaves to bounty brokers filling recruitment quotas. He left the army briefly, but returned in 1867 and had a series of run-ins with civilian and military courts. In the 1880s, he was charged with "conduct unbecoming an officer" for reneging on a poker debt. Although his dismissal from the army had been ordered, powerful Ohio friends had intervened and saved his military career with an appeal to President Grover Cleveland.[17]

Despite his tarnished record, Smith was given a command when war broke out with Spain, and he was assigned to Cuba, where he was wounded once more, shot in the chest at San Juan Heights. After the Cuban fighting was over, Smith led American infantry ashore at Manila in 1899 to fight the Philippine rebel forces that had begun to challenge the American occupation of the islands, previously held as a colony by Spain.

Smith led his men personally against guerrilla forces and soon made his name as an unrelenting warrior, uninterested in polite niceties or diplomacy and swift to mete out his own brand of battlefield justice. "He burnished his no-nonsense reputation by building an open-air prison fashioned from steel rails," wrote Gregg Jones.

"Within weeks, 'Smith's Cage' had sixty inmates. Turnover was rapid as Smith's military courts cranked out a flurry of capital murder convictions against captured guerrillas."[18] Smith's relentlessly punitive approach to the native population filtered down through the ranks.

It is a story as old as war itself—men pushed into extreme circumstances take extreme measures, especially when questions of race, ethnicity, and language are part of the equation. As columnist and historian Max Boot has put it, "Although wars against guerrillas tend to be particularly savage, atrocities are endemic to all wars, not just colonial ones. When men are thrust into kill-or-be-killed circumstances, the constraints of civilization often slip off with shocking ease."[19]

Like Boot, many observers have attributed this kind of behavior in war to the stresses of combat, especially in a guerrilla situation. But Philip Zimbardo, the Stanford psychologist famed for his experiment in which students role-playing as prison guards quickly descended to brutality, takes a different view. Having studied the Vietnam-era My Lai atrocities in which American killed civilians, and in his role as expert witness for some of the defendants in the Abu Ghraib prison abuses in Iraq, Zimbardo wrote, "It is time for the reader to be juror and to decide whether what took place [in Abu Ghraib] was merely the work of those 7 'bad apples,' or that of a corrupt system, a 'rotten barrel,' that has sacrificed the basic human values of rule by law, honesty, and adherence to the Geneva Conventions in the cause of its obsession with the so-called 'war on terror.'"[20] War, and not just the Iraq War, Zimbardo argued, is the rotten barrel.

Edward Tick, a psychotherapist who has worked with returning veterans from Vietnam and both the Afghan and Iraqi wars, has explained, "What are we denying about our warmaking? We deny our own complex human nature, including our capacities for greed, evil and doing harm, clinging instead to the belief in our innocence and goodness."[21]

From the earliest days of the fighting in the Philippines, there were instances of prisoners shot "while trying to escape" and whole towns torched after American telegraph wires were cut. American soldiers began to adapt the interrogation techniques known as the "strangling torments" first employed by torturers during the Spanish Inquisition. It had traveled to the Philippines with the Spanish Empire and was first used to "propagate the faith." American soldiers quickly learned of it, apparently from Filipino collaborators working with U.S. troops, and from insurgents who used the technique on American prisoners or Filipino collaborators. Americans called it the "water cure," which sounds very much like the "waterboarding" method of interrogation, which is now considered a form of torture under U.S. Army policy.*

A prisoner was bound, lying on his back, under a water tank holding as many as one hundred gallons. The faucet was opened and a stream of water, often dirty, was fed down into his opened mouth through a bamboo pipe. His throat was held so the prisoner was forced to swallow the water. Sometimes salt was added to the mixture to make the torture more effective. The sensation of drowning and suffocation was made worse as the Americans sometimes pummeled the stomach of the victim. The prisoner either talked or died.

Whether it was useful and effective or not—the reliability of any information obtained under torture is suspect because the victims

---

* In 2009, President Barack Obama banned the use of waterboarding and other forms of torture in questioning anyone in U.S. custody. According to *Time* magazine, "An executive order signed by Obama now requires that interrogations of anyone in U.S. custody follow what's known as the Army Field Manual.... The book lays out 19 interrogation techniques permitted by law and prohibits nine categories of others, including waterboarding, used by the Central Intelligence Agency during the Bush Administration, as well as forcing prisoners to be naked, as happened in the Abu Ghraib prisoner scandal." Kate Pickert, "The Army Field Manual," *Time*, January 26, 2009, http://content.time.com/time/nation/article/0,8599,1873897,00.html#ixzz2r2zLz5lO.

often tend to say anything the torturer wants to hear—the "water cure" was liberally employed by American forces. "Investigations into the scale of its use by American troops," historian Brian Linn wrote, "produced such contradictory testimony as to preclude any reliable conclusions, but it appears that the use of torture steadily increased."[22]

Smith was promoted to brigadier general in March 1901, after which he ordered a scorched-earth campaign on the island of Samar to "pacify" Balangiga. Navy gunboats, a 300-man Marine unit, and eventually 4,000 soldiers were employed to herd more than 300,000 civilians into "reconcentration zones," essentially prison camps. By December 31, 1901, Americans had killed or captured 759 supposed rebels known as *insurrectos* and destroyed tons of rice, 1,662 houses, and 226 boats.[23]

While the use of the "water cure" caused some dismay back home when it was first reported, far worse was yet to come. In his most notorious command, Smith issued orders to Marine major Littleton W. T. "Tony" Waller: "I want no prisoners. I wish you to kill and burn. The more you kill and burn, the better you will please me."[24] Children over ten years of age were included in his soon-to-be-infamous order in which he said he wanted to turn the area into a "howling wilderness."

A widely admired marine who had gained heroic stature and international renown during the Boxer Rebellion, a violent uprising aimed at removing mostly Western foreign powers from China in 1900, Major Waller was, in historian Linn's judgment, "[a]n ambitious and ruthless officer with a fondness for the bottle."[25] Waller later claimed he was appalled by Smith's order. But he and his two companies of marines cut an incredibly destructive swath across Samar's towns and villages for a twenty-five-mile stretch. Like General Sherman's army slashing its way through the Confederate interior in the Civil War, and army tactics used against Native Americans during the Indian wars of the late nineteenth century, Waller's marines went on a campaign of ruthless destruction, burning hundreds of houses, destroying crops and fishing boats, and killing thirty-nine men.

With this first round of destruction under his belt, Waller then set off with two hundred marines on a long search-and-destroy mission that was a disaster by any reasonable measure. Food shortages, torrential rain, malarial swamps, and leeches made the trek an epic of misery as Waller and his men hacked their way through the jungle from December 28, 1901, until January 19, 1902. "Ten marines had either died or disappeared and an eleventh was to die shortly," writes Linn. "Starving, barefoot, their clothes in rags, some crazed by their exertions, the marines were literally helpless, their rifles and ammunition carried by their porters." But, Linn adds, "This botched patrol was transformed into an epic of courage and leadership, and later historians all too willingly accepted the myth."[26]

When he and his men returned to their base, Waller was told of a plot by some locals to murder the marines. He reacted by ordering the execution of eleven Filipino civilians in January 1902 in retribution for the marines who had died under his command. "Americans had used harsh tactics since the beginning of the Philippine War," assessed journalist Stephen Kinzer. "But the summary execution of eleven Filipinos who were working for them, and who had committed no apparent crime, was too much for commanders to ignore. They ordered the offending officer court-martialed on charges of murder."[27]

———————

Massacres of American soldiers met with harsh revenge attacks. Atrocities committed against civilians. Torture of prisoners. Concentration camps. Summary execution of civilians. None of this sounds like America at war in a simpler, more "civilized" era in the nation's history.

But fighting in the Philippines—long before World War II or

Vietnam—meant that young Americans were caught up in a remote war half a world away from their homes and farms, in a land of jungles, diseases, strange religions, and languages so foreign to most Americans that it hardly seemed real. This was America at war in the first years of the twentieth century, an important chapter in American history that is missing from many textbooks.

How had America come to a long, costly war in the Philippines, just thirty-five years after the nation was so completely devastated by the Civil War, under a president, a devout Christian, who had fought in that conflict and professed to hate war? It is a largely untold tale of military history and an expanding American empire at the dawn of the twentieth century that deserves to be understood.

On February 15, 1898, the USS *Maine* lay in the harbor at Havana, Cuba. A few weeks earlier, the battleship had arrived at the Caribbean island ninety miles from Florida to keep a watchful eye on "American interests." America's interests, in fact, were in seeing that the Cubans, who were then battling colonial Spain for the island's independence, succeeded in their rebellion.

At 9:40 on that February night, a terrible explosion shattered the stillness in Havana Harbor. Most of the crew were sleeping or resting in the enlisted quarters in the forward part of the ship when the *Maine* blew up. Of the 374 officers and sailors on board, 266 lost their lives in the disaster: 260 died in the explosion or shortly thereafter, and six more died later from injuries. An investigation by American naval authorities attributed the explosion to a mine, without placing responsibility on the Spanish.[28]

But public opinion was another matter. "Remember the *Maine*! To hell with Spain!" soon became a national rallying cry, trumpeted by an enthusiastic, jingoistic, and competitive press that was eager for war headlines to boost circulation. At the heart of this battle were the rival Hearst and Pulitzer newspapers in New York, where the long pitched struggle for newspaper readers ultimately came to define the

phrase "yellow journalism"—audacious headlines, aggressive reporting, populist politics, cartoons and abundant illustrations, and a
heavy dose of human interest, true crime, and jingoism. In New York,
the *Journal*, a Hearst paper, sold one million copies on February 18
with a front-page illustration purportedly showing how the explosion
had been detonated from land.

Within weeks, the nation was on a war footing and Congress was
pressing a reluctant President McKinley to hit hard at Spain. "The
*Maine*'s destruction did not cause America to declare war on Spain,"
according to the U.S. Navy's official Naval History and Heritage
Command, "but it served as a catalyst, accelerating the approach to a
diplomatic impasse."[29]

On April 21, 1898, America declared war for the third time in its
history. The war lasted a little more than one hundred days and initially was not very costly to the United States. But the conflict, which
ended officially on August 13, 1898, was clearly a turning point in the
nation's history, signaling America's emergence as a power player on
the global stage.

The tensions between Spain and the United States rose out of the
attempts by Cubans to liberate their island from Spanish colonial
control. Lasting most of a decade from 1868 to 1878, the first Cuban
insurrection was unsuccessful but drew American sympathies to the
revolutionaries. At the close of the nineteenth century, anti-Catholic
propaganda and animosity still ran thick in white Anglo-Saxon
Protestant America, and no small part of the anti-Spanish venom
expressed by Americans was due to the fact that Spain was a Catholic
country.

Intense anti-Catholic sentiment had arrived in America with the
first English Protestant settlers and had hardened over more than two
centuries. Nineteenth-century America was rife with conspiracy the-
ories suggesting that Catholic immigrants wanted to take over America and install the pope in a new American Vatican; such notions

were widely shared in pulpits and editorial pages. Tinged with violent anti-immigrant sentiment—the Irish and later Italians were the chief villains in this scenario—the deep-seated hatred of "papists" would boil over in laws limiting Catholic rights in early America; pitched battles like Philadelphia's anti-Catholic, anti-Irish Bible Riots in 1844; and the angry nativist movement that produced the vitriolic Know-Nothing party of the mid-nineteenth century. Ridding Cuba and other Spanish territories of Catholics ranked just slightly behind taking control of these islands for their commercial and military value and was draped in the language of the Monroe Doctrine, an early-nineteenth-century president's warning that Europe should stay out of the Americas.

When a second bid for independence by Cuban revolutionaries began in April 1895, the Spanish government had dispatched General Valeriano Weyler y Nicolau with orders to pacify the island. Known as "the Butcher" in the American press, he was determined to deprive the rebels of support by forcibly removing the civilian population in the troublesome districts to areas near military headquarters, essentially creating concentration camps. Spanish policy resulted in the starvation and death of more than one hundred thousand Cubans. There was outrage in many sectors of the American public, fueled by stories in the "yellow press"—the highly sensationalized reporting that Hearst and Pulitzer papers practiced at the time and so named because of a famous cartoon of the period called *The Yellow Kid*. The Hearst and Pulitzer reports, along with a powerful American lobby that wanted to expand overseas, created pressure on two presidents, first Grover Cleveland and then William McKinley, to end the fighting in Cuba and eliminate Spanish control.

Since the early years of the century, when Jefferson sought to purchase Cuba from Spain, some Americans had looked longingly at the nearby island as a potential piece of a larger United States. In 1823, when he was secretary of state, future president John Quincy

Adams said the island would be in American hands in fifty years. In 1848, President James Knox Polk offered $100 million to Spain for the island, and President Franklin Pierce raised the ante to $130 million in 1854.[30] By the end of the nineteenth century, America's expansionist appetite and the political lobby favoring an American empire had only grown stronger. President McKinley was confronted by a powerful group of men who saw the situation in Cuba as a chance to intervene and expand American power overseas.

Chief among these aggressive expansionists was Henry Cabot Lodge, an influential senator from Massachusetts, and his best friend, Theodore Roosevelt (who once complained that McKinley had "the backbone of an éclair"), recently appointed assistant secretary of the navy. Both Harvard men (separated by nine years there) and published historians—Lodge earned one of Harvard's first PhDs in the subject of history—they shared a bedrock Republicanism and a worldview that was far more interested in a global American presence than that of the newly elected McKinley. "The President [McKinley] wanted nothing so much as four years of peace and stability, so that corporate interests he represented could continue their growth," wrote Roosevelt biographer Edmund Morris. "He was by nature a small-town son of the Middle West, who shied away from large schemes and foreign entanglements....But as a Civil War veteran, he had a genuine horror of bloodshed."[31] Like several presidents before him, McKinley offered to purchase Cuba from Spain.

When pro-Spanish forces in Havana instigated riots in January 1898, the official reaction in Washington, D.C., was concern for the safety of Americans in the country. But that was a convenient cover for the real objective of removing Spain from the picture. In January, President McKinley sent the second-class battleship USS *Maine* from Key West, Florida, to Havana, after clearing the visit with a reluctant government in Madrid.

After the *Maine*'s destruction, Spanish officials and the crew of a civilian steamer acted quickly to rescue survivors and care for the wounded. The U.S. Department of the Navy immediately formed a board of inquiry to determine the reason for the *Maine*'s destruction. The inquiry, conducted in Havana, lasted four weeks. The condition of the submerged wreck and the lack of technical expertise prevented the board from being as thorough as later investigations would be. In the end, they concluded that a mine had detonated under the ship. The board did not attempt to fix blame for the placement of the device.*

When the navy's verdict was announced, the American public reacted with outrage. Fed by inflammatory newspapers blaming Spain for the disaster, the public had already placed guilt squarely on the Spanish government. Although he continued to press for a diplomatic settlement to the Cuban question, President McKinley accelerated military preparations, including an especially aggressive naval expansion, under the guiding hand of Assistant Secretary of the Navy Theodore Roosevelt.

The Spanish position on Cuban independence hardened, and on April 11 McKinley asked Congress for permission to intervene. On April 21, the president ordered the navy to blockade Cuba, and Spain followed with a declaration of war on April 23. Congress responded with a formal declaration of war on April 25, made retroactive to the start of the blockade.

Though only two generations removed from the killing fields of Gettysburg and Cold Harbor, a younger, daring, muscled-up America appeared to be itching for a fight. "While President McKinley hoped to the last to avoid war," argues Gregg Jones, "millions of Americans

---

* Subsequent investigations by the U.S. Navy have determined that an external mine was not the likely cause of the explosion. Rather, it may have been set off by the spontaneous combustion of coal stored in a bunker next to the ship's magazine, which held a large quantity of ammunition.

clamored to prove the nation's fighting worth to the world. Fishermen and farmers, coal miners and carpenters, steelworkers and store clerks flocked to join the Army, Navy, or Marine Corps. Bands dusted off Civil War tunes, and flags sprouted from homes and offices.... Pent-up emotions erupted across the country."[32]

When the war began, Assistant Secretary of the Navy Roosevelt abruptly resigned his government post in what historian H. W. Brands called "one of the most impetuous and least responsible acts of his thirty-nine years of life." At the Navy Department, wrote Brands, he "might have had significant influence on the outcome of the war he had helped precipitate." Instead, with the assistance of Washington friends, Roosevelt enlisted and was given a commission in the First Volunteer Cavalry, which the press christened the Rough Riders. Chafing to get into action, Roosevelt was afraid that the war would end before he had the chance to "bloody his lance."[33]

McKinley had reluctantly moved toward a war footing. "I have been through one war," the president said after the *Maine* explosion. "I have seen the dead piled up, and I don't want to see another."[34]

But once the war was on, he became an aggressive and effective wartime president. First he called for 125,000 volunteers, more than twice what was expected. McKinley remembered that Lincoln's call for 75,000 volunteers at the beginning of the Civil War in 1861 had been too small, and he was determined to avoid the same mistake.

At the time, America had a fairly small regular army. As in American wars past, it was expected that a large force of volunteers would be added to the core of regular soldiers and officers. Among the regular troops called up were black units of the Twenty-Fourth and Twenty-Fifth Infantry and the Ninth and Tenth Cavalry, the famed Buffalo Soldiers, who had spent most of the previous years either fighting Indians in the Southwest or fighting civilians in the mine and railroad labor wars.

These troops would constitute almost a quarter of the force

sent to Cuba. One reason they were called into action there was the mistaken notion that African Americans were somehow impervious to tropical disease; they were even known as "immunes." On the way to ports to ship out to Cuba, they had confronted racist attacks in Florida, and on the voyage to Cuba, historian Evan Thomas noted, "the black regiments—veteran buffalo soldiers in the Ninth and Tenth Cavalry, raw recruits in the Twenty-fourth and Twenty-fifth Infantry—were kept below decks in the most squalid conditions."[35]

But the Buffalo Soldiers were a sideshow, overshadowed by the press fascination with the most famous unit headed to Cuba. This was the First Volunteer Cavalry, organized and subsidized by Theodore Roosevelt, a semiprivate army that initially relied on cowboys and Roosevelt's other friends from his ranching days in South Dakota. Easterners, including some of Roosevelt's Harvard classmates and other Ivy Leaguers, soon increased their number. Some had learned their horsemanship playing polo. One was a Harvard quarterback, another a Yale track man. They became darlings of the press that was sent to cover the war. "But they owed much of their glory," Gail Buckley argues, "as well their lives to Buffalo Soldiers, who came to their rescue in three important battles: the 10th Cavalry at Las Guási-mas; the 25th Infantry at El Caney ('Hell Caney'); and the 9th and 10th Cavalries at San Juan Hill."[36]

In all three battles, the black troops were singled out for their bravery and credited with saving the day. But the credit would be short-lived.

While the exploits of the Rough Riders got most of the press attention, it was Roosevelt who was turned into a hero of the first magnitude, first by the war correspondents in his tow, such as Rich-ard Harding Davis, who wrote that "Roosevelt, mounted high on horse-back, and charging the rifle-pits at a gallop and quite alone, made you feel that you would like to cheer."[37]

That sort of cheerleading would soon make his name. Roosevelt was then relatively unknown outside his native New York, where he had been a reform-minded member of the Police Commission. But Roosevelt hardly needed a booster section. Not to be outdone by war correspondents, he later provided his own accounts of the battles—accounts that were filtered through an outsized ego and ambition. As H. W. Brands notes, "Reviewers poked fun at Roosevelt's egotism. Rumor claimed that the publisher had run out the uppercase *I* in setting the type."[38]

But more troubling than his egotism was Roosevelt's revisionism, especially when it came to the Buffalo Soldiers. In his initial battle reports, Roosevelt had praised the black troops, but he would later change his story. "In his published recollections, he condescended to the black soldiers, describing them as utterly dependent on their white officers," wrote Evan Thomas. "Roosevelt's racial attitudes were moderate, but only relatively speaking."[39]

Gail Buckley's assessment is even more damning. "Roosevelt, who had promised he 'would never forget' the ties that bound him to the Buffalo Soldiers, began to betray them shortly after San Juan Hill. Though he once said that 'no one can tell whether it was the Rough Riders or the men of the 9th who came forward with the greater courage to offer their lives in the service of their country,' he now claimed that all black accomplishment was the result of white leadership. Worse, he invented a canard of encountering black troops drifting away from the battlefield and forcing them at gunpoint to return. That account was challenged in the black press."[40]

When Theodore Roosevelt arrived in Cuba with the Rough Riders he was far from a household name—the "Teddy bear" fame would come much later. Born into a wealthy New York family, he had been a sickly child who suffered from asthma. His father, whom he idolized, believed that vigorous exercise and a manly life—along with frantic carriage rides to force cold night air into his lungs—would solve the problem. Fascinated by natural science and history, he had been mostly tutored at home, but he went on to attend Harvard. While too small for football, which he loved, he rowed and boxed instead, always trying to build up his rather spindly body. Many historians and biographers have suggested that Theodore Roosevelt's ardor for war and the military life may be traced to the fact that his father, twenty-nine years old when the Civil War began, had hired a substitute to fight in his place. Such a tactic was not unusual for wealthy young men, and it was completely legal at the time. But Theodore's obvious and almost desperate passion for winning battlefield glory has been widely interpreted as the younger Roosevelt's attempt to erase this perceived stain on his family's honor.

Roosevelt's stark betrayal of the black soldiers in Cuba also contradicts to some degree the image of Roosevelt as a progressive, especially since one of his first acts as president was to invite the prominent black educator and leader Booker T. Washington to dine in the White House. It was an unprecedented act that outraged people in the former Confederacy as well as many other Americans of the day who disapproved of any "race mixing," or miscegenation, as it was then called.

But setting aside Roosevelt's later revised version of events, the fact remains that the July 1 battle at San Juan that made him a household name was not the deciding battle in the Cuban campaign. Roosevelt himself wrote that night that his troops were on the edge of a disaster. "We have won so far at a heavy cost.... We *must* have help—thousands of men, batteries, and *food* and ammunition."[41]

On July 3, the war in Cuba was actually won not by a heroic charge up a hill on land, but in a completely separate naval victory. When a five-ship Spanish squadron sailed out of Santiago Harbor in what amounted to a suicide mission, it was destroyed quickly by American naval power. "The endgame was ragged," recounted Evan Thomas. "The *Colón*, the last ship to be hunted down, slowly lost speed. The engine room crew, drunk on brandy, had mutinied. When the ship surrendered, Americans found the stokers' bodies in the boiler room; they had been shot by their officers for shirking. The battle was over by 1:00 p.m. Only one American sailor died, his head blown off by a Spanish shell."[42] The Spanish lost 323 men, about a fifth of their crews and officers.

The loss of her navy at Santiago sealed the fate of Spain's global empire, once the richest and most powerful of any European nation. A few weeks later, a peace protocol was signed. But the question of Cuba and nearby Puerto Rico, another Spanish possession claimed by the victorious Americans, was not all that was on the table. In a history-changing, single-handed judgment, President McKinley had determined that America was going to keep the Philippines, also a Spanish colony, largely overlooked in the run-up to the war with Spain.

He later told a group of Christian missionaries that his decision had been divinely inspired. "I am not ashamed to tell you, gentlemen, that I went down on my knees and prayed to Almighty God for light and guidance more than one night. And one night it came to me this way—I don't know how it was, but it came: (1) That we would not give them back to Spain—that would be cowardly and dishonorable; (2) that we would not turn them over to France or Germany...that would be bad business and discreditable; (3) that we could not leave them to themselves—they were unfit for self-government...and (4) that there was nothing left for us to do but take them all, and to educate the Filipinos, and *uplift and civilize and Christianize them....*" (emphasis added).[43] It should be noted that Roman Catholicism had been introduced centuries earlier by the Spanish and so was well established in the Philippines at the time of McKinley's divine inspiration.

Theodore Roosevelt and Senator Lodge were firmly behind the annexation decision. The Treaty of Paris, signed on December 10, 1898, made it official.

While the war in Cuba had attracted most of the press attention, the fate of the Spanish Empire and the outcome of the war had already been largely determined on the other side of the world, before a single shot was ever fired in Cuba.

Commodore George Dewey commanded an American squadron of five modern cruisers and two gunboats. On April 30, just days after the war was declared, Dewey's flotilla approached the expansive bay that led to Manila, the capital of the Philippines. He had been warned of mines and advised to send a supply ship through first. But eager to put his name in the naval history books, he tossed aside caution. The crusty sixty-year-old commodore had battled the Confederacy with Admiral David Farragut, who had become a navy legend for announcing, "Damn the torpedoes [mines]. Full speed ahead" at Mobile Bay in August 1864 during the Civil War. Now Dewey said, "I've waited sixty years for this opportunity. Mines or no mines, I am leading the squadron in myself."[44]

On April 30, finding Subic Bay empty of Spanish ships, Dewey ordered the squadron to push on toward the port city of Manila. Sailing in darkness, the squadron passed the island fortress of Corregidor and then cruised into the harbor. With Dewey's flagship in the lead, the ships cruised single file. A shore battery fired on the American ships just before midnight, but the shots fell harmlessly into the sea.

The American squadron traveled the twenty-three miles from the mouth of the harbor to the city of Manila. As dawn broke on May 1, another shore battery fired, again leaving the American vessels unharmed. Now alert to the American approach, the Spanish fleet of seven antiquated warships, some of which were not seaworthy, had been moved to an anchorage nearby at the Cavite naval station.

Hoping to avoid any damage to the city of Manila in a battle with the Americans, the Spanish commander also thought that this maneuver would give his sailors a better chance to survive if their ships went down. By morning light, the Americans sighted the Spanish ships, sitting at anchor to steady their guns. Just before 6 a.m.,

Dewey uttered the words that would enter American naval history and lore, telling the captain of the *Olympia*, "You may fire when ready, Gridley." But it was John Jordan, a black gunner's mate, who led the crew that actually fired the first American shots of the Spanish-American War—not in Cuba but from Commodore George Dewey's flagship in Manila Bay.[45]

George Dewey was a Vermonter, born in 1837 in the Green Mountain State, well inland from the ocean. As a young man, he had aspired to attend West Point, but when he failed to win an appointment to the military academy* he went to the relatively new and far less prestigious U.S. Naval Academy at Annapolis, Maryland, instead. The Naval Academy had its beginnings in 1845 as a naval school in a former army fort after a notable mutiny aboard the *Somers*, a training ship for naval apprentices. Initially it had seven professors for a class of fifty midshipmen who were also apprentices. But in 1850, it was expanded as the United States Naval Academy, with a four-year requirement. Dewey entered in 1854, graduated from the academy in 1858, and was commissioned a navy lieutenant in 1861 after the Civil War broke out.

During the Civil War, Dewey served with Admiral Farragut and was with his fleet during the Battle of New Orleans. When Ulysses S. Grant attacked the citadel of Vicksburg in 1863, Dewey was aboard a ship that ran aground and took heavy Confederate fire. He scuttled the damaged ship and jumped into the Mississippi to save a wounded comrade. In the years of relative quiet after the Civil War ended, Dewey had cultivated political friends, including his home state senator Redfield Proctor, an otherwise colorless figure who, like President McKinley, was initially reluctant to go to war. But in a

---

* Admission to the service academies traditionally required an application process that included a nomination from a politician, usually from a congressional representative of the applicant's home state.

single speech to the Senate after a fact-finding trip to Cuba, Proctor emerged as an influential war hawk.

More significantly, Dewey had struck up a friendship with Theodore Roosevelt at the Metropolitan Club, a posh Washington gentlemen's preserve both frequented. It was a meeting place for Washington power brokers of the day in Congress and the military, along with lawyers, writers, and scientists who shared the belief, in Edmund Morris's words, that America's "Manifest Destiny called for the United States to free Cuba, annex Hawaii, and raise the American flag supreme over the Western Hemisphere."[46]

By now a published naval historian and former member of the New York Police Commission, Roosevelt was a reform-minded politician with outsized ambitions. When the war with Spain broke out, he was serving as assistant secretary of the navy in the McKinley administration, a post secured by Roosevelt's good friend Senator Henry Cabot Lodge of Massachusetts.

Roosevelt and Dewey shared more than a social circle. Both were eager for glory and advancement and thought America needed to expand its global power through the navy. In describing Dewey, Roosevelt biographer Morris writes that the sixty-year-old commodore possessed "personal ambition in inverse proportion to his age and height (five feet, five inches). Over three decades of undistinguished peacetime service had not quenched his lust for battle."[47]

But in late February, it was Acting Navy Secretary Roosevelt whose appetite for war was even larger than Dewey's. With no higher authorization, he cabled Dewey, then at port in British colonial Hong Kong: "KEEP FULL OF COAL. IN THE EVENT OF DECLARATION OF WAR."[48]

"In a stroke of breathtaking audacity (and questionable authority)," historian Gregg Jones commented, "Theodore Roosevelt had just set in motion America's conquest of the Philippines."[49] Dewey pressed his captains to load up on coal and ammunition. He enthusiastically obeyed Roosevelt's orders and steamed off for the Philippine islands once war had officially been declared on Spain.

This "other war" with Spain, fought half a world away from Cuba, was going to be a struggle over the Philippines. Encompassing more than seven thousand islands across more than a half million square miles of Pacific Ocean, the Philippine archipelago had been part of Spain's global empire for more than three centuries, almost since the time Ferdinand Magellan had circumnavigated the globe and reached the islands in 1521. In 1543, another Spanish sailor first named only the islands of Samar and Leyte in honor of the Spanish king Philip II, and the name Philippines was later extended to the entire archipelago. Its three major island groups included Luzon, the largest, most populous island and site of the capital, Manila.

The Philippine population, spread over this vast and in many places largely unexplored territory, defied easy description, including tribal groups with many ethnic differences and a large Muslim population on some of the islands as well as many Roman Catholics. "Within individual islands," historian Brian McAllister Linn noted, "mountains, swamps, jungles and bodies of water further separate the inhabitants. As geographers have noted, the term 'Filipino' is no more accurate in describing a people of one race and culture than is the term 'American.' "[30]

By the time Americans arrived in the Philippines, the Spanish had actually created a Spanish-language public educational system. With a fairly vibrant economy by nineteenth-century colonial standards, a class of comparably well-educated and affluent Filipinos had begun to emerge in some parts of the country, which had a population of nearly eight million by the beginning of the twentieth century.

But the Philippines' sheer size, geography, history, and diverse populations all posed daunting challenges to any would-be conqueror. Most Americans, including President McKinley, had no clue where the Philippines were or who lived there.

As Dewey's flotilla pounded the Spanish, little accurate fire was returned. Commodore Dewey ordered five passes, each successive run bringing the American guns closer to bear on the Spanish ships. Informed at 7:35 a.m. that some of the guns were running low on ammunition, Dewey ordered a withdrawal from the assault to consult with his other captains and redistribute ammunition for some of the guns. When told later that morning that the reports of low ammunition were incorrect, Dewey ordered the squadron to return to the attack.

Shortly after noon, with the entire Spanish fleet in flames, the Spanish hoisted the white flag of surrender. A few days later, on May 4, Dewey officially recorded: "I am happy to report that the damage done to the squadron under my command was inconsiderable. There were none killed and only 7 men in the squadron very slightly wounded. As will be seen by the reports of the commanding officers which are herewith inclosed [sic] several of the vessels were struck and even penetrated, but the damage was of the slightest, and the squadron is in as good condition now as before the battle."[51]

The Spanish fleet had been completely destroyed, with a loss of 381 of its 1,200 men. Among the Spanish dead was a shore battery commander who shot himself in the head after the inglorious defeat. The Battle of Manila Bay was a complete victory for Dewey over the Spanish, in what has been described as the "most one-sided naval victory in history."[52]

———————

Now what? Dewey commanded only two thousand men. How to hold the city of Manila, let alone an archipelago spread over hundreds of thousands of square miles of ocean? And exactly what was Dewey supposed to do with his conquest?

Dewey used the Spanish telegraph office to request orders and troops to control the city, if not the whole archipelago. Back in Washington, McKinley, jubilant at word of Dewey's decisive victory, had turned to a map. He later confessed that he "could not have told where those darned islands were within two thousand miles."[53] But McKinley had already ordered five thousand men to the Philippines, the first contingent of a force that would quickly grow.

In the aftermath of Dewey's quick and relatively inexpensive victory at sea, the rest of the Spanish forces in the Philippines did not simply surrender and head for home. The Spanish still held Manila and other significant land fortifications. An all-out American invasion and conquest of the colonial capital would have required far more than a naval assault. There were also diplomatic complications along with the incredibly difficult issue of what was going to become of the island territory and its inhabitants, many of whom wanted to be rid of the Spanish.

In this Dewey had to contend with another complicating factor: Filipino rebel leader Emilio Aguinaldo. In 1894, then twenty-four-year-old Aguinaldo had joined a secret rebel group that was trying to win Philippine independence from Spain, just as the Cubans were. Plagued by internal conflicts, the rebels led a brief uprising based on the northern island of Luzon, after which Aguinaldo and his group accepted a Spanish peace deal that came with the pledge of reforms for the islands, but without any actual promise of independence. Promised amnesty by the Spanish, Aguinaldo left the Philippines in late 1897 for Hong Kong and voluntary exile. He had also accepted a large payment—essentially a payoff—from the Spanish government, which clearly thought it cheaper to bribe Aguinaldo and other rebels than fight them. But as one historian noted, "He did not stay bought."[54] Aguinaldo banked the cash, biding his time while in Hong Kong. Then he and his men formed a Philippine government in exile, and awaited the promised Spanish reforms. They never came.

When the American conflict with Spain began to heat up, Dewey and other Americans sought out Aguinaldo in Hong Kong. With unwritten assurances from American diplomats and Dewey—but never any actual promise of Philippine independence—Aguinaldo was asked to join the American cause against Spain. Dewey arranged for his transportation back to Manila, and when Aguinaldo arrived on May 19, he believed the Americans would depart as soon as the Spanish did. He was mistaken.

Aguinaldo soon declared himself dictator for the duration of the crisis, charting a certain collision course with the American occupiers. Though the young rebel leader thought of himself as the Philippine nation's George Washington, the reality is, as usual, more complex. "Aguinaldo had emerged as the most important leader of Luzon's nationalist movement," wrote historian Brian McAllister Linn. "And for better or worse, he would continue to shape the course of anticolonial resistance. His admirers depict him as a gallant, steadfast patriot whose primary failing was believing that others, particularly the Americans...were as honorable as he. To his critics, he was an opportunistic warlord, a treacherous and prevaricating military incompetent."[55] Historian Stanley Karnow characterized the Filipino resistance this way: "Aguinaldo and his staff were egregiously inept."[56]

After the Spanish navy's defeat, Aguinaldo rebuilt his fighting force. He used some of the cash he had been given by the Spanish to buy arms, supplementing a few thousand captured Spanish rifles given to him by Dewey. His forces grew as thousands of Filipinos who had once worn Spanish uniforms as part of Spain's colonial army joined his ranks. Soon there were some thirty thousand men in Aguinaldo's fledgling army near Manila. They still expected that the Americans would leave, a belief that Aguinaldo maintained for the rest of his life.

McKinley had not yet announced his divinely inspired decision to annex the Philippines, but Dewey's victory had resulted in one early example of what has come to be known as the Pottery Barn rule, sometimes attributed to Secretary of State Colin Powell during the invasion of Iraq in 2003: "You break it, you own it."\* In the Spanish-American War this meant the United States was responsible for the future of the Philippines and its inhabitants.[57]

Dewey learned President McKinley had dispatched another twenty thousand men on ships steaming out of San Francisco and bound for the Philippines, the president expecting that the conflict with Spain there would not end with a single naval battle. The first contingent of these troops, commanded by Major General Wesley Merritt, arrived on June 30, more than a month after departing California.

Like Dewey, Merritt was a Civil War veteran, and also a veteran of the Indian campaigns in the West. He was a highly respected and well-regarded soldier, at that time the army's second-ranking officer. But when he arrived in the Philippines, he did not know what his job was. He had already told McKinley, "I do not yet know whether it is your desire to subdue and hold all of the Spanish territory in the islands, or merely seize and hold the capital."[58] He had not yet received a presidential reply.

But first he had to deal with the Spanish still occupying Manila. And that is when Dewey and Merritt scripted a lovely *paso doble*, a Spanish dance for two, with the cooperation of their enemies. The idea of a ceremonial war is an ancient one, in which mock battles are substituted for real ones to spare any bloodletting. Just as many individual duels once concluded with both parties firing their pistols harmlessly into the air or deliberately missing their opponent to maintain personal honor without doing any actual damage, the

---

\* Powell was quoted as saying that in Bob Woodward's book *Plan of Attack*. Powell later attributed the idea to *New York Times* columnist Thomas Friedman, who had referred to a "pottery shop," not Pottery Barn.

Spanish and Americans were about to craft an epic staged battle that would keep international reputations intact without more casualties. But as with many artificial events, reality intruded harshly. The coming battle for the city of Manila and control of the Philippines would be one of those disastrous tragicomedies.

It commenced in late July, after Merritt arrived and joined forces with Dewey—now Rear Admiral Dewey—to secretly negotiate the surrender of Manila by the Spanish in an orchestrated second Battle of Manila. The plan seemed simple enough. On August 13, Dewey's ships were to lob a few shells harmlessly at the Spanish forts. His flagship would then raise a signal and the Spanish would surrender. The exercise was to be over by afternoon with no casualties, a show battle that allowed the Spanish troops to return home claiming that they had fought bravely against an overwhelming force.

According to the script, the Spanish troops would defend an outer line of trenches but not use their heavy guns. In exchange, the Americans would not blast the city with naval guns and promised the Spanish that the Filipino forces, which had been left completely out of the planning of this staged performance, would be kept out of the city.

But this *paso doble* of polite surrender was poorly choreographed. When given the order to fire on Spanish positions, Dewey's gunners assumed they had been given the wrong range for their targets and actually shelled the Spanish garrisons, which were supposed to be safe from harm. Dewey quickly had to pull his ships out of position. On land, the "fake surrender" had also come undone. Thinking that they were marching to destroy the Spanish, Filipino fighters joined the Americans who were supposed to attack the Spanish trenches. Seeing the attack actually taking place, the Spanish began to fire in return. When the "mock" battle was over, six Americans and forty-nine Spanish soldiers had died. And as historian Karnow records, "The phony fight for Manila further strained the already threadbare ties between the Americans and Filipinos."[59]

On August 16, when word reached the Philippines from America that the war between the United States and Spain had ended four days earlier, there was already hostility building between the Americans and their Filipino "allies." Unbeknownst to the American forces in Manila—or the Filipinos whose fate and future independence were presumably hanging in the balance—a peace protocol had been arranged between Spain and the United States on August 12. Under its terms, the future of the Philippines would be decided at a peace conference to be held in Paris in December. When that meeting concluded on December 10, the Philippines had been ceded by Spain to the United States. America's Filipino allies had no say in the matter.

By that time, Aguinaldo had already issued his declaration of independence from Spain, naming himself military dictator, and in June 1898 he had proclaimed a revolutionary government in which he was president.

As word of the Spanish defeat crossed the oceans, German and Japanese naval ships soon arrived in Manila Bay, looking to see if they might find a strategic advantage and new colonial bases in the Pacific. Their presence merely confirmed to Dewey and other American expansionists that the Philippines were a prize worth keeping.

Just as the "end of combat operations" in May 2003 was actually the beginning of a long, deadly Iraqi insurrection, America was soon neck-deep in a long and deadly insurrection in the Philippines.

———

"Is the Government willing to use all its means to make the natives submit to the authority of the United States?" That was the question that Dewey and Merritt cabled to President McKinley when the peace treaty with Spain was formalized. The president replied that the Philippine insurgents must recognize American authority.

Learning this and feeling betrayed by the Americans, Aguinaldo's people took up arms in early February 1899 when they saw that their former rulers had simply been replaced by a new American colonial rule. Many Filipinos were not going to recognize America's claim of authority without a struggle.

Fighting began around Manila on February 4, 1899, as Filipino forces attacked the American army, but they were driven from their trenches by naval gunfire supporting an American counterattack. After several days of combat, the Americans had quashed the uprising.

A few weeks later, Congress passed legislation keeping the regular army at 65,000 men, but authorized an additional 35,000 volunteers for the "Philippine emergency," for which there was no formal declaration of war. In addition, McKinley ordered the army to demonstrate that the "mission of the United States is one of benevolent assimilation, substituting the mild sway of justice and right for arbitrary rule."

This was the American idea of "nation building" at the dawn of the twentieth century. Before a civilian administrator arrived in the Philippines, the U.S. Army had begun to build highways, transportation, and public health facilities. New railroads, bridges, and telegraph and telephone lines began to bring the Philippines more rapidly into the twentieth century. And the public-health arm of the military virtually eliminated smallpox and other epidemic diseases, while reducing infant mortality.

These were all well-intentioned goals, couched in the paternalistic language of caring for America's "little brown brothers," in the memorable phrase of William Howard Taft, the future civilian administrator of the Philippines (and future president). But paternalism and the benevolent guiding hand of the Americans was not what Aguinaldo and his followers had bargained for when the young rebel leader agreed to return to the Philippines with Commodore Dewey.

The first volunteer regiments arrived from the United States in

November 1899. But McKinley's "benevolent assimilation" and "mild way of justice" was neither completely benevolent nor especially mild. The *insurrectos* fought back. Under Aguinaldo and other commanders, the Filipino rebel leadership had first attempted to use conventional battlefield tactics, but superior American firepower and command tactics quickly defeated them. With their poorly armed and organized army shattered, the Filipinos shifted to guerrilla tactics. They hoped they could bog down the U.S. forces in a war the Americans couldn't win and in doing so strengthen the growing anti-imperialist movement in the United States—a large and growing political force that was attacking McKinley and his policies. Aguinaldo and his allies believed that continuing their armed struggle would weaken McKinley in his 1900 race against Democrat William Jennings Bryan, an outspoken opponent of the war. They also thought that they could win other Asian allies against a new Western colonial power.

Another crucial part of the insurgents' tactics was a deliberate attempt to terrorize Filipinos who had taken positions in the American-sponsored government. These collaborators were attacked by Aguinaldo's forces or forced to pay what Aguinaldo called "fines" collected by the rebels at gunpoint in what was becoming a Filipino civil war. However, Aguinaldo did not enjoy broad popular support.

When threats of violence and financial penalties failed to accomplish the task, Filipinos allied with the Americans were hacked to death or buried alive in an increasingly violent insurgency aimed at turning Filipinos against the American occupation.

Witnessing these atrocities, some American soldiers began to do what soldiers throughout history have done: They retaliated in kind. It was at this time that the "water cure" began to be used by American forces with greater regularity.

By May 1900, when General Arthur MacArthur, a Civil War veteran, arrived in the Philippines to take command of the American troops battling the "insurrection," the American efforts were in disarray. As an eighteen-year-old lieutenant, MacArthur had achieved hero's status at the Battle of Chickamauga in November 1863. With the Twenty-Fourth Wisconsin, he took his unit's colors to the top of Missionary Ridge. Shouting "On, Wisconsin!" MacArthur stood up to withering Confederate fire that had already killed three other color-bearers. General Philip Sheridan later recommended him for the Medal of Honor.*

Even as he needed more troops, MacArthur was ordered to dispatch some of his men to China to help suppress the Boxer Rebellion, the violent anti-foreign uprising that was sweeping imperial China in opposition to the Great Powers—six European countries, the United States, and Japan—which then dominated China. McKinley had ordered American troops to participate in the brigades of Western troops sent to rescue foreign diplomats and missionaries in the foreign Legation Quarter in Peking.

The military effort in the Philippines was also complicated by the arrival of new civilian commissioners, led by William Howard Taft, who was dispatched to establish a new civil government in the Philippines. Many point to the 1901 arrival of Taft—the future twenty-seventh president of the United States—as first civilian administrator, or governor-general, of the Philippines as a turning point in the era. While he would lock horns with military commanders, especially General Arthur MacArthur, Taft compiled an impressive record that won admiration in Washington and among many Filipinos, despite his famously condescending reference to them as "little brown brothers."[60]

---

* He was awarded the Medal of Honor in 1890 for his bravery at Missionary Ridge. His son Douglas MacArthur also won the Medal of Honor. Only two other fathers and sons have won the high honor—Theodore Roosevelt and his son General Theodore Roosevelt Jr., who served in World War II.

An Ohio attorney who would later lead the Supreme Court (the only former president to date to do so), Taft carried with him to the Philippines a constitution with a Bill of Rights modeled on the first ten amendments to the U.S. Constitution, absent the right to trial by jury and the right to bear arms. Taft also negotiated with the Vatican the purchase of 390,000 acres of church-held property in the Philippines for $7.5 million. Through low-cost mortgages, this land was later sold to tens of thousands of Filipinos.[61]

But Taft's uneasy relationship with MacArthur—who departed in 1901—was frayed from the start, as Stanley Karnow wrote: "MacArthur refused from the outset to recognize Taft's mandate. And even snubbed the commissioners on their arrival. Instead of meeting their ship personally, he sent an aide to conduct them to his office—where, as Taft quipped, 'the frigid greeting dried his perspiration.'"[62]

Squabbles over unclear lines of power arose between the American military and civilian authorities. As the insurrection gained momentum, American casualties mounted, and more troops were sent to the Philippines. At the same time, MacArthur increased the recruitment of pro-American Filipinos and allowed the use of "military necessity" and "retaliation" to develop harsher measures against the guerrillas, both in the field and in court, where the result of this martial law was that prisoners went "to the gallows with far more regularity," as Brian McAllister Linn wrote.[63] MacArthur's policies meant that captured guerrillas were deported, imprisoned, or in some cases simply executed. The Americans also established a new Filipino political party, hoping to build a pro-American opposition to Aguinaldo's independence movement.

The draconian American tactics were in place and effectively eliminating the resistance when, in March 1901, General Frederick "Foghorn" Funston led a mixed American-Filipino force that captured the rebel leader. After a hundred-mile forced march, during which the men nearly starved, the American-led Filipinos tricked Aguinaldo into believing that they were rebel reinforcements.⁶⁴ The Filipino scouts, known as Macabebes, marched into the camp and seized Aguinaldo, who was taken to Manila. Aguinaldo was held there until April 19, when, as the face of the rebellion, he issued a proclamation accepting American sovereignty and authority and calling for an end to the armed resistance.* By the end of the summer, there were only two sizable guerrilla forces still active, on the island of Samar and in Batangas, a region on the large island of Luzon, where Manila is located. Even with Aguinaldo's capture and capitulation, the pacification of these last bastions of the Filipino insurgency would add to the levels of brutality and violence, with repercussions that reached all the way to the White House.

By then, one key piece of Aguinaldo's strategy—the hope for McKinley's defeat in the 1900 presidential race—had also been dashed. McKinley won reelection over the isolationist William Jennings Bryan as the American people basically ignored the Democrat's anti-imperialist campaign against McKinley, who ran on the slogan "Four More Years of the Full Dinner Pail." With an economy booming and the war with Spain over, McKinley could run on prosperity and peace, even though the Philippine conflict raged on. In fact, McKinley's new running mate for vice president was the popular face of America's new global empire, the governor of New York, young Theodore Roosevelt.

As assistant secretary of the navy, Roosevelt had spearheaded the

---

* His influence blunted, Aguinaldo remained a major figure in the nation's politics for decades. After an unsuccessful run for president of the Philippines in 1935, Aguinaldo later broadcast pro-Japanese propaganda on the radio when Japan took the Philippines during World War II. He also urged Americans in the Philippines under General Douglas MacArthur to surrender, advice that was ignored. Jailed after Japan was defeated, Emilio Aguinaldo was later granted amnesty and the Philippines gained their independence in 1946. Becoming a symbolic elder statesman, he died in 1964 at the age of ninety-four.

buildup of the navy's strength before the war and issued the orders to Dewey to sail to Manila, fully understanding the importance of these islands in a new American global empire.

But in September 1901, the hero of San Juan Hill was in the White House. And if anything, President Roosevelt was even less interested than McKinley had been in negotiating with the Filipinos. The man who spoke softly and carried a big stick was going to use that stick on the Philippine insurrection. And after the massacre at Balangiga, the president had passed those orders down the line.

It was classic Roosevelt strategy—brute force, or "hit the line hard," as he liked to say in football jargon. In this case, the big stick was the combination of aggressively battling the insurgents; destroying their food stores and sources of civilian support; "reconcentrating" Filipinos into controllable territories (just as the American Indians had been removed to reservations during the nineteenth century); punitive taxes; and torture when necessary. It was accompanied by a touch of "speaking softly." The viable Philippine civil structures that had been built under Taft's largely benign if paternalistic administration would ultimately be corrupted and rigidly stratified along class, ethnic, and religious lines, in a "nation" of multiple languages, cultures, faiths, and competing ethnic groups.

With these strategies in place, Roosevelt simply declared an official end to the hostilities on July 4, 1902; the insurrection in the Philippines was over. Roosevelt backdated his proclamation so it symbolically fell on America's Independence Day.

The financial cost of the insurrection was $400 million—twenty times the price paid to Spain for the islands. More than 125,000 troops saw service in the Philippines, out of which approximately 4,374 Americans died; that contrasts with the 379 Americans lost in Spanish-American War combat. An estimated 16,000 Filipino soldiers and another 20,000 civilians also died in three and a half years.

As journalist and historian Stephen Kinzer noted: "Filipinos remember those years as the bloodiest in their history. Americans quickly forgot that the war ever happened."[65]

## AFTERMATH

While fighting in the Philippine campaign was technically over by April 1902, there had been persistent rumors and increasing newspaper reports of atrocities committed by Americans in the early months of the war. Prior to that time, military censorship had limited many of the worst stories coming out of the insurrection. When that censorship was lifted in 1901, papers including the *New York Post* began to run stories claiming that American troops "have been pursuing a policy of wholesale and deliberate murder."[66] While partisan newspapers defended the Republican policies, the mounting accusations emerged as one of the first political firestorms of Theodore Roosevelt's administration. Horrified by the atrocities committed on Samar, the American public was tiring of the endless struggle. Senator George Hoar, an opponent of the war, heard the rumors and demanded a Senate investigation. While Democrats would lead the charge, fellow Republicans, hoping to unseat the young Roosevelt as president in 1904, began to pile on.

And there were more voices in the American anti-imperialist camp, including that of celebrated author Mark Twain, who found no humor in the war and accused America of "debauching her honor." (In 1902, Twain had also written a scathing antiwar short story–prose poem titled "The War Prayer," which was not published until 1916, six years after his death.) Twain went so far as to suggest that the American flag be redesigned with the "white stripes painted black and the stars replaced by the skull and crossbones."

Theodore Roosevelt—the young Roosevelt, not the elder statesman whose face was to be carved on Mount Rushmore—faced heavy opposition. Though far from a vocal advocate of civil rights, Roosevelt had already set off a vicious controversy by inviting the African-American educator Booker T. Washington to become the first black man to dine at the White House, an action that unleashed an angry storm of racist rebukes and the lasting enmity of the Old South as well as death threats and hate mail aimed at the White House and Washington's Tuskegee Institute. Among the critics was the South Carolina senator Benjamin R. Tillman, who said, "The action of President Roosevelt in entertaining that nigger will necessitate our killing a thousand niggers in the South before they learn their place again."[67]

On the political side, one of the most powerful Republican leaders of the time, Senator Mark Hanna of Ohio—a kingmaker who had largely been responsible for putting his friend McKinley in the presidential chair—was being touted as a possible 1904 candidate. No fan of Roosevelt—he had been aghast when the New York governor was added to the 1900 Republican ticket—Hanna was reluctantly considering a bid to unseat him. At the same time, General Nelson Miles, commanding general of the United States Army, was also eyeing a run at the White House.

At sixty-one, Miles was a noted Civil War hero, having enlisted when the war began. A veteran of major action, Miles had been wounded four times and later received the Medal of Honor. After the war, he had commanded U.S. troops during the Indian wars, claimed credit for the capture of Chief Joseph of the Nez Percé, and led the campaign against Geronimo. He was also in overall command of the forces that fought the Sioux, a campaign that led to the death of Chief Sitting Bull on December 14 1890. Miles was not in the field during the massacre at Wounded Knee later that month, when the U.S. Army gunned down more than three hundred Sioux, including women and children. Miles was nonetheless sharply critical of the commanding officers there. Later he was in charge of the federal troops sent to quell the labor unrest in the Pullman Riots of 1894. Roosevelt biographer Edmund Morris described General Miles as "a splendid specimen of bristling military masculinity. If he wore more gold braid, silver stars, and polished leather than seemed necessary for national security, few begrudged him his glitter."[68]

Miles was not averse to using the Philippines controversy to advance his political ambitions. He and Roosevelt were already at odds, with Roosevelt dismissing Miles as a "brave peacock."[69] After becoming president, Roosevelt had publicly embarrassed Miles and then issued an official reprimand after Miles discussed a military matter with the press. Their personal animosity boiled over into public display and soon became a political rivalry. Miles made no secret that he was eager to challenge Roosevelt with a nomination from either main party.

Miles took the controversy to another level when he attempted to travel to the Philippines to investigate reports of atrocities committed by Americans. He was denied permission to make the trip, and that refusal spurred Roosevelt's enemies in Congress to ask for documents related to the alleged atrocities.

To counter, Roosevelt suggested a Senate hearing to air these charges. Begun in January 1902 and under the control of Senator Henry Lodge, Roosevelt's old friend and ally, the hearings never gained much public traction. However, the senators were stunned when William Howard Taft, the civilian governor of the Philippines, testified about the "water cure":

> What I am trying to do is state what seemed to us to be the expla-
> nation of these cruelties—that cruelties have been inflicted; that
> people have been shot when they ought not to have been; that there
> have been in individual instances of water cure, that torture which
> I believe involves pouring water down the throat so that the man

swells and gets the impression that he is going to be suffocated and then tells what he knows, which was a frequent treatment under the Spaniards, I am told—all these things are true.[70]

———

For the most part, war-weary Americans wanted the troops home from the far-off Asian islands. In April 1902, the controversy was back in the headlines as reports emerged of Filipinos being flogged, strung up by their thumbs, and tattooed for identification purposes. But the Lodge Committee report, released on April 11, merely caused some sputters of outrage while defenders of the Roosevelt administration dismissed the allegations as minor, occasional incidents. As the Senate hearings were still under way, however, Major Tony Waller had gone on trial in March 1902 for the deaths of civilians and other atrocities committed against Filipinos in the Samar province.

At a court-martial convened in Manila, Waller confessed to ordering the execution of eleven men without trial. But he argued that it was defensible under Civil War orders issued by President Lincoln (General Order 100) that codified treatment of prisoners of war, but also decreed stiff penalties for civilian suspects. Waller did not initially blame his commander, General Jacob Smith, now known as "Hell Roaring Jake" for the actions taken in the Samar region. But he testified in court to Smith's orders that he told Waller to "kill and burn," to make Samar "a burning wilderness," and sanctioned killing Filipinos as young as ten.

In April, just as the controversy was bubbling up and President Roosevelt was coming under increasing fire over the issue, the court acquitted Waller. Once presumed to be a lock to lead the Marine Corps, Waller was permanently tarred. He would be passed over for several promotions. General Smith was indicted and also tried; though subsequently convicted, he was merely "admonished."[71]

The brief sensation of these trials quickly faded from the headlines. In May 1902, Cuba was granted its independence, blunting some of the most virulent anti-imperialist rhetoric in the country. Medal of Honor winner Leonard Wood, also the presidential physician and Rough Riding hero of Cuba, had been named the island's military governor. During his time there, Wood had overseen an effort to eradicate yellow fever on the island and had a spectacular success. The United States had also built thousands of schools, paved Havana's streets, and added sewer and water systems to the city.* But Cuban independence created a largely American-overseen puppet government and the Cuban constitution included such pro-American stipulations as the right to military intervention and a perpetual lease on Guantanamo Bay. (U.S. troops returned to Cuba in 1906 when President Roosevelt ordered an invasion and occupation that would last for nearly four years: Guantanamo, of course, is still in American hands, as is the territory of Puerto Rico, also won from Spain after the war.)

When President Roosevelt declared on July 4, 1902, that the Philippine insurrection (war had never been declared by Congress) was over, he was already moving on to grander schemes. The Senate had just agreed to his ambitious design to build a strategic waterway across Central America through Panama, which was then a Colombian province. During the war, newspapers had tracked the progress of the naval vessel *Oregon* heading for Cuba. It had taken weeks to round South America. "Colonel Roosevelt" was going to fix that. He would make sure that the long-planned canal across Panama got built.

Back in the Philippines, while the conflict might have been over as far as President Roosevelt was concerned, it was really just beginning

---

* Wood went on to perform a similar role the Philippines, later returning to the United States to become the army chief of staff in 1910 under President Taft.

for some other Filipino people. The end of the Philippine insurrection did not mean peace for the islands.

Resistance continued. It would continue with nearly a decade of intense guerrilla warfare as the Moros—Muslims concentrated on some of the southern Philippine islands, and on Mindanao in particular—began to confront American forces. The Spanish had named them Moros because of their resemblance to the Moors of North Africa. Dressed in gaudy turbans, and carrying the sharp knife called a *kris*, the Moros kept up a quiet war with America from 1902 until 1913. "For fourteen years, the Moros had fought the Americans as they had fought the Spaniards," commented military historian James R. Arnold. "But when it came to kris versus Krag [a type of rifle carried by U.S. troops], the kris could not win. All the Moros had accomplished was to show yet again that they were not afraid to die."[72]

The decade-long war against the Moros became one of America's most hidden and overlooked conflicts. But the soon-to-be-legendary "Black" Jack Pershing, who commanded the U.S. troops in the final battle, at Bud Bagsak, would not be so ignored. His nickname came from the fact that Pershing was one of the commanders of the black troops, the Buffalo Soldiers, who had fought against Indians, in Cuba, and later in the Philippines. (According to biographer Frank E. Vandiver, he was derisively known as "Nigger" Jack for that service, the name only later softened.) Pershing's service against the Mexican rebel leader Pancho Villa and later as commander of the U.S. forces sent to Europe in World War I is well-known. His role in the Philippines is largely overlooked.

After Pershing's victory, a civilian administrator took over and the Moro resistance subsided. Most Americans had largely ignored the war against the Moros, a decade-long commitment of troops in a faraway place. By 1920 the American government exerted little influence over "Moroland." But the struggle of the Moros did not end there.

In October 2012, the government of the Philippines announced a deal with Moro rebels that was aimed at ending a three-decade-long struggle between the Moros and the government. That struggle had claimed an estimated 120,000 lives and displaced more than two million people.[73]

Nearly a year later, in September 2013, the *New York Times* reported, "Rebel Rifts Confound Philippines," and that "the quest for peace in the southern Philippine island of Mindanao, one that goes back more than a century, remains as difficult as ever."[74]

As for Balangiga, its memory has not been completely forgotten, either. Two church bells had been taken from Balangiga's church, scene of the 1901 massacre. Stamped with a coat of arms of the Franciscan missionaries, these bells were the same ones that rang that morning to announce the attack on the American garrison.

The men of Company C returned to the United States in 1904 and brought the bells with them. Two were left at a post in the United States and a third bell was taken to Korea, when the company was later posted there. In 1997, to celebrate the hundredth anniversary of the Philippines' declaration of independence from Spain, the country requested the return of the "Bells of Balangiga." To Filipinos, the bells are a reminder of the reprisals in which American troops were ordered to kill anyone over ten years old. To the men of Company C and the people who still honor the bells at a Wyoming air force base where they are kept, the bells are a memorial to fallen comrades.[75]

As of 2012, the bells remain in the control of the United States.

———

"I believe we intend to build up a good navy," said Theodore Roosevelt at the beginning of the new century. "But whether we build up a respectable army or not I do not know; and if we fail to do so, it may well be that a few years hence…we shall have to learn a bitter lesson."[76]

Roosevelt was more prophetic than he knew.

The following year, he delivered on his promise of a navy.

To demonstrate America's new global power, Roosevelt dispatched sixteen new battleships, all painted white, on a round-the-world voyage. This was the Great White Fleet, Roosevelt's crowning achievement as he left office after his second term. The nation celebrated this achievement, as it would the completion of the Panama Canal, the signature project begun during his first term. (The canal was not completed until 1914, under President Woodrow Wilson.)

With the canal and the Great White Fleet, America had declared its coming of age as a player on the world stage. Now the U.S. Navy would be the big stick to the world.

But the fleet carried another message, as Gail Buckley notes in her history of blacks in the American military. "In 1907, the 'Great White Fleet,' a brand new American battle fleet, all painted white, sailed around the world, the aim being to impress Japan with the power of the Caucasian race. The Great White Fleet represented the new all-white Navy—the first Navy in American history without black sailors. Blacks became stewards and messmen, replacing Japanese Americans, who were now seen as a security risk."[77]

To be accurate, there were some black sailors on the Great White Fleet, according to the Naval Institute. The navy's new recruiting policy, however,

was not designed to attract members of one class of citizens, African-American men, who made up an eighth of the American male population. Although the Navy had not yet become segregated and there were still black sailors among the ranks of the petty officers, the Navy of 1907 could not escape the racial attitudes of the American society of the time....In rapid order, black sailors were relegated to the ranks of the mess men or to the laborious and hot work of the engine room crew, as members of which they would eat and sleep separately from the rest of the crew....Of the many hundreds of photographs of sailors in the world cruise of the Great White Fleet, only two have been identified that clearly include black sailors.[78]

When the Great White Fleet returned in February 1909, Roosevelt was nearing the end of his second term, with a U.S. Navy that was now second only to that of England's Royal Navy in number of heavy ships. The remaining years prior to the onset of World War I saw the army and navy involved in few major conflicts. The Moro War continued, but mostly out of sight of the public. When "Black" Jack Pershing went from fighting the Islamic tribes in Mindanao to Mexico in hot pursuit of Pancho Villa under President Wilson in 1916, it was far from all-out war. And Wilson would campaign on the idea that "He Kept Us Out of War" in that presidential election year.

The campaign slogan was in reference to the fighting in Europe that had begun in August 1914. Most Americans—and Wilson was with them—wanted to stay out of the conflict. When it became clear that the outcome of that war could affect America's future, two million American men were sent to the trenches of Europe.

It was not until then—with the conflict that was later called World War I under way in Europe and America contemplating what its role in the conflict should be, if any—that the regular army was given an ambitious makeover under the National Defense Act, in 1916.

Spurred by a Preparedness Movement, the law increased the size of the army to 75,000 men over five years. It also created a college-based training program for officers, the Reserve Officers' Training Corps (ROTC), in which 80,000 men enrolled during World War I. At the same time, the National Guard would expand to 400,000 Guardsmen, who had a dual oath to both state and federal government. "Guardsmen could be compelled to serve abroad for unlimited amounts of time in national emergency, but they would go to war as guard units, not as individuals," as Millett and Maslowski explained.

The War Department would establish physical and mental standards for Guard enlistees and retained the right to screen Guard officers for fitness. This would create a much larger pool of trained junior officers for an enlarged wartime army, if war should come.[79]

World War I brought the United States to full stature as an international military power, but the costs were frightful. In just two hundred days of combat, 53,402 American fighting men were killed in action; another 200,000 were wounded. Disease largely associated with the influenza pandemic of 1918, which claimed an estimated 30–50 million lives worldwide,[80] also took another 57,000 soldiers' lives at home and abroad. "Americans who fought in France," Millett and Maslowski concluded, "knew they had participated in a critical turning point in their nation's military history. They had gone to Europe, and they had fought a mass, industrialized war with allies against a modern national army noted for its expertise. 'Over there' they had seen the face of future war."[81]

The dreadful consequences of what was called "the war to end all wars" reinforced America's isolationist tradition and mood, as did fears of the growing threat of Bolshevism and socialism, which had been set loose in Russia and elsewhere in Europe. Fear of the foreign only increased in the first Red Scare of the 1920s, with federal and local crackdowns on anarchists and socialists.

That isolationist sentiment was further cemented as the forces of European fascism in Hitler's Germany and Mussolini's Italy threatened America's First World War allies, England and France. But when war came again to Europe in 1939, President Franklin D. Roosevelt was unable to follow the course he preferred. Constrained by a Congress that passed five different neutrality acts—and by the Great Depression, which kept the United States from spending more on its military—FDR could only watch and plan. He knew Hitler posed a threat to America's security. And he, like other military planners, also knew that another pressing threat loomed as an increasingly militarized Japanese Empire—allied with Germany and Italy in the Axis—aggressively followed its plan to dominate the Pacific.

But the reluctance of Americans to get involved disappeared on December 7, 1941:

> Yesterday, December 7, 1941—a date which will live in infamy—the United States of America was suddenly and deliberately attacked by naval and air forces of the Empire of Japan.
>
> The United States was at peace with that nation and, at the solicitation of Japan, was still in conversation with its government and its emperor, looking toward the maintenance of peace in the Pacific.... The attack yesterday on the Hawaiian Islands has caused severe damage to American naval and military forces. I regret to tell you that very many American lives have been lost.... Yesterday, the Japanese Government also launched an attack against Malaya. Last night, Japanese forces attacked Hong Kong. Last night, Japanese forces attacked Guam.
>
> Last night, Japanese forces attacked the Philippine Islands.
>
> Last night, the Japanese attacked Wake Island. And this morning, the Japanese attacked Midway Island....No matter how long it may take us to overcome this premeditated invasion, the American people, in their righteous might, will win through to absolute victory.
>
> —Franklin D. Roosevelt's war message to Congress
> (December 8, 1941)[82]

## Chapter Four

→⭢⭠←

# Berlin Stories

### Berlin, Germany—April 1945

"Well, then. Who is going to take Berlin: are we or are the Allies?"[1]

—*Soviet Union leader Joseph Stalin*
*(April 1945)*

"The radio announced that Hitler had come out of his safe bomb-proof bunker to talk with the fourteen to sixteen year old boys who had 'volunteered' for the 'honor' to be accepted into the SS and to die for their Führer in the defense of Berlin.... These boys did not volunteer, but had no choice, because boys who were found hiding were hanged as traitors by the SS as a warning.... When trees were not available, people were strung up on lamp posts."[2]

—*Berlin resident Dorothea von Schwanenfluegel*
*(April 1945)*

"Russia is not going to give up anything that she considers essential to her well-being without a fight and I mean a *fight*."[3]

—*U.S. Army general Jack Whitelaw (August 1945)*

"I hate war as only a soldier who has lived it can, only as one who has seen its brutality, its futility, and its *stupidity*."[4]

—*General Dwight D. Eisenhower (January 10, 1946)*

# Milestones in World War II

## 1938

**September 30** Under the Munich Pact, the British and French allow
Hitler to annex the Sudetenland, an area of Czechoslovakia with a
largely German-speaking population.

## 1939

**August 23** Germany and the Soviet Union sign the Nazi-Soviet
Non-Aggression Pact (also referred to as the German-Soviet
Non-Aggression Pact and the Ribbentrop-Molotov Pact).

**September 1** Germany invades Poland.

**September 3** France and Great Britain declare war on Germany.

**September 28** Germany and Russia partition Poland, which Russia
invaded from the east on September 17.

**October 11** In a letter to President Roosevelt signed by Albert Ein-
stein, several physicists explain the potential for an atomic bomb;
Roosevelt orders a plan to develop such a weapon and share information about it with the British. This is the beginning of the
army-run "Manhattan Project."

## 1940

**March 18** Italy's Mussolini and Hitler announce Italy's formal alliance with Germany against England and France. Mussolini calls
this the "Axis" on which Europe will revolve.

**May–June** Germany invades France and the Low Countries. By June 22 a pro-German government is installed in the city of Vichy.

**July 20** Congress authorizes $8.5 billion for the construction of a two-ocean U.S. Navy capable of meeting threats in both the Atlantic and Pacific. The Army Air Corps, first created in 1926 and the predecessor of the U.S. Air Force, is also authorized to expand to 7,800 combat aircraft.

**December 29** In a year-end "fireside chat," Roosevelt says that the United States will become the "Arsenal of Democracy" as peacetime factories shift to war production.

### 1941

**March 11** The Lend-Lease Act is signed into law; it allows the United States to "lend" military equipment to other nations with deferred payments. Under the law, the United States arms the Allies fighting Nazi Germany but is not actually engaged in combat.

**June 22** Germany invades Russia; two days later, President Roosevelt promises U.S. aid to the Soviets under Lend-Lease.

**September 8** The Siege of Leningrad (now St. Petersburg, Russia) begins. Lasting almost nine hundred days until January 1944, it is considered the most lethal siege in history, with millions of civilian and military deaths, many of them from starvation, disease, and exposure in the severe Russian winters. More Russians die in Leningrad alone than British and American soldiers and civilians during the whole of World War II.[5]

**December 7** The Japanese attack the U.S. Navy base at Pearl Harbor, Hawaii, and declare war on the United States.

**December 8** Roosevelt requests a declaration of war on Japan. The Senate vote is unanimous in favor; the House approves 388–1, with pacifist Jeannette Rankin, the first woman elected to the House, the lone dissenter.

**December 11** Responding to the state of war between the United States and Japan, Germany and Italy declare war on the United States.

## 1942

**August 22** The Battle of Stalingrad (now renamed Volgograd) begins; among the war's bloodiest battles, it produces combined Axis-Soviet casualties (dead, wounded, missing, and captured, as well as civilians) estimated at 1.72 million.

## 1943

**July 10** Allied forces begin an assault that captures the strategic island of Sicily, giving the Allies control of Mediterranean shipping and a base from which to launch an invasion of mainland Italy.

## 1944

**February 20–27** A massive bombing campaign by the U.S. Army Air Forces is begun against German aircraft production centers. On March 6, more than six hundred U.S. bombers make their first raid on Berlin.

**June 6** D-Day, the Allied invasion of Normandy, commences just after midnight.

**December 16** In the Battle of the Bulge, Nazi Germany's last major counteroffensive, Allied troops are pushed back in Belgium's Ardennes Forest. After two weeks of heavy combat in brutal winter weather, this last-gasp German attack is defeated.

## 1945

**February 1** One thousand American bombers strike Berlin.

**February 4–11** The Yalta Conference is held in this Crimean city, with Churchill, Stalin, and an ailing Roosevelt discussing plans for the final assault on Germany and laying the groundwork for the postwar division of Europe among the Allies.

**April 11** U.S. troops reach the Elbe River in Germany. They halt there and meet advancing Russian troops in the city of Torgau on April 25.

**April 12** President Roosevelt dies at his retreat in Warm Springs, Georgia. Vice President Harry S. Truman is sworn in as president.

**April 28** In Italy, communist partisans execute former dictator Mussolini.

**April 30** Hitler marries his longtime mistress, Eva Braun, in his bombproof Berlin bunker. He then poisons her and kills himself. His remains are never recovered.

**May 7** The Germans formally surrender to General Eisenhower at Rheims, France, and to the Soviets in Berlin. President Truman pronounces the following day V-E (Victory in Europe) Day.

**June 5** At Potsdam, in defeated Germany, the United States, Russia, England, and France agree to split occupied Germany into eastern and western halves, and to divide Berlin, which is within the eastern, Russian-occupied half of Germany.

**August 6** The U.S. B-29 Superfortress *Enola Gay* drops an atomic bomb on Hiroshima, Japan. Three days later, on August 9, a second bomb is dropped on the city of Nagasaki. The Soviet Union declares war on Japan, launching an invasion of Manchuria, China, which has been under Japanese control.

**September 2** General Douglas MacArthur, Supreme Commander of Allied Powers in Japan, accepts the country's formal, unconditional surrender aboard the USS *Missouri* in Tokyo Bay.

*Berlin, Germany*
*April–May 1945*

Hell had been unleashed.

In the early hours of April 16, 1945, the people of Berlin were shaken from their beds by the sound of distant thunder and what felt like an earthquake. Pictures fell from walls and telephones began to rattle off their hooks and ring on their own.[6] But the faraway noise and shaking ground was not nature's fury. It meant that a day of reckoning had arrived. The Red Army was approaching.

In January, Berliners had heard the Soviet offensive described on their radios as "a mass invasion, to be compared in scale and significance with the past comings of the Mongol hordes, the Huns and Tatars."[7] Two and a half million Soviet soldiers—Russians, Ukrainians, Poles, and others from the Eastern European lands now in the Kremlin's grasp—were racing toward Berlin with tens of thousands of tanks and armored vehicles, supported by 7,500 aircraft. Coming from the east, they outnumbered the German defenders by at least ten to one, and they mercilessly crushed German resistance, smashing their way toward Hitler's lair. Although the Red Army tanks were still more than thirty miles from the city, the roar and rumbling reverberated right into the crumbling, trembling heart of the Thousand-Year Reich.

Marshal Zhukov, one of the Soviet commanders, threw his forces at the German defenses without regard for casualties. As the battle between the Red Army and the last lines of Nazi defense raged on the Seelow Heights, east of Berlin, over the next three days, 30,000

Russians would die and the Germans would lose 12,000 men to the relentless Soviet push to bring Nazi Germany to its knees.[8]

But some Berliners still believed the propaganda they heard: that the brave German defenders would hold back the "new storm of Mongols." Others hoped that the Americans and British, also sweeping through the German heartland, from the west, might arrive first. Mordant Berliners joked that the optimists were learning English and the pessimists Russian.

In spite of the daily pounding from British and American bombers, some determined Berliners still braved the danger, desperate to retain a veneer of normal life. Some went to their offices. Others rushed out to line up at the few open bakeries and food shops, hoping to fill their shelves before the siege began.[9] There was no more milk in the stores, a thirty-four-year-old diarist* noted, adding, "That means that children are going to die."[10]

By April 20, Adolf Hitler's birthday, there was still no sign of the Soviets in the city. In previous years, the Führer's birthday had been triumphantly marked in Berlin with festive celebrations. This day, the usual propaganda pronouncements promised a swift defeat of the approaching Allied armies, then called on German teenagers to join the home guard defending the Reich. Many Berliners still believed some last-minute German miracle would scatter their enemies, a last-gasp aura of the "master race" invincibility that the German people had made an article of faith since Hitler's rise to power. There were even rumors going around of a mysterious and frightful new super-weapon that would turn back the enemy at the gates.

---

* The unnamed woman in this story is a journalist who anonymously published her account of life in besieged and occupied wartime Berlin in 1954. Written in diary form, it told of the two months in 1945 when the Soviet armies invaded. The diary's author died in 2001 without revealing her identity and the book was reissued in 2003 under the title *A Woman in Berlin*. Historian Antony Beevor and other authorities are convinced of the accuracy of the book's description of the horrors of life in Berlin in the spring of 1945.

But the American and British air forces had a forceful and unpleasant birthday greeting for Hitler. Their bombers unleashed a particularly heavy raid on Berlin to mark the date. The Royal Air Force had been raiding Berlin since 1940. The American Eighth Air Force had begun combined fighter and bomber raids over Germany as well. On March 6, 1944, the "Mighty Eighth" had sent more than 700 heavy bombers and 800 escort fighters on a nighttime raid, the first American strike on the German capital. Nearly a year later, on February 3, 1945, more than 900 bombers and 550 fighter escorts, the largest force ever sent against a single city, struck Berlin. American forces targeted German government centers and railway stations filled with civilian refugees.[11] But the American targets also included factories, such as the Daimler-Benz tank factory in Berlin, attacked by B-17 bombers escorted by the Tuskegee Airmen—the all-black unit of fliers known as the Red Tails and commanded by Benjamin O. Davis Jr.*

Now on April 20, with the Soviet army at Berlin's outskirts, the Allied pilots knew that Hitler's Birthday Raid would be their second-to-last attack on the German capital.

The writing on the wall was clear—and most Berliners could read it. Their illusions of invincibility had been shattered, replaced by a new inevitability. The anonymous woman recorded in her diary, "It's true; the war is rolling towards Berlin.... What was yesterday a distant rumble has now become a constant roar. We breathe the din; our ears are deafened to all but the heaviest guns.... We are ringed in by barrels, and the circle is growing smaller."[12]

The far-off sounds of Soviet artillery finally gave way to the shelling of Berlin on April 21. Any optimism for the city's miraculous

---

* Son of the first African-American general in the U.S. Army, Benjamin O. Davis Jr. was the fourth black man to graduate from West Point, where he had been shunned by white classmates, who refused to eat with him. Following his distinguished service with the Tuskegee Airmen in World War II, he later became the first African-American general officer in the U.S. Air Force.

deliverance was now buried in the rubble of a massive bombing campaign. The U.S. Eighth Air Force had delivered the final American air raid on Berlin, the 363rd of the war. When the death from the air raids ceased, it was replaced by Soviet shelling.

Just before noon, artillery shells began to burst over downtown Berlin, shocking the shoppers at a department store, among other Berliners still in the streets. As Soviet gunners found their range, the deadly artillery assault left people writhing in agony in the city's streets. As historian Cornelius Ryan put it, "Berlin had become the front line."[3]

With Red Army tanks and snipers advancing on the desperate German capital, Hildegard Knef, a beautiful nineteen-year-old actress, was in a German soldier's uniform, wearing a helmet and carrying a machine gun and a few grenades. She was not outfitted for a movie role. She was on the run with her boyfriend, Ewald von Demandowsky, a film producer in Joseph Goebbels's Nazi propaganda machine. As the Soviets approached, Demandowsky had been pressed into service in the *Volkssturm*.* Donning a uniform, Knef had joined her lover, hoping to stave off, or somehow escape, the Russian assault.

Inside his Berlin bunker in the Reich Chancellery a few days earlier, Adolf Hitler had called for the German people to rise up against the Allied threat and to make a last-ditch effort to defend the Fatherland. Propaganda minister Goebbels issued a call to form a wall on which the "Asian hordes" would be smashed. Demandowsky and Knef were joining tens of thousands of average Germans who were trying to hold back an onslaught of more than one million Red Army soldiers who were eager to wreak havoc and win vengeance for the invasion of Russia and other Eastern European nations by Germany.

---

* The word is translated as "Folk assault," but it was a militia home guard formed by the Nazi Party, and its members, mostly older men, lacked training and weapons.

The old men and the young boys, along with a handful of women, in the ranks of the German home guard joined a broken contingent of regular German army soldiers who had been pushed back to Berlin by the Allied advances of the past few months. Millions of Americans and British were coming from the west and their Red Army allies were pressing from the east in a punishing pincer movement—combined with a relentless Allied air bombing campaign—that was rolling up German armies and leaving the Reich in ruins.

And just as other German cities had been decimated by the American and British bombing campaigns, much of Berlin had been reduced to piles of smoldering rubble. Hamburg, a coastal port, had been hard hit in repeated strikes that began in the summer of 1943. Thousands of Germans had been trapped inside air raid shelters there, literally roasted alive by the fires started by incendiary bombs. In one of the most infamous attacks, the medieval city of Dresden had been firebombed over the course of two days in February. With high explosives and incendiary bombs, the Royal Air Force (RAF) and the United States Army Air Forces (USAAF, predecessor to the U.S. Air Force) had devastated the city, killing an estimated twenty-five thousand men, women, and children in a city of questionable military value and prized for its architectural beauty and historic heritage.[14]

In the basement of a Berlin building, the anonymous diarist—who had worked for a publisher until two weeks earlier—huddled with neighbors behind a blast door weighing a hundred pounds, with rubber seals around the edges. The building's basement, like many in Berlin, had been converted into a neighborhood bomb shelter, its ceiling supported by heavy timbers. In orderly German fashion, Berliners were assigned to specific shelters. The diarist observed her shelter-mates, most clutching the battered suitcases they carried as they raced down belowground at the sound of the air raid alarms: the baker's wife; the pharmacist's widow; a young man in gray trousers who turned out to be a woman; three elderly dressmakers; a curtain seller who had no curtains to sell; a bookseller and his wife; an elderly businessman, his wife, and their teenage daughter; the retired post-master and his wife. They were, as the "pale-faced blonde" wrote, "a community of discards, unwanted at the front, rejected by the civil defence." In the shelter they now shared, the young woman wrote, "We call it cave, underworld, catacomb of fear, mass grave."[15]

The next day, April 22, trying to keep a semblance of normal life in what was once one of Europe's most cosmopolitan cities, people shopped and looked for newspapers for any word of their possible fate. But "news" in Berlin had been reduced to gossip and swirling rumor. With only the whispered reports of the approaching Red Army's location to go on, the diarist had searched the city for food.

"They're handing out what are officially called advance rations—meat, sausage, processed foods, sugar, canned goods and ersatz coffee," she recalled. "I took my place in line and waited in the rain for two hours.... A crowd is milling around the corner butcher's in an endless queue on both sides, people standing four abreast in the pouring rain. What a mess! What else can I do? I have to sit it out and wait. Our days are accented with flak and artillery fire."[16]

On that April 22, as the realization finally struck home that his plans were ruined, Adolf Hitler ranted in his Berlin bunker, casti-gating his generals and armies for the disaster that had befallen his Reich. "Eventually he collapsed into an armchair, drained and weep-ing," historian Antony Beevor writes. "He said quite openly for the first time that the war was lost....Hitler went on to say that because he could not die fighting, because he was too weak, he would simply shoot himself to avoid falling into the hands of the enemy."[17]

When one of his generals suggested that a German army then battling the American troops in the west could move back to Berlin and perhaps save the city from the Red Army, Hitler's mood changed abruptly. He invited the general to sit down to a dinner of sand-wiches, cognac, and chocolates. Hitler then insisted that his orders to the army be broadcast over the radio, which announced, "The Führer has issued orders from Berlin that units fighting [the] Americans rapidly be transferred east to defend Berlin."[18]

In the approaching Red Army, Berlin's defenders were facing one of the most extraordinary collections of troops in World War II, if not military history. Lacking the necessities and comforts supplied to British and American troops, including razors, knives, candles, or pencil and paper, the Red Army was issued vodka. They also operated with what military historian Max Hastings terms "a willingness to accept almost unlimited casualties" together with "knowledge of the draconian penalties awaiting those who flinched or failed."[19] According to Hastings:

> The advancing Soviet legions resembled no other army the world had ever seen. A mingling of old and new, Europe and Asia, high intelligence and brutish ignorance, ideology and patriotism, technological sophistication and the most primitive transport and equipment. T-34s, artillery and katyusha rocket launchers were followed by jeeps and Studebakers and Dodge trucks supplied under Lend-Lease, then by shaggy ponies and columns of horsemen, farm carts and trudging peasants from the remote republics of Central Asia, clad in foot cloths and rags of uniform. Drunkenness was endemic.... The only discipline rigorously enforced was that which required men—and women—to attack, fight, and to die. Stalin and his marshals cared nothing for the preservation of civilian life or property.[20]

Knowing of the Red Army's reputation for wanton ruthlessness toward Germans, Berliners grasped at the slimmest straw of hope that General Walther Wenck and seventy thousand troops would ride to

Berlin's rescue like Wagner's operatic Valkyries sweeping in to choose the winners on a mythical battlefield. In the chaotic atmosphere of Berlin under siege, other rumors spread like wildfire, including the optimistic report that the Americans and British would get to Berlin before the Russians; it offered a faint chance of a better outcome.

At the same time, the Soviet propaganda machine unleashed an airdrop of leaflets aimed at German soldiers and civilians promising them "safe conduct" if they surrendered. Another assured the women of Berlin that they had nothing to fear.

But General Wenck had other ideas about what to do with his troops. Perhaps Wenck knew that Hitler's last battle plan was a dream, the demented fantasy of a crazed dictator's last moments.* Believing that Hitler's order was the doomed delusion of a man gone mad, and lacking tanks to battle the Soviets, Wenck instead hoped to open up a corridor for German soldiers and civilians to escape the approaching Red Army and the senseless fighting.[21]

When one of the remaining German armies met the Red Army in a forest south of Berlin, the result was an epic massacre on both sides. One eyewitness who survived the Soviet onslaught said, "In this mess of metal, wood and something unidentifiable was a dreadful mash of tortured human bodies....In the surrounding forest—corpses, corpses, corpses, mixed with, I suddenly noted, ones who were still alive." The Soviet artillery and air bombardment had wreaked havoc on the remnants of Wenck's forces sent to try to help Germans escape west toward the approaching Americans. Close to 30,000 Germans

---

* In assessing Hitler's mental state at this moment in history, Antony Beevor writes in *The Fall of Berlin 1945*, "The debate over Hitler's degree of insanity or madness can never be resolved," adding that one observer of the German leader in his final days was "convinced that '[Hitler's] mental sickness consisted of hypertrophic self-identification with the German people.' This may well explain why he felt that the population of Berlin should share his suicide" (*The Fall of Berlin 1945*, p. 276).

were buried in the forest. At least 20,000 Soviet troops died there, too.[22]

By April 25, more than one million Red Army soldiers had encircled the city, which was now down to about 90,000 defenders, of whom 45,000 were soldiers from the depleted German army and the other half from the ill-equipped, ill-trained *Volkssturm*.

For two members of that militia, Hildegard Knef and her lover, Ewald, the arrival of the Soviets almost didn't matter. As they ran from the crumbling front lines of defense and pitched battles in the streets of Berlin, a German officer accused them of trying to desert and arrested them. Having survived the Russian onslaught so far, Knef now faced execution in a city that was in its death throes.

She had already seen the bodies of other German "deserters" hanging from trees. Executioners from the German SS (the Nazi Party's armed "Protective Squadron") had begun to hang anyone who placed a flag of surrender on their home or soldiers who were trying to escape the ranks.

But as Knef and Ewald awaited their fates, a Russian shell burst on the scene. Suddenly, the bodies of dead and dying Germans surrounded the lovers, and they were able to make a run for it, escaping with their lives. Then, just as suddenly, another German officer stopped them. Knef thought their luck had run out and another fanatical Nazi officer would shoot them on the spot. But when she removed her helmet to show him that she was a woman, the young officer laughed and let the pair go, tossing them a bar of chocolate.[23]

When the Russians finally reached the city on April 27, Knef and thousands of other German women expected the worst, and with good reason. Refugees from the eastern regions of Germany that had already fallen to the Red Army had streamed into the city with beastly tales of what the Russian soldiers had done to women there as they had advanced into East Prussia. One woman told Knef that her sister's breasts had been cut off while her husband was crucified against a door.[24]

Earlier in 1945, Nazi propaganda minister Goebbels had been able to dispatch camera teams to film in the East Prussian territory that had fallen to the Soviets. The corpses of German women and girls who had been raped and murdered by drunken Red Army soldiers were shown on newsreels in Berlin. "The images on the Nazi newsreels had been so appalling," notes historian Antony Beevor, "that many women presumed they were part of a gross exaggeration by the 'Promi,' the propaganda ministry."[25]

As Knef and a few other remnants of Berlin's ragtag defenders sought shelter from the Red Army's devastating onslaught in a garden shed, the teenage actress turned soldier heard the sound of screams nearby. "I stand there in my hole, in the water, keep a firm hold on the machine gun and the pistol, peer through the glasses over the yard... hear screams, dreadful heartrending screams, high, thin, shrill. I call out softly to the next hole... 'What's that screaming?' 'Russians in that house over there started on the women.'"[26]

The Berlin that the Soviet armies were assaulting with such lethal and brutal vengeance was far removed from the beautiful capital Americans had known from a dozen years earlier when "[n]icely dressed men and women sat in the Romanisches Café, drinking coffee and wine,"[27] historian Erik Larson recounted. The German capital's immaculate and orderly streets, fashionable shops, and dazzling gardens were world-renowned, the roads filled with the latest motorcars. The fabled boulevards and grand hotels had once welcomed Greta Garbo and Charlie Chaplin. The Tiergarten, the equivalent of Central Park, offered acres of trees and walkways leading to the celebrated

Brandenburg Gate and a wealthy shopping and residential neighborhood. It was also home to a celebrated zoo.*

Now beneath Berlin's famed zoo there was an air raid shelter. In November 1943, the zoo was hit by an Allied air attack. Berliner Ursula Gebel remembered, "I had been at the elephant enclosure and had seen six females and one juvenile doing tricks with their keeper. That same night, all seven were burnt alive.... The hippopotamus bull survived in its basins, [but] all the bears, polar bears, camels, ostriches, birds of prey and other birds were burnt. The tanks in the aquarium all ran dry; the crocodiles escaped, but like the snakes they froze in the cold November air. All that survived in the zoo was the bull elephant named Siam, the bull hippo and a few apes."[28]

The human toll would soon be much greater. After one USAAF attack, Berliner Karl Deutmann wrote, "We heard, behind the meter-thick walls of our bunker and for more than one hour, nothing but the awful rumbling and thunder of the carpet of falling bombs, with the lights flickering and sometimes almost going out.... When we left the bunker the sun had disappeared, the sky darkened with clouds. Fed by numberless big fires, a vast sea of smoke hung over the whole of the inner city.... In the Neuburgerstrasse...the girls' trades school had been hit; hundreds of girls had been sheltered in the cellar. Later the parents were standing in front of the shattered bodies, mangled and stripped naked by blast, no longer able to recognize their own daughters."[29]

In Berlin, with prototypical German efficiency and planning, shelters had been built to accommodate the city's population, but not the vast numbers of refugees streaming into the besieged capital. The city of more than three million had grown to more than four million as

---

* This Berlin will be familiar to readers of Erik Larson's bestseller *In the Garden of Beasts*, which presents a rich view of Germany and Berlin in particular at the dawn of the Nazi era in 1933.

refugees from other parts of Germany under Allied attack crowded into the city's five separate railroad stations each day.

And then there were the city's three hundred thousand foreign workers, most from European countries defeated by Germany earlier in the war. Identifiable by letters painted on their clothes, they were forbidden to seek safety.

"The air raid shelters themselves, lit with blue lights, could provide a foretaste of claustrophobic hell," recounted Beevor, "as people pushed in bundled in their warmest clothes and carrying small suitcases containing sandwiches and thermos. In theory all basic needs were catered for in the shelters.... Water supplies ceased when mains were hit, and the *Aborte*, or lavatories, became disgusting, a real distress for a nation preoccupied with hygiene."[30]

The best-protected shelters went to Nazi officials, especially the Führer and his inner circle, according to Max Hastings. "Hitler devoted vast resources to his personal safety: 28,000 workers and a million cubic centimeters of concrete—more than the weight of materials employed throughout 1943–44 on all Germany's public shelters—were used to construct his East Prussian and Berlin bunkers."[31]

With the largest shelters either restricted or overloaded, many Berliners were assigned to reinforced basements. The diarist was assigned to the subterranean refuge of a neighboring building, and huddled there once more with her neighbors. It was Friday, April 27, and the Russians were already in the city. When some Red Army soldiers entered the basement, their officer reassured the Berliners that Stalin had declared "this sort of thing"—meaning the rape of women—was not to happen and left.

The diarist, a journalist who had traveled widely before the war and spoke some Russian, checked to see if the Red Army soldiers were gone. But they were not. Two had stayed behind. Grabbing her wrists, they jerked the woman along a corridor. She struggled, but the two men tore off her suspender (garter) belt and forced her to the ground. When the door opened and three more Russians entered, one a woman in officer's uniform, the attackers stopped their assault. The two Russian rapists jumped up and departed with their comrades.

Left lying there, the young woman was able to gather herself and returned to the basement, where the other Germans stared at her.

"My stockings are down to my shoes, my hair is disheveled. I'm still holding onto what's left of my suspender belt. I start yelling. 'You pigs. Here they rape me twice in a row and you shut the door and leave me lying like a piece of dirt.' "[32]

Two days later, as the ring of Soviet armies tightened around the dying city, the man who had set Germany on this course signed his last will and testament. In the early hours of April 29, Hitler married his longtime mistress, Eva Braun, in his Berlin bunker.

Told the next day that Berlin's defenders were nearly out of ammunition, Hitler and Braun committed suicide. She took poison; he used a shot to the temple. Their bodies were cremated by loyal followers in a garden not far from Hitler's bunker in the Reich Chancellery. Under the terms of Hitler's will, Grand Admiral Karl Dönitz, the German naval commander, became the president of Germany. It was Dönitz who would soon officially surrender to the Allies, bringing the war in Europe to a close.

The shock of the Red Army's arrival in Berlin was more than just a grotesque nightmare that confirmed the worst fears of Berliners, and would play out mercilessly in the city in the months ahead. It was the end of the world as Berliners knew it. The people of Berlin, the home of the Thousand-Year Reich, had been pummeled by air strikes, more than three hundred of them since early 1944, when the daily raids on the city began.

The air war had been designed by the American command, which felt it could turn the tide of war. For months, the Americans bombed by day and the Royal Air Force bombed by night. In the eight months between September 1944 and April 1945, the U.S. Eighth Air Force and the Royal Air Force dropped 729,000 tons of bombs on Germany—more ordnance than they had delivered in all of the previous months of the war combined.[33]

Before 1943, Allied bombing raids had been costly to British and American fliers, as German fighters were able to down a significant number of Allied bombers. But late in 1943, the Americans began to mass-produce long-range fighters—a fast single-seater called the P-51B Mustang. With external auxiliary fuel tanks that could be jettisoned when empty, the Mustang could escort bombers as far as Berlin from British bases. As British military historian Andrew Roberts explains, "Once the Mustangs established dominance over the German skies, shooting down large numbers of Messerschmitts flown by experienced pilots, thereby allowing Allied bombers to destroy Luftwaffe [German air force] factories, the next stage was to destroy the synthetic-oil factories without which new German pilots could not even complete their training."[34]

American industrial prowess was the most crucial piece of the wartime equation. In 1944, Germany built 40,000 warplanes; the United States turned out 98,000.[35]

The USAAF and the RAF took different approaches to bombing. While the RAF had embarked on a strategy of wrecking German cities, the USAAF was "doctrinally committed to precision bombing," as Max Hastings records. But, Hastings also notes, "Bombing did not make the decisive impact upon civilian morale that the British aspired to achieve: factories continued to produce and orders to be obeyed."[36] Besides that, as Roberts points out, "The distinction between area and precision bombing was often blurred by the fact that German armaments, ball-bearing and synthetic oil facilities, as well as submarine dockyards, railway marshaling yards and other targets deemed morally acceptable by post-war armchair strategists, were very often located in built-up areas and near schools, hospitals and the tenement housing of their workers. As a senior USAAF officer joked at a post-war seminar, 'The RAF carried out precision attacks on area targets, while the USAAF carried out area attacks on precision targets.' The difference...was often marginal."[37]

Still, air superiority—in American industrial output, in the destruction of German war-making capacity through the bombing campaigns, and in air support over land battles—was a crucial underpinning to the eventual Allied victory. Following the November 1942 turning-point victory of the British over the Axis armies at El Alamein in Egypt, legendary German field marshal Erwin Rommel* wrote, "Anyone who has to fight, even with the most modern weapons, against an enemy in complete control of the air, fights like a savage against modern European troops, under the same handicaps and with the same chance of success."[38]

While it was presumed that the strategic bombing had been costly to the German economy and morale, a survey initiated by President Roosevelt later revealed that the bombing was devastating but did not work "conclusively." Just as the British economy had survived the German Blitz, the Germans were able to shift production from one factory to another and continue producing aircraft and other equipment. Again, as Hastings recorded, "German production remained remarkably high: as late as September (1944), 3,538 aircraft of all types were built, of which 2,900 were fighters. But the Luftwaffe's total 1944 output of 34,100 combat aircraft was dwarfed by the Allies' 127,300... and the Germans' loss of pilots was calamitous."[39]

By the end of 1944, Berlin had increasingly become the focus of the unrelenting air strikes. "The statistics of destruction had increased

---

* A World War I veteran, Erwin Rommel was one of Germany's most successful, admired, and popular military leaders. In command of the German defenses on June 6, 1944—D-Day—Rommel was later implicated in the failed "July 20" (1944) plot to assassinate Hitler. Because of his popularity, Rommel was not publicly executed but forced to take cyanide; his death was attributed to an earlier war injury.

almost hourly; by now they were staggering," Cornelius Ryan writes. "Three billion cubic feet of debris lay in the streets.... Almost half of Berlin's 1,562,000 dwellings had sustained some kind of damage, and every third house was either completely destroyed or uninhabitable. Casualties were so high that true accounting would never be attainable. But at least 52,000 were dead and twice that number were seriously injured—five times the number killed and seriously injured in the bombing of London."[40]

The agony of the bombings was bad enough. Far worse for many Germans was the fear of what was to follow. Around Berlin, even as the Führer and his propaganda minister Goebbels issued calls for heroic resistance, the people knew that the Red Army was at the gates. The hell of the bombing campaign that had forced once-proud Berliners to cower in fetid bomb shelters, lacking basic sanitation and sufficient food, would be small compared to what the people of Berlin, especially the women and girls, expected to see once the Soviet forces took the city.

And when the Red Army arrived, their worst fears were realized. Young or old, it did not matter. In his account of the battle for Berlin, Nicholas Best recounts the horrors. "Hannelore von Cmuda, aged only seventeen, was raped repeatedly by drunken troops, then shot three times and left for dead. Anneliese Antz was dragged from her mother's bed just before dawn and taken screaming to an apartment, where a Soviet officer roughly assaulted her. Her sister Ilse was stripped naked by another soldier who mistook her half-starved body for a man's before realizing his mistake and raping her. 'That's what the Germans did to Russians,' he told her, after he had finished."[41]

The widespread sexual violence was an inhuman orgy of pent-up rage at the Germans, often fueled by alcohol. The men of the Soviet armies knew how the Germans had brutalized the people of their countries after they had invaded. Hitler and Stalin had made a non-aggression pact before the war started, then divided a conquered Poland in 1939. But Nazi war plans included the ultimate conquest of Soviet Russia. Long before he took power, Hitler had made no secret of his hatred of Russia's Bolshevism. He also wanted Russia's enormous natural resources and to enslave its vast population as a labor force.

Many Americans familiar with the Normandy invasion on D-Day as a "turning point" know little of what the Soviets—and generations of Russians—called the "Great Patriotic War": the massive effort to turn back Hitler's invasion of the USSR. Code-named Operation Barbarossa, Hitler's invasion of the Soviet Union began in June 1941 and is considered the greatest invasion in the history of warfare, as an estimated four million Axis soldiers were sent to the Soviet Union. As Axis armies advanced across a broad front into the Soviet Union, millions of Russians, Poles, and other Eastern Europeans were enslaved in concentration camps and labor camps and murdered by the Nazis.

These camps and the enormity of the Nazi crimes had been revealed as the Red Army made its push into Germany. Russian prisoners of Nazis had been caged and starved to death by the millions. "By February 1942, almost 60 percent of 3.35 million Soviet prisoners in German hands had perished," wrote Max Hastings. "By 1945, 3.3 million were dead out of 5.7 million taken captive."[42]

These atrocities came on top of the grotesque numbers of dead in besieged Soviet cities such as Leningrad and Stalingrad, where the casualties were astronomical and unthinkable. According to Hastings, "Since the 1917 Revolution, the population of the Soviet Union had endured the horrors of civil war, famine, oppression, enforced migration and summary injustice. But Barbarossa transcended them all in the absolute human catastrophe that unfolded in its wake, and eventually became responsible for the deaths of *27 million* of Stalin's people, *of whom 16 million were civilians*" (emphasis added).[43]

That was the level of death and destruction that had fueled the vengeance aimed at Germans., meted out in response to the savagery experienced by the Russians and other Eastern Europeans under German hands.

Sweeping into the eastern province of Germany, the Red Army had already shown its ruthlessness, first toward the retreating Nazi soldiers and then, as the German armies were destroyed, more indiscriminately at the civilian population. The frenzy of violence only increased with their arrival in the heart of the Third Reich. "Within a couple of days," wrote historian Antony Beevor, "a pattern emerged of soldiers flashing torches in the faces of women huddled in the bunkers to choose their victims. This process of selection, as opposed to the indiscriminate violence shown earlier, indicates a definite change. By this stage Soviet soldiers started to treat German women more as sexual spoils of war than as substitutes for the Wehrmacht [the overall term for German defense forces] on which to vent their rage."[44]

According to Beevor, estimates of rape victims from the city's two main hospitals ranged from 95,000 to 130,000. One doctor deduced that out of approximately 100,000 women raped in the city, an estimated 10,000 died as a result, mostly from suicide. The death rate was thought to have been much higher among the 1.4 million estimated victims in East Prussia, Pomerania, and Silesia. Altogether, at least two million German women are thought to have been raped, and a substantial minority, if not a majority, appear to have suffered multiple rape.[45]

To many of those who had been victims of the Nazi onslaught, the wholesale destruction of the Third Reich and the devastation brought down on its civilians was nothing more than rough justice. The monstrous assault on Germany's women was taking place even as the Red Army continued its frenzied race to conquer the German capital. For Soviet leader Joseph Stalin's commanders, the grand prize was the Reichstag, Germany's parliament building. Stalin had pitted his generals against one another, daring them to be the first there. The Russians wanted to fly their flag over the dome of the Reichstag in time for May Day, the international celebration of socialism. And they achieved their goal. On May 1, 1945, the red hammer and sickle flag flew over Germany's fallen capital.

———————

Why is the horrific story of the capture and occupation of Berlin by a Soviet army counted as a significant tale of American military history? In fact, many postwar American World War II narratives ignored or at least underplayed this ultimate battle for Germany's capital for a very simple reason: The Americans did not take part in the land battle and wouldn't reach Berlin for several weeks after the city fell. The British and American role in attacking Berlin had been the large-scale air campaign meant to bomb Germany into submission. In postwar American history books, the contribution of the Soviet Union in fighting Hitler—along with the astonishing toll the war had taken on Russia—was largely brushed aside as the tensions between the American and Western European countries on the one side and the Soviet Union and its bloc of communist nations grew increasingly fraught during the Cold War.

During the war in Europe against Nazi Germany, the idea of a future confrontation between the United States and Stalin's Soviet Union was well down on the list of wartime concerns for President Franklin D. Roosevelt and Winston Churchill, England's wartime prime minister. In the 1930s, as Hitler came to power in Germany, both men had been focused on defeating Hitler.

Adolf Hitler made no secret of his plans for German domination of Europe. From the start, he announced that he wanted to reunite the German-speaking peoples separated when the map of Europe was redrawn following the Treaty of Versailles, which ended World War I. He also pledged to rearm Germany so that it would never be forced to accept terms as it had at Versailles in 1919. By 1935, Germany was committed to a massive program of militarization, modernizing its armaments and requiring universal military service.

American attempts to avoid entanglement in these "European" problems led to passage of the Neutrality Act in 1935, which barred the sale of munitions to all belligerents. Facing strong isolationist sentiment led by prominent Americans, including famed pilot and American hero Charles Lindbergh and the automaker and industrialist Henry Ford, as well as key members of Congress, Roosevelt had to swallow the unpleasant pill of remaining on the sidelines.

America's official position remained neutral, and ultra-isolationists of the America First Committee, like Charles Lindbergh, seemed to be in the majority. Lindbergh had visited and openly admired a rebuilt Germany under Hitler as preferable to the "Godless" Soviets. Cautioning that no European nation could stand up to Hitler's Germany, Lindbergh voiced racial sentiments that had more than a whiff of Aryan sensibility and published an article in *Reader's Digest* stating that "our civilization depends on a Western wall of race and arms which can hold back . . . the infiltration of inferior blood."[46]

Like President Woodrow Wilson before World War I, Franklin D. Roosevelt professed a desire to avoid American involvement in this war. Saying, "America actively engages in the search for peace," he recommended "quarantining" the aggressors, without specifically identifying the Germans.

In March 1938, Germany absorbed Austria in the Anschluss (annexation), and in September of that year Hitler demanded the return of the Sudetenland, a German-speaking area that had been incorporated into Czechoslovakia after World War I. At a conference in Munich in late September 1938, the prime ministers of Great Britain and France acceded to Hitler's demand and pressed the Czechs to turn over the land. That was simply Hitler's prelude to a more ambitious land grab. Recognizing the lack of resistance, Hitler boldly took the rest of Czechoslovakia in early 1939. He next set his sights on Poland, demanding that the city of Danzig (modern-day Gdansk) be made part of Germany. Hitler now had Roosevelt's full attention, but Roosevelt lacked the votes at the time even to overturn the Neutrality Act, which prevented him from arming France and Great Britain for the war that everyone now knew was coming.

In August 1939, Germany and the Soviet Union signed their non-aggression pact, a prelude to an attack on Poland begun by Germany on September 1, 1939. France and England could stand by and appease Hitler no longer and both countries declared war on Germany on September 3. Two weeks later, the Soviets invaded Poland from the east and the country was partitioned between the Germans and Soviets.

Hitler sought a quick, decisive victory that would crush France and give Germany almost total control of Western Europe. In World War I, the British and French had been able to fend off the German offensive, leading to the long, agonizing years of vicious but inconclusive trench warfare. But in 1939, the Nazis' plan was for something far more decisive. The Nazi onslaught, the Blitzkrieg ("lightning war"), leveled resistance in Denmark, Norway, the Netherlands, and Belgium. Following the stunning fall of France, and after the British and French armies had been sent reeling from Dunkerque, a French town on the Strait of Dover, Hitler controlled most of Western Europe by the summer of 1940.

Still handcuffed by the political atmosphere in America, a determined Roosevelt, dismayed at the unwillingness of the American people to recognize the threat from Germany, was able to force through Congress a stopgap "cash and carry" law allowing Great Britain and France, the chief allies, to buy arms from the United States. And without proper legal authority, FDR began to sell "surplus" American arms to the British.

In September 1940, just months before the presidential election, Roosevelt was able to push through the Selective Service Act, which imposed military conscription—even though America was officially at peace and isolationism remained a powerful campaign issue in the November election. Running for an unprecedented third term, Roosevelt defeated Republican Wendell Willkie. Previously an interventionist, Willkie had followed public opinion and turned isolationist. And in an October 30, 1940, campaign address in Boston, Roosevelt himself told America's mothers and fathers, "Your boys are not going to be sent into any foreign wars."[47]

After the fall of France, FDR came up with the idea of "trading" aging American destroyers to the British in exchange for naval bases, the deal that was the prelude to the Lend-Lease Act, which eventually allowed the United States to "loan" military equipment to the Allies in return for future repayments "in kind."

Roosevelt simply and brilliantly explained Lend-Lease to the American people at a December 1940 press conference: "Suppose my neighbor's house catches fire. If he can take my garden hose and connect it up with his hydrant, I may help him put out the fire. Now what do I do? I don't say to him, 'Neighbor, my garden hose cost me fifteen dollars; you have to pay me for it.' What is the transaction that goes on? I don't want fifteen dollars—I want my garden hose back after the fire is over."

Then came Pearl Harbor. The fire wasn't over. It had spread wildly across the globe.

At 7 a.m., Hawaiian time, on Sunday, December 7, 1941, two

U.S. Army privates saw on their mobile radar screens more than fifty planes that seemed to be appearing out of the northeast. When they called in the information, they were told it was probably just part of an expected delivery of new B-17s coming from the mainland United States. What they saw was actually the first wave of 183 Japanese planes that had arrived at Hawaii after taking off from Japanese carriers and struck the American naval base with complete surprise.

At 7:58 a.m. the Pearl Harbor command radioed its first message to the world: "AIR RAID PEARL HARBOR. THIS IS NOT A DRILL." An hour later, a second wave of 167 more Japanese aircraft arrived. The two raids, which had lasted only minutes, accounted for eighteen ships sunk, capsized, or damaged, and 292 aircraft, including 117 bombers, damaged or wrecked. And 2,403 Americans, military personnel and civilians at the base, had been killed, with another 1,178 wounded.

The following afternoon, President Roosevelt requested and won a declaration of war against Japan. With that done, Germany declared war on America under the terms of a treaty negotiated with Italy and Japan in September 1940, establishing the so-called Axis. Soon America was at war with Germany and Italy as well as Japan. (Although there were official congressional declarations of war against the three Axis members in 1941, there were actually a total of six World War II war declarations. In June 1942, war was also declared on Bulgaria, Hungary, and Romania—all German allies.)[48]

There is little question that Roosevelt viewed Japan as America's entrée into the European war. But he and Churchill, along with military leaders such as Chief of Staff George C. Marshall and Dwight D. Eisenhower—who had been appointed commander of the American forces a week after Pearl Harbor—all agreed that the Pacific war would be pushed to the backburner and the war in Europe would come first. They also agreed that keeping the Soviet Union as an ally was essential to victory.[49]

A small island nation with limited resources but great ambitions, Japan sought to control the resources and economy of the Asian-Pacific world. That put the highly militarized and industrialized empire on a collision course with the Western nations that had established a colonial presence in the Pacific and Asia and had their own plans for exploiting that part of the world.

Japanese-American relations were already bad in the 1930s, and worsened when the Japanese sank an American warship, the *Panay*, on the Yangtze River late in 1937; it was a clear violation of all treaties and an outright act of war. But America was not ready to go to war over a single ship. Attempting to influence the outcome of China's struggle against Japan, Roosevelt loaned money to the Nationalists in China and began to ban exports to Japan of goods that eventually included gasoline, scrap iron, and oil.

But it was increasingly clear that the Japanese were intent on dominating the Asian world, and they proved themselves quite ruthless in achieving that goal. In Nanking, China, a campaign of rape, murder, and looting committed by the invading Japanese between December 1937 and March 1938 ranks with the worst atrocities in history. An estimated 250,000–300,000 Chinese in Nanking were killed in Japan's attack and occupation of the city beginning in December 1937, often called "the Rape of Nanking."[50]

Japan's wartime record of treatment of conquered people would mirror the worst excesses of the Nazis. Military policy toward prisoners of war—civilian or military—was exceptionally brutal, with many documented accounts of events such as the Bataan Death March, anthrax experiments on prisoners, and the machine-gunning and beheading of survivors of merchant ships sunk by Japanese submarines.[51] Many Koreans still carry historic grudges against the Japanese for the cruelty of their wartime rule, including slave labor and the forced prostitution of thousands of Korean women as sex slaves, who were made to work in brothels servicing Japanese soldiers during Japan's occupation of Korea.*

The Japanese, according to war trial records, also killed at least 131,000 Filipinos. Late in the war, when U.S. forces were poised to retake the Philippines in 1945, there was also a savage round of rapes, mutilations, and executions of Filipinos in Manila by the Japanese. In one such documented incident, 250 starving civilians at St. Paul's College in Manila were herded into a school building and told there was food inside. The Japanese then detonated explosives inside the school, finishing off any survivors with hand grenades.[52]

By late 1941, it had become more than apparent to Roosevelt and many in his administration that war was coming between Japan and the United States—two speeding engines on a breakneck collision course. American and foreign diplomats in Japan dispatched frequent warnings about the Japanese mood. Nearly a year before the Pearl Harbor attack, Joseph Grew, the U.S. ambassador in Tokyo, had wired a specific warning about rumors of an attack on Pearl Harbor. And more significantly, the Japanese diplomatic code had been broken by American intelligence. Almost all messages between Tokyo and its embassy in Washington were being intercepted and understood by Washington.

But this is where human error, the frailty of judgment, and overconfidence bordering on arrogance—and perhaps even American and British racial attitudes—take over. Supremely assured of their defenses, the navy commanders on Pearl Harbor had been warned about the possibility of attack, but little was done to secure the island. The "little

---

* "During Japan's occupation in World War II, as many as 200,000 women were rounded up across Asia to work as sex slaves—the Japanese euphemism is 'comfort women'—for the Japanese Army. Many of the women came from China and South Korea but others were from the Philippines, Indonesia and Taiwan." Carol Giacomo, "Did Japan Need Comfort Women?," *New York Times*, May 15, 2013.

yellow men," as Churchill sometimes disparaged the Japanese and as Roosevelt thought of them, were believed to be incapable of such a feat of arms. Most American military planners expected a Japanese attack to come in the Philippines, America's major base in the Pacific; the American naval fortifications at Pearl Harbor were believed to be too strong to attack, as well as too far away for the Japanese. There was also a sense that any attack on Pearl Harbor would be easily repulsed. The general impression, even back in the navy secretary's office in Washington, was that the Japanese would get a bad spanking, and America would still get the war it wanted in Europe.

While conspiracy theorists maintain that the attack on Pearl Harbor was deliberately "invited" or "welcomed" by FDR in the hopes of pulling America into the war and that specific warnings were ignored or disregarded, many historians rebut the idea. But there is no question that the devastation of the American installation at Pearl Harbor was totally unexpected. Even today, the tally of the attack is astonishing.

A day after the surprise Japanese strike, Roosevelt delivered his war message to Congress. The long-running battle between American isolationists and interventionists was over.

———————

The long road to Berlin that began in earnest for the United States after the Pearl Harbor attack on December 7, 1941, would take the nation's military to the precipice many times. The story of fighting a devastating and costly war on two fronts—in Europe and in the Pacific—is an epic tale of American resourcefulness and ingenuity as well as battlefield courage. Perhaps more than anything else, America had been able to outproduce its enemies as the nation was turned into what Roosevelt himself called the "Arsenal of Democracy."

During the war, America produced some 297,000 planes, 86,000 tanks, 2.4 million trucks and jeeps, 12,000 ships, and enormous quantities of other vehicles, arms, and munitions. As was true in World War I, America's industrial capacity to mass-produce war materials provided a significant key to victory.

"The 'Arsenal of Democracy' policy also assumed that the American scientific-engineering community would ensure that the armed forces enjoyed technological superiority over the Axis," wrote military historians Allan R. Millett and Peter Maslowski. "After some pulling and hauling between the various military and civilian components of the research and development community, the administration established the Office of Scientific Research and Development under Dr. Vannevar Bush.... An active lobbyist for war-related research, Bush won an important early battle by winning draft exemptions for 10,000 critical scientists and engineers." As America went on full war footing, university and industrial research laboratories turned to war projects with generous government funding.[53]

The most obvious and far-reaching product of this collaboration between government, industry, and academia was the Manhattan Project, which would eventually create the atomic bomb. But other developments that emerged from this collaboration included radar, sonar for detecting submarines, drugs to combat infection and tropical diseases, as well as many specific weapons and innovations, like amphibious vehicles and bomb guidance systems.

Over the course of the next few years, from early 1942 through August 1945, American troops would fight in a series of legendary battles around the globe. Far-off battlefields on both the European and Pacific fronts soon became part of American military legend: North Africa, Anzio, Sicily, the beaches of Normandy, the Bulge in Europe; in the Pacific Theater, Midway, Guadalcanal, Iwo Jima, Tarawa, and Okinawa.

But not Berlin, seat of Hitler's empire and home of the Führer himself.

As the war against Nazi Germany was winding down, Supreme Allied Commander General Dwight D. "Ike" Eisenhower, America's greatest World War II hero, made the decision to allow the Soviet Red Army to complete the capture of Berlin in April and May 1945. With the war nearly won in the early months of 1945 as the Allies began the last push into the German heartland, Eisenhower's decision was far-reaching. He would leave Berlin to the Russians, in fact confirming a decision made earlier at the summit meeting of Roosevelt, Churchill, and Stalin at Yalta.

It was a decision with which some of his British allies disagreed, including most famously and vociferously Winston Churchill. It would become a vehicle for a sharp political attack against President Eisenhower by Senator Joseph McCarthy, who when he began his notorious campaign against communist espionage and influence in America accused the general of surrendering Berlin and East Germany to the communists. But in wartime 1945, a domestic political controversy down the road was not on Eisenhower's radar. He had only one overriding goal: End the war as quickly as possible, with as little loss of American life as possible.

By the end of February 1945, Eisenhower had almost three million U.S., British, French, Canadian, and other Allied troops at his command to push the last of the German armies back and finish off the Nazis. The Soviets had four million men moving quickly across a two-hundred-mile front from the east. By the end of February, the Soviets were already near Berlin.

"It was clear to Eisenhower," wrote Eisenhower biographer Jean Edward Smith, "that the Red Army would reach the German capital long before the Allies."[34]

Without letting on, the cagey Stalin—a dictator whose brutality places him alongside history's worst mass murderers—sent a telegraph message to Eisenhower. "Berlin has lost its previous strategic significance. Therefore the Soviet Supreme Command is thinking of assigning second-level forces to the Berlin side."[55]

But the Soviet leader clearly prized Berlin as a trophy, and he was going to challenge his generals to race each other to the German capital. In their desire to satisfy Stalin, his commanders would sometimes recklessly and ruthlessly sacrifice thousands of Red Army soldiers in frontal assaults in the sprint to Berlin.

Why did Stalin want Berlin so badly in the first place?

"Stalin was determined to win the race even if the Americans declined to compete," Stalin biographer Robert Service concluded. "He was worried that the USA and the United Kingdom might do a deal with the Germans for an end to the fighting. This could lead to a joint crusade against the Soviet Union; and even if this did not happen, the Germans might surrender to the Western allies and deprive the Soviet Union of post-war gains."[56]

Berlin was the jewel in the crown that Stalin desperately wanted to symbolize the communist victory over fascism for the Russian people and Soviet republics. Certainly the prestige that would come with entering the fallen capital of the Nazi Reich was uppermost in Stalin's mind. It would be a propaganda coup to show the world that the Red Army, which suffered losses on a massive scale in World War II—along with the many millions of civilian Russian lives lost—had delivered the fatal blow to Germany.

But far more significant than mere propaganda value was the redrawing of the boundaries of postwar Europe. Political dominion over Eastern Europe by the Soviets was Stalin's chief aim.

At the Yalta Conference in February 1945, Stalin had joined a then seriously ailing Franklin D. Roosevelt and Winston Churchill in signing the Declaration on Liberated Europe, in which the three Allied leaders pledged that after the war ended and stability had been achieved, European nations would have democratically elected governments. In hindsight it was a pledge that Stalin clearly had no intention of honoring.

A few weeks after Germany formally surrendered on May 8, the German capital remained under Soviet control. At a meeting at a palace in Potsdam, fifteen miles from downtown Berlin, in July and August 1945, Stalin conferred with Roosevelt's successor, President Harry Truman. Roosevelt had died on April 12, 1945, of a cerebral hemorrhage. At this meeting, the four main Allied countries—the British, France, the United States, and the Soviet Union—made the agreement to split occupied Germany into eastern and western halves, and also to divide Berlin, which was within the eastern, Soviet-occupied half of Germany.

Stalin also had another important trump card, which he was ready to play. The Soviet Union had never declared war on Japan, and the American war effort in the Pacific was grinding through a series of costly and brutal battles for the islands that were a series of stepping-stones leading to a potential American invasion of the Japanese mainland. Before his death, Roosevelt and then his successor Truman, along with America's military brain trust, wanted Stalin to declare war on Japan. The Soviet dictator would eventually do so, but not out of charity toward his allies. The Soviets and Japan were going to compete for power and influence in the Asian-Pacific world and Stalin wanted to get what he could out of any peacetime bargain as an ally.

But there was yet another even more compelling reason that Stalin was so eager to capture Berlin. Stalin's intelligence agents had informed him that Nazi scientists inside the city were working on developing the atomic bomb. Long before Stalin met President Truman at Potsdam, the secrets of the American Manhattan Project had already made their way to the Kremlin through the extensive efforts of the Soviet espionage network. Stalin knew that the Americans were nearly done developing the atomic bomb, but Eisenhower was in the dark. When he decided to allow Stalin to take Berlin, America's supreme commander in Europe still didn't know about the atomic bomb. It was only at the Potsdam Conference in July 1945 that Eisenhower learned of the atomic bomb's existence, when Truman announced a successful test of the weapon in New Mexico.* He was also informed then that the United States was preparing to drop the bomb on Japan unless the Japanese surrendered.

When told of the bomb by War Secretary Stimson, Eisenhower was, in the words of biographer Jean Edward Smith, "overcome by depression" and "appalled." As Smith quotes Eisenhower: "I voiced to him [Stimson] my grave misgivings, first on the basis of my belief that Japan was already defeated and that dropping the bomb was completely unnecessary, and secondly because I thought that our country should avoid shocking world opinion by the use of a weapon whose employment was no longer mandatory as a measure to save American lives....I disliked seeing the United States take the lead in introducing into war something as horrible and destructive as this new weapon was described to be."[57]

Joseph Stalin had no such moral misgivings; the Soviets had been pursuing their own atomic program for years.

Given all of Eisenhower's other stated reasons for leaving Berlin to the Soviets, it is unlikely this information would have altered his tactical thinking in the spring of 1945. But it is now clear that one of the chief reasons for Stalin to secure Berlin was to reach the Kaiser Wilhelm Institute for Physics. Stalin believed that the Nazi quest for an atomic bomb was being carried out there and that the research laboratory might have the uranium the Soviets needed. The Soviets

---

* In his own memoir, *Crusade in Europe*, Eisenhower wrote, "I did not know then, of course, that an army of scientists had been engaged in the production of the weapon" (p. 443). However, General Leslie Groves, the head of the secret Manhattan Project, had alerted Eisenhower to the possible use of a radiation weapon by the Germans prior to the D-Day landings of June 6, 1944.

also wanted to capture German scientists capable of processing that uranium.[58]

The Third Reich was an early leader in the race to develop the atomic bomb. The Germans had a wealth of scientists and a plentiful supply of uranium from the Congo. The great British military historian John Keegan wrote forebodingly, "The men who produced the V-1 [the first cruise missile] were aeronautical technicians of the first class. Had Hitler had the vision to devote a proportion of Germany's scientific effort similar to that given to other weapon programmes to nuclear weapons, it is possible, with the V-weapons, he could have won the war. The Nazi nuclear research programme was dissipated between too many competing research organisations."[59] Historian Michael Dobbs agreed: "The German atomic project had failed to live up to its potential due to infighting among the scientists and a lack of interest from Nazi officials.... Nevertheless, the essential components were all in place, scattered across a no-man's land between the advancing American and Russian armies."[60]

In March 1945, a U.S. bombing raid destroyed a German factory where uranium ore was being processed. The location was within the future Soviet zone and the raid was meant to deny the Russians the uranium. Another raid turned up uranium at a salt mine in Germany, and an American team that had been responsible for destroying or otherwise sabotaging the German atomic program had also captured several key German physicists, even as Stalin was getting ready to assault Berlin.

On arriving in Berlin, the Russians found the Kaiser Wilhelm Institute wrecked. But they also found the blueprints of the German nuclear project, revealing that the Germans were well behind the Americans and the Soviets in the race to develop an atomic weapon.

Later, the Russians uncovered some of the German uranium hidden on the outskirts of Berlin. They also captured several German scientists and "invited them," for a few days, as one of the scientists later noted, in the most profound sense of an invitation you can't refuse. But the "few days" lasted a decade for the Germans who were held by the Soviets. The Russians had their prized German scientists and tons of high-grade uranium. As Dobbs summarized in his history of these developments, "The Americans may have been correct in believing that they had been dealt a royal flush in the form of the world's first atomic bomb. But the nuclear poker tournament was far from over. In fact, it had barely begun."[61]

## AFTERMATH

By July 1945, when President Truman met with Winston Churchill and Stalin in Potsdam, not far from the ruins of downtown Berlin, it was a carefully choreographed victors' moment. American and British armies had moved into the devastated and divided city of Berlin. The weeks of battle had left it in ruins, most of its infrastructure destroyed, its buildings looted, and its civilian population, largely reduced to beggar status, in shock.

But on the afternoon of July 31, what was soon to be known as the Cold War between America and the Soviets already had turned very hot.

Responding to a report of looting by Russian troops, American soldiers went to one of Berlin's railroad stations. Thousands of refugees from eastern Germany, now in Soviet control, were pouring into Berlin. These "Displaced Persons"—as they would come to be officially called—were frisked by Red Army soldiers as they arrived in the station, usually carrying everything they owned in meager suitcases and bags. Many of the Soviet soldiers were taking watches, currency, and other valuables from the refugees. As the station was in the American sector of divided Berlin, the Americans felt obligated to protect the "Displaced Persons." When an American soldier tried to stop three Russians who were walking away with some loot, one appeared to reach for a gun. The American soldier shot the Russian, a major. He died two days later.

For the two former Allied nations now in occupied Berlin, the exuberant greetings exchanged when the two armies met in February 1945, just a few months before at the Elbe River, had been replaced by growing tensions and animosities.

A more typical incident was described by historian Michael Dobbs. It was an exchange between American general Frank "Howlin'" Howley, commandant of the American sector in Berlin, and his Russian counterpart:

> "You must control and discipline your troops," the American commanding general lectured his Soviet counterpart. "You can't expect us to let them run wild in our sector, looting and shooting, without doing something about it."
>
> "Maybe they had a few drinks and the wine caused them to get out of hand," conceded the Russian general. "But we don't shoot Americans when they come in our sector."

The American general explained that shooting first was "an American tradition, growing out of frontier days when 'the man who shot first lived.'" Dobbs adds, "History does not record what the Russians made of the patently self-serving explanation."[62]

But the incident was part of the increasingly dangerous divide between Soviets and Americans, who clearly possessed a "cowboy" attitude. During the first five months in Berlin, Americans shot and killed ten Russians, according to Dobbs, while suffering zero casualties.[63]

It would also be impossible to recount the brutal tale of the Soviet "rape of Germany" without exploring the behavior of Americans in occupied Europe. For a long time, postwar history offered a portrait of a largely one-dimensional Greatest Generation army that had fought heroically on the beaches of Normandy and across the heart of Germany, to be welcomed by the liberated people of France and Germany. Images of smiling girls welcoming happy-go-lucky GIs were captured and reproduced in America's magazines. And to be sure, there were many such scenes.

Here again, facts are troublesome things. While rape of European women by Americans during the occupation occurred at nowhere near the rampaging levels of the Red Army in Berlin, it certainly occurred. "In the summer of 1944," Mary Louise Roberts wrote in *What Soldiers Do*, "Norman women launched a wave of rape accusations against American soldiers, threatening to destroy the erotic fantasy at the heart of the operation. The specter of rape transformed the GI from rescuer-warrior to violent intruder."[64]

The sexual assaults committed by American GIs were not limited to France. In Germany, where Eisenhower had issued a widely ignored "non-fraternization" order during the occupation, American officials had to recognize the ugly truth. Saul K. Padover, an American officer in the Psychological Warfare section (and later a prominent American historian), wrote, "The behavior of some of the troops was nothing to brag about, particularly after they came across cases of cognac and barrels of wine. I am mentioning this only because there is a tendency to think that only Russians rape and loot. After a battle, soldiers are pretty much the same."[65]

But there was an equally disturbing side of this story in the official American response. When American officials prosecuted soldiers for rape or other crimes against civilians, they overwhelmingly targeted the relatively small number of black troops in occupied Europe. According to historian Michael Hitchcock, "Evidence from U.S. Army records shows conclusively that although blacks were a small statistical minority of U.S troops in the European Theater—less than 10 percent—they were targeted by French and American authorities alike, as the scapegoats for widespread American misbehavior and sexual violence. Black American soldiers were charged and convicted and punished for crimes against French people in numbers vastly disproportionate to the statistical presence."[66]

While clearly dwarfed by the number of mass rapes of German women by Soviet soldiers, the relatively small number of German rapes by Americans reported by the judge advocate general—552 cases were considered by the JAG in Berlin—surely must have been underreported. With venereal disease also spreading among troops, and the issue of rape troubling American authorities, General Eisenhower lifted his "fraternization" ban in July 1945, acknowledging the reality that it was a failure.

———

In a war of such catastrophic death and destruction on a mind-boggling scale, the fall of Berlin stands as one of the most gruesome chapters in that terrible conflict, as the widespread rape and massacre of German civilians by Soviet troops followed. But American wartime history has largely ignored the story, overlooked because the Americans were not involved and the Soviet role in World War II was being disposed of in an Orwellian "memory hole," disappearing from the "Good War" narrative. Still, it is fair to ask if an American and British attempt to take Berlin would have made a meaningful difference.

Assessing Eisenhower's decision to "allow" the Soviets to take Berlin, Max Hastings concluded, "It is hard…to make a plausible case that any of this changed the postwar political map of Europe, as the supreme commander's detractors claimed. The Allied occupation zones had been agreed upon many months earlier, and confirmed at the Yalta summit in February [1945]. The Russians got to Eastern Europe first. To have frustrated their imperialistic purposes, sparing central Europe from a Soviet tyranny in succession to that of the Nazis, it would have been necessary for the Western Allies to fight a very different and more ruthless war, at much higher cost in casualties....Such a course was politically and militarily unthinkable, whatever Churchill's brief delusions that eastern European freedom might be recovered by force."[67]

This battle, and its impact, stand as a crucial piece of usually over-looked American history because of the decision-making that was involved. Just as significant are the long-term reverberations of the Soviet control of Berlin. As Germany and Berlin were divided into East and West sectors by the victorious allies, Berlin would become the hot-button center of Cold War intrigue and potential atomic war for a good part of the next half century.

After the war and over the coming years, Berlin emerged as the lightning rod for international Cold War tensions, as the divided city lay completely within East Germany, the larger Soviet area of control. In 1947, the United States proposed the European Recovery Program, or Marshall Plan, which aimed to improve European economies in part through American aid. The three zones of Berlin controlled by the Western powers—zones later to be merged into a single West Berlin—agreed to use the same currency. But the Soviet Union refused to accept the Marshall Plan, bemoaning "American economic imperialism."

Stalin saw the Recovery Program as an attempt to undermine communist control and he authorized a blockade of western Berlin, which began on June 24, 1948. Unable to travel through Soviet-occupied Germany to reach the city, the Western powers began the Berlin Airlift, supplying the western sectors of the surrounded city by air. This stalemate persisted for nearly a year, with neither side willing to back down. At last, on May 12, 1949, the Soviets lifted the blockade after the Western powers had increased deliveries each month of that year.

Despite the promises made at Yalta, where the agreements with

Roosevelt and Churchill had included democratically elected governments in Europe, Stalin was clearly installing ruthless communist
governments in the Eastern European countries the Kremlin would
control with an iron fist.

In the years that followed, what Winston Churchill would
famously call the Iron Curtain divided Europe. By the time Stalin
died on March 5, 1953, he had established a rigidly enforced Soviet
hold over much of Eastern Europe, turning countries like Poland,
Hungary, and Czechoslovakia into client police states where any
whiff of dissent was squashed by secret police and Soviet tanks.

In the face of that repression, some 2.5 million East Germans,
attempting to escape the poor economic conditions and police-state
policies of the Soviet-sponsored East German government, had fled
to West Berlin by 1961. To halt these escapes, that year the East Berlin
government began building a wall dividing the two city sectors. At
first a simple barbed wire fence, the Berlin Wall eventually grew to
a nearly hundred-mile-long concrete barricade topped by a smooth
pipe and barbed wire to prevent people from scaling it. Eventually
the infamous barrier was bolstered by the addition of anti-vehicle
trenches, guard posts, soldiers patrolling with dogs, and raked sand
that showed any footprints. By the time the barrier was removed on
November 9, 1989, nearly two hundred people had been killed while
trying to make it over the infamous Wall.

———

Hildegard Knef, the young actress who attempted to make a stand
against the Red Army, was captured and sent to a Soviet prison camp
in Poland. She eventually made her way back to East Berlin and continued her stage, film, and singing career. She died of emphysema in
2002 at age seventy-six.

The anonymous journalist who wrote of life in the Berlin siege also survived. As the city was going to be divided, she wrote a last diary entry dated June 22, 1945: "I have to find a flint lighter for the stove; the matches are all gone. I have to mop up the rain puddles in the apartment. The roof is leaking again....I have to run around and look for some greens along the street kerbs, and queue for groats [a form of crushed cereal grain]. I don't have a feeding time for my soul....God knows what we'll all end up eating. I think I'm far from any life threatening extreme, but I don't really know how far. I only know I want to survive—against all sense and reason, just like an animal."[68]

———

Dwight D. Eisenhower came home from the war as America's greatest hero—a role once held by George Washington and Ulysses S. Grant, both future presidents. President Harry Truman reportedly offered to serve as Eisenhower's vice president if the conqueror of Hitler wanted to run as a Democrat in 1948. Expressing little interest in politics, Ike declined and then served as the president of Columbia University from 1948 to 1952, taking leave to lead the recently created North Atlantic Treaty Organization (NATO) as supreme commander. After a second approach to run for the White House by Democratic president Truman, Eisenhower declared himself a Republican, accepted the party's 1952 nomination, and won easily in a landslide. One of his stated campaign pledges was to end America's involvement in Korea, a Cold War confrontation that had boiled over into an open war, with Communist China waiting on the fringes.

When he took office in 1953, Eisenhower had somewhat altered his views on atomic weapons and pushed his military advisers to find, according to John Lewis Gaddis's Cold War history, "ways in which the United States might use both strategic and recently developed 'tactical' nuclear weapons to bring the fighting to an end."[69] But a year later, in March 1954, when the United States tested a new thermo-nuclear device at Bikini Atoll, the results changed Eisenhower's mind. Once opposed to the use of the bomb at Hiroshima and Nagasaki, he was more convinced by the results of a test known as "Bravo," when the test blast—750 times the size of the Hiroshima bomb—spread radioactive fallout for hundreds of miles.

The race for Berlin's atomic secrets long over, the Soviets had successfully tested their first atomic bomb in August 1949. By the early 1950s, the United States and Soviet Union—soon to be joined in a nuclear club that included Great Britain (1950), France (1962), and China (1964)—possessed weapons capable of ending civilization. Men like Winston Churchill and senior Soviet leader Georgii Malen-kov, the latter one of the three men who initially succeeded Stalin on his death in 1953, now believed that such weapons could never be used. It would mean "equality of annihilation," as Churchill told the House of Commons.[70]

Americans and the rest of the world had entered the era of nuclear deterrence and eventually "mutual assured destruction."

On March 5, 1953, shortly after President Eisenhower had taken office in January, America's World War II ally turned Cold War adversary Joseph Stalin died. With a power struggle under way for leadership of the Soviet Union and Cold War tensions running high, Eisenhower a few weeks later delivered an address known as the "Cross of Iron" speech.[71] Outlining how many schools and power plants could be built and how many people could be fed with the millions of dollars being allocated for Cold War weaponry, Eisenhower warned, "Under the cloud of threatening war, it is humanity hanging from a cross of iron."

Born in Texas and raised a barefoot Kansas farm boy, the hero of World War II and now leader of the free world saw a global scene utterly transformed. The Europe that existed before World War II was gone. Under Stalin, the Soviet Union had expanded its military strength, installed Soviet-style police-state governments throughout Eastern Europe, and exploded an atomic weapon. China, once dominated by Western colonial powers, had fallen to Mao Zedong's communist rule in 1949.

All the rules of war and national security had been rewritten. Throughout most of its history, America had fought its wars and gone back to "normal" once the fighting had ended.

There would be a new normal. In this new global landscape, as military historians Allan R. Millett and Peter Maslowski wrote, "The creation of nuclear weapons and their adaptation to intercontinental bombers stripped the shield of time and space from American security. Amid the casualties of World War II lay the corpse of traditional American defense policy....Instead of waiting for general war to engulf the United States or depending upon the nation's industrial and manpower potential to discourage potential enemies, the United States adopted the strategy of deterrence."[72]

Before the advent of these weapons, and the jets and missiles to carry them across oceans, the United States was content to remain safe within its borders, largely avoiding involvement in overseas conflicts and responding to a security emergency when necessary. Americans had a generally long history of keeping out of foreign business—unless it coincided with emerging American interests, as it had in the Philippines and in numerous other small incursions and invasions America had undertaken in the early twentieth century.

But the new realities of the American century, as it was being called, the need to expand American businesses beyond domestic markets into emerging international markets, taking a share of natural resources overseas—oil chief among them—and a superpower confrontation with the Soviets meant that protecting America from threats to its security and economic future could no longer be left to the oceans that separated the United States from the world. Gone too were the days of the iconic American boys who left farms, jobs, colleges, and sweethearts behind to grab their guns and defend the nation. The much-revered but somewhat mythical Minuteman narrative, in which brave Americans dropped what they were doing and stood up to defend their country, would no longer suffice in a world in which communism was on the march and national security now called for an army that could fight two wars at the same time.

The new reality of deterrence meant possessing weapons of mass destruction while also creating a standing, professional global military force so powerful that it could meet any conventional military challenge, and whose very existence could in theory stave off any threats. In 1950, the recently created National Security Council produced a document known as the "Bible of American National Security." As military historians Fred Anderson and Andrew Cayton described it, "The document, whose contents were soon to be an open secret, pledged the United States to massive defense spending to be prepared for war at a moment's notice. It assumed that the struggle against international communism permeated all aspects of American life."[73]

From domestic politics to defense budgets and every foreign policy issue confronting America, Cold War considerations now drove America's decision-making. One of the most consequential of those decisions was a peaceful one intended to rebuild free market economies in war-ravaged Western Europe, but named for a former soldier. In 1948, the United States embarked on the most successful of its postwar undertakings in creating the European Recovery Program—best known as the Marshall Plan.

It was first described in a June 5, 1947, commencement address at Harvard by George C. Marshall, then Truman's secretary of state. One of the chief architects of the World War II victory as Franklin D. Roosevelt's army chief of staff, Marshall described a program that became a \$13 billion* effort to rebuild the capitalist democracies of war-torn Europe. This ambitious foreign aid package spawned a remarkable period of swift economic recovery and growth, rebuilding devastated industries and cities in sixteen Western European nations, including the western portion of defeated Germany. Twenty-two European countries had been invited—including Poland, Czechoslovakia, Hungary, Bulgaria, and Albania—all future communist states. The sixteen European states that accepted America's help and terms were Britain, France, Italy, Belgium, Luxembourg, the Netherlands, Denmark, Norway, Sweden, Switzerland, Greece, Turkey, Ireland, Iceland, Austria, and Portugal.

The Soviet Union and Spain (then under General Francisco Franco's fascist rule) were not invited. But the Soviets made sure, as Anthony Judt pointed out, "No future Communist states took part in the European Recovery Program or received a dollar in Marshall aid."[74]

The Marshall Plan was the plowshares side of the Cold War. But the swords were still there. Buttressing the trade relations between the United States and these European countries was the creation of the North Atlantic Treaty Organization (NATO) on April 4, 1949, a military alliance of the United States and Western European democracies to fend off threats from Soviet-dominated Eastern Europe. In the words of the NATO treaty, "An armed attack against one or more of them...shall be considered an attack against them all."

For nearly half a century, from the end of World War II until the Berlin Wall came down in 1989 and the Soviet Union collapsed in the 1990s, Europe was a nuclear-armed camp, with opposing conventional

---

* "A Marshall Plan at the beginning of the twenty-first century," notes Anthony Judt in *Postwar*, "would cost about \$201 billion."

and atomic weapons aimed across the continent. The United States and its European allies in the late 1940s prepared for another land war or potential nuclear exchange, hoping to contain communism and deter another war for Europe.

The stark reality of the Cold War—the political, economic, and military threat communism represented to Americans—and the fears it engendered also transformed America's entire defense structure after World War II. And American airpower, demonstrated in the bombing assault on Berlin, would move to the head of the class. The army and navy, the traditional backbone of America's defenses, would be supplanted by the Strategic Air Command (SAC), created in 1946, which would become the nation's first line of defense and deterrence as SAC bombers were charged with delivering America's growing nuclear stockpile.

In 1947, during the Truman administration, the National Security Act began completely realigning America's military structure to streamline the nation's defense readiness and increase efficiency in what had become a huge bureaucracy during World War II.

Under the law, the cabinet-level War and Navy departments that had existed since the early days of the republic were merged into the National Military Establishment, changed in 1949 to the Department of Defense, and led by a civilian secretary of defense. In another crucial reorganization, the Joint Chiefs of Staff (JCOS) was created to bring together the heads of the separate services, including the newly created U.S. Air Force, which had formerly been the U.S. Army Air Forces. The role of the air force in the nation's defenses would quickly lead to the new service winning the largest share of growing defense budgets. The act also created several new agencies that are now fixtures of the American landscape: The Central Intelligence Agency (CIA) grew out of the wartime spy agency known as the Office of Special Services (OSS); the National Security Council

(NSC)* was formed to advise the president on all national security issues; and the National Security Resources Board was born as an agency that advised the president on manpower, natural resources, and science issues in times of mobilization for war.

The Department of Defense would also be increasingly identified as "the Pentagon," after the iconic five-sided structure in which it is housed. Groundbreaking for the Pentagon—the world's largest office building, with five million square feet of floor space when completed—took place in 1941. The new building was dedicated in January 1943, an incredible achievement given wartime constraints and the building's size (occupying some 115 acres) and design complexity.

With wartime manpower shortages, black workers had helped to complete the massive building project, creating job-site racial tensions. When Franklin D. Roosevelt toured the nearly completed facility, he asked why it had so many washrooms and learned a harsh reality. Virginia state law at the time required segregated bathrooms and so the Pentagon was built with separate toilet facilities for whites and blacks, although they were never identified that way.

The U.S. military was totally segregated during World War II and immediately afterward, although black units were largely commanded by white officers. That changed in one sweeping stroke of

---

* The NSC is not to be confused with the NSA, or National Security Agency. Created in 1952, the NSA was originally charged with monitoring communications and gathering electronic intelligence. The NSA is at the center of the controversy created when Edward Snowden, working as an independent contractor for the NSA, leaked a massive trove of NSA secrets over the Internet. Among those documents were budget figures showing that the total intelligence budget request in 2012 was more than $52 billion, with the CIA requesting $14.7 billion and the NSA $10.8 billion, according to the *New York Times*. See Scott Shane, "New Leaked Document Outlines U.S. Spending on Intelligence Agencies," August 29, 2013, http://www.nytimes.com/2013/08/30/us/politics/leaked-document-outlines-us-spending-on-intelligence.html?hp&pagewanted=all&_r=0.

Harry Truman's pen when he issued Presidential Order Number 9981 on July 26, 1948, desegregating the American armed services.

In a Defense Department history of the integration of the armed forces, Brigadier General James Collins Jr. commented, "The integration of the armed forces was a momentous event in our military and national history.... The experiences in World War II and the postwar pressures generated by the civil rights movement compelled all the services—Army, Navy, Air Force, and Marine Corps—to reexamine their traditional practices of segregation. While there were differences in the ways that the services moved toward integration, all were subject to the same demands, fears, and prejudices and had the same need to use their resources in a more rational and economical way."[75]

During the Korean War, American forces fought for the first time in completely integrated units. Many historians of the military and the civil rights era have pointed to the gradual full integration of the American military as a pivotal step in the wider acceptance of integration in American society over the next few decades. Once the brotherhood of the foxhole proved that black men in Korea served with bravery, patriotism, and sacrifice—qualities African-American soldiers had proven in battle since the Revolution and every American conflict since—long-harbored racial attitudes in the army gradually improved. When the meritocracy of the army finally allowed blacks to move up the ranks, it was another significant step for civil rights.

The Cold War had fundamentally changed American society and the way it thought about war. In his farewell speech as president, Dwight Eisenhower famously spoke about the transformation of American military power:

> Until the latest of our world conflicts, the United States had no armaments industry. American makers of plowshares could, with time and as required, make swords as well. But now we can no lon-

ger risk emergency improvisation of national defense; we have been compelled to create a permanent armaments industry of vast proportions.... This conjunction of an immense military establishment and a large arms industry is new in the American experience. The total influence—economic, political, even spiritual—is felt in every city, every State house, every office of the Federal government.... In the councils of government, we must guard against the acquisition of unwarranted influence, whether sought or unsought, by the military industrial complex.[76]

The other most significant change in how America was battling communism's spread was the growing involvement of the newly created Central Intelligence Agency. What was once the province of the army—gathering and analyzing military intelligence—or the State Department—cracking diplomatic codes and reading other people's mail—was now going to be the business of America's new generation of professional spies. With fewer than two thousand veterans of the wartime OSS left by the end of 1945, America had no meaningful intelligence-gathering capability as the Cold War opened. And as Tim Weiner writes in his history of the CIA, "There would be no coherent intelligence reporting in the American government for many years to come."[77]

The CIA was born without a specific mandate to conduct secret operations overseas. Initially built with a small budget, the agency was always caught up in the turf wars fought between the Pentagon and State Department, which both wanted to exert control over intelligence and America's foreign policy. But the CIA's early leaders bent a piece of the National Security Act that blandly stated the agency would perform "other functions and duties related to intelligence affecting the national security." As Weiner writes, "In time, hundreds of major covert actions—eighty-one of them during Truman's second term—would be driven through the loophole." The loophole widened when the CIA was specifically instructed to execute "covert psychological operations designed to counter Soviet and Soviet-inspired activities."[78]

After successfully sponsoring a coup in Iran in 1953, which replaced the elected Soviet-leaning government with the pro-American shah, the CIA was emboldened. And when Cuba fell to Fidel Castro's Soviet-sponsored communists on January 1, 1959, the CIA's role was expanded to a nearly obsessive mandate to overthrow Castro, with mostly disastrous results for the new administration of John F. Kennedy.

In 1960, Kennedy had campaigned against Richard Nixon, Eisenhower's vice president, on a so-called missile gap that existed between the United States and the Soviet Union. Following his extremely close victory over Nixon, Kennedy was going to cement his anticommunist credentials in Cuba, at the Bay of Pigs. Planned by the CIA, the Bay of Pigs invasion in April 1961 proved a debacle for President Kennedy when a CIA-backed army of Cuban rebels was caught on the beaches of Cuba in a failed counterrevolution that left Castro even stronger.

Emboldened by this stinging American military and propaganda defeat, the Soviets began to move missiles into Cuba, countering U.S. Jupiter missiles that had been placed in Turkey as a threat to the Soviets. This set off the next nuclear showdown, in the Cuban Missile Crisis of October 1962, and a negotiated end to a tense confrontation that nearly led to all-out war. It concluded in part with a secret U.S.-Soviet agreement to remove the missiles from Turkey, "a secret sweetener that promised the withdrawal of U.S. missiles from Turkey within six months after the crisis was resolved," as Graham Allison described it an *Foreign Affairs* on the fiftieth anniversary of the crisis. "The sweetener was kept so secret that even most members of the ExComm [an ad hoc Executive Committee] deliberating with Kennedy on the final evening were in the dark, unaware that during the dinner break, the president had sent his brother Bobby to deliver this message to the Soviet ambassador."[79]

The world had tiptoed past a nuclear showdown that could have, by some estimates, "led to the deaths of 100 million Americans and over 100 million Russians."[80] But Kennedy would remain preoccupied with the anticommunist fight there and in other hot spots around the world.

The next superpower showdown was already under way. Vietnam, a small country in Southeast Asia, was also a divided nation. Once known as French Indo-China, Vietnam had won its independence from France after a long, bitter struggle, and the country was partitioned into North and South in 1954. At the time, Eisenhower had warned that if Vietnam fell to communism, it would be like a "falling domino."

Once barely known to most Americans, Vietnam would soon become a household word.

## Chapter Five

→><←

# The "Living-Room War"

### *Hué, South Vietnam—February 1968*

"If we must fight, we will fight. You will kill ten of my men but we will kill one of yours. And in the end it is you that will tire."[1]
—*North Vietnamese Communist Party leader Ho Chi Minh*
*(September 1946)*

"Finally, you have broader considerations that might follow what you would call the 'falling domino' principle. You have a row of dominoes set up, you knock over the first one, and what will happen to the last one is the certainty that it will go over very quickly. So you could have a beginning of a disintegration that would have the most profound influences."
—*President Dwight D. Eisenhower (April 1954)*

"There were more scenes of soldiers, crouching and standing, firing toward the distant line of trees, and later, up in the sky, far in the distance, the two helicopters....CBS correspondent Morley Safer came on to say that there had probably been only three or four Vietcong snipers, that nobody knew whether or

not the southern troops had killed them, and that was the way
it often was in Vietnam."[2]

—*Michael Arlen (1966)*

"It was the strangest thing we have ever gotten mixed up with.
We didn't understand the Vietnamese or the situation, or what
kind of war it was. By the time we found out, it was too late."[3]

—*General Bruce Palmer Jr. (1975)*

"You should never let television on the battlefield."[4]

—*General Maxwell Taylor (1987)*

# Milestones in the Vietnam War

## 1963

**November** Officers from the Army of the Republic of Vietnam (ARVN) overthrow the government of President Ngo Dinh Diem in a CIA-backed coup. ARVN officers assassinate President Diem and his younger brother, Ngo Dinh Nhu.

**November 22** President John F. Kennedy is assassinated; Vice President Lyndon B. Johnson becomes president.

**December** By year's end, the number of American advisers in Vietnam increases to 16,300, and the CIA begins training South Vietnamese guerrillas as part of an ambitious covert sabotage operation against the North.

## 1964

**August 7** Congress passes the Gulf of Tonkin Resolution, authorizing President Johnson to "take all necessary measures to repel any armed attack against the forces of the United States and to prevent further aggression."

**August 26** President Johnson is nominated for a second term by the Democrats, pledging before the election to "seek no wider war." Johnson defeats Republican candidate Barry Goldwater in a landslide.

## 1965

**March 2** Operation Rolling Thunder, the sustained bombing of North Vietnam, begins. It will continue until October 31, 1968, with occasional suspensions.

**March 8** U.S. Marines, the first American combat troops in Vietnam, are assigned to protect the air base at Da Nang.

**December 25** President Johnson suspends bombing in an attempt to get the North to negotiate. By year's end, American troop strength reaches nearly 200,000.

## 1966

**January 31** The bombing of North Vietnam is resumed. By year's end, American troop strength in Vietnam is nearly 400,000.

## 1967

**January 5** American casualties in Vietnam for 1966 are announced: 5,008 killed and 30,093 wounded. (Totals since 1961 are 6,664 killed, 37,738 wounded.)

**October 21** Two days of antiwar protests take place in Washington, D.C.

**December 8** The wave of American antiwar protests becomes more organized and grows larger. In New York, 585 protesters are arrested, including Dr. Benjamin Spock and poet Allen Ginsberg. By year's end, U.S. troop strength stands at nearly half a million.

## 1968

**January 21** Vietcong and North Vietnamese regulars attack the American garrison at Khe Sanh. A strategic hamlet that had been heavily fortified as a staging point for attacks on the Ho Chi Minh Trail—the main supply route from the communist North to rebels in the South—it is the scene of one of the war's most hard-fought battles.

**January 31** The Tet Offensive begins during what was a negotiated cease-fire to mark the Lunar New Year.

**February 25** After twenty-six days of fighting, the city of Hué is recaptured by American and South Vietnamese forces.

**February 29** Defense Secretary Robert McNamara resigns; he is replaced by Clark Clifford.

**March 12** Senator Eugene McCarthy, an opponent of the war, loses to President Johnson in the New Hampshire Democratic primary by only three hundred votes.

**March 16** Following McCarthy's near upset of Johnson, Senator Robert F. Kennedy announces that he will campaign for the Democratic presidential nomination.

**March 31** In a television address, President Johnson announces a partial bombing halt, offers peace talks, and then stuns the nation by saying he will not run again.

*Hué, South Vietnam*
*January 31–February 25, 1968*

Bam!...There was no mistaking what this noise was. A rocket, one of the enemy's largest missiles, had landed not fifty feet from where I was sleeping."

Captain George Smith and the other men in his bunker grabbed boots and "steel pots"—their standard army helmets—as the surprise attack began. An army information officer who had spent much of his time in Vietnam at a typewriter, Smith was now in the thick of the fighting in the fortress city of Hué.[5]

James Mueller, who had arrived in Vietnam as a clerk typist, was also in bed in his "skivvies."

"I scrambled out of my cot, ripped away the protective mosquito net, donned my helmet liner and steel pot and slipped on my flak jacket. In a matter of seconds, I had my carbine and ammunition and was out the door with my shower shoes on. My fellow hooch mates always made fun of me because I never took time to put on my uniform. So there I was in combat gear in my underwear and shower shoes. To me, speed was the most important thing—I wanted to stay alive."[6]

The onslaught began a little after 3:30 a.m., when a rocket and mortar barrage rocked the predawn quiet. Coming during a formal ceasefire, the shock of the surprise attack was soon followed by thousands of North Vietnamese soldiers storming across the lightly defended bridges and lotus-choked moats of Hué. They surged through the great stone entrances of the Citadel, Hué's fortress compound, and into the heart of Vietnam's former imperial city.[7]

Inside the Citadel, a small garrison of South Vietnamese army defenders barely managed to hold off the thousands of Hanoi's best-trained regulars descending on the old capital. For the Americans in the MACV* compound in the city's newer section, the sneak attack was sudden and fierce.

"American officers and men inside the high-walled U.S. advisers' compound scrambled into bunkers and gun positions dressed only in the undershirts and skivvies they were wearing when awakened," newsman Don Oberdorfer later recorded. "A young radio operator, a draftee with only a few more days of Vietnam duty, fired at attackers from an exposed position in an unfinished tower. They finally blasted him down with a B-40 rocket. It took five hours for him to die."[8]

By 7 a.m., the communist flag of North Vietnam was flying over Vietnam's former imperial capital.

Located a few miles inland from the China Sea in central Vietnam, Hué (pronounced "way") was a charming old city of graceful streets, serene temples, and grand imperial buildings, including the imposing nineteenth-century palace compound known as the Citadel, which dominated the city's old half. The three-square-mile, fortresslike Citadel was built in 1802 for Emperor Gia Long, who unified modern Vietnam in the nineteenth century. It was also the site of a palace that Gia Long had built for himself, modeled on the famed Chinese imperial palace the Forbidden City in what is now Beijing.

Tacitly considered an "open city"—that is, one that was not being bombed or attacked—because of its cultural and religious significance in Vietnam, Hué had been spared most of the fighting during the war's early years. Besides the Citadel, Hué was the home of the country's most prestigious university, a prominent Catholic high school, and a cathedral, along with Buddhist temples.

In Buddhist tradition, the city was said to be like a lotus flower

---

* "Military Assistance Command, Vietnam," and pronounced "mac-vee."

growing from the mud and slime. That floral image was the reason for Hué's other most notable feature. The Perfume River, named for its legendary fragrant scent, wandered through the city dividing the old imperial capital from its newer sections. The city was so placid and seemingly removed from the war, South Vietnamese army officers, it was said, paid bribes to be posted there.

With a population of about 140,000 in 1968, Hué was the third-largest city in Vietnam when the predawn attack began and, like Paris or London, it stood as an iconic symbol. Hué symbolized all Vietnam, not a nation divided by civil war. "Hué embodied the tradition and values of the past and a clear sense of time remembered," as *Washington Post* correspondent Oberdorfer recalled. "Its bittersweet charm and faded glory were deeply affecting to almost every visitor. The city radiated a haunting attraction difficult to define or fully explain."[9]

All that would change as the venerable and charmed city was swept up in some of the most deadly fighting and worst urban violence of the Vietnam War, starting in the early hours of January 31, 1968. John Laurence, a CBS correspondent on the scene, would somberly note, "After being spared most of the misery of two Indochina wars over the past twenty years, the citizens of Hué were now condemned to suffer the worst of it all at once."[10]

The city had been targeted as part of a highly coordinated, nationwide surprise attack of unexpected ferocity and strength that had been planned for months. Combining guerrilla units of the Vietcong with North Vietnamese regular forces, an estimated eighty thousand North Vietnamese soldiers and Vietcong struck simultaneously across much of South Vietnam. Their offensive hit five major cities, including heavily defended Saigon and the American embassy there, thirty-five of South Vietnam's provincial capitals, and fifty other locations. It was an ambitious assault meant to spark a popular uprising and demoralize or defeat the United States and the Saigon regime it supported.

Apart from the vast numbers of troops and daring of its scope, the attack's timing was what made it so stunning. Coming as the divided nation marked the Tet holiday, the traditional Vietnamese Lunar New Year, the offensive was unleashed even as a weeklong nationwide cease-fire had been declared by the warring sides to allow the country to celebrate. For the Vietnamese, Tet was Easter, Christmas, New Year's Day, and Thanksgiving rolled into one week of celebration. A festive season of flowers and gift giving, Tet was a time when many Vietnamese traveled home to be with their families. Whether communist, Buddhist, or Roman Catholic, many Vietnamese still venerated the Tet holiday as one of family and national tradition. It was also a holiday marked with fireworks that filled villages and hamlets around the country.

But in 1968, the explosions that rolled across South Vietnam were not celebratory pyrotechnics. Although U.S. military intelligence had picked up signs of increased enemy activity in the days before the Tet surprise attack, and the North Vietnamese and Vietcong had launched a heavy attack on an American base at Khe Sanh, not far from Hué, about two weeks earlier in January, the American and South Vietnamese guard was clearly down as the cease-fire approached.

The most audacious strike by the Tet attackers exploded in the very heart of Saigon, the South Vietnamese capital. At about 2:45 a.m. on January 31, 1968, a small Peugeot truck and a battered taxicab carried a small group of Vietcong sappers* who blew a hole in the wall of the brand-new U.S. embassy compound. A handful of Vietcong fighters, wearing South Vietnamese army uniforms, held parts of the embassy compound for the first six hours of the offensive,

---

* Sappers were traditionally considered combat engineers who dug trenches and other fortifications (see chapter 1). In Vietnam, American soldiers used the term to refer to Vietcong commandos who worked in small units, often planting bombs, booby traps, and other explosive devices, rather than performing more traditional combat roles.

which was aimed, according to Hanoi radio reports, at overthrowing the South Vietnamese government of President Nguyen Van Thieu. The next day, President Thieu declared martial law throughout South Vietnam.

The scenes of Saigon and the supposedly impregnable American embassy under attack shook Americans instantly, because the revolution was now being televised—almost as soon as it happened. Broadcast correspondents had begun to use satellite transmission instead of sending film back to the United States to be processed and later aired. What was once a process requiring days to get filmed news reports from Vietnam onto the air had become live "on-the-spot news." Vietnam would be anointed the Living-Room War. And those images were going to have a profound effect.

"It did not matter to the American public that the platoon of sappers did not actually break into and seize the embassy building, although they had plenty of B-40 rockets and explosives with which to do so," wrote Neil Sheehan, a *New York Times* correspondent in Vietnam. "It did not matter in the United States that the Vietnamese Communists failed to topple the Saigon regime and foment a rebellion by the urban population.... What mattered to the American public was that this defeated enemy could attack anywhere and was attacking more fiercely than ever before. The winning of the war was not coming 'into view.' The war in Vietnam was never going to be won. Nothing had been achieved by the outpouring of lives and treasure and the rending of American society. The assurances the public had been given were the lies and vaporings of foolish men."[11]

What American armchair generals and living room spectators were seeing was a different kind of "reality television," before that term was coined. And the reality was quickly becoming clearer, as Don Oberdorfer commented. "Vietnam was America's first television war. And the Tet offensive was America's first television superbattle."[12] The city of Hué would soon become the epicenter of that superbattle.

The defense, and later the recapture, of the city initially fell to a group of South Vietnamese troops and a small contingent of American soldiers in the MACV compound. Even as hell broke loose across South Vietnam and the American command continued to focus most of its attention and resources on the battle being fought at Khe Sanh, two companies of marines reinforced the Americans in Hué. The first arrived by the highway and was forced to fight their way into the city; the other came by boat on the Perfume River.

The shorthanded rescue effort was hamstrung from the start by the most basic problems of any war—confusion and poor intelligence. "Unfamiliarity with the city streets forced the Marines to use maps from a local gas station and the police headquarters," writes journalist and military historian James S. Robbins. These problems were compounded as the face of the battle changed, Robbins adds. "On day seven, the day the original Tet ceasefire was supposed to have ended, the Marines in Hue moved west, clearing the city block by block with massive firepower.... The enemy would disappear as Marines seized parts of the city, then reappear in the cleared areas at night. Most Marines had not been trained for or experienced urban combat."[13]

Lieutenant Colonel Ernest C. Cheatham, a Korean War veteran who had briefly played defensive tackle in the NFL, commanded one of the Marine groups. "We had to blow our way through every wall of every house," he told a combat reporter on the scene. "It's a shame we have to damage such a beautiful city. In this kind of fighting, we're like a football team....Four men cover the exits of a building, two men rush the building with grenades, while two men cover them with rifle fire. We hope to kill them inside or flush them out for the four men watching the exits. Then taking the next building, two other men assume the hairy job of rushing the front. It sounds simple, but the timing has to be just as good as a football play."[14]

As few other battles in history have been recorded and reported, journalists and cameramen who were there documented the fight for Hué. And the pictures and stories they sent back home would change the arc of American politics and history.

One of those journalists was a young writer for *Esquire*, Michael Herr. "Almost as much as the grunts and the Vietnamese, Tet was pushing the correspondents closer to the wall than they'd ever wanted to be," he recorded in his book *Dispatches* (1977).* "I realized later that actual youth had been pressed out of me in just the three days that it took me to cross the sixty miles between Can Tho and Saigon."[15]

Arriving a few days into the battle to retake the city, Herr described the "damp gloom" and the "cold and dark" that hung over Hué as the marines he was covering fought house-to-house in the counterattack. Dead bodies bobbed in the moat of the old imperial city and littered all its approaches. When the battle was over, Herr wrote, "70 percent of Vietnam's one lovely city was destroyed, and if the landscape seemed desolate, imagine how the figures in that landscape looked."[16]

The toll taken on the marines was steep. "By the end of the week, the [Citadel] wall had cost the Marines roughly one casualty for every meter taken, a quarter of them KIA [Killed in Action]," recounted Herr. "1/5, which came to be known as the Citadel Battalion, had been through every tough battle the Marines had had in the past six months, they'd even fought the same NVA [North Vietnamese Army] units a few weeks before.... They all knew how bad it was, the novelty of fighting in a city had become a nasty joke, everyone wanted to get wounded."[17]

---

* In addition to his acclaimed book, Herr also cowrote the Academy Award–nominated screenplay for Stanley Kubrick's film *Full Metal Jacket* (1987) with Kubrick and Gustav Hasford, whose novel *The Short-Timers* was the basis for the film, in which the Battle of Hué is featured.

What was wrong with this picture was that the American public had been told that the war was going well by military leaders such as General William Westmoreland, head of the MACV. The jolting ease with which the South Vietnamese and American forces had been attacked and nearly overwhelmed in so many places at once, coupled with the brutality of the Tet Offensive, was a thunderbolt that made front-page headlines and led the nightly network news. Perhaps the most devastating single scene had taken place in Saigon, where national police chief General Nguyen Ngoc Loan strode up to a bound prisoner on a Saigon street, leveled his revolver, and put a bullet in the man's brain. This scene was captured by the Associated Press photographer Eddie Adams and by an NBC television camera, and the shockingly close-range killing became an indelible and iconic image of the war.[18]

The stark contrast between the incurably optimistic and reassuring reports of military press officers at Saigon's "Five O'clock Follies," as their press conferences were known, and the reality of reporters caught in combat and witnessing the fury of the Tet fighting soon came home to America in a remarkable series of events. Accepted all too blithely by reporters and American anchormen, the army's blatant lies about the conflict and how it was progressing were now on view in living color.

Before Tet, Americans had mostly seen neatly packaged news reports. As writer Michael Arlen famously put it two years before Tet, in his 1966 *New Yorker* article titled "Living-Room War":

> The cumulative effect of these three- and five-minute clips, with their almost unvarying implicit deference to the importance of purely military solutions…and with their catering…to a popular democracy's insistent desire to view even as unbelievably complicated a war as this one in emotional terms (our guys against their guys), is surely wide of the mark, and is bound to provide these millions of people with an

excessively simple, emotional and military-oriented view of what is, at best, a mighty unsimple situation.[19]

For Americans back home, Tet made it clear suddenly and dramatically that the Vietnam story was far more complex and dangerous than they believed. A number of very experienced and respected journalists were also undergoing an awakening, and for some, the wake-up call came in Hué.

In his offices in New York at CBS News's broadcast center, legendary broadcaster Walter Cronkite—"America's Most Trusted Man"—had heard the noise of wire service machines clattering on the first day of Tet on January 31, 1968. Reading about the multiple attacks spread across Vietnam, he asked colleagues, "What the hell is going on? I thought we were winning the war."[20]

In the latter months of 1967, after more than two years of bitter fighting in Vietnam, General Westmoreland, the senior American commander, had been doing his best to convince Americans that the United States and its allied forces were making significant headway. Westmoreland had been appointed head of MACV not long after Kennedy's death, chosen by Maxwell Taylor, former army chief of staff who had left the army but returned to the Kennedy administration to investigate the 1961 Bay of Pigs fiasco in Cuba.

A decorated World War II veteran, Taylor was a ramrod-straight soldier, fourth in his 1922 West Point class, and was the first American general to parachute onto the beaches of Normandy on D-Day with the 101st Airborne Division. After the war, he served as West Point's superintendent from 1945 to 1949, where he is credited with the written codification of the academy's traditional Honor Code, which at its heart states: "A cadet will not lie, cheat, steal, or tolerate those who do." Later commander of Allied troops in West Berlin, Taylor was sent to Korea after the outbreak of the Korean War. He was serving as army chief of staff when President Eisenhower ordered troops from the 101st Airborne Division (without any of its black troops) to Little Rock, Arkansas, in 1957 to enforce a federal court's desegregation order—the first time federal troops had been used in the South since Reconstruction.

In 1959, Taylor resigned from the army and wrote *The Uncertain Trumpet* (1960), a book highly critical of Eisenhower's military policy, which had included a shift to airpower and nuclear deterrence as the country's first line of defense. During the 1960 presidential campaign, the book was read and admired by John F. Kennedy and his brother Robert, later the U.S. attorney general and most influential adviser to his brother.

After delivering his report on the Bay of Pigs fiasco, Taylor stayed on as Kennedy's personal military adviser, effectively replacing the chairman of the Joint Chiefs of Staff and becoming one of the main architects of America's involvement in Vietnam. In 1962, he was formally given the Joint Chiefs post and held it until 1964, when he retired to become Lyndon Johnson's ambassador to South Vietnam.*

William Westmoreland was another of the World War II generation whose experiences in North Africa and Italy had been his path to promotion. Like Maxwell Taylor, Westmoreland had served as the superintendent of West Point, where he "was best remembered for rejecting a plan to hire Vince Lombardi to coach the academy's football team," Thomas E. Ricks notes.[21] The first army general to attend Harvard Business School while on active duty, Westmoreland had never studied at the Army War College nor the Command and General Staff College. In his history of Vietnam, Stanley Karnow said

---

* Not long before his death in 1987, Taylor told journalist Stanley Karnow that America's involvement in Vietnam had been "both a blunder and a lesson." According to Karnow, Taylor said, "Until we know the enemy and know our allies and know ourselves, we'd better keep out of this kind of dirty business. It's very dangerous." See Karnow, *Vietnam: A History*, p. 23.

Westmoreland, like Taylor, represented a new breed of army leadership. "Westy was a corporate executive in uniform, a diligent, disciplined organization man who would obey orders. Like Taylor, he saw the war as essentially an exercise in management—and together they began to 'Americanize' the effort."[22] Karnow's assessment was more recently echoed by Ricks, who described Westmoreland as representative of a new American type, the "organization man," more grounded in management than leadership—a key distinction.

Translated to the battlefield of Southeast Asia, that meant Westmoreland believed he could defeat the enemy through conventional warfare. But Vietnam was not North Africa's Kasserine Pass or the plains of Europe, and the North Vietnamese were not Rommel's Nazi panzer tank divisions. His optimism was based on the reported "body count" of dead Vietcong guerrillas and North Vietnamese Army regulars. It was corporate-style war by the numbers—numbers often inflated by field commanders who wanted to make their "quotas" as if they were measuring factory output or productivity numbers.

In mid-November 1967, General Westmoreland was brought home from Vietnam to the United States to "revive the country's flagging spirit," as Stanley Karnow put it. He told reporters that he was "very, very encouraged" by recent events, and at an appearance on NBC's *Meet the Press*, he said American troops would be able to begin withdrawing "within two years or less." With his consistently upbeat accounts of how things were going in the war, Westmoreland expressed the clear belief that a corner had been turned.[23] At the National Press Club, he claimed, "We have reached an important point when the end begins to come into view."[24]

"Westmoreland resolutely pursed his strategy of attrition with a series of search-and-destroy operations," wrote historian Karnow. "And the enemy 'body count' mounted astronomically." But the misleading or inflated numbers provided to reporters were coming at a cost that was also climbing sharply, as Karnow noted. "By the end of 1967, the U.S. troop presence was up to nearly half a million, an increase of a hundred thousand during the year, and American soldiers killed in action exceeded nine thousand—bringing total battlefield deaths for the past two years to more than fifteen thousand. More than a million and a half tons of bombs had been dropped since the air strikes began on both the north and south. But the war was deadlocked."[25]

With almost uncontested air superiority, the United States eventually dropped more tons of bombs on North Vietnam than had been dropped on Europe in World War II. But the overwhelming air assault did not diminish the will of the North Vietnamese and could not blast North Vietnam "back to the Stone Age,"[26] in the memorable phrase of Air Force general Curtis LeMay, who had commanded the air strikes on Japan, including firebombings, in the final days of World War II.

Like millions of Americans to whom he had delivered the news and the "official version" of events in Vietnam, Walter Cronkite had listened respectfully to Westmoreland and usually accepted his reports at face value—and Cronkite was no stranger to war. During World War II, he had been a correspondent flying above the action when troops hit the beaches of Normandy; he had parachuted into Holland with the 101st Airborne and followed American GIs at the Battle of the Bulge, a devastating last-ditch effort by the Germans in the waning days of World War II. Through most of the early years of American involvement in Vietnam, Cronkite had often accepted the president's view that the United States was in a postwar struggle with communism, as well as General Westmoreland's pledge that there was "light at the end of the tunnel" in Vietnam.

All that began to change with the first reports of the Tet Offensive. Cronkite decided to see Vietnam for himself. "Uncle" Walter donned combat gear once more and went to Hué.

On February 6, Cronkite flew from New York to San Francisco

and then on to Tokyo, before finally arriving in Saigon on February 11, 1968. Outfitted in flak jacket and army helmet, he began to tour the Vietnamese countryside. General Westmoreland reassured Cronkite that Hué, which had been attacked on the first day of Tet, was once again in the control of the Americans and South Vietnamese.

But the veteran reporter could see for himself that the truth was far different. Cronkite biographer Douglas Brinkley wrote, "As Cronkite and company headed up Highway 1 [the main north-south road of Vietnam] to Hué, they realized that Westmoreland had lied. The Marines were still trying to retake the city. 'The Battle was still on in Hué when I got up there,' Cronkite recalled. 'It lasted twenty-seven days.'"[27]

Once in Hué, the legendary newsman, his face familiar to millions, found himself in the line of fire again. James Mueller, the former army typist, recalled his momentary surprise inside the embattled American command compound: "I had run an errand upstairs...and was coming down the steps of the open stairwell when I ran into Walter Cronkite and two members of his film crew. All of a sudden a hail of sniper fire came from the direction of the Perfume River. As bullets whizzed by my head, I ran down the steps and sprinted across the open courtyard, trying to avoid getting shot by snipers."[28]

Once more, as he had at Normandy and the Bulge, Cronkite could see for himself what American grunts were experiencing. But now he was also witnessing how the Pentagon and official Washington had been fundamentally misleading the American people.

In purely military terms, the Tet Offensive was suppressed fairly quickly in most parts of South Vietnam as the U.S. Army and South Vietnamese ARVN forces counterattacked. But in Hué, the battle would go on for nearly a month in street-by-street fighting of a kind not experienced before by American soldiers in Vietnam. There had been some pitched battles and plenty of jungle fighting in Vietnam. Bombers had struck the North for years, especially in Hanoi. But gunfights in narrow streets and air strikes called in on a major population center in South Vietnam were part of a new phase in the fighting. Unwilling to commit more troops to Hué while the battle for Khe Sanh was still being fought, General Westmoreland did not order sufficient reinforcements to Hué. As Neil Sheehan later wrote, "He abandoned the battle to the ARVN and a couple of reinforced battalions of Marines."[29]

It would be a battle with a brutal new face. Soon after taking the city in early February, North Vietnamese political officers had begun rounding up hundreds of civilians and members of the South Vietnamese government in Hué. Vietcong fighters took advantage of the chaos to "settle scores," as one writer put it. Foreigners in the diplomatic corps and working for aid agencies were also being arrested. It was not immediately clear whether they were being detained or sent back to Hanoi, the North Vietnamese capital, or executed.

But the fates of a large number of the missing citizens of Hué were soon revealed. It was a bright and sunny morning in March 1968 when U.S. Army information officer Captain George W. Smith accompanied a group of Vietnamese women and children to a large field outside the city. The families stopped and dug in the ground. "The smell attacked my senses like a blast of hot air from an oven," Smith recalled. "It was a sour, pungent odor that reminded me of decaying garbage. This first whiff was the worst."[30]

It was the smell of death as Vietnamese families uncovered the putrefying corpses of what has been called the "worst bloodbath of the conflict."[31] Although the numbers are still disputed, as many as three thousand Vietnamese and foreigners may have been massacred in the monthlong siege of Hué during Tet.

For the twenty-five days that the North Vietnamese held large portions of the city, it is believed that they carried out one of the most notorious atrocities of the war: preplanned, targeted executions of select officials, military personnel, and others loyal to the Republic of Vietnam. According to claims made in documents captured at the time, historian Nick Turse later wrote, "During this occupation, the revolutionary forces 'eliminated 1,892 administrative personnel, 38 policemen, 790 tyrants, 6 captains, 2 first lieutenants, 20 2d lieutenants and many noncommissioned officers.' In all, 3,000 or more people have been killed in the massacre."[32]

According to journalist-historian Neil Sheehan, "They rounded up current and retired officials, civil servants, police officers, anyone connected to the regime or a known sympathizer, and killed them. Most of the victims were shot; some were beheaded; others were buried alive. The number of victims is impossible to establish with precision. One careful estimate put the toll at 3,000. The killings were as stupid as they were cruel. The massacre gave substance to the fear that a bloodbath would occur should the Communists ever win the war in the South."[33]

But in spite of the large American media presence in Vietnam and Hué, these atrocities purportedly committed by the communists went largely unreported to the American public. "Despite its scale and brutality," James S. Robbins wrote in a recent reassessment of Tet, "the Hue massacre was virtually unnoticed in the United States at the time and is now largely forgotten.... The Hue Massacre was a natural expression of Communist revolutionary doctrine, the type of incident common in totalitarian systems. The NLF [National Liberation Front], acting under specific orders from Hanoi, sought to jump-start the revolution by physically eliminating the 'ruling class' at one stroke."[34]

The "fog of battle" certainly confused the picture. As U.S. and South Vietnamese forces launched counterattacks to take back the city, it was difficult to separate citizen from soldier. Reporting on the marines as they fought from street to street, the CBS television correspondent John Laurence asked Lieutenant Colonel Ernie Cheatham what would happen to innocents trapped between them and the enemy. "I'm pretty sure they are civilians that we would consider bad guys right now," Cheatham replied. "The others—if there's somebody in there right now, they're Charlie [Vietcong] as far as we're concerned."[35]

With little regard for civilian casualties, U.S. Navy ships lobbed 7,670 shells into Hué, and Marine Corps aircraft flew dozens of sorties, dropping napalm and five-hundred-pound bombs on residential neighborhoods. With the rules of engagement changed, any building in Hué was fair game, and Hué's churches, pagodas, and other historic buildings previously off-limits were soon targeted. Whole neighborhoods were reduced to rubble or burned out with napalm attacks.

While the Tet Offensive was put down quickly in some parts of Vietnam, the fighting in Hué would be long and deadly, though this clearly contradicted what the American public had been led to believe.

Like James Mueller, the reporters working for other newspapers, wire services, and networks were amazed to see Cronkite striding through Hué's streets in combat gear. "Like the younger correspondents," wrote Douglas Brinkley, "he slept on the bare floor of a Vietnamese doctor's house that had been turned into a pressroom. He ate C rations and used the overflowing latrine. No one thought he acted like a bigwig or was bigfooting. Cronkite operating in Hué was a sight to behold."[36]

Cronkite left Hué in a helicopter two days after he arrived, flying out alongside the body bags of a dozen dead marines. Following a few more days spent reporting in Saigon, Cronkite was set to return home and tell America what he had seen in Tet's aftermath.

It was not a pretty picture. By the twentieth day of the battle, CBS correspondent John Laurence said, "All anyone could think about was staying alive. Foul-smelling smoke drifted up from the burned-out shells of houses and buildings and garbage and blackened the low clouds hanging over the Citadel....Dead bodies lay in the streets. Food was scarce, nerves frazzled. The noise of the battle was loud and incessant. Artillery shells, mortars, rifle bullets, machine gun tracers, tank cannon, hand grenades, gas grenades, rocket artillery, recoilless rifles and even shells from the long heavy guns of U.S. Navy destroyers in the South China Sea whooshed overhead with shrieking whistlescreams and burst upon the pulverized remains of the city....Madness was in the air."[37]

On the morning of February 24, the communist flag was torn down and the South Vietnamese flag raised over the remains of the Citadel. Hué, city of the Perfume River, was in ruins. A medical student in the Hué Civilian Hospital later said, "Hué has nothing now, nothing. It is not only the loss of our buildings and monuments, it is the loss of our spirit. It is gone."[38]

-----

Early in 1968—an American presidential election year—America's involvement in Vietnam was already deep and escalating. American involvement in Vietnam and much of Southeast Asia came after World War II, but the roots of Western involvement in the region date to 1862, when France took control of parts of the Vietnamese Empire.

After World War I, a young man named Nguyen Sinh Cung—changed at age ten to Nguyen Tat Thanh, one of a number of aliases—left Vietnam for Paris, where he tried to influence President Woodrow Wilson and the victorious Allies to allow Vietnamese self-determination at the Versailles peace talks in 1918. Born in 1890, Nguyen Tat Thanh had been educated at Hué's prestigious Quoc Hoc High School. When his efforts to win Vietnam's independence failed, he joined the French Communist Party in 1920 and traveled to China and later Moscow in 1924, returning in secret to

Vietnam in 1941. He took the nom de guerre Ho Chi Minh ("He Who Enlightens") at that time and formed the Viet Nam Doc Lap Dong Minh Hoi (League for the Independence of Vietnam), an umbrella resistance group better known as the Vietminh. In 1945, the Japanese seized control of French Indochina, allowing the Vietnamese emperor Bao Dai to declare his independence from France. It was during that time that Ho Chi Minh emerged to battle both Japan and China, still under Nationalist control, and Vietnam's traditional antagonist. (China would fall to the communists in 1949.)

In the immediate aftermath of Japan's World War II defeat in August 1945, Ho Chi Minh declared Vietnam's independence, citing Thomas Jefferson and the Declaration of Independence as he did so. He wrote a letter to President Truman requesting support for Vietnam's independence.[39] The Democratic Republic of Vietnam (DRV) encompassed the whole country and Ho dissolved the Communist Party to form a coalition government with other nationalists. In 1946, France recognized the DRV as a free state, but within the French Union. Later that year, the French and Vietnamese would begin to fight the First Indochina War.

By 1950, with U.S. troops fighting in Korea, it was President Truman who first granted military aid to France for its war against Ho Chi Minh's rebels in Indochina.

In May 1954, President Eisenhower was presented with a plan to assist the French army, then trapped in a fight-to-the-death battle against a Vietnamese rebel army at the fortress of Dien Bien Phu. Named "Operation VULTURE," it called for the use of small tactical atomic bombs. Two American aircraft carriers, according to Thomas E. Ricks, were in the South China Sea, "with small nuclear bombs in their weapons lockers."[40] Army Chief of Staff Matthew Ridgway opposed their use; President Eisenhower concurred and the plan to use them in Vietnam was shelved. According to biographer Jean Edward Smith, Eisenhower told a national security aide, "I certainly don't think that the atomic bomb can be used by the United States unilaterally. You boys must be crazy. We can't use those awful things against Asians for the second time in less than ten years. My God."[41]

Eisenhower decided against both the use of tactical atomic weapons and the provision of direct military support to the French in their doomed stand at their base at Dien Bien Phu; Eisenhower also vowed not to send ground troops to the country.[42]

At an April 1954 multinational conference in Geneva, convened to settle issues related to the conflicts in Korea and Indochina, Vietnam was partitioned into two zones, with the North controlled by Ho's Vietminh organization and the South aligned with the United States and the Western powers. Elections were scheduled to determine Vietnam's future in 1956. But the South's President Diem, elected in a fraud-riddled 1955 referendum with CIA backing, refused to participate in this national vote, and the elections were scuttled, only worsening the division. Brutality, torture, and assassinations soon became common on both sides. The increasingly corrupt South Vietnamese government installed in Saigon under President Diem had the full backing of the CIA and both the Eisenhower and Kennedy administrations. In the communist North, where the communists had purged noncommunist nationalists from the Vietminh, thousands of peasant farmers were also killed or imprisoned in labor camps under communist "land reform." As the conflict between North and South grew, the North Vietnamese leadership created a group to enlarge the so-called Ho Chi Minh Trail—actually an elaborate system of trails, communications networks, and supply routes that ran through Laos and Cambodia—and infiltrate the South, beginning a campaign of assassination that claimed the lives of four thousand South Vietnamese government officials a year between 1959 and 1961.[43]

That was the situation on the ground after President Eisenhower left office in 1961. President Kennedy continued to supply money and arms and eventually dispatched military advisers into South Vietnam as it struggled to battle the communist North and Vietcong* guerrillas operating throughout the country. In February 1962, the American Military Assistance Command, Vietnam (MACV) was formed in Saigon to coordinate the American efforts to keep the anticommunist government of South Vietnam viable. By the end of 1963, with Kennedy dead and Lyndon B. Johnson in the White House, some fifteen thousand military advisers had been committed in support of the anticommunist Saigon government.

Before the ferocious battle for Hué began, most Americans would be hard-pressed to find the city on a map, let alone understand its illustrious past. At best, some might have recalled a scene from May 1966, when Thanh Quang, a Buddhist nun in her fifties, entered Hué's Dieude temple courtyard. It was before dawn as she assumed the lotus position, her simple gray robe billowing around her. Then a companion doused her with gasoline and Thanh Quang lighted a match, setting herself ablaze. The nun burst into flames, with thick, acrid black smoke rising over her body as the fire consumed her. Another companion fed peppermint oil onto Thanh Quang's burning body in an attempt to suppress the stench of burning flesh.[44]

The odor quickly overwhelmed the floral fragrance of the Perfume River.

By the time American journalist Stanley Karnow arrived on the scene, crowds had gathered around the nun's upright, burning body, appealing to the Buddha to ease her suffering. "Her body was still erect," Karnow recalled, "the hands clasped in prayer. The religious rite was fast becoming a political episode."[45]

The reason for the Buddhist nun's stunning act of self-immolation

---

* The Communist National Liberation Front, organized at the end of 1960, was first called "Vietcong," or Vietnamese communists, by the Diem government, according to Stanley Karnow's *Vietnam* (p. 245).

soon became clear. As Thanh Quang's blackened figure continued to smolder, companions of the nun passed around copies of a letter she had written to President Lyndon B. Johnson. In it, she condemned America for its continuing support of the South Vietnamese government in Saigon, dominated by Roman Catholic Vietnamese who had been suppressing Vietnam's Buddhists just as the Vietnamese emperors and later the French colonial government once did.

For years, Americans had been warned by political and military leaders, like Eisenhower, that Vietnam was about "falling dominoes"—the threat of a Soviet-backed communist dictatorship overwhelming a "democratic" American ally, as had been the case in Korea. Most were unaware of the legacy of Buddhist-Catholic antagonism that was a part of the complicated rivalries that had splintered the country beyond the partition of communist North and noncommunist South. As Karnow wrote, "[President] Diem counted on the thousands of Catholics who had fled south after the 1954 partition as his core constituency. He coddled them with key military and civilian posts, business deals and property privileges."[46] Corruption and class divisions, along with religious conflicts, riddled Vietnam's politics and economy, as did the fundamental struggle between North and South.

After a 1963 military coup, President Ngo Dinh Diem was removed and murdered by his generals, leading to a succession of military regimes in Saigon. By 1967, the South Vietnamese government was led by President Nguyen Van Thieu and Prime Minister Nguyen Cao Ky—a flamboyant pilot who with Thieu was installed after another coup. This regime continued to suppress the Buddhists, leading to more dramatic protests by other Buddhists. When more suicides followed, President Johnson called them "tragic and unnecessary," and asked the South Vietnamese people to support the Thieu government as it waged war against North Vietnam's communist regime.

The CIA was also in the thick of things, having helped foster the coup that toppled President Diem in 1963 and then acting surprised when the army officers who overthrew him executed Diem. The initial report from the CIA in Saigon was that Diem had committed suicide. Like much of what the CIA in Vietnam reported, that proved false.

As recorded by Tim Weiner, Lucien Conein, the CIA operative who was involved with the mutinous generals, later told a Senate hearing, "I was part and parcel of the whole conspiracy."[47] Nicknamed "Black Luigi," Conein had been in Indochina to fight the Japanese and was once allied with Ho Chi Minh, staying on in Vietnam to become a charter member of the CIA, which, according to Weiner, "created South Vietnam's political parties, trained its secret police, made its popular movies, and printed and peddled an astrological magazine predicting that the stars were in Diem's favor. It was building a nation from the ground up."[48]

Following the assassination of John F. Kennedy a few weeks after the Diem coup, Lyndon B. Johnson became president, retaining many of his predecessor's "best and brightest"—journalist-historian David Halberstam's decidedly uncomplimentary phrase for Kennedy's key advisers. With the complicity of the CIA, they were determined to find a Vietnamese version of Pearl Harbor in order to escalate America's military involvement in Vietnam with at least a glimmer of legitimacy. It came in August 1964 in the Gulf of Tonkin, a large bay in the South China Sea between the coast of North Vietnam and southern China.

Supporting a CIA program that sent saboteurs into North Vietnam, the U.S. Navy had posted warships in the Gulf of Tonkin, loaded with electronic eavesdropping equipment that enabled them to monitor North Vietnamese military operations and provide intelligence to the South Vietnamese commandos.

On August 2, 1964, one of these ships, the USS *Maddox*, reported being attacked, in what remains one of the most controversial incidents in recent American military history. Another American destroyer, the *Turner Joy*, joined the *Maddox*, along with jets from an American aircraft carrier, to strike at four North Vietnamese gunboats thought to have fired on the American ships. Two days later, both American vessels were sent back into the area to "show the flag" in a demonstration of American power after the first incident. While in the Gulf of Tonkin, a radar operator on the *Turner Joy* saw some blips, and another radar operator on the *Maddox* reported seeing incoming torpedoes. Both the *Maddox* and *Turner Joy* opened fire and kept firing for two hours. But there was never any confirmation that either ship had actually been fired on, or that North Vietnamese gunboats were even there.

Much later, the radar blips would be attributed to weather conditions and jittery nerves among the crew. According to Stanley Karnow, "Even Johnson privately expressed doubts only a few days after the second attack supposedly took place, confiding to an aide, 'Hell, those dumb stupid sailors were just shooting at flying fish.'"[49]

But in the confusion and haste to find a reason to attack North Vietnam, the "intelligence" was shaped to fit Johnson's needs.

At the time, the National Security Agency (NSA) had clearly buried the facts in making its reports to Johnson and his military advisers. Only decades later, in 2005, would the NSA ultimately reveal: "The overwhelming body of reports, if used, would have told the story that no attack had happened. So a conscious effort ensued to demonstrate that the attack had occurred." The intelligence was "deliberately skewed to support the notion that there had been an attack."[50]

But Lyndon Johnson had all that he needed. Without waiting for a review of the situation, he ordered an air strike against North

Vietnam in "retaliation" for the "attacks" on the U.S. ships. American jets flew more than sixty sorties against targets in North Vietnam. One bitter result of these air raids was the capture of downed pilot Everett Alvarez Jr., the first American POW of the Vietnam War. He would remain in Hanoi prisons for eight years.

President Johnson followed up the air strike by calling for passage of the Gulf of Tonkin Resolution. This proposal gave the president the authority to "take all necessary measures" to repel attacks against U.S. forces and to "prevent further aggression." The resolution not only gave President Johnson the almost unrestrained powers he needed to increase American commitment to Vietnam, but also allowed him to blunt Republican presidential candidate Barry Goldwater's accusations that Johnson was "timid before Communism."

On August 7, 1964, the Gulf of Tonkin Resolution passed the House unanimously after only forty minutes of debate. In the Senate, there were only two voices in opposition, Senators Wayne Morse (D-Oregon) and Ernest Gruening (D-Alaska). What Congress did not know was that the resolution had been drafted in June, weeks before the Tonkin incident took place.

"Lyndon Johnson had been ready to bomb North Vietnam for two months," Tim Weiner recounted. "On his orders, in June 1964, Bill Bundy, the assistant secretary of state for the Far East, brother of the national security adviser [McGeorge Bundy], and a veteran CIA analyst, had drawn up a war resolution to be sent to Congress when the moment was ripe."[51] After the vote, Walt Rostow, a national security adviser to President Johnson and one of the men chiefly behind the resolution, remarked, "We don't know what happened, but it had the desired result."[52]

More to the point and in his down-home style, Johnson remarked that the Tonkin Resolution was "like granny's nightshirt. It covered everything."[53]

For the next few years, Johnson would escalate America's involvement in Vietnam, eventually putting half a million troops into the country and relying on an increasingly unpopular draft to fill out the military manpower needs. Through most of that time, public opinion polls showed support for Johnson's policies. But the mood was beginning to change as 1968 rolled around.

When North Vietnamese and Vietcong troops launched the wave of simultaneous attacks on South Vietnamese and American forces in major cities, towns, and military bases throughout South Vietnam at three o'clock in the morning of January 31, 1968, it was not only a military turning point in the war. It was far more significant in the impact it was to have on Americans at home.

By mid-February, two weeks into the offensive, Washington was estimating that enemy casualties had risen to almost 39,000, including 33,249 killed. Allied casualties were placed at 3,470 dead, one-third of them Americans, and 12,062 wounded, almost half of them Americans.

When the Tet Offensive ended and the last communist attackers were finally dislodged from the Imperial Citadel at Hué, General William C. Westmoreland compared the fighting to the Battle of the Bulge in 1944, Nazi Germany's last major drive in World War II. "Although the enemy has achieved some temporary psychological advantage, he suffered a military defeat," the general said at a Saigon press conference.

Little did Westmoreland know that the struggle in Vietnam would continue for another seven years, and that a war-weary United States would withdraw. Nor did he know that his ill-suited comparison to an epic American victory was about to crumble.

Back in New York City, Walter Cronkite prepared an account of the Vietnam he had just visited. Airing on February 27, 1968 at 10 p.m. Eastern Time, Cronkite's *Report from Vietnam* was mostly eyewitness reporting from a trusted veteran reporter, viewed by millions of Americans who saw air raids and Vietnamese villages in ruins.*

The images were completely at odds with what America had been told for a very long time. As Cronkite biographer Douglas Brinkley explained, "Cronkite made a powerful case that President Johnson was misleading the American public about the dire situation in Vietnam."[54] Cronkite, the man who had told America about JFK's tragic death and the triumphs of the space program, concluded by facing the cameras and saying:

> To say that we are closer to victory today is to believe in the face of the evidence the optimists who have been wrong in the past. To suggest we are on the edge of defeat is to yield to unreasonable pessimism. To say that we are mired in stalemate seems the only reasonable, yet unsatisfactory, conclusion....But it is increasingly clear to this reporter that the only rational way out then will be to negotiate, not as victors, but as honorable people who lived up to their pledge to defend Democracy and did the best they could. This is Walter Cronkite. Good night.[55]

## AFTERMATH

A few weeks after Cronkite's broadcast, General Westmoreland was relieved of command and given the job of army chief of staff. Then, on March 31, after nearly losing the New Hampshire Democratic primary to antiwar challenger Senator Eugene McCarthy, Johnson stunned the American public by announcing he would not seek reelection.

There have been many reports that after Cronkite's broadcast,

---

* According to Nielsen surveys, *CBS Evening News* and NBC's *Huntley-Brinkley Report* were seen in more than 100 million homes during the first week of Tet.

Lyndon B. Johnson said to an aide, "If I've lost Cronkite, I've lost the country." According to biographer Douglas Brinkley's *Cronkite*, there are several versions of this quote, including, "If I've lost Cronkite, I've lost Middle America."

As Brinkley recounted, "Just what President Johnson really said about the 'Cronkite Moment,' as it is known in the history books, has been mired in scholarly controversy....It doesn't make any real difference. The important point is that Cronkite had grabbed America's attention about Vietnam in a way that would have been impossible for LBJ to have missed."[56]

Public opinion polls at the time confirmed the loss of support. According to Johnson biographer Robert Dallek, "The polling numbers showed a 'new wave of pessimism on Vietnam.' In early March, 40 percent of Americans thought it was a mistake to have sent troops to fight. Forty-one percent believed it was right. Only 35 percent saw the conflict ending in less than two years."[57]

In other words, Westmoreland and President Johnson also became casualties of Tet. Defense Secretary Robert S. McNamara, one of the driving forces behind American involvement and escalation, also left office in the waning days of Tet in February 1968. But he hadn't left in response to Tet. By mid-1967, McNamara had come to realize that the war effort was essentially futile and he advised Johnson to stop the bombing and negotiate peace. His split with Johnson on policy led to his resignation. Taking a post as head of the World Bank, McNamara did not discuss defense issues or policy for years, until he confessed in a 1995 memoir that the war was "wrong, terribly wrong."[58]

But it was more than the doubts of his defense secretary or Walter Cronkite that forced Johnson's decision. Johnson's health was poor and his wife, Lady Bird, wanted him to step aside. He was also confronting the growing costs of a war that was adding a sharp inflationary spiral to the American economy as the Pentagon budget, driven by the war, grew to half the entire federal budget. And there was a sharply negative reaction to a story that Johnson was going to call for more troops. Finally, he was now confronting an old political adversary—Robert F. Kennedy, the former attorney general and chief political adviser to President John F. Kennedy. Now a senator from New York, Robert Kennedy had begun a campaign to replace Johnson on the Democratic ticket in 1968 and was attracting a passionate antiwar following. As Dallek concluded, "The war had become an unshakable burden."[59]

The purely military situation—although no such thing really exists—was not without irony. With a few notable exceptions—at Hué, Khe Sanh, and Cholon—most of the fighting of the opening phase of the Tet Offensive was over in a few days as the American and South Vietnamese forces overcame the initial surprise and responded with superior firepower. The citizen uprising that the communists had been counting on to take down the U.S.-backed Saigon government failed to materialize. "By any objective measure, the Tet offensive was a disaster for the Communists," journalist Max Boot wrote in a recent history of what he terms "America's Small Wars."

"But that was not how it was perceived in the United States," argued Boot. "Americans were shocked by the Vietcong's ability to mount such an extensive offensive. For months, they had been assured by their leaders that there was 'light at the end of the tunnel.' Now they perceived nothing but darkness."[60]

Was the United States losing while winning? The Vietnamese communist forces had suffered horrendous casualties; some estimates ranged as high as forty thousand killed. Their losses continued to grow as subsequent fighting extended into the fall of 1968. By the time the offensive had run its course, the Vietcong guerrilla forces had been crippled and the North Vietnamese Army would carry out the communists' major combat operations during the rest of the war. Truong Nhu Tang, the Vietcong's minister of justice, who was imprisoned in Saigon during the offensive, later said, "The Front's armed forces had suffered agonizing and irreplaceable losses during the frontal assaults of Tet. What might happen to the Northern main-force divisions in the meat grinder of American air power was anyone's guess.... All this suggested strongly that some kind of negotiated settlement was at least as likely an outcome as a decisive military resolution."[61]

The Americans had clearly won the tactical victory. But the sheer scope and ferocity of the offensive and the vivid images of the fighting on the nightly television news convinced many Americans that the Johnson administration had lied to them, and the president's credibility plummeted. Perhaps more important, the offensive shook the administration's own confidence and led to a reevaluation of American strategy. When General Westmoreland asked for an additional 206,000 troops to "take advantage of the situation," President Johnson balked.

As the Tet Offensive began, there had been a powwow at CIA headquarters. In Tim Weiner's account, the director of the CIA, Richard Helms, called in all of his Vietnam experts on February 1, 1968. All were—or soon would be—in accord on some basic points, including the fact that Westmoreland had no coherent strategy. They also agreed, according to Weiner, that "[i]t was useless to send more American troops. If the government and the army of South Vietnam did not pull together and fight the enemy, the United States should get out.... The army of South Vietnam [was] shattered and the two leaders at one another's throats. American soldiers were unable to defend the nation's cities; American spies were panicked and demoralized. Hanoi had won its greatest political victory since 1954, when it handed the French their final defeat at Dien Bien Phu.

"Helms personally gave the president the deeply pessimistic conclusions. They destroyed all but the last of LBJ's enormous political will."[62]

By the end of March 1968, almost 4,000 Americans had died in Tet Offensive battles that raged from rice paddies to hilltops to more than 30 of South Vietnam's 44 provincial capitals. The number of enemy dead had climbed to more than 58,000. More than 14,000 South Vietnamese civilians, men, women, and children, also had died.[63]

Cronkite's broadcast on that February night has been seen as the straw that broke Lyndon B. Johnson's back. There is a belief that Cronkite—and the American media in general—had been responsible for shifting popular opinion and influencing the course of the American war effort. There is also a belief that the media had done so in a misleading way. In a book that stirred considerable debate, *The Big Story*, the late journalist Peter Braestrup—a veteran of Korea, where he had been wounded, and who worked in Vietnam during Tet as a correspondent for the *Washington Post*—contended that "crisis journalism" had veered from reality in describing the offensive. His view holds that the media version of Tet influenced the public's perception of the war and changed American attitudes about Vietnam. It is a narrative that has been embraced by many commentators who think that the United States had the upper hand and might have "won" in Vietnam.

But there is another widely held view that Walter Cronkite and the American media were merely catching up with the rest of America— not leading it. As Stanley Karnow put it, "Public 'support' for the war had been slipping steadily for two years prior to Tet—a trend influenced by mounting casualties, rising taxes, and, especially, the feeling that there was no end in view. For a brief moment after the Tet offensive began, Americans rallied behind the flag in a predictable display of patriotic fervor. But their mood of despair quickly returned as the fighting dragged on, and their endorsement of the conflict resumed its downward spiral."[64]

Whether it was Cronkite who specifically influenced Johnson to step aside or not, his broadcast changed the conversation in America.

"If you watched the *CBS Evening News*, Walter Cronkite sounds like a Pentagon spokesman in 1965 and 1966," *New York Times* reporter and Vietnam War historian Neil Sheehan later commented. "I hope I'm not making Mr. Cronkite angry by saying this. But he's essentially repeating—in an enthusiastic way—what he's being told. It is only after 1968, after Tet '68—the communist Tet Offensive of '68 which disillusioned the public—that you find an antiwar bias coming into the news media in general. You find figures like Cronkite really questioning the war."[65]

Cronkite himself worried that he had gone too far. Later blasted about whether his February 25, 1968, broadcast had demoralized troops, he worried that he had betrayed the fighting men in Vietnam. As James H. Willbanks pointed out in a history of Tet, "The role of the media during the Vietnam War remains controversial, and there has been a long-standing argument that the coverage of the war and particularly the Tet offensive ultimately led to the American defeat in Vietnam."

But as Willbanks himself concluded, "All the reports, news photos, and film footage, good or bad, only served to add velocity to a situation made bad by the credibility gap that had begun to develop well before the Communists launched their offensive in 1968.... This was the same impression that many Americans had of the bitter fighting that they saw on their televisions during the Tet Offensive."[66]

The controversy over the media's role—and especially Cronkite's place in Vietnam history—is only one part of the disputes that continue to rage over Tet and Vietnam.

The other controversy that lingers over Hué's part in this ghastly history is the fate of the missing. After the battle, much of the ancient city was a pile of rubble as an estimated 40 percent of its buildings were destroyed. Besides 116,000 homeless civilians, there were 5,800 civilians reported killed or missing.

In the months after the battle, mass graves were uncovered in the areas surrounding the city, as George Smith had witnessed. While the reports of an atrocity committed by American troops at the Vietnamese village of My Lai began to emerge in November 1969 in a story broken by investigative journalist Seymour Hersh and which received wide media attention, the purported atrocity killings in Hué attracted little American notice at the time.

Later reports would attribute the deaths to a North Vietnamese program of "retribution killings" aimed at South Vietnamese government officials, religious leaders, and others identified by Hanoi as "collaborators." But in his recent history of Vietnam, *Kill Anything That Moves*, Nick Turse pointed to the massive U.S. counterattack bombings as potentially responsible for much of the Tet death toll in Hué. What's more, Turse argued that after Hué was taken, " 'Black teams' of South Vietnamese assassins moved in, reportedly torturing and 'disappearing' those accused of collaborating with the revolutionary forces, including women and children."[67]

While still the Vietcong minister of justice, Truong Nhu Tang described asking a North Vietnamese official about atrocities in Hué during Tet. "He expressed his sorrow and disappointment about what had happened, and explained that discipline in Hué had been seriously inadequate. Fanatic young soldiers had indiscriminately shot people and angry local citizens who supported the revolution had on various occasions taken justice into their own hands....I did not find this explanation particularly satisfying. But I must also admit that neither did I pursue the issue. In the context of a bloody and atrocious conflict, the events in Hué were not, for me at least, the kind of stunning blow that forces the reconsideration of basic assumptions."[68] (After the fall of Saigon, a disillusioned Truong Nhu Tang saw the violence that swept the country as North Vietnamese forces took over, and he fled the country for exile in Paris, where he later recorded his memoirs, published in 1985.)

According to Willbanks, "We may never know what really happened at Hué, but it is clear that mass executions did occur and that reports of the massacre there had a significant impact on South Vietnamese and American attitudes for many years after the Tet Offensive and would ultimately contribute to the abject panic that seized South Vietnam when the North Vietnamese launched their final offensive in 1975."[69]

The American political fallout from Tet, and the Vietnam War in general, continued as President Johnson completed his term in 1968. When the Democratic National Convention opened in Chicago that summer, in the midst of antiwar protests and a violent police response, the Democrats nominated Hubert Humphrey, Johnson's vice president. The Republicans later selected Richard M. Nixon, who sounded a tough law-and-order campaign theme. Many Americans—Nixon called them the Silent Majority—were angry over the racial and antiwar protests sweeping the nation, and the assassinations of Martin Luther King Jr. and Robert F. Kennedy earlier in the year had seemingly torn the fabric of American society apart.

But in 1968, the war became for Americans not just the big issue, but the only issue. Hoping to put a negotiated peace within reach before he left office, Johnson came to suspect that Republican candidate Nixon was trying to scuttle American efforts to reach a settlement with North Vietnam at the Paris negotiations through a close and powerful political ally, Anna Chennault, the Chinese-born widow of famed World War II aviator General Claire Lee Chennault. Anna Chennault had close connections to the South Vietnamese regime.

"Johnson was convinced that Nixon knew and had even ordered the initiative to discourage Saigon from coming to the peace talks," wrote Johnson biographer Robert Dallek. "He had good reasons for his suspicions."[70] Johnson was considering going public with these assertions about Nixon's actions, even describing them as "treasonous" in private talks. On November 3, Nixon called Johnson directly to deny the reports. No last-minute peace accord—which presumably would have helped Humphrey—was reached. Dallek, in his summary of this campaign incident, maintains that the contact was made on Nixon's behalf and writes, "In 1997, [Anna] Chennault acknowledged that Nixon and Mitchell [John Mitchell, later Nixon's Attorney General]...knew everything. 'I was constantly in touch with Mitchell and Nixon,' she said."[71] President Johnson did not press the issue at the time, believing that Nixon was likely to win and that the controversy, if exposed, would be too dangerous for the country.

In one of the closest presidential elections of modern times, the Republican ticket of Richard Nixon and Spiro Agnew defeated Democrat Hubert Humphrey, with third-party candidate George Wallace, the segregationist governor of Alabama, drawing more than 9 million votes in the November 1968 race. (With more than 13 percent of the popular vote, Wallace and running mate Air Force general Curtis LeMay, who publicly disavowed Wallace's segregationist views, won five states and forty-six electoral votes in one of the best third-party showings in presidential history.)

At year's end, American troop strength in Vietnam was at 540,000. The Paris Peace Accords between the warring parties continued as Nixon took office, even as President Nixon and National Security Advisor Henry Kissinger ordered the secret bombing of communist bases in Cambodia, expanding the war without congressional authority. While Nixon pursued these two tracks of talking peace while escalating the war, the American antiwar movement moved from college campuses to large cities, drawing wider popular support. At the end of 1969, the draft deferments were replaced by a lottery system to reduce criticism of the Selective Service System as unfair. The last draftee to serve in Vietnam was called up on June 30, 1973.

Early in 1972, another presidential election year, Nixon announced that a secret negotiation between Kissinger (who became secretary of state in September 1973) and North Vietnam's Le Duc Tho had produced an eight-point peace plan. The two men were awarded the Nobel Peace Prize in 1973, but Le Duc Tho declined the honor, saying, "Peace has not been established in South Vietnam."[72]

Nixon won a second term in 1972 in a landslide victory, humbling the Democratic antiwar candidate George McGovern. A formal cease-fire agreement was announced on January 27, 1973.

On January 22, a few days before the cease-fire was announced, Lyndon B. Johnson died of a heart attack at his Texas home. Once one of the most powerful politicians in American history, he had left office in defeat and disgrace. His management of the war in Vietnam had completely overshadowed his substantial domestic accomplishments in areas of civil rights, health care, and economic justice.

Before the year's end, an increasingly war-wary and war-weary Congress passed the War Powers Act, over President Nixon's veto. In a sharp blow to executive powers under the Constitution, the law restricted the president's power to deploy and maintain U.S. forces in an area of hostilities without congressional consent. The legislation required the president to inform Congress within forty-eight hours of committing troops to military actions, with a sixty-day limit unless the president requested and received congressional authorization or a declaration of war for such actions.

Congress's override of the presidential veto was possible because Nixon had been weakened by Watergate, the political scandal and constitutional crisis created by the break-in at the Democratic Party's national offices by men working for the Nixon reelection campaign. Their arrest and the subsequent cover-up of the involvement of the White House and the FBI led to congressional investigations and constitutional arguments over executive power that forced Nixon's resignation even as American involvement in Vietnam wound down and combat troops were withdrawn from the country in March 1973.

After Nixon resigned in August 1974, his successor, Gerald Ford, watched on television as North Vietnamese forces overran Saigon on April 29, 1975. The Vietnam War was finally over.

———

The end of the fighting in Vietnam was not a good time for the Pentagon. Or Washington, D.C., for that matter. Or the CIA.

The war's long, slow crawl toward a negotiated peace came as the Watergate scandal finished the presidency of Richard Nixon in the disgrace of a resignation before near-certain impeachment. He had promised "peace with honor." He left office in 1974 before peace had been achieved and with any remnants of his personal honor destroyed, although by the time of his death twenty years later in 1994, Nixon's reputation as an elder statesman had been partially rehabilitated.

But in his fall, Nixon had taken the CIA down with him. "The final blow," Tim Weiner wrote, "was [Nixon's] admission that he had ordered the CIA to obstruct justice in the name of national security."[73] The CIA was further damaged during the presidency of Gerald Ford, when Senate hearings held in 1975 revealed the full extent of the agency's illicit doings alongside its many failures in its key mission of providing good intelligence.

The Vietnam fiasco, Watergate, other domestic espionage, the Senate Church Committee hearings on the CIA—named for Intelligence Committee chairman Senator Frank Church—all combined for a toxic mix that helped the relatively unknown governor of Georgia, Jimmy Carter, retake the White House for the Democrats in 1976.

A navy officer, Carter had served on nuclear warships, and he would make the reduction of the nuclear threat a centerpiece of his presidency. Coming to office in the wake of Vietnam, Carter brought with him a determined noninterventionism and hopes for peaceful diplomatic resolutions to world problems. The most significant transformation of the American military during the period had begun in 1973, with a transition to an all-volunteer army, a move that was coupled with sharp cuts to the Pentagon budget in Vietnam's aftermath.

Carter achieved a major diplomatic breakthrough when he brokered a peace treaty between Israel and Egypt. Bringing Anwar Sadat of Egypt* and Menachem Begin to Washington to seal what was known as the Camp David Accords in 1978 seemed to produce a new high note in American diplomatic history.

But Carter's undoing came a year later in another part of the Middle East as Iran, which Carter himself had called "an island of stability," exploded in an Islamic revolution. Since 1953, when the CIA had overthrown Iran's elected government and installed the shah, Iran had been a reliable ally of the United States. A friendly oil-producing country that then bordered the Soviet Union, Iran provided an important counterbalance and the United States was willing to overlook the shah's repressive police-state tactics while they served American interests. That all changed after the shah was overthrown in November 1979; Iranian students took sixty-six Americans hostage at the American embassy in Tehran during the Islamic revolution.

The Carter administration's military response—an attempted rescue—ended in disaster when helicopters carrying Special Operations forces crashed in the Iranian desert, killing eight Americans. The episode, combined with the Soviet Union's armored invasion of Afghanistan in 1979, seemed to symbolize America's—and Carter's—powerlessness, not only in the Middle East but globally. When Carter's approval ratings hit a post–World War II presidential low, the way was clear for Ronald Reagan's landslide election in 1980.

---

* Islamic fundamentalist army officers assassinated Anwar Sadat in 1981, dashing hopes for a broader Middle East settlement as the treaty with Israel was seen as the principal motivation for his assassination.

Promising to cut taxes, reduce America's deficit, and rebuild America's military, Reagan swept into office despite the fact that one of his Republican primary opponents had said that his goals could only be accomplished with "smoke and mirrors." Another primary opponent famously called Reagan's plans "voodoo economics." This was George H. W. Bush, and he became Reagan's vice president.

But with a compliant Congress and the understanding that his plan required grand defense budgets, he declared a "Reagan Doctrine"—a combination of fierce anticommunism, more conventional forces stationed around the world, and preparedness for sustained nuclear or nonnuclear conflict with the Soviet Union. "Communicating his proposals with a relaxed, jocular militancy that soothed his constituents and frightened the rest of the world," commented military historians Allan R. Millett and Peter Maslowski, "the president proposed and Congress accepted—without major alteration—six years of increased defense spending, the longest sustained peacetime investment in the armed forces in the twentieth century. The authorizations in this honeymoon represented a 56 percent increase over Carter's last defense budget."[74]

Reagan's muscular militarism was matched by his rhetoric—he famously called the Soviet Union an "evil empire" and stood in Berlin to rhetorically tell Soviet leader Mikhail Gorbachev, "Tear down this wall."

Eventually, of course, the Berlin Wall was torn down, after Reagan left office. And then the Soviet Union itself fell, in an astonishing burst of mostly peaceful protest and mobilization within the Soviet-dominated Eastern Bloc.

But the Cold War's sputtering end came from a combination of forces far more potent than Ronald Reagan's powerful anti-Soviet rhetoric. As Millett and Maslowski summarized:

Jimmy Carter, Ronald Reagan and George Bush all supported the sturdy military opposition that contributed to the collapse of the Soviet Union....But in the end, the exhaustion of the Russian people, the patriotic endurance of the national minorities in the Soviet Union, the rebelliousness of the member states of the Warsaw Pact, and the greed and moral poverty of the Communist party brought the Soviet Union down. Although the United States could find some comfort in its role in the demise of Soviet Communism, it could not claim that military strength alone had provided a new measure of national security. [75]

Reagan's role in the end of the Cold War is rightly celebrated—if perhaps embellished and overstated. And the Cold War triumph over the "evil empire" sometimes masks two disastrous events on Reagan's watch—again in the part of the world that had long bedeviled so many American presidents: the Middle East, with its combination of Israeli-Arab tensions, oil politics, and rising Islamic fundamentalism.

On October 23, 1983, a truck bomb exploded underneath the barracks of a U.S. Marine force stationed in Beirut, Lebanon. The marines had been deployed there in the wake of an Israeli invasion of Lebanon, as "peacekeepers" sent to police a cease-fire. In the blast, 260 men died, 220 of them marines and some CIA operatives. The marines were withdrawn from Lebanon a few months later. "Their failed deployment," Tim Weiner noted, "had been doomed by a near total lack of accurate intelligence."[76]

In a stunning operation that prompted criticism that the Reagan administration was deflecting attention from Beirut and the attack by terrorists, the U.S. invaded Grenada on October 25, 1983, a few days after the truck bombing. A tiny Caribbean island with a population of 91,000 in the Lesser Antilles, the former British colony had come under socialist rule following a coup four years earlier, and Cuban workers, including some combat engineers and special forces, were building an airstrip on the island. The rapid and successful overthrow of the island's regime was purportedly made to rescue American students attending a medical college on the island—though the students later mostly expressed surprise at the idea of needing to be rescued.

The invasion was sharply criticized by both of America's closest allies, Canada and the United Kingdom—the latter of which was led by Reagan ally and confidante Prime Minister Margaret Thatcher. The United Nations later called it a "flagrant violation of international law." But the Grenada invasion, clearly designed to show that the United States was not a "paper tiger," played well with the American audience and even inspired a chest-thumping and highly fictionalized film, *Heartbreak Ridge*, directed by and starring Clint Eastwood. "It requires a certain crazy vision to transform the American invasion of Grenada into the equivalent of Iwo Jima," said one reviewer.[77]

The Pentagon review of the Grenada operation was even less enthusiastic. Three years after the invasion, a declassified Pentagon study found serious problems with the operation, largely caused by hasty planning, compounded by the old woes of war—confusion, poor communications, and faulty intelligence. Reporting on the Pentagon assessment, *New York Times* reporter John H. Cushman Jr. wrote:

> An almost total lack of intelligence data about the situation on the island, brought on when a Central Intelligence Agency operative refused to fly there as a crisis enveloped the island's radical Government, was followed by critical failures of military communications and faulty tactics.... While the operation has been criticized for poor coordination, and has been cited to support arguments for legislation that will soon reorganize the Joint Chiefs of Staff, newly published details from the Pentagon's assessment go well beyond what was known previously. As portrayed in the report, the mission's flaws included mistaken information about the strength of the

island's defenses, a decision to land Army rangers in daylight hours and, above all, a nearly crippling lack of communications between the Army, Navy, Air Force and Marine units that took part in the invasion.[78]

Another Reagan foray into Middle East politics also resulted in tragedy and fiasco. A TWA jetliner bound for Rome was hijacked after its takeoff from Athens on June 14, 1985. The hijackers were Shiite Muslims demanding the release of seven hundred Muslim prisoners held by Israel. After the plane was landed in Beirut and held there for seventeen days, Robert Dean Stethem, a U.S. Navy diver on board, was shot and killed, his body dumped on the tarmac in Beirut.[79]

Reagan quietly pressured the Israelis to release some prisoners they held—meeting the hijackers' demands. Then his CIA director, William Casey, proposed making a deal to win the release of other hostages. With Reagan's approval, 504 American TOW missiles were sent to Tehran, America's avowed enemy and supporter of terrorism.* And like that, as Tim Weiner notes, "[t]wo pillars of Reagan's foreign policy—no deals with terrorists, no arms for Iran—tumbled down in secret."[80]

For the next two presidents, George H. W. Bush and Bill Clinton, the terrorist threat, the rising tide of Islamic fundamentalism, and the rivalries between Iran and Iraq—which had fought a long, bloody war for the most part of a decade—presented the greatest military threats.

The region's instability led to the Persian Gulf War in 1991, under George H. W. Bush. A response to Iraqi dictator Saddam Hussein's

---

* The profits from the arms deal were then transferred illegally to anti-communist rebels in Nicaragua, known as the "Contras," in what became known as the "Iran-Contra Affair," almost resulting in Ronald Reagan's impeachment.

invasion of Kuwait, Operation Desert Storm was a quick, devastating air and ground assault proving that the United States military could easily handle a conventional-style threat. Under Clinton, the major military undertaking was a NATO-sponsored air war against Serbia. It was an attempt to end a brutal civil war that had split the former Yugoslavia, which had dissolved in the post–Soviet Union era into warring groups with regional and religious differences.

But the greatest threats would still come from the Middle East, as Saddam Hussein's Iraq continued to create international tension. When he refused to cooperate with United Nations weapons inspectors in 1998, President Clinton ordered a three-day bombing attack. That was also the year that Al Qaeda, a then-obscure terrorist group, bombed two American embassies in Africa. A wealthy Saudi expatriate named Osama bin Laden, who had gone to Afghanistan to fight the Soviets in the 1980s, led the shadowy organization. Bin Laden remained in Afghanistan when the country fell to Islamic extremists known as the Taliban.

American efforts to track, capture, or kill bin Laden had been unsuccessful when Clinton left office in January 2001.

Then four airplanes were hijacked on September 11, 2001.

## Chapter Six

*→>-<←*

# The Bridge over the River Euphrates

*Fallujah, Iraq—March 2004*

"We arrived in Fallujah to see people gathered around two burned-out S.U.V.'s.... Two bodies were on the ground, their jackets still smoking.... Then my attention turned to the bodies swinging mutilated from the bridge."[1]

—*Abdulrazzaq al-Saiedi (March 31, 2004)*

"I just joined to help Americans.... I never want her to ever have to worry about anybody coming into our country. I'd rather kill 'em in their backyard than have 'em come into our backyard.... The more I kill the less I've got to worry about coming into my country."[2]

—*U.S. Marine corporal Willy Wold (November 12, 2004)*

"It sucks. Honestly, it feels like we're driving around waiting to get blown up."[3]

—*Specialist Tim Ivey (July 27, 2006)*

"Blackwater provides a valuable service. They protect people's lives. And I appreciate the sacrifice and the service that the Blackwater employees have made."[4]

—*President George W. Bush (September 2007)*

"War is business and business is very good."[5]

—*Jeremy Scahill, Blackwater (2007)*

"I don't think anyone had the grand illusion that Fallujah or Ramadi was going to turn into Disneyland, but none of us thought it was going to fall back to a jihadist insurgency."[6]

—*Former marine Adam Banotai (January 2014)*

# Milestones in the War in Iraq

## 2001

**September 11** Armed hijackers take over four jets and attack the World Trade Center in New York City and the Pentagon in Washington, D.C.; one of the jets crashes in Pennsylvania before reaching its target (presumed to be in Washington, D.C.).

**October 7** The United States and allied nations attack Afghanistan in response to the 9/11 attacks; the stated aim is to overthrow the Taliban government, which allowed the Al Qaeda terror group to train and plan its mission in Afghanistan.

**November** In the aftermath of 9/11, a group of senior U.S. military planners begin preparations for a possible invasion of Iraq.

## 2002

**November 27** After the UN Security Council declares Iraq in breach of a disarmament resolution, Iraq allows weapons inspectors to return to the country in search of banned weapons of mass destruction (WMD).

## 2003

**March 19** "Operation Iraqi Freedom" commences with U.S. air strikes. Iraq's military forces, including the feared Republican Guard, are quickly overwhelmed, and many of the troops melt into the civilian population. There is no evidence of any chemical or biological weapons used by the Iraqis.

**April 9**  U.S. Marines topple a statue of Saddam Hussein in a major square in Baghdad.

**April**  Order in Iraq begins to break down amid widespread looting.

**May 2**  Aboard the USS *Abraham Lincoln*, under a banner reading "Mission Accomplished," President Bush declares the "end of major combat operations" in Iraq.

**May 6**  L. Paul Bremer is appointed to supervise the occupation of the country, now being swept by chaos, replacing retired general Jay Garner. On May 9, Bremer disbands the entire Iraqi military and intelligence services. He also announces that some fifty thousand members of Saddam Hussein's Baath Party are barred from any government work.

**August 19**  A bombing attack on UN headquarters in Baghdad kills more than twenty people, including the UN special representative, Sergio Vieira de Mello. The UN closes its Iraq mission.

**December 13**  Saddam Hussein is captured.

## 2004

**January 4**  The Bush administration concedes that its prewar arguments about extensive stockpiles of WMD appear to have been mistaken.

**March 31**  Four American employees of a private security contractor, Blackwater, are killed in the city of Fallujah and two of the bodies are hung from a bridge.

**April 30**  Photographs of prisoners at Abu Ghraib prison abused by U.S. soldiers are first published. Seven soldiers are later convicted of torturing and humiliating Iraqi prisoners, but no senior officers are charged or punished.

**November**  President Bush is reelected to a second term.

## 2005

**March** A presidential commission concludes that "not one bit" of prewar intelligence about chemical, biological, and other weapons in Iraq was accurate.

## 2006

**February 22** A mosque in Samarra, one of the holiest sites for Shiite Muslims, is bombed. The attack leads to a dramatic escalation of sectarian violence, with Shiites attacking Sunnis in large-scale killings.

**November 7** In U.S. midterm elections, the Republicans lose control of the House of Representatives, largely as a result of growing opposition to the war. Secretary of Defense Donald Rumsfeld steps down and is replaced by Robert Gates, a moderate who had been privately critical of the war.

**December 6** The Iraq Study Group, formed earlier to analyze the situation in Iraq, concludes that it "is grave and deteriorating" and "U.S. forces seem to be caught in a mission that has no foreseeable end."

**December 30** Saddam Hussein is hanged, following separate trials for "crimes against humanity" and genocide.

## 2007

**January 10** The presidential campaign to replace George Bush begins; President Bush announces a "surge" of additional troops in Iraq. General David Petraeus is assigned to implement the new strategy.

## 2008

**November 4** Barack Obama, a critic of the Iraq War who had voted against it in the Senate and campaigned to end it, is elected president. Obama asks Secretary of Defense Gates to remain in the post.

**November 27** Iraq's government approves an agreement calling for the withdrawal of U.S. forces by December 31, 2011. By September 2009, the U.S. troop presence in Iraq will decline to 130,000. (There will still be tens of thousands of private American contractors doing Defense Department work in Iraq at that time.)

## 2010

**August 31** President Obama declares an end to the seven-year combat mission in Iraq.

## 2011

**May 1** President Obama announces that Osama bin Laden was killed at his compound in Pakistan by a Navy SEAL team.

**September 15** The Obama administration announces the withdrawal of 33,000 "surge troops" from Afghanistan as part of the pledge to withdraw all U.S. troops by 2014.

**December 15** The war in Iraq is declared over as U.S troops are withdrawn.

*Fallujah, Iraq*
*March 31, 2004*

Shoes for his barefoot soldiers: As Civil War legend once had it, that was why Robert E. Lee took his army north to Gettysburg in 1863.

But kitchen equipment? Battles and wars are not supposed to rise and fall over pots and pans.

In the middle of one of Iraq's most dangerous areas, a little more than a year after the American "shock and awe" assault on Iraq had commenced in March 2003, four experienced combat veterans were riding shotgun on a truck convoy passing through Fallujah, the City of Mosques. This pair of two-man teams was not providing advance reconnaissance for the U.S. Marine force encamped nearby. They weren't guarding a load of deadly ammunition, high-tech weaponry, or even high-level diplomats. Their assignment was simple, even absurdly mundane in a war zone: Escort three trucks detailed to collect a supply of cooking equipment left behind by the U.S. Army in Fallujah and deliver it back to another American military base.

On March 31, 2004, Scott Helvenston, Wesley Batalona, Jerry Zovko, and Michael Teague, all experienced soldiers, were working as guards for Blackwater USA, a private contracting security firm. They weren't the Mall Cop variety security detail, guarding shops and an array of food courts. Earning about six hundred dollars a day, they might be more accurately called mercenaries or soldiers of fortune, although they were technically called private security contractors.

On this day, their mission as contract security officers was to provide an armed escort for trucks belonging to Eurest Support Services

(ESS), a large-scale food service company that operates field kitchens for military services, mining and exploration companies, and construction companies in harsh and often dangerous locations.

The four men were riding in two Mitsubishi Pajero sport utility vehicles, much lighter and much more vulnerable than Humvees to roadside bombs. Driving on Iraq's Highway 10 about thirty miles west of Baghdad, they were heading into one of Iraq's most combustible locations, a hardscrabble industrial city of some 140,000 people, many of them seething at the American forces.

It was a little more than a year since the United States had invaded Saddam Hussein's Iraq. And it was less than one year since President George W. Bush had famously declared, "Major combat operations are over." After landing a plane on the deck of the aircraft carrier USS *Abraham Lincoln* on May 1, 2003, the president made that assertion with a large red, white, and blue banner reading "Mission Accomplished" hanging behind him.

The four men were shepherding three empty Mercedes flatbed trucks, driven by Iraqis, which were scheduled to pick up the kitchen equipment from the recently vacated base of the 82nd Airborne in Fallujah. Just a week earlier, on March 24, the U.S. Army had moved out and turned control of Fallujah over to the care of the U.S. Marines, who had pitched their tents on the outskirts of the city.

Whatever short-lived joy some Iraqis may have felt at seeing the dictator Saddam Hussein deposed, captured, and imprisoned by December 2003 had already been replaced by a sour mood of resentment at the American "occupiers" in the early days of 2004. As the *New Yorker*'s George Packer wrote, "In the summer of 2003, the enemy brought it on, as President Bush had taunted them to do, and the U.S. military found itself enmeshed in a guerrilla war for the first time since the Vietnam War. In the early summer, it was still safe for an American to jog along the east bank of the Tigris in the morning, to lunch on chicken cordon bleu at a nice restaurant in western Baghdad's heavily Baathist Mansur district, and even to walk out at night to visit nearby friends. By late fall of 2003, such actions would still be possible but foolhardy."[7]

Centuries-old religious hatred between Sunni and Shiite Muslims in Iraq; power plays in the new political landscape of an oil-rich nation; ethnic rivalries born with modern Iraq's "creation" in the wake of World War I; decades of a fearsome, brutal, and corrupt dictatorship under Saddam; and even ancient tribal feuds: All of these ingredients fed a poisonous brew of violence and resentment at the American occupation. And Fallujah, in Anbar Province, had become one of the most combustible cauldrons of that resentment.

Before setting off for Fallujah, the Blackwater men were uneasy. One of them, former Army Ranger Wes Batalona, complained to a friend that the team had never worked together before. Under the terms of its contract, Blackwater was supposed to supply these convoy security missions with two SUVs, each carrying three guards per vehicle: a driver, one man riding shotgun, and a third man in back with a heavy machine gun. Instead, the foursome set out that morning with just two men per car, each vehicle missing their rear gunner. The SUVs were only outfitted with a steel plate as extra armor. And the men had not been given maps.

But they did possess serious skills. Whether Army Ranger or Navy SEAL, all had been trained to deal with danger of the most unexpected kind. In the lead car and in charge of the mission was Jerry Zovko, a thirty-three-year-old Croatian-American, "built like a sequoia" and fluent in five languages, including Arabic. Zovko had served in the 82nd Airborne and had been deployed in Yugoslavia, his parents' homeland. His buddy, the driver, was forty-eight-year-old Wes Batalona, a Hawaiian who had been a paratrooper and a twenty-year Army Ranger vet, with experience in Panama and then Somalia in 1993. After a stint training Iraqi soldiers, Batalona had been back in Hawaii, working as a security guard at a hotel, "chasing local kids out of the pool," before his buddy Jerry Zovko convinced him to return to Iraq.[8]

Bringing up the rear, the second car carried Scott Helvenston, thirty-eight and an eleven-year veteran of the Navy SEALs, and Michael Teague, also thirty-eight, a former member of the Special Ops unit known as the "Night Stalkers," a reservist who had won a Bronze Star while serving in Afghanistan.

The four men had spent the night before they set off at Marine base Camp Fallujah. But the men kept their distance from the leathernecks. Had they spoken to the marines, the Blackwater team might have learned that the Americans were already in the midst of a major offensive meant to assert control over the increasingly restive city, where elements of the radical Islamist movement and remnants of Saddam's army were beginning to aggressively strike back at the American occupation.

Just a day before, a Marine convoy had hit an IED (improvised explosive device), the insurgents' weapon of choice in Iraq. Iraqi fighters had attacked the marines, killing one. In fact, nine marines had died in fighting around Fallujah in the previous eleven days. Whether the four Blackwater men knew that Fallujah was already a hornet's nest of anti-American sentiment and rising anger, or if they felt pressured by their employer to get on with the mission, would remain an unanswered question.[9]

The main road through Fallujah, Highway 10, passed through a strip of restaurants, small shops, and cafés. Attempting to clamp their control over the city and limit new fighters and weapons from reaching Fallujah, the marines had blocked off several nearby roads, adding to the traffic congestion on the city's main highway. As the Blackwater convoy neared the city on this morning, the street was crowded with people. When a small group of masked men detonated an explosive device, the streets cleared and the shopkeepers shuttered their doors.

The masked men were Iraqi insurgents who had been tipped off to the convoy and been told, according to some reports, that it was led by a group of CIA agents. Riding in civilian-style SUVs, armed, and wearing sunglasses, the Blackwater team certainly looked the part. *Washington Post* senior Pentagon correspondent Thomas Ricks later reported that there had been a leak about the convoy from a source in Baghdad's "Green Zone," the heavily defended headquarters of the U.S. occupying forces.[10]

As the two cars driven by the contractors and bracketing the flat-bed trucks rolled into the city, the convoy slowed in the heavy traffic, which was worsened by the explosion. Then, abruptly, the convoy came to a complete halt on the city's main thoroughfare.

Without warning, the sound of machine gun fire split the air. Bullets ripped into the vehicles as Iraqi insurgents dashed into the street and sprayed both Pajeros with automatic weapons. "With no armor plating on the vehicles, the four men inside were riddled with bullets," wrote journalist Bing West in his account of the Fallujah attack. "They had no chance to fire back."[11]

Scott Helvenston was fatally wounded. In a scene of sudden and utter chaos and savagery, a mob of men had jumped on the hood of his car, firing into the vehicle and pounding on the windshield. As chants of *Allahu Akbar!* (God is great) filled the air, the attackers departed and a large crowd of Iraqis moved in. Soon more than a dozen young men joined in the assault on the cars. According to one eyewitness, Michael Teague survived the shooting but was dragged from the SUV. Attacked with bricks and shovels by the cheering mobs, Teague was bludgeoned to death and then partially dismembered.

Helvenston and Teague had been in the rear SUV, which was hit first. As soon as Jerry Zovko and Wes Batalona, in the lead car, realized they were being ambushed, they gunned their vehicle in an attempt to escape. But it was too late. "Within moments, they found themselves in a hail of gunfire as their jeep slammed into another vehicle," Jeremy Scahill recounted. "Zovko's head was blown apart.

Batalona's Hawaiian shirt was full of bullet holes, his head slumped over."[12]

What happened next was a spontaneous outburst of barbarous rage that would soon jolt the world. "The looters swarm, pouring out of alleys and shops and apartments," as journalist Sean Flynn recorded the scene. "Wes's carbine is yanked off his neck. A teenager in white trousers vaults the hood of the lead Pajero, reaches through the passenger window, grabs Jerry's gun, jerks the strap over his lolling head. More hands reach in, taking bullets and radios....Kids bring cans of gasoline, soak the Pajero, light them on fire....There's a mob on the highway now, people streaming toward the oily smoke. No Iraqi police stop them. No Iraqi firefighters come with hoses and water."[13]

" 'Where is Bush?' shouted a boy no older than ten, as he ground his heel into a burned head," according to Peter Baker's account of the Bush White House. " 'Let him come here and see this!' "[14]

All four Americans were soon dead, either shot or beaten to death. But the macabre death orgy didn't stop there. And the whole world would soon see. "Egged on by older men, boys dragged the smoldering corpses on the pavement and beat the charred flesh with their flip-flops to show that Americans were scum under the soles of their shoes," wrote West, a Vietnam combat veteran, former Pentagon official, and military writer "embedded" with the Marines in Iraq. "A body was ripped apart, and a leg attached to a rope was tossed over a power line above the highway."[15]

The mob then tied two of the bodies to a nearby car and dragged them to the main bridge across the Euphrates, a span American soldiers had nicknamed the "Brooklyn Bridge." Some Iraqi men climbed the bridge's rusting beams and suspended two of the bodies upside down. The charred, lifeless remains of Scott Helvenston and Mike Teague were left to dangle over the river for ten hours.[16]

"We arrived in Fallujah to see people gathered around two burned-out S.U.V.'s," wrote Abdulrazzaq al-Saiedi, an Iraqi journalist working for the *New York Times*, who witnessed the immediate aftermath of the attack and later recounted the mixture of fear and revulsion he felt as an Iraqi:

> My reporter's instincts carried me, almost against my will, through the sea of rioters, to where the bodies of the contractors had been dragged.... A boy of about 10 was kicking one of them, yelling, *"Pacha, pacha,"* the name of an Iraqi dish made from the head of a sheep. It crossed my mind that this child could not be human. Then my attention turned to the bodies swinging mutilated from the bridge. I felt briefly disoriented.... I pretended to be part of the crowd. "These Americans deserve this destiny!" I yelled. I knew I would be the fifth body if I were exposed as a reporter for a U.S. paper.[17]

Accounts of the deadly ambush and the grisly murders and mutilation of the Americans spread quickly around the world. Other journalists soon arrived to capture the aftermath of the attack, and Iraqi insurgents later released their own videotape of the gruesome scene as the corpses dangled obscenely from a rusted bridge over the Euphrates River.

If Vietnam had been the television war, Iraq had become the online war, as jihadist websites became the means for instantly and globally transmitting information and propaganda without the strictures of network editors or government censors. "The whole world watches," journalist Flynn later wrote. "And now the war in Iraq looks nothing at all like a liberation. It looks like Mogadishu all over again "[18]

The sickening scenes of the hanging bodies and the burning corpses went viral. And when the news broke in America, the carnage grimly recalled the 1993 incident made famous in the book and subsequent film *Black Hawk Down*, in which two American helicopters were downed by rocket fire and their pilots captured in Mogadishu, Somalia. The chopper pilots were killed and their mutilated and desecrated bodies dragged through the city's streets. At the time of the Fallujah attack, American newspapers noted that the four victims were civilians. But few Americans made a distinction between the U.S. soldiers who had died in Somalia and the American contractors murdered in Iraq; as journalist Sean Flynn noted, they were "civilians working for a private company...that has reaped millions from the war in Iraq."[19]

To that point, most Americans probably assumed that the war in Iraq—like most American wars—was being fought by America's highly trained, highly motivated men and women of the armed services. But the deaths of the contractors underscored a new reality in the way America went to war. Seeking efficiency, the American defense establishment had increasingly turned to private, for-profit firms to do some of the work of war. If corporate America had discovered outsourcing to contain costs, and more government operations—from office cleaning to running prisons—were being "privatized," the Pentagon had learned some new tricks as well. While the journalists embedded with the troops told stories of American fighting men and women in Iraq, the story of the other war—the for-profit war—had been largely ignored.

In Fallujah and the surrounding countryside, the distinction that the Americans were not soldiers was lost on many Iraqis. Their "victory over America" was heralded from mosques, of which there were more than two hundred inside the city and the surrounding towns.[20] The announcements boasting of a victory also heralded a new phase in the year-old Iraqi conflict and the repercussions sent the American chain of command into a whirling frenzy. The civilian and military leadership in Iraq soon got the message from Washington and passed it along down the line. To the American military command in Baghdad, as journalist Thomas E. Ricks recounted it, the word came down: "'Go in and clobber people' was the way one officer remembered it."[21]

At an April 1, 2004, press briefing in Baghdad, Brigadier General Mark Kimmitt said, "Quite simply, we will respond. It's going to be deliberate, it will be precise, and it will be overwhelming."[22]

The "deliberate, precise, and overwhelming" task of "clobbering" Fallujah and regaining control of the city was handed over to the marines then camped outside of the city. Although Marine commanders on the scene "resisted suggestions for a full-fledged assault on the city, arguing for a more targeted approach," in Peter Baker's account of events, they were overruled. Lieutenant General Ricardo Sanchez favored an indirect approach. But he would later remember Defense Secretary Donald Rumsfeld telling him, "No, we've got to attack. We need to make sure that Iraqis in other cities receive our message."[23]

On April 5, only days after the Blackwater contractors were killed and a little more than a year after the fall of Baghdad, the U.S. launched Operation Vigilant Resolve, a coordinated maneuver that involved surrounding the city in an attempt to capture the individuals responsible for the attack as well as anyone else involved in what was now being called "the Iraqi insurgency."

As many of the marines quickly realized, they were going to be engaged in intense, house-to-house combat for the first time since the deadly urban fighting in Hué, Vietnam, in 1968. The fight would be against the mushrooming ranks of Iraqi insurgents and foreign fighters who had flocked to Fallujah. This enemy was much better equipped and trained than American intelligence expected it to be.

But in the twenty-first-century world of a war fought with unmanned drones and laser-guided missiles, the marines would still do it "old school" in a style that George Washington, Ulysses S. Grant, or Jack Pershing would have understood. Correspondent Robert D. Kaplan, embedded with the marines outside Fallujah, wrote, "It was decided that when Bravo Company penetrated the city along with Alpha and Charlie, all fanning out in different directions in the industrial zone of the city, marines would affix bayonets to their M-16 assault rifles. The point was mainly psychological: to show the people of Al-Fallujah that the marines truly meant business."[24]

Even as Vigilant Resolve was rolled out, the marines did not think that they would have to "pacify" Fallujah by themselves. After all, this was the newly liberated Iraq and there was a reconstituted, U.S.-trained and -supported Iraqi army that was expected to pull its weight in restoring order to the country. As part of the grand American plan to train the Iraqi army to eventually take over the nation's security, Iraqi troops from the American-trained Iraqi Civil Defense Corps were supposed to be involved in the Fallujah operation. But on the dawn of the invasion, the Iraqis balked.

"As the assault on Fallujah began," wrote Ricks in *Fiasco*, "commanders ordered an Iraqi battalion to go help the Marines there. It was the first time the U.S. military had sought to involve the newly formed postwar Iraqi army in its major combat operations, and it led to major disappointment. To the chagrin of U.S. commanders, the 620-man 2nd Battalion of the Iraqi Armed Forces refused to join the battle." Of 695 soldiers on the rolls, 106 deserted and another 104 refused to leave their base, Ricks reported. He cited a veteran army planner who said, "That was stunning. It was the first real attempt to use Iraqi forces, and it just flopped."[25]

Although willingly preparing to defend their newly liberated country from foreign assault or invasion, the revived Iraqi army did not plan on going to battle against their fellow Iraqis in what was already exploding into a widespread civil war, compounded by an influx of foreign fighters drawn to Iraq by the idea of jihad against America. The problem worsened when the Iraqi forces came under fire from Iraqi insurgents in what was also the renewal of a complicated ancient sectarian conflict between rival Sunni and Shiite Muslims in the country. Follow-up assessments showed that their American sponsors had also poorly equipped the Iraqi forces. A congressional watchdog, the Government Accountability Office (GAO), found the supplies going to Iraqi forces months behind schedule and that many of the units lacked the most basic fighting equipment, including helmets, radios, rifles, and ammunition.[26]

The Fallujah attack on the contractors had also taken place just as the 2004 American presidential race was getting under way. As often happens in war, the military world was smashing headlong into the political world. Most of these collisions end badly as good military policy is often trumped by electioneering and politicking. Successful politicians don't necessarily make successful military leaders, and vice versa. Rare is the general who makes a good president—Washington, yes; Grant, no—and perhaps even rarer are politicians who make good generals (see Benjamin Butler, discussed in chapter 2).

After the Fallujah news broke in Washington, D.C., President George W. Bush told donors at a Marriott hotel campaign dinner on March 31, "We still face thugs and terrorists in Iraq who would rather go killing the innocent than accept the advance of liberty. This collection of killers is trying to shake our will. America will never be intimidated by thugs and assassins. We are aggressively striking the terrorists in Iraq. We will defeat them there so we do not have to face them in our own country."[27]

That fundamental concept—defeating the terrorists so "we don't have to face them in our own country"—had always been the ostensible reason that America was in Iraq, taken there by George W. Bush (President #43) a little more than twelve years after his father, President George H. W. Bush (President #41), had also taken America to war against Saddam Hussein's Iraq. Eliminating Iraq's supposed "weapons of mass destruction" and ridding Iraq of Saddam—"regime change"—were the other rationales.

Having succeeded Ronald Reagan in 1989, under whom he had served as vice president, the elder President Bush had witnessed the stunning unraveling of communism in Europe in his first two years at the helm. The Berlin Wall, long a symbol of the conflict with Soviet communism, had come crashing down. The Evil Empire—the former Soviet Union—had disintegrated into a collection of independent republics. Long Soviet-dominated Eastern Bloc countries, such as Poland and Czechoslovakia, shifted swiftly to free market democracies in a turnabout that was as sudden as it was remarkable. East and West Germany were again joined as a single country. Former antagonists petitioned to join NATO, and the borders that once bristled with barbed wire and guard posts were replaced by an open European Union, which eventually did not even require passports for one to travel from one member country to the next.

The Cold War was over. George H. W. Bush, who had been the youngest naval pilot in history when he left Yale to enlist after Pearl Harbor, was the president on hand to usher in what he thought would be a New World Order.

But even as the Evil Empire unraveled with stunning velocity, and a half century of Cold War tension and proxy wars wound down, the elder Bush's presidential high point was to come in a part of the world that had confounded every American president since Truman: the Middle East. In Bush's case, the crisis came from Iraqi dictator Saddam Hussein's August 1990 invasion of neighboring oil-rich Kuwait. Mobilizing the United Nations against Saddam Hussein, Bush first ordered Operation Desert Shield, a defensive move to protect the vast oil fields of neighboring country Saudi Arabia. Although there was considerable rhetoric about protecting freedom and liberty, it was difficult to make a case that the United States was going to war to defend democracy. Kuwait and Saudi Arabia were feudal monarchies with little interest in democracy or human rights.

A quick strike by Iraq's army into the Saudi kingdom would have given Iraq control of more than 40 percent of the world's oil reserves, a frightening prospect considering Saddam's proven willingness to measure up to his chief role model, Joseph Stalin. With United Nations approval, the United States spearheaded a coalition of thirty-nine other nations in Operation Desert Storm, a devastating air war, followed by a swift, decisive ground offensive.

# The Bridge over the River Euphrates

On February 28, 1991, the coalition ended all military operations at 8 a.m., about one hundred hours after the ground attack began. American losses for the operation were 148 killed in action and 7 missing in action. The Gulf War lasted forty-two days: thirty-eight days of intense air strikes and four days of ground fighting. The U.S.-led coalition routed Saddam's army, overran Kuwait and southern Iraq, and liberated Kuwait.

In halting the offensive against Iraq without assaulting Baghdad and possibly overthrowing Saddam Hussein, President Bush and his advisers had fulfilled the United Nations terms of the action against Iraq. During the Gulf War, those advisers included Defense Secretary Dick Cheney, who would become George W. Bush's highly influential vice president, and General Colin Powell, chairman of the Joint Chiefs of Staff and later secretary of state under the younger Bush.

The Persian Gulf War had been fought with basic operating principles that the United States should have vital national security interests, overwhelming strike capabilities with an emphasis on ground forces, and widespread public support before taking military action. These were the underpinnings of what became known as the Powell Doctrine. After leaving the army, Powell elaborated on these ideas in a *Foreign Affairs* article:

> When the political objective is important, clearly defined and understood, when the risks are acceptable, and when the use of force can be effectively combined with diplomatic and economic policies, then clear and unambiguous objectives must be given to the armed forces. These objectives must be firmly linked with the political objectives. We must not, for example, send military forces into a crisis with an unclear mission they cannot accomplish—such as we did when we sent the U.S. Marines into Lebanon in 1983. We inserted those proud warriors into the middle of a five-faction civil war complete with

terrorists, hostage-takers and a dozen spies in every camp, and said, "Gentlemen, be a buffer." The results were 241 dead Marines and Navy personnel and a U.S. withdrawal from the troubled area.

When force is used deftly—in smooth coordination with diplomatic and economic policy—bullets may never have to fly. Pulling triggers should always be toward the end of the plan, and when those triggers are pulled all of the sound analysis I have just described should back them up.[28]

During the Gulf War in 1991, several members of the George H. W. Bush administration had pushed for pressing the attack all the way to Baghdad. But Joint Chiefs chairman Powell, along with Secretary of State James Baker and National Security Advisor Brent Scowcroft, won the debate that time around. As Scowcroft and President Bush wrote in *A World Transformed* (1998), "Had we gone the invasion route, the United States could conceivably still be an occupying power in a bitterly hostile world. It would have been a dramatically different—and perhaps barren—outcome."[29]

They were profoundly prophetic words. But others have disagreed ever since. In *How Wars End*, Gideon Rose, the editor of *Foreign Affairs*, argued, "The Bush [41] Administration thought a full loaf in Iraq was too expensive to purchase and many agreed. As the president was fond of saying, 'not gonna do it—wouldn't be prudent.' But in the unforgiving marketplace of geopolitics, buying only half a loaf didn't eliminate the costs. It just meant they would be paid in other ways, at other times, by other people."[30]

The Persian Gulf War had devastated Iraq's infrastructure and fighting capability. But early estimates of as many as one hundred thousand Iraqi soldiers killed and a great number of civilian deaths later proved to be greatly inflated. According to a documentary on the Gulf War by the PBS series *Frontline*, "There were an estimated 10–12,000 Iraqi combat deaths in the air campaign and as many as

10,000 casualties in the ground war....The Iraqi government says 2,300 civilians died during the air campaign."[31]

But Iraqi roads, bridges, factories, and oil industry facilities were demolished. Water purification and sewage treatment facilities could not operate without electric power. A continuing trade embargo caused serious economic problems. In March 1991, Kurdish and Shiite Muslim uprisings broke out with encouragement from President Bush, who had promised American support, which never came.

By April 1991, Saddam Hussein's Iraqi troops had brutally crushed these rebellions. His actions were later classified as crimes against humanity, and included the use of chemical weapons against the Kurds, an ethnic minority in northern Iraq. At the same time, Iraq accepted the terms of a formal cease-fire agreement and the UN Security Council officially declared an end to the war. In the cease-fire agreement, Iraq agreed to the destruction of all its biological and chemical weapons, its facilities for producing such weapons, and any facilities or materials it might have for producing nuclear weapons. After the formal cease-fire, the UN continued the embargo to pressure Iraq to carry out these terms.

Following George W. Bush's election in 2000, the United States and the United Kingdom continued to bomb Iraqi air defense systems while enforcing the no-fly zones established by the United Nations after the 1991 war.

Then, in the wake of the terrorist attacks of September 11, 2001, as preparations were made to attack Al Qaeda and its sanctuaries in Afghanistan, Secretary of Defense Donald Rumsfeld and other officials in the younger President Bush's administration expressed an immediate interest in attacking Iraq. As Jeremy Scahill recorded it, "'The agenda was very clear from the night of 9/11,' General Hugh Shelton, at the time Chairman of the Joint Chiefs of Staff and the most senior military adviser to President Bush, told me. He said that Rumsfeld and [Undersecretary of Defense Paul] Wolfowitz 'immediately began pressing for an attack on Iraq.... Although there wasn't one shred, not one iota of evidence that would say [9/11] was linked to Iraq.'"[32]

The war in Afghanistan was aimed at toppling the Taliban, the country's fundamentalist Islamic regime, which had allowed Osama bin Laden's Al Qaeda to plot the September 11 attacks from there. Begun on October 7, 2001, and lasting a little more than two months, the U.S. military effort had succeeded. The Taliban was ousted, though some of its leaders and Al Qaeda forces had escaped into the wild mountainous region between Afghanistan and neighboring Pakistan, including a remote area called Tora Bora. In Kabul, Afghanistan's capital, Hamid Karzai was installed with American support as the head of a new provisional Afghan government. American troops, along with those of a handful of other nations, continued to occupy Afghanistan with hopes of stabilizing a new government and continuing the destruction of Taliban and Al Qaeda forces.

The American military effort in Afghanistan was under the command of General Tommy R. Franks, who led the war, which was fought in extremes of heat and cold, from an air-conditioned center in Tampa, Florida, home of the U.S. Central Command. While Franks and the military would win high praise from civilian bosses in the Bush White House and Pentagon, the assessment was not universally shared: "The warning signs about Franks began flashing in late 2001, with his bumbling effort to capture Osama bin Laden in Tora Bora," wrote Thomas E. Ricks in a damning appraisal of Franks as a "two-time loser" in *The Generals*. "Coming just three months after the attacks of 9/11, the Tora Bora fight provided the best chance American forces had to kill or capture the al-Qaeda leader. Yet Franks seemed inattentive, almost as if the battle were someone else's problem."[33] Specifically, Franks had rejected requests from CIA officers in the area for U.S. Army or Marine support in sealing the escape routes from Afghanistan into Pakistan (where bin Laden would eventually be killed by Navy SEALs in 2011). He later declined to provide adequate artillery support to infantry units that had trapped a large number of Al Qaeda fighters.

In an account of the hunt for bin Laden, Peter L. Bergen seconded the critique. "The man responsible for the deadliest terrorist attack in U.S. history, along with many of his top lieutenants, was making his escape. Why was there no effort to put more American boots on the ground?" asked Bergen. There was a fear that Afghans would resent the troop presence, Bergen answered, and a "risk-averse" Pentagon feared that a great many casualties even in pursuit of bin Laden would be unacceptable.[34] There would be no more soldiers, journalist Kurt Eichenwald also wrote of the Tora Bora episode. "Tommy Franks's position was firm."[35]

Years later, Franks would defend his Tora Bora actions. "My decision not to add American troops to the Tora Bora region was influenced [by]...the comparative light footprint of coalition troops in theater, and the fact that these troops were committed to operation ongoing across Afghanistan, the amount of time it would take to deploy additional troops would likely create a 'tactical pause' which would run the risk of losing the momentum our forces were enjoying...and uncertainty as to whether bin Laden was in fact in Tora Bora."[36]

To many observers of the war in Afghanistan, the Bush administration had already taken its eye off the ball, quickly shifting their focus and attention to Iraq. In December 2001, Secretary of Defense Rumsfeld was pressing General Franks for "options on Iraq" and Franks later presented an existing eight-hundred-page contingency plan. Unsatisfied, Rumsfeld asked for a revision, which Franks presented on December 12, 2001, the same day that Al Qaeda leaders left Tora Bora.[37]

One year after the 9/11 attacks, President Bush spoke at the United Nations, demanding that Iraq eliminate its weapons of mass destruction, refrain from supporting terrorism, and end the repression of its people. These three reasons became the ostensible justification for

America's going to war in Iraq, in what is considered the first preemptive war in American history, to achieve "regime change," that is, to eliminate Saddam Hussein as Iraq's leader.

In a post-9/11 America, the Powell Doctrine was about to be shoved aside for what became known as the Bush Doctrine, formally outlined in *National Security Strategy of the United States*, published on September 17, 2002 (and updated in 2006). It read, in part:

> The security environment confronting the United States today is radically different from what we have faced before. Yet the first duty of the United States Government remains what it always has been: to protect the American people and American interests. It is an enduring American principle that this duty obligates the government to anticipate and counter threats, using all elements of national power, before the threats can do grave damage. The greater the threat, the greater is the risk of inaction—and the more compelling the case for taking anticipatory action to defend ourselves, even if uncertainty remains as to the time and place of the enemy's attack. There are few greater threats than a terrorist attack with WMD.
>
> To forestall or prevent such hostile acts by our adversaries, the United States will, if necessary, act preemptively in exercising our inherent right of self-defense. The United States will not resort to force in all cases to preempt emerging threats. Our preference is that nonmilitary actions succeed. And no country should ever use preemption as a pretext for aggression.[38]

Many commentators have noted that Iraq was in fact a preventive rather than preemptive war—a distinction worth noting. A *preemptive war* or strike is an accepted concept that means an attempt to repel or defeat an impending threat. A *preventive war* or strike, on the other hand, describes a war launched to destroy a potential threat from an enemy when no attack is imminent. In a discussion sponsored by the U.S. Army, Colin S. Gray, who worked as an adviser to the British and American governments, wrote of this distinction: "Preventive war...refers to the option of shooting on suspicion. In an age of weapons of mass destruction (WMD), it could be too late to shoot if one waits for suspicion to be verified by hostile behavior."[39]

Responding to the Bush policy statement a few days after its release, the *New York Times* Editorial Board warned, "Striking first to prevent aggression is not unreasonable when dealing with groups like Al Qaeda, which operate independently of the restraints that govern the behavior of most nation-states....But when these pugnacious strategies become the dominant theme in American conduct, overwhelming more cooperative instincts, the nation risks alienating its friends and undermining the very interests that Mr. Bush seeks to protect."[40]

Unlike his father, who had mustered a large coalition of nations in 1991, President George W. Bush decided to go to war over the objections of many of America's Western allies and the United Nations. The principal exception was Great Britain, although Spain and Italy also joined in the initial invasion of Iraq.

When National Security Advisor Condoleezza Rice raised fears of "a mushroom cloud," Americans were already dazed and confused by the complexity of a Global War on Terrorism (GWOT)* against a stateless enemy pledged to America's destruction by any means. The constant barrage of fearful warnings about America's exposure to attack by small groups of suicidal terrorists willing to use any means and supposedly seeking nuclear weapons quickly ratcheted up the tension in a country already on edge since the attacks of 9/11. And while consistently connecting Saddam Hussein's Iraq to Al Qaeda and the 9/11 attacks—despite a lack of evidence—the United States went to war, unprovoked, against Iraq in March 2003.

---

* An executive order of President Bush created the Global War on Terrorism Service Medal (GWOTSM) in March 2003.

Once again under the command of Tommy Franks, the initial offensive was swift and overwhelming, the famous "shock and awe" campaign. Baghdad and much of Iraq were quickly devastated by American airpower. Less than six weeks after the assault began on March 19, 2003, American troops were in nominal control of Baghdad. They had been accompanied by embedded journalists who were offering a close-up—if largely Pentagon-sanctioned—version of events. The Defense Department had learned one key lesson in Vietnam—to try to control the flow of information and images that Americans would see on the nightly news.

In the view of many critics, this media strategy is deeply flawed, as British investigative journalist Phillip Knightley pointed out: "No matter how determined embedded correspondents may have been to maintain their distance and objectivity, once the war had started, almost without exception, they soon lost all distinction between soldier and correspondent and began to use 'we' in their reports.... Clive Myrie of the BBC said an embedded correspondent could feel under pressure in a tight situation to help his unit out."[41]

As journalists riding in American tanks or Humvees entered the fallen city of Baghdad, they soon reported that fears of a powerful Iraqi counterattack, possibly including chemical weapons, were completely overblown. Under the staggering power of American air strikes, the Iraqi armed forces had been either destroyed or quickly surrendered. Or they had melted back into the general population, taking a great deal of weaponry with them. It was this quick and seemingly decisive success that allowed George W. Bush to take to the deck of the aircraft carrier USS *Abraham Lincoln* in what became known as the "Mission Accomplished" moment on May 1, 2003.

But almost immediately after the invasion, Iraq had begun a dizzying spiral out of control into complete chaos. Warnings of a postwar occupation demanding more American forces on the ground to control a country that had been repressed for decades by a ruthless dictator had simply been ignored by the architects of the Iraq War, including Donald Rumsfeld, the secretary of defense, who was battling for control of the war in Iraq with Colin Powell's State Department.

General Eric Shinseki, the army chief of staff, had serious concerns that there were not sufficient troops to secure the country, an opinion he expressed in testimony to Congress on February 25, 2003. The remark struck at the core of the Bush-Cheney-Rumsfeld plan to get into Iraq with a "light footprint." "The idea was to get in and get out, turning the country over to a new generation of Iraqis as quickly as possible," Peter Baker wrote. Two days later, Rumsfeld assistant Paul D. Wolfowitz, who had pressed for action against Iraq since the days following September 11, publicly rebutted Shinseki's estimate of needing several hundred thousand troops as "wildly off the mark."[42] Wolfowitz told Congress, "It's hard to conceive that it would take more forces to provide stability in post-Saddam Iraq than it would to conduct the war itself and to secure the surrender of Saddam's security forces and his army."[43]

Shinseki was overruled, his opinions publicly dismissed by General Franks and Defense Secretary Rumsfeld. Shinseki's treatment by the Rumsfeld Pentagon was, in the view of many observers, a public humiliation that Shinseki, a decorated veteran, did not deserve. Afterward, air force major general Charles Dunlap Jr. wrote, "The treatment of Army General Eric Shinseki after testifying honestly (and, as it turns out, accurately)...is widely viewed as an object lesson of the most negative type."[44*]

---

* A Vietnam veteran and the highest ranking Asian-American in American history before 2009, General Shinseki retired as scheduled in June 2003. In 2006, one of Franks's successors, General John Abizaid, told Congress that Shinseki had been correct. President Obama, taking office in January 2009, appointed General Shinseki to the cabinet-level post of director of veterans affairs. In June 2014, Shinseki was forced to resign from that post in the wake of a new scandal involving revelations of deeply flawed, and possibly fatal, medical treatment of veterans at several V.A. hospitals.

The atmosphere in Baghdad and much of occupied Iraq had become like a school day when the teacher leaves and a substitute takes over—multiplied by many thousands. If Saddam was the "mean teacher" who kept class quiet and the school bullies in line, the United States was the gullible substitute. Only here, the bullies weren't just rifling the school lockers. They were tearing the country apart, piece by piece.

Remnants of the old Iraqi regime, Islamic fighters surging into the country to fight America in a jihad, and various sects within Iraq kept up a steady insurgency. There was also constant conflict between the U.S. military and the American civilians charged with overseeing the occupation and transition to a new Iraqi government.

The first American civilian chief of the Defense Department's—not the State Department's—Office of Reconstruction and Humanitarian Assistance (ORHA), Jay Garner, proved no match for the infighting in Washington and Baghdad. A retired lieutenant general, Garner had overseen Operation Provide Comfort following the Gulf War in 1991 and was credited with saving thousands of lives in the Kurdish region in northern Iraq near Turkey. But Garner was unequal to the new task, perhaps an impossible one for any administrator. "If one thought of postwar Iraq as a limited humanitarian operation, as opposed to an open-ended political-military undertaking more vast and complex than anything the United States had attempted since the end of World War II, Garner had the right stuff," wrote George Packer.

But occupying Iraq was not going to be about making sure there were enough tents, food, and medicine for wartime refugees. Iraq was going to be rebuilt from scratch with the noblest intention of creating a Western-style democracy that would inspire others in the Middle East. Unfortunately, this was fool's gold.

Iraq was created in the aftermath of World War I, in 1918, when the Allied victors carved up the remnants of the Ottoman Empire, which had aligned with Germany in that conflict. Iraq was ruled by the British under a League of Nations mandate, and in 1932 it became independent under a monarchy, which was overthrown in a 1958 military coup, when King Faisal II was killed. Saddam Hussein took over the country in another coup in 1979 and—with Joseph Stalin as his inspiration—began a ruthless dictatorship in which enemies were purged and dissent crushed. In 1980, he took Iraq into a nearly decade-long war against neighboring Iran and in 1990 he launched an invasion of Kuwait, which brought about the Persian Gulf War. In other words, Iraq's history as a nation had been brief and brutal.

Jay Garner's Herculean task was going to be undercut by Iraqi infighting. Ahmad Chalabi, a wealthy Iraqi leader in London exile with close ties to the Defense Department, by many accounts wanted to be given control of Iraq by the Bush administration. According to Packer, "Without informing the White House or military commanders, [the Pentagon] had flown Chalabi and seven hundred followers— with American uniforms and weapons—from northern Iraq.... The idea was to give Chalabi a head start in the race to power."[45] Chalabi was also seated near First Lady Laura Bush during the president's State of the Union address on January 20, 2004. According to Bob Woodward, the president wasn't happy that the seat had been given to him.

Chalabi was also believed to be the chief source of the "hyped" intelligence about weapons of mass destruction that Bush had used to take the country into the war.[46] Chalabi was later dumped by the U.S. government, which raided his home in Baghdad and suspected him of spying for Iran and informing the Iranians that the U.S. had broken Iran's secret communications code.[47] (No action was taken against Chalabi, who remained in Iraqi government positions and continued to live in Baghdad in "full pasha mode," as a biographer put it. "Unfortunately for Chalabi, the one entity he never succeeded in winning over was the Iraqi people," wrote *Salon*'s Laura Miller. "He failed every electoral test thereafter. In 2004, a poll found him to be Iraq's "least-trusted public figure.")[48]

Subverted by the Defense Department that had appointed him, and with mounting unease in Washington over his shaky performance as the looting in Baghdad spread around the country, Jay Garner was told by Defense Secretary Donald Rumsfeld that he was going to be replaced. After just three weeks, L. Paul Bremer III, an ally of the neoconservative wing in the White House, was installed as the new civilian administrator in Iraq in Garner's place.[49]

"Garner was a fall guy for a bad strategy," a Defense Department official later told Packer. "He was doing exactly what Rummy [Rumsfeld] wanted him to do. It was the strategy that failed."[50] In April 2004, about a year after Garner's removal, Paul Krugman of the *New York Times* wrote, "Last month Jay Garner, the first U.S. administrator of Iraq, told the BBC that he was sacked in part because he wanted to hold quick elections. His superiors wanted to privatize Iraqi industries first—as part of a plan that, according to Mr. Garner, was drawn up in late 2001."[51] When Garner later met President Bush and complimented his successor Bremer, Bush reportedly told him, perhaps in jest, "I didn't choose him [Bremer]. Rumsfeld chose him."[52]

Routinely wearing combat boots with his business suits, Bremer stepped on a great many toes belonging to both Iraqis and the U.S. military commanders. One of his first major decisions was to outlaw members of Saddam's Baath Party and the Iraqi army, a decision that, as Stephen Kinzer wrote, "[l]eft more than 300,000 young men, all armed and trained in military tactics, without work and seething with anger against the occupier."[53]

The decision not only created a large, well-armed, out-of-control fighting force, but also backfired as most of the country's civil servants were without jobs. Many of them had been managers, civil servants, and engineers who ran basic services and utilities that had been severely damaged or destroyed by the bombing campaign. Clean water and electricity soon became precious commodities in Iraq's approaching summer heat.

But perhaps the most misunderstood element of a post-Saddam Iraq was the deep sectarian divide that would be opened between competing Sunni and Shiite Muslims. The fundamental religious dividing line within Islam between Sunni and Shiite dates back centuries, to the death of the Prophet Muhammad in 632, leading to a dispute over who would succeed the founder of Islam. More than 1,300 years later, the theological differences between Sunni and Shiite—like the schism that separated Christians after the Protestant Reformation—were intensified by political, economic, and class distinctions and discrimination. For a rough Western equivalent, consider Northern Ireland, where an essential religious difference—Catholic versus Protestant antagonism—created centuries of deadly political and economic repercussions.

If anything, the mixture of religion and political oppression in Iraq was far more volatile and combustible, waiting to explode in a deadly paroxysm of anti-American and sectarian rebellion and bloodshed. And that conflict was playing out in spades in Fallujah, even as President Bush prepared to campaign in 2004 for a second term.

That was the situation on the ground as Bremer and the military command sought some control over a situation that was going from bad to worse. Predictions of an insurgency had been brushed aside. The Americans in nominal control of Iraq appeared helpless as the violent resistance spread. The mistakes of the Bush administration in overestimating Saddam's threat and military capabilities and underestimating what it would take to control Iraq after Saddam's defeat were matched by military mistakes. "American generalship in Iraq in 2003 and the following years is too often a tale of ineptitude exacerbated by a wholesale failure of accountability," Pulitzer Prize–winning Pentagon correspondent Thomas E. Ricks charged. "The war began badly, with Tommy R. Franks failing to understand the war he was fighting."

Franks retired not long after the fall of Baghdad, wrote a bestselling memoir, and enjoyed the rewards of the high-paid speechmaking circuit. His successor, Ricardo Sanchez, concluded Ricks, "[u]nder-stood the conflict even less.... Iraq was boiling over, the Pentagon and the Bush Administration were in denial, and he was trying to deal with this while operating in a confused command structure that generated constant friction between him and L. Paul Bremer III."[34]

When the images of the bodies hanging from the bridge over the River Euphrates found their way around the world, the pictures made the anarchy in Iraq manifest. There was understandable revulsion and anger, as some headlines read: "Iraqi Mob Mutilates 4 American Civilians" (*Chicago Tribune*) and "Americans Desecrated" (*Miami Herald*). This was not the friendly greeting to liberators that Americans had been told by their political leaders to expect from a grateful Iraqi nation.

Were average Iraqis glad to be freed from the iron grasp and reign of terror of a murderous despot? Undoubtedly yes. But that did not mean they were more interested in being occupied by the United States. Naïvely expecting newly liberated Iraqis to adopt a Western-style democracy, the administration was completely unprepared for the anger and resentment that had been unleashed in a country that had suffered for decades under a repressive monster, his sadistic sons, and the dreaded army and police. That Iraqi rage exploded in the first major blowback at Fallujah, a city that had been largely overlooked in prewar planning, which had been focused on securing Baghdad.

Outraged by what they had seen take place in Fallujah, many Americans may have been hearing the name of the city for the first time. But the city was not unfamiliar to the American military. They had been there since the beginning of the war. Fallujah and nearby Ramadi are major cities of Anbar Province, a vast desert area in western Iraq (bordering Saudi Arabia, Jordan, and Syria) and home of many conservative Sunni Arabs. Both Fallujah and Ramadi had been taken without much shooting and local Iraqi leaders were in control when Americans arrived in April 2003. But its vast size and border with Syria made Anbar difficult to police.

And the American military footprint had become large and clumsy. All the talk of boots on the ground—a favorite cliché among tough-sounding politicians and journalists—meant that heavy-footed Americans had quickly become unwelcome liberators. Resentments bottled up by people who had lived for decades under Saddam's thumb did not go away at the sight of the Stars and Stripes. Iraqis had lived for much of their recent history with an impression of America as a dangerous foe, aligned with Israel, the Arab world's archenemy.* It was a lesson that might have been learned a century earlier in the Philippines, where an American "liberation" also had quickly turned into an occupation resented by many Filipinos.

In Fallujah, the weight of the occupation had already turned deadly. For a brief time after the "shock and awe" invasion of March 2003, there had been a window of opportunity for a peaceable accommodation in Anbar Province. "The province was ready to cooperate with the coalition," according to George Packer. "If only the Americans had stayed outside the cities, then crowds wouldn't have gathered to protest, and soldiers wouldn't have fired on the crowds, as they did in Fallujah on April 28 and 30, killing eighteen civilians, and Iraqis wouldn't have retaliated with grenades and automatic weapons, and the second war wouldn't have begun."[55]

Just as the American army's tough tactics had once fed resentment in Balangiga and other Philippine locations in 1902 and again in Vietnam, the heavy-handed American presence would stoke Iraqi anger. Civilians had been killed. The American forces, not Saddam's torturers or Republican Guard, had done the killing. Replacing one dictator with what was seen as an occupying army—long viewed as the enemy of Iraq and Islamic people—had only deepened the

---

* Besides the enmity of the overall Israeli-Arab conflict, Israeli jets had bombed Iraq in 1981, successfully destroying an Iraqi nuclear reactor, using modified American F-16 jet fighters.

explosive resentment in a country that was restive, divided, and armed to the teeth with the weaponry of Iraq's former army.

Another crucial factor—also one predicted by critics of the invasion—came into play. The Iraqi resistance was fed by an influx of foreign fighters who saw Iraq as the new battlefield in the jihad against America. Their ostensible leader was Jordanian-born terrorist Abu Musab al-Zarqawi, who had begun his career as a militant in Afghanistan. He had entered Iraq in 2002 and sought to establish his group, Tawhid al-Jihad, as, in the words of Michael Gordon and Bernard E. Trainor, Iraq's "franchise of Al-Qaeda: the group responsible for some of the earliest suicide bombings against civilian targets in Baghdad."[56]

Angry at the occupation and stoked by foreign fighters streaming across Iraq's porous borders (Anbar had been compared to the Vietnam-era Ho Chi Minh Trail as a conduit for guerrilla fighters and arms), the Iraqis were seething. But news of so many Iraqi civilian deaths in Fallujah never found its way to the American headlines, as did the later deaths of the four contractors. Nor did the Marine firefight in Fallujah three days after they arrived in late March 2004 garner much attention. A thirty-six-hour gun battle that began when patrols went looking for high-level officials of the old Saddam regime had left at least fifteen Iraqi civilians dead. It was compounded a few days later when news of the assassination of a prominent Islamic leader in Palestine by an Israeli missile strike was announced. The long-held hatred of Israel was simply one more reason to resent America, Israel's chief ally and strongest defender.

That was just part of the background that left the city boiling with anti-American rage when the four Blackwater contractors drove through the city.

If combat operations were over, as the president had claimed a year before, it was impossible to know it in Fallujah. Backed by tanks and armored vehicles, twenty-five hundred marines went into the city on April 5, 2004, to "clobber them" in Vigilant Resolve. The fighting went on inconclusively for a few weeks in what would be called the "First Battle of Fallujah." Despite the abject failure of most of the Iraqi forces called in—Marine commander Jim Mattis called the Iraqi security forces "little more than a jobs program"[37]—the marines began to make significant headway in taking Fallujah. And they were working successfully with the lone Iraqi unit, the Thirty-Sixth Commando Battalion, that performed well for the first few days of the fight.

Like Hué in 1968, the fighting in Fallujah was tough, street-by-street, deadly grunt work. As journalist and historian Robert Kaplan, an eyewitness to the operation, put it, "There was nothing fancy about this: the Marines slugged it out three steps forward, two steps backward. This was the classic, immemorial labor of infantry, little different from the way it had been practiced in Vietnam, World War II, and earlier back to the Greeks and Romans. Commanders inserted grunts and waited for them to be attacked, using the opportunity to break the enemy over the contact line.... There was still a place in this world for old-fashioned infantrymen."[38]

In firefights around the city, the heroism of many of the marines was no different in Fallujah than it had been in places like Guadalcanal and Iwo Jima in an earlier generation. But as casualties mounted, so did reports of collateral damage. With no way to distinguish fighters in the deadly crossfire, marines shot civilians—some mistakenly, some accidentally. Insurgent mortar rounds meant for Americans were also killing Iraqi children instead.

The marines may have had plenty of "Vigilant Resolve," but this was not shared in political circles. The reports of civilian casualties were part of the reality of brutal combat in a major urban center, spawning second thoughts among political leaders in both Baghdad and Washington. Fearful that controversy in Fallujah might undermine planned Iraqi elections, the Bush administration pulled the plug on the First Battle of Fallujah. After telling his commanders on April 7 to "kick ass" against the Shiite cleric Muqtada al-Sadr's Mahdi Army as well as the insurgents in Fallujah, President Bush had to throttle back. "On April 8, [Lieutenant General Ricardo] Sanchez was ordered to halt the offensive," wrote Peter Baker. "Once again, the marines were furious. Having launched the operation over their own objections, they now wanted to finish it. [General John] Abizaid flew to Fallujah on April 9 to tell the marine commander, Major General James Mattis, whose pants were spattered with blood. Mattis exploded."[59]

As Kaplan, an observer embedded with the Marines, wrote, "The focus of the media klieg lights on Al-Fallujah…was central to the decision—made at the highest levels of the U.S. government—to call a cease-fire that would end the Marine assault. This happened just as the Marines, strengthened by the arrival of a whole new battalion, may have been about to overrun the insurgents.…[The] decision to invest Al-Fallujah and then pull out just as victory was within reach demonstrated both the fecklessness and incoherence of the Bush administration."[60]

Words like *feckless* and *fiasco* increasingly came to define the fighting at Fallujah and the overall performance of the Bush administration in Iraq. "The Fallujah debacle led Sanchez to call those days in March and April 'a strategic disaster for America's mission in Iraq,'" White House correspondent Peter Baker concluded. "Taken together, [Sanchez] said, 'our actions had undeniably ignited a civil war in Iraq.'"[61]

The decision to pull the Marines out of Fallujah was complicated because the fighting had spread to other cities in Anbar Province. There was a sharp escalation in attacks at nearby Ramadi, and in other cities including Baghdad and Najaf, where forces of the rabidly anti-American Shiite cleric Sadr began an offensive against Americans. The radical Shiite clerics forces were partly inflamed by Bremer's order to shut down a newspaper that was run by Sadr on March 28, one more fuse lit in the powder keg of Iraq. "In padlocking the gate," wrote Baker, "they touched off a violent and sustained backlash from Sadr and his supporters in Baghdad, Najaf, and other Shiite areas."[62]

In Najaf, it was later revealed, Blackwater personnel had also played a prominent role in the fighting against Sadr's well-equipped and highly motivated militia forces. With growing internal divisions between Iraqi Sunni and Shiite accelerating into a sectarian civil war, the situation in Iraq was quickly spiraling out of American control, despite assurances from Americans like spokesman Dan Senor, who said at the time, "We will not allow the country to head down the path toward destabilization."[63]

Under intense international political pressure and with the Iraqi Governing Council balking and threatening to disband, the White House called off the Marines. General Stanley McChrystal later wrote, "Bush ordered the assault stopped."[64]

Control of the city was handed over to an Iraqi general, who formed the Fallujah Brigade, which, as one American officer said, "was made up of the people we'd been fighting against." Supposedly allied with the American military and the Iraqi government, members of the brigade soon switched sides, either joining the insurgents or turning weapons over to them.[65]

The Iraqi general, it turned out, had been a senior member of Saddam Hussein's Republican Guard. When American commanders in Iraq learned whom they had put in charge, they removed the general. But the Fallujah Brigade melted away within weeks, with many of its men joining the insurgency.

Having lost face in Fallujah in what the insurgents were trumpeting as "victory," the Marines withdrew at the end of May and the city continued to serve as a magnet for anti-American fighters. That insurgency, a guerrilla war that threatened to reverse the swift American victory over Saddam's forces, was a surprise to military planners. But it shouldn't have been.

"The CIA issued several secret prewar intelligence reports warning of the possibility of an insurgency," Packer wrote. "The first suicide bombings hit American checkpoints around the time Baghdad fell; a few weeks after that, what the military called improvised explosive devices, or IEDs, began blowing up convoys in the capital. General Franks's achievement in toppling the regime in just three weeks, hailed at the time as a brilliant new form of warfare, allowed thousands of Iraqis to melt away into the population or to go into hiding to fight another day. Franks and the administration's civilian leaders would later describe the chaos and insurgency that followed the fall of the regime as the inadvertent consequences of the war plan's 'catastrophic success.' As it turned out there was nothing inadvertent about it."[66] General Eric Shinseki's warnings, dismissed by Rumsfeld, Wolfowitz, and the army brass, had been all too accurate.

Despite the mounting costs of the insurgency and considerable American outrage prompted by the publication of photographs in late April 2004 showing abuse of Iraqis held by Americans at the Abu Ghraib prison, domestic opposition to the war was fairly muted in 2004 as the presidential campaign got under way.

Ever since President James Madison was reelected during the War of 1812, conventional American political wisdom has held that wartime presidents are insulated from defeat. It is not always that simple, but it did prove true for President George W. Bush. Even though the war planning, invasion, and post-invasion occupation had become highly visible and disastrous failures, the war itself did not prove to be a major issue in the 2004 election, in which President Bush won a second term, defeating Senator John Kerry of Massachusetts. A decorated Vietnam War veteran, Kerry had turned against American involvement in Vietnam, joined a group of veterans opposed to the war, testified in Congress about it in 1971, and thrown away some of his combat medals. For that, he was attacked sharply during the 2004 presidential campaign in a series of negative "Swift Boat" advertisements that questioned his loyalty and service record.

It was on the day that George Bush secured his second term that the American forces returned to Fallujah in what would be known as

Operation Phantom Fury, or the "Second Battle of Fallujah." On a cold, rainy November 8 day, 6,500 marines, 1,500 army soldiers, and 2,000 Iraqi troops began a concentrated assault on the city with air strikes, artillery, armor, and infantry. The fighting was intense, the toughest urban fighting seen by the U.S. military since Hué.

Once off-limits to American troops who had orders not to attack holy places, Fallujah's mosques had become fighting positions for the insurgents, who used them as a shield. That soon changed. One Marine squad entered a mosque in south Fallujah and initially found one dead and five wounded fighters. As they continued their sweep through the mosque, the marines found another nine armed men. "There was the momentary 'holy shit' pause, followed by the pulse wave of fear that violence is imminent," Kevin Sites, a journalist embedded with the Marines, later recounted. "[Corporal Willy] Wold yelled, 'Shoot him,' to the first Marine, who blasted the man in front of him. Pushing in, Wold fired into the group on the left, putting rounds into the mass of men, who were close enough to hug."[67]

Sites, on assignment for NBC, had videotaped one of the wounded Iraqis before his death. He later claimed in his book that the incident led to several wounded Iraqi prisoners being shot.[68] According to National Public Radio, which aired the unedited footage after NBC rejected it, "Sites' video shows five men wounded from the previous day's fighting lying on the floor of the mosque. One Marine can be heard shouting to others that a man was only 'playing dead.' A Marine corporal appears to fire a round from his weapon into the Iraqi's head, and another Marine says, 'Dead now.' "[69]

But as in every battle, there were moments of extreme valor as well. On November 15, 2004, Marine sergeant Rafael Peralta had volunteered for a house-clearing mission and was hit several times by enemy fire. As two other marines entered the house, an insurgent threw a grenade at them. Peralta, according to eyewitness accounts, pulled the grenade under his body, absorbing the explosion and saving his fellow marines from certain death.*

By nightfall on November 9, the U.S. troops had almost reached the heart of the city. In house-to-house fighting and searches, U.S. troops uncovered bomb factories and more than four hundred weapons caches. They also uncovered prison cells where Iraqis had been tortured by the insurgents, whether foreign or other Iraqis. When residents were allowed to return to the city in mid-December, U.S. officials reported, "more than half of Fallujah's 39,000 homes were damaged, and about 10,000 of those were destroyed."

But the killers of the Blackwater contractors were not apprehended and never would be. As Jeremy Scahill concludes about the Fallujah battle, "Hundreds more Iraqis were killed, thousands more forced from their homes, as the national resistance against the [American] occupation grew stronger and wider."[70] On November 14, the Marines reopened the bridge over the Euphrates. They hung a sign on it reading: "This is for the Americans of Blackwater that were murdered here in 2004, Semper Fidelis. P.S. Fuck You."[71]

## AFTERMATH

Although the resistance in Fallujah had been blunted by the second offensive in November 2004, the Iraqi insurgency that had been sparked there and in cities like Ramadi and Najaf continued to rage like wildfire across the country in 2005. In fact, as Thomas Ricks wrote in *The Gamble*, "In 2005, the United States was close to losing the war in Iraq.... It would take nearly 12 more months, until late in 2006,

---

* Peralta was recommended for a Congressional Medal of Honor, according to former defense secretary Robert M. Gates, who described the incident in his 2014 memoir, *Duty*. Gates had approved the recommendation but had to withdraw it when evidence suggested that Peralta could not have pulled the grenade under him. "Regardless," wrote Gates, "there is no doubt he was a hero."

for senior officials in the Bush administration and the U.S. military to recognize that the U.S. effort was headed for defeat. Then, almost at the last minute, and over the objections of nearly all relevant leaders of the U.S. military establishment, a few insiders...managed to persuade President Bush to adopt a new more effective strategy built around protecting the Iraqi people."[72]

This was the beginning of the Surge, the much-discussed strategy overseen by General David Petraeus, and widely credited with changing the course of the war in Iraq. By doubling the U.S forces around Baghdad and putting in place a counterinsurgency program, the number of attacks on U.S. forces fell sharply between 2007 and 2008. The U.S. military had gone from near defeat in 2006 to the point at which American troops were ultimately able to depart in December 2011, the American combat mission officially over, with the ultimate fate of Iraq still very much in the air. Security had been improved, but the possibility of a stable, democratic Iraq, allied with the United States, was a fantasy.

And while General Petraeus and his approach were widely hailed, not every analyst agreed that the Surge was solely responsible. The *Washington Post* writer Bob Woodward pointed to three other more nuanced elements of the turnaround:

- A covert program to locate and kill key leaders in Al Qaeda and the Iraqi insurgency. Lieutenant Gen. Stanley McChrystal, commander of the Joint Special Operations Command (JSOC), led the program.
- The "Anbar Awakening," which cut deals and won over tribal leaders, mostly Sunni sheiks, who opposed the Shiite-led Iraqi government. A similar program paid thousands of Iraqis to join what Petraeus called "Concerned Local Citizens."
- A sudden decision by the militant cleric Muqtada al-Sadr to suspend the operations of his powerful Mahdi militia in return for the Americans ceasing operations in Sadr City, a vast

slum within Baghdad that was the center of al-Sadr's political and military strength. The cleric also vowed to become more involved with Iraqi politics.[73]

"In fact, the term used to describe the campaign that American forces pursued beginning in 2007 is a misnomer," wrote military analyst and historian Andrew Bacevich. "Rather than a 'surge,' something like an 'accommodation' is more apt, capturing the shift to buying off insurgents instead of seeking to defeat them."[74]

———

When the Marines entered Fallujah in the aftermath of the attacks on the contractors, most Americans had not heard of Fallujah or Blackwater. But as Joseph Neff and Jay Price later wrote in the *Raleigh News and Observer*, "Almost overnight, the issue of private contractors in Iraq was put on the map. The Marines in charge of the area didn't know the Blackwater team would be traveling that day into the dangerous city of Fallujah, but four days later they were ordered to invade the city and find the killers; this was not the original plan they had had for quelling the insurgency in the area."[75]

As the deadly Iraqi insurgency grew, with fighting spreading around the country, Fallujah and the death of the contractors took a backseat to other headline news in Iraq, including the explosive controversy over the Abu Ghraib prison torture. But Blackwater would be back on the front pages in 2007. On September 16, a Blackwater convoy escorting U.S. diplomats in Baghdad opened fire on the crowded Nisour Square with grenade launchers, machine guns, and sniper fire. In the shooting, seventeen Iraqis were killed. The four men, hired to guard American diplomats, said insurgents ambushed them. The case outraged Iraqis, who demanded that the men be tried in Iraq. Instead, they were later charged with manslaughter and weapons violations and tried in the

United States in 2008. A federal judge dismissed the case, ruling that the Justice Department had withheld evidence.*

Blackwater USA was a private military company founded in 1997 by two former Navy SEALs, Al Clark and Erik Prince; Prince was described in the *New York Times* as "the scion of a fabulously wealthy, deeply religious family that is enmeshed in Republican Party politics."[76] With powerful friends in Congress and former politicians on Blackwater's board, it quickly became a success, like many other private security contractors (PSCs). In the post–Cold War world, these companies had grown up to provide services that the Pentagon was no longer able or willing to perform. As historian Andrew Bacevich, an army officer for twenty-three years, explained, "In deciding that a post–Cold War army could do more with less, senior leaders had, wittingly or not, opened the door to an expanded contractor presence, which soon enough translated into a veritable contractor dependency."[77]

If the government was looking to privatize certain functions, even Pentagon and intelligence functions, PSCs were there to meet those needs and turn handsome profits. In 2001, Vice President Cheney had reportedly sanctioned a CIA killing program to hunt down or assassinate people around the world, either with drones or hit teams. It was temporarily shelved, according to *New York Times* journalist Mark Mazzetti, who documented this program in *The Way of the Knife*, noting that it was outsourced to Blackwater.[78] "Erik Prince was already a favorite son of the Bush Administration and was looking to burrow

---

* In 2013, the Justice Department brought fresh charges against four former contractors employed by Blackwater, according to the Associated Press. "An appeals court reinstated the case in 2011, saying that Judge Ricardo Urbina, now retired, had wrongly interpreted the law. Prosecutors again presented evidence to a grand jury. Blackwater Worldwide is under new ownership and is headquartered in Virginia. It is now called Academi." "Case Against Contractors Resurfaces," Associated Press, October 17, 2013, http://www.nytimes.com/2013/10/18/us/case-against-contractors-resurfaces.html?ref=blackwaterusa. On October 22, 2014, a jury found four former Blackwater contractors guilty on criminal charges stemming from the 2007 shooting.

deeper into America's clandestine establishment. Prince had arrived on the scene with impeccable timing. The CIA couldn't find enough of its own personnel to meet the demands of its large covert station in Kabul [Afghanistan] and Baghdad, and the spy agency turned to Blackwater's private guards for secret missions—from protection of CIA officers to intelligence gathering to snatch-and-grab operations—that had once been reserved only for fully trained CIA employees."[79]*

Supplementing the CIA, Blackwater and other private contractors were at full bore in Iraq. "As of the summer of 2007, there were more 'private contractors' deployed on the U.S. government payroll in Iraq (180,000) than there were actual soldiers (160,000)," wrote Jeremy Scahill. "This meant the U.S. military had become the junior partner in the coalition that occupies Iraq. The existence of a powerful shadow army enabled the waging of an unpopular war with forces whose deaths and injuries went uncounted and unreported."[80]

Iraq had proven a veritable gold mine for these contractors, according to Bacevich. "When post-9/11 wars expected to be very short turned out to be very long, contractors lined up at the door to claim the boodle on the other side. Soldiers once viewed the battlefield as their exclusive jurisdiction. Now they learned to share it with the likes of KBR (Kellogg Brown Root, a subsidiary of Halliburton], DynCorp, Engility (formerly L-3MPRI), and Academi (formerly Xe, previously Blackwater USA), hired to perform security, training, and logistics functions over which the military itself had once exercised responsibility." In Iraq and Afghanistan, these well-connected contractors were awarded contracts worth billions. KBR led the pack with $40.8 billion in contracts during the decade after 9/11.[81]

---

* "No killing operations were carried out during this phase of the hit-team program," according to Mazzetti. "Prince and [former CIA operative and Blackwater employee Enrique] Prado had overseen the training of Blackwater teams, but Prince blames 'institutional osteoporosis' for why the Blackwater assassins were never dispatched to kill terrorists." Mazzetti, *The Way of the Knife*, p. 124.

In 2007, the House Committee on Oversight and Government Reform, chaired by Democrat Henry Waxman of California, investigated Blackwater and its role in Iraq. In late September 2007, the committee released a detailed report on the massacre of the four Blackwater contractors. According to the executive summary of the report:

> These eyewitness accounts and investigative reports conflict with Blackwater's assertion that they sent the team out with sufficient preparation and equipment. They portray a company that ignored multiple warnings about the dangers of traveling through Fallujah, cut essential personnel from the mission, and failed to supply its team with armored vehicles, sufficient threat intelligence, or even maps of the area. Blackwater's own employees described its conduct as "flat out a sloppy…operation."…"Why were they sent into the hottest zone in Iraq in unarmored underpowered vehicles to protect a truck? They had no way to protect their flanks because they only had four guys."[82]

Among its findings:

- Blackwater, a for-profit company, used unarmored vehicles to save money and cut essential personnel from the mission to escort flatbed trucks on their way to pick up kitchen equipment. An internal Blackwater report said Blackwater's contract paid for armored vehicles, but "management in North Carolina…made the decision to go with soft skin due to the cost."
- Blackwater ignored the warnings of a British security firm, which had twice turned down the same mission "due to the obvious risk of transporting slow-moving loads through such a volatile area."
- Blackwater impeded the congressional investigation by claiming key documents were classified. The documents, however, were not officially secret, despite the efforts of Blackwater's general counsel—formerly the military's top auditor—to prevent their

disclosure. He made two unsuccessful trips to the Pentagon to persuade defense officials to alter the status of damaging documents to "classified."[83]

According to the committee report, Blackwater USA employees had been involved in nearly two hundred shootings in Iraq since 2005, "in a vast majority of cases firing their weapons from moving vehicles without stopping to count the dead or assist the wounded." The Oversight Committee also placed blame on the State Department for failing to exercise restraint or supervision over the employees of Blackwater, which had been paid $832 million under a security contract.[84]

During the hearings, Erik Prince, founder and chief executive of Blackwater USA at the time, told the committee that his nearly one thousand armed guards in Iraq were not "trigger-happy mercenaries." Said Prince, "They call us mercenaries. But we're Americans working for America protecting Americans." He said he welcomed additional oversight and testified that he was providing a needed service at reasonable cost. Members of the committee disputed that, citing the $1,222 the company charged for each day of work by its guards.[85]

---

In his stinging assessment of the Iraq War three years after it began in March 2003, *Washington Post* Pentagon correspondent and Pulitzer Prize winner Thomas E. Ricks wrote in *Fiasco*, "It now seems likely that history's judgment will be that the U.S. invasion of Iraq in the spring of 2003 was based on perhaps the worst war plan in American history."[86]

There was an abject failure of the Bush war planners to adequately prepare for the war in Iraq—a war built on faulty assumptions and predetermined concepts. More tragically, the occupation that followed certainly falls into the category that Barbara Tuchman once defined as folly: "Wooden-headedness....It consists of assessing a situation in terms of preconceived fixed notions while ignoring or rejecting any contrary signs."[87]

That was the tragic story of America's involvement in Iraq—at enormous cost to the Iraqi people, the Americans who fought there, and the American Treasury.

Those costs, like the costs of all wars, were not borne equally.

General Tommy Franks retired from the army, effective July 7, 2003. He wrote a memoir, *American Soldier*, which became a bestseller. He also joined the boards of several corporations, including Bank of America and the children's restaurant chain Chuck E. Cheese,[88] and appeared at the 2004 Republican National Convention to endorse George W. Bush for a second term. In December 2004, he was awarded the Presidential Medal of Freedom by President Bush. At the same time, the same honor was bestowed on George Tenet—who had retired as head of the CIA following severe criticism for the intelligence failures prior to September 11, 2001, and the faulty intelligence on Iraq—and Jerry Bremer, the civilian administrator of Iraq. "The decision shocked Washington," recounted journalist Peter Baker. "The three awardees, critics were quick to point out, had been at the heart of the biggest mistakes of the Iraq War—the false intelligence, the heavy-handed occupation, and postwar plans more intent on pulling troops out than properly securing the country."[89]

In 2008, Franks also accepted one hundred thousand dollars from the Coalition to Support America's Heroes, a charity supposedly organized to help veterans, for allowing his name to be used on the letterhead of a solicitation letter. When Congress later investigated them and another charity aimed at assisting veterans for "questionable spending practices," Franks severed his relationship with the coalition. According to the *New York Times*, "A spokesman for General Franks said at the time that the general also made several speeches for the charity and ended his support 'when he learned that the percentage of money raised that was going to the troops was less than 85 percent.'" (The *Washington Post* reported that the charity actually spent 25 percent on veterans.)[90]

———

General David Petraeus, who was widely credited with the Surge strategy, later became director of the Central Intelligence Agency, appointed by President Barack Obama. In November 2012, a revelation of an extramarital affair ended his government career. His appointment to teach a seminar at the public City University of New York came under fire in 2013 when it was reported he would receive two hundred thousand dollars for teaching the seminar and two public lectures; he later agreed to teach the course for one dollar. In May 2013, Petraeus was hired by the Wall Street firm of Kohlberg Kravis Roberts to lead the new KKR Global Initiative as chairman.[91]

———

Prior to the CIA appointment, Petraeus had been called on to replace General Stanley A. McChrystal as commander of U.S. forces in Afghanistan following a separate controversy. A West Point graduate (1976) and the son of a Vietnam veteran and army general, McChrystal rose through Special Forces ranks to become the top officer of U.S. and coalition forces in Afghanistan. However, in June 2010 *Rolling Stone* published an article written by the late Michael Hastings titled "The Runaway General." Hastings quoted the general's men making disparaging remarks about President Obama and members of his administration, though McChrystal was not quoted directly as being critical of the president.[92] After a brief White House meeting, McChrystal offered his resignation. At a press conference announcing the move, President Obama said, "The conduct represented in the recently published article does not meet the standard that should be set by a commanding general. It undermines the civilian control of the military that is at the core of our democratic system. And it erodes the trust that's necessary for our team to work together to achieve our objectives in Afghanistan."[93]

McChrystal also wrote a memoir, *My Share of the Task*, in which he described a Defense Department inquiry into the allegations made in the *Rolling Stone* article. "The investigations," he wrote, "could not substantiate any violations of Defense Department standards and found that 'not all of the events occurred as portrayed in the article.'" McChrystal also noted, "I would accept First Lady Michelle Obama's request to serve my country again, this time on the board of advisers for Joining Forces, a White House initiative for service members and their families."[94]

Following his departure from the army, McChrystal was made Senior Fellow at Yale University, teaching a graduate-level seminar called "Leadership." He also joined several corporate boards and established a consulting firm. In 2011, he backed a call for a national service system, going beyond a military draft. "We have let the concept of service become dangerously narrow, often associated only with the military," he wrote. "This allows most Americans to avoid the sense of responsibility essential for us to care for our nation—and for each other. We expect and demand less of ourselves than we should."[95]

———

Erik Prince, facing mounting legal problems in the United States, sold Blackwater. In 2011 he was in Abu Dhabi, the glittering seaside capital of the oil-rich United Arab Emirates, to reportedly create a secret American-led mercenary army. According to a *New York Times* story based on corporate documents obtained by the paper and interviews with former employees of Blackwater and American officials, the billionaire Prince was building a private army, which the *New York Times* reported was "intended to conduct special operations missions inside and outside the country, defend oil pipelines and skyscrapers from terrorist attacks and put down internal revolts, the documents show. Such troops could be deployed if the Emirates faced unrest in their crowded labor camps or were challenged by pro-democracy protests like those sweeping the Arab world this year [the Arab Spring]."[96]

---

After Abdulrazzaq al-Saiedi, the Iraqi journalist working for the *New York Times*, returned to Baghdad after seeing the bridge at Fallujah, he resolved to quit his job with the paper, citing the dangers of the position. He had already lost his brother, who had died in one of Saddam's prisons. After having lost two Iraqi colleagues at the *Times*, both of them murdered, he did quit and moved to Cambridge, Massachusetts, to pursue a graduate degree. There he met Donna Zovko, the mother of Jerry Zovko, one of the murdered contractors, who had come to attend an event at Harvard.

"Zovko told me that she was not angry with the Iraqis who murdered her son," wrote al-Saiedi. "Instead, she empathized with Iraqi mothers who lost children to the American forces."[97]

Corporal Willy Wold of the U.S. Marines died on November 10, 2006. His autopsy revealed that he was using a variety of prescription drugs that included Prozac, clonidine, and Klonopin, and methadone, for which Wold had no prescription. According to Kevin Sites, his death came "just two days before the two-year anniversary of the day he had shot the six Iraqi men in the mosque."[98]

---

In November 2013, nine years after the two battles for Fallujah, the *New York Times* reported that a series of bomb blasts killed at least twenty-seven people in nine attacks all across Iraq. The violence was part of the continuing sectarian warfare between Sunnis and Shiites in Iraq. Near the end of the story, the reporter wrote, "The mayor of the western town of Fallujah, Adnan Hussein, was assassinated by a sniper."[99]

That news did not make most front pages in America. But in early January 2014, nearly ten years after the four Blackwater contractors drove into Fallujah, the embattled Iraqi city was again in the news. Sunni militants fighting under the banner of Al Qaeda had secured nearly full control. A few months later, on January 4, 2014, black-clad Sunni militants destroyed the Fallujah police headquarters, planted their flag atop government buildings, and decreed that the city was part of a new independent state.[100]

To some of the marines who had fought in those streets a decade earlier, the sight was both shocking and disturbing. "I don't think anyone had the grand illusion that Fallujah or Ramadi was going to turn into Disneyland, but none of us thought it was going to fall back to a jihadist insurgency," said Adam Banotai, who had been a twenty-one-year-old sergeant and squad leader in November 2004. "It made me sick to my stomach to have that thrown in our face, everything we fought for so blatantly taken away."[101]

James Cathcart, who had been a nineteen-year-old marine in 2005, told the *New York Times* about seeing a young female marine assigned to Fallujah to search Iraqi women at checkpoints. In June 2005, he watched as a bomb blew up the truck carrying her and the other women marines back to their base. "'I wanted to get with that girl, and then the next day I was seeing pieces of her all over the side of the road,' said Mr. Cathcart, now 28, who says he was discharged with post-traumatic stress disorder and is now unemployed in Colorado. 'Lives were wasted, and now everyone back home sees that,' he said. 'It was irresponsible to send us over there with no plan, and now to just give it all away.'"[102]

# Afterword

→>‹‹←

"Any future defense secretary who advises the president to again send a big American land army into Asia or into the Middle East or Africa should have his head examined."[1]

—*Defense Secretary Robert M. Gates (2011)*

"Prior to the attacks of September 11, the Pentagon did very little human spying, and the CIA was not officially permitted to kill. In the years since, each has done a great deal of both, and a military-intelligence complex has emerged to carry out the new American way of war."[2]

—*Journalist Mark Mazzetti (2013)*

"So, even as we aggressively pursue terrorist networks—through more targeted efforts and by building the capacity of our foreign partners—America must move off a permanent war footing. That's why I've imposed prudent limits on the use of drones—for we will not be safer if people abroad believe we strike within their countries without regard for the consequence....And with the Afghan war ending, this needs to be the year Congress lifts the remaining restrictions on detainee transfers and we close the prison at Guantanamo Bay—because we counter terrorism not just through intelligence and military action, but by remaining true to our constitutional ideals, and setting an example for the rest of the world."[3]

—*President Barack Obama (January 28, 2014)*

When Republican challenger Mitt Romney opposed President Obama during the 2012 presidential campaign, it marked the first time since World War II that neither major-party candidate had any military experience. With the nation still at war, the campaign was missing the sort of meaningful conversation about military matters of the sort debated by Richard Nixon and John F. Kennedy in 1960. One of the few times the subject of defense came up led to a memorable exchange, when Governor Romney criticized President Obama over the size of the U.S. Navy. Obama replied, "You mention…that we have fewer ships than we did in 1916. Well, Governor, we also have fewer horses and bayonets, because the nature of our military's changed."[4]

Fewer, yes, but America still has bayonets.

The leap in time from Yorktown in 1781 to Fallujah in 2004 is a giant step in time of 223 years. But the marines who went into that Iraqi city did so just as Alexander Hamilton, John Laurens, Lafayette, and the men of the First Rhode Island did at Redoubt No. 10—with "cold steel."

The scenes change. The uniforms change. Many of the weapons change. But the sense of duty and honor, loyalty, and courage were traits held in common—just like the bayonets both generations of American soldiers used.

Set that fact against some of headlines regarding America's armed forces in recent times:

"How a U.S. Citizen Came to Be in America's Cross Hairs"
"Obama Ends 'Don't Ask, Don't Tell' Policy"
"Pentagon Is Set to Lift Combat Ban for Women"
"Two Men Married at West Point Chapel for the First Time"

"Reports of Military Sexual Assault Rise Sharply"

"Baffling Rise in Suicides Plagues the U.S. Military"

"Despite Administration Promises, Few Signs of Change in Drone Wars"

"Military's 'Iron Man' Suit May Be Ready to Test This Summer"[5]

And perhaps most sadly but not surprisingly:

"Severe Report Finds V.A. Hid Waiting Lists at Hospital"

We have exchanged some of the bayonets and M-16s for joysticks that control drones from air-conditioned comfort thousands of miles from the target and the sophisticated tools of cyberwar that can infect an enemy's computer command and control systems with deadly viruses. Women fly combat missions and will increasingly find a place on the battlefield. Hundreds of thousands of American women in uniform were deployed in Afghanistan and Iraq; more than 130 of them died in the two wars.[6]

This is the face of the American military in the dawning years of the twenty-first century. America's professional soldiers today are better educated, more lethal, nimbler, more powerful—and certainly more diverse—than any of the Founding Fathers could have envisioned when they debated the wisdom of a standing army and the constraints they would place on it. Certainly they did not envision blacks and women as part of that fighting force.

The face of the army—and all of the other uniformed services—has changed with the face of America.

But the American military community as it exists after more than a decade of constant war since September 11, 2001, is looking down the barrel of a long, new century.

Most of the two million men and women who went to war since 9/11 are back at home. Slightly more than half remain in the armed services, where, as Thom Shanker of the *New York Times* wrote, "Many are struggling—like America's ground forces over all—to find relevance in the face of an uncertain future."[7]

With the war in Iraq over and the war in Afghanistan winding down, the army is reducing its forces to 490,000 troops, down from a post-9/11 peak of 570,000. Future Pentagon budget cuts may force the numbers lower.

The stark reality of a Pentagon with new financial restraints became clear in late 2013. The federal government had been hit by a so-called "sequester," which called for automatic budget cuts when Congress and the president were stalemated over the budget. The Defense Department, even in the midst of war, was not immune. The air force grounded its combat squadrons as money ran out for flying hours; only warplanes assigned over Afghanistan and the Persian Gulf were allotted full rations of fuel and munitions. Other services were also affected, raising serious questions about readiness to respond to an emergency, whether a sudden armed conflict or a natural disaster.

Senator Jack Reed, a Rhode Island Democrat and West Point graduate who served in the Army Rangers and was on the Senate Armed Services Committee at the time, said the sequester-imposed budget slashing had done more than injure the military's "premium on readiness." He told the *New York Times* the budget battles had demanded a new definition of America's role in the world. "Do we want to be able to shape the environment, or do we want to be prepared to react to it?" he asked. "Can we afford to shape the world—or can we afford not to?"[8]

While the cuts mandated by the sequester were eventually restored, the Pentagon faced a leaner future. The country was left with the kind of questions that had plagued the Founders. What kind of defense did America want? Need? And what can it afford?

Army major general H. R. McMaster, who led the Third Armored Cavalry Regiment in Iraq in 2005 and 2006, wrote, "Budget pressures and persistent fascination with technology have led some to declare an end to war as we know it....Future wars will pose different problems and involve different conditions of course. But war will continue to follow its important age-old truths."[9]

As the six stories in this book illuminate, wars are fought for reasons of power, self-interest (including self-defense), and fear. And those deeply held human factors are not going away, even as the weaponry employed by the United States changes and the Pentagon balances its need for new systems with manpower needs, health care for veterans and active-duty members, and an array of issues that don't include simply figuring out how many tanks and airplanes the country actually needs and can afford.

To put that in a different context, think about where the next war will be fought. Of course, there are people at the Pentagon whose job that is. Consider, for instance, the conflict over shrinking natural resources and what that means for competition in the Arctic. In 2013, the Pentagon released a study of its strategy for competing for those resources in the Arctic as climate change transforms the region where the United States has interests along with Canada, Denmark, Finland, Iceland, Norway, Russia, and Sweden.[10] As the polar ice cap melts, a new potential source of natural resources, trapped beneath Arctic ice, is opened up. History's record on the competition for new resources has not been kind. So the Pentagon prepares for missions in polar cold instead of desert heat.

The practicalities of war—budget constraints, regional conflicts, competition for natural resources, changing technologies that have brought the digital age to the "Field of Mars"—all factor into the decisions America must make about its military.

But there is another, all too human side of the equation, mostly paid by the small fraction of the population who actually don military uniforms and train for a role in which they could lose their lives. The problems that confront American veterans and service men and women are significant and disturbing—particularly when we hear so much lip service paid to honoring those who serve. The scandal, exposed in 2014, over long waits for treatment at V.A. hospitals around the country is the most recent and visible of these problems. But there are many other long-standing issues related to America's veterans. Chief among them:

*Suicide:*

"Over the course of nearly 12 years and two wars, suicide among active-duty troops has risen steadily, hitting a record of 350 in 2012," according to a report in the *New York Times*. "That total was twice as many as a decade before and surpassed not only the number of American troops killed in Afghanistan but also the number who died in transportation accidents last year."[11]

Related issues of mental health problems and drug addiction are factors in those disturbing statistics.

*Homelessness:*

The 2012 Annual Homeless Assessment Report to Congress, prepared by the U.S. Department of Housing and Urban Development, estimates there were "62,619 homeless veterans on a single night in January in the United States." While the number represented a 7.2 percent decline since 2011 and a 17.2 percent decline since 2009, it is still a figure that speaks to the nation's ability to avert its eyes from its troops after they come home.[12]

*Sexual Assault:*

The Defense Department recently reported that in 2011, "About 26,000 men and women in the military were sexually assaulted...up from 19,000 in 2010."[13]

Each of these issues underscores the great disconnect between the American people and the current professional military. Before the Vietnam-era shift to an all-volunteer army, much higher percentages of Americans typically served in the military, especially in wartime emergencies, whether by enlistment or conscription.

Warning about the danger of this trend toward a permanent "warrior class," former army officer and history professor Andrew Bacevich wrote, "From pulpit and podium, at concerts and sporting events, expressions of warmth and affection shower down on the troops. Yet when those wielding power in Washington subject soldiers to serial abuse, Americans acquiesce. When the state heedlessly and callously exploits those same troops, the people avert their gaze. Maintaining a pretense about caring about soldiers, state and society actually collaborate in betraying them."[14]

That trend has only accelerated as the military has shifted to drone warfare, in which the killing is done remotely—admittedly at much less physical risk to American soldiers. The increasing reliance on privatization through the use of security contractors, as outlined in the Fallujah story, simply adds to the insulating layer of invisibility over the American way of war. It is much easier to conceal or avert our eyes from the dirty work that is being done in America's name. But perhaps that carries the moral danger of becoming a little too easy.

To borrow from the old expression, making war is like making sausage (and legislation): If you see how it's done, you lose respect for it.*

Plunging into the stories behind these six battles has often been a disheartening exercise in the "evils that men do." The double-edged sword of war—courage, self-sacrifice, and duty matched by folly, cowardice, and atrocity—hangs over our heads. The new American way of war has helped distance so many Americans from what the battlefield means to the people in or near it that the dangling sword seems less threatening.

---

* The line, "Laws, like sausages, cease to inspire respect in proportion as we know how they are made," is often attributed to Otto von Bismarck, the nineteenth-century Iron Chancellor of Germany. However, the original has been traced to the *Daily Cleveland Herald*, quoting the lawyer-poet John Godfrey Saxe on March 29, 1869, according to Fred Shapiro, editor of *The Yale Book of Quotations*.

In *What It Is Like to Go to War,* Vietnam veteran and novelist Karl Marlantes movingly wrote about war's attractions and threats. "We must be honest and open about both sides of war," cautioned Marlantes. "The more aware we are of war's costs, not just in death and dollars, but also in shattered minds, souls and families, the less likely we will be to waste our most precious asset and our best weapon: our young. The more we recognize the feelings of transcendence and psychological and spiritual intensity of war, the easier it will be to prevent their appeal from clouding our judgment about going to war the next time."[15]

"War the next time." It would be nice to wish that away. But history is a hard taskmaster. The questions don't go away.

What kind of military should America have? What does it need? And must we go to war? What do we want as a nation done in our name?

During the American Civil War, a little more than 150 years ago, the British philosopher John Stuart Mill wrote, "War is an ugly thing, but not the ugliest of things: the decayed and degraded state of moral and patriotic feeling which thinks that nothing is *worth* a war, is much worse. When a people are used as mere human instruments for firing cannon or thrusting bayonets, in the service and for the selfish purposes of a master, such war degrades a people. A war to protect other human beings against tyrannical injustice; a war to give victory to their own ideas of right and good, and which is their own war, carried on for an honest purpose by their free choice—is often the means of their regeneration."[16]

The lessons of these six battles are manifold. Men fight, sometimes for good reason, but often not. War is a brutal and bestial affair that can bring out the best and worst in people. Politicians and generals make woefully unwise decisions, usually out of arrogance, ignorance, or self-delusion. And the least powerful and the innocent usually pay the greatest price for those woeful decisions.

It would be the height of folly to suggest that the real, simple lesson of these six battles is that all wars are unnecessary and unavoidable. The most naïve among us must realize that war is too much a part of human nature. And certainly there have been necessary and just wars. However, it is also fair to believe that we can be far more creative and intelligent about preventing future wars—that we can, to borrow from Lincoln once more, discover the "better angels of our nature." But judging from this long, bloody, and all too sad history, it is difficult to be too optimistic about that celestial vision.

# Acknowledgments

Throughout my career, I've said many times that an author's name goes on the cover, but a great many people go into making every book happen. This book was made possible through the combined efforts of some great teams of people who have assisted me in researching, writing, editing, and producing this material, as well as some who have been working with me over the course of my writing career. I am grateful to all of them and would like to express my sincere gratitude here.

At Hachette Books, I've been pleased to work with interim publisher Martha Levin, publisher Mauro DiPreta, Paul Whitlatch, Bob Castillo, Tom Pitoniak, Lauren Shute, Rebecca Lown, Betsy Hulsebosch, and Rebecca Berger. I am also indebted to Alex Gigante for his legal wisdom. And a very large thank-you goes to Sydny Miner, who ably stepped in to edit this book with great care and sensitivity and provided many wise and useful questions and suggestions along the way. It has been a pleasure to work with her and all of the Hachette Books team. For all of them, I am exceedingly thankful.

The seed for this book began with my former editor Elisabeth Dyssegaard. Thanks to her as well.

For many years, I have worked with the team at the David Black Literary Agency, and they are not only wonderful representatives but good friends as well. Thanks to David Black, Sarah Smith, Susan Raihofer, Luke Thomas, Antonella Iannarino, and Gary Morris.

My other publishing partners include the people at Random House Audio who produce the audio editions of my books. They have always been gracious, and I am grateful for the support of Amy Metsch, Dan Zitt, Katherine Punia, Heather Dalton, Jennifer Rubins, Kaiulani Kaneta, Skip Dye, and Michael Gentile.

In the course of the past three years, I have been actively reaching out to teachers and librarians across the country, hoping to share my love of history and its importance. I am so grateful to all of them for the important work they do every day. Finally, I thank my family for their support and love. My children, Colin and Jenny, have always been my greatest source of pride and happiness. And the person who has made all of this possible deserves the greatest gratitude. To my wife, Joann, who bears all, thank you always!

# Bibliography

## General Overview

Ambrose, Stephen E. *Duty, Honor, Country: A History of West Point*. Baltimore: Johns Hopkins University Press, 1999.

Anderson, Fred. *A People's Army: Massachusetts Soldiers and Society in the Seven Years' War*. Chapel Hill: University of North Carolina Press, 1984.

—————. *Crucible of War: The Seven Years' War and the Fate of Empire in British North America, 1754–1766*. New York: Vintage, 2000.

Anderson, Fred, and Andrew Cayton. *The Dominion of War: Empire and Liberty in North America, 1500–2000*. New York: Penguin, 2005.

Aptheker, Herbert, ed. *A Documentary History of the Negro People in America*. Vol. 1, *From the Colonial Times Through the Civil War*. New York: Citadel Press, 1990.

Bacevich, Andrew J. *Breach of Trust: How Americans Failed Their Soldiers and Their Country*. New York: Henry Holt/Metropolitan Books, 2013.

Bamford, James. *Body of Secrets: Anatomy of the Ultra-Secret National Security Agency*. New York: Anchor Books, 2002.

Berlin, Ira. *Many Thousands Gone: The First Two Centuries of Slavery in North America*. Cambridge, MA: Belknap/Harvard University Press, 1998.

Boot, Max. *The Savage Wars of Peace: Small Wars and the Rise of American Power*. New York: Basic Books, 2002.

Brown, Dee. *Bury My Heart at Wounded Knee: An Indian History of the American West*. New York: Henry Holt, 1970.

Buckley, Gail. *American Patriots: The Story of Blacks in the Military from the Revolution to Desert Storm*. New York: Random House, 2001.

Carroll, Andrew, ed. *Letters of a Nation: A Collection of Extraordinary American Letters*. New York: Broadway Books, 1997.

Chenoweth, Avery, and Brooke Nihart. *Semper Fi: The Definitive Illustrated History of the U.S. Marines*. Revised and updated ed. New York: Sterling, 2010.

# Bibliography

Cohen, Eliot A. *Conquered into Liberty: Two Centuries of Battles Along the Great Warpath That Made the American Way of War.* New York: Free Press, 2011.

———. *Supreme Command: Soldiers, Statesmen, and Leadership in Wartime.* New York: Free Press, 2002.

Colbert, David, ed. *Eyewitness to America: 500 Years of American History in the Words of Those Who Saw It Happen.* New York: Pantheon, 1998.

Cutler, Thomas J. *A Sailor's History of the U.S. Navy.* Annapolis, MD: Naval Institute Press, 2005.

Davis, Paul K. *100 Decisive Battles: From Ancient Times to the Present.* New York: Oxford, 1999.

Gaddis, John Lewis. *The Cold War: A New History.* New York: Penguin, 2005.

Giangreco, D. M. *United States Army: The Definitive Illustrated History.* New York: Sterling, 2011.

Hedges, Chris. *War Is a Force That Gives Us Meaning.* New York: PublicAffairs, 2002.

———. *What Every Person Should Know About War.* New York: Free Press, 2003.

Jaffe, Steven H. *New York at War: Four Centuries of Combat, Fear, and Intrigue in Gotham.* New York: Basic Books, 2012.

Keegan, John. *Intelligence in War: The Value—and Limitations—of What the Military Can Learn About the Enemy.* New York: Knopf, 2002.

Kinzer, Stephen. *Overthrow: America's Century of Regime Change from Hawaii to Iraq.* New York: Times Books, 2006.

Knightley, Phillip. *The First Casualty: The War Correspondent as Hero and Myth-Maker from the Crimea to Iraq.* Baltimore: Johns Hopkins University Press, 2004.

Kretchik, Walter E. *U.S. Army Doctrine: From the American Revolution to the War on Terror.* Lawrence: University Press of Kansas, 2011.

Larson, Edward J., and Michael P. Winship. *The Constitutional Convention: A Narrative History from the Notes of James Madison.* New York: Modern Library, 2005.

Levy, Leonard. *Original Intent and the Framers' Constitution.* New York: Macmillan, 1988.

———. *Origins of the Bill of Rights.* New Haven, CT: Yale University Press, 1999.

Maddow, Rachel. *Drift: The Unmooring of American Military Power.* New York: Crown, 2012.

Madison, James. *Notes of the Debates in the Federal Convention of 1787.* New York: Norton, 1987.

# Bibliography

Marlantes, Karl. *What It Is Like to Go to War.* New York: Atlantic Monthly Press, 2011.

Michino, Gregory F. *Encyclopedia of Indian Wars: Western Battles and Skirmishes, 1850–1890.* Missoula, MT: Mountain Press, 2003.

Millett, Allan R., and Peter Maslowski. *For the Common Defense: A Military History of the United States of America.* New York: Free Press, 1994.

Peters, Gerhard, ed. *The Presidency: A to Z.* 4th ed. Washington, DC: CQ Press, 2008.

Quarles, Benjamin. *The Negro in the Making of America.* New York: Collier/Macmillan, 1987.

Ricks, Thomas E. *The Generals: American Military Command from World War II to Today.* New York: Penguin Press, 2012.

Rose, Gideon. *How Wars End: Why We Always Fight the Last Battle.* New York: Simon & Schuster, 2010.

Scahill, Jeremy. *Dirty Wars: The World Is a Battlefield.* New York: Nation Books, 2013.

Schlesinger, Arthur M., Jr. *The Almanac of American History.* New York: Barnes & Noble, 1993.

Schultz, Eric B., and Michael J. Tougias. *King Philip's War: The History and Legacy of America's Forgotten Conflict.* Woodstock, VT: Countryman Press, 2000.

Sheppard, Ruth, ed. *Empires Collide: The French and Indian War, 1754–63.* New York: Osprey, 2006.

Sites, Kevin. *The Things They Cannot Say: Stories Soldiers Won't Tell You About What They've Seen, Done or Failed to Do in War.* New York: Harper Perennial, 2011.

Stampp, Kenneth M. *The Peculiar Institution: Slavery in the Ante-Bellum South.* New York: Vintage, 1984.

Toll, Ian W. *Six Frigates: The Epic History of the Founding of the U.S. Navy.* New York: Norton, 2006.

Tuchman, Barbara W. *The March of Folly: From Troy to Vietnam.* New York: Random House, 1984.

Turse, Nick. *The Changing Face of Empire: Special Ops, Drones, Spies, Proxy Fighters, and Cyberwarfare.* Chicago: Haymarket Books, 2012.

Walzer, Michael. *Just and Unjust Wars: A Moral Argument with Historical Illustrations.* 4th ed. New York: Basic Books, 2006.

Weiner, Tim. *Enemies: A History of the FBI.* New York: Random House, 2012.

———. *Legacy of Ashes: The History of the CIA.* New York: Anchor Books, 2008.

Whipple, A. B. C. *To the Shores of Tripoli: The Birth of the U.S. Navy and Marines.* New York: William Morrow, 1991.

Witt, John Fabian. *Lincoln's Code: The Laws of War in American History.* New York: Free Press, 2012.

Wright, James. *Those Who Have Borne the Battle: A History of America's Wars and Those Who Fought Them.* New York: PublicAffairs, 2012.

Zacks, Richard. *The Pirate Coast: Thomas Jefferson, the First Marines, and the Secret Mission of 1805.* New York: Hyperion, 2005.

Zimbardo, Philip. *The Lucifer Effect: Understanding How Good People Turn Evil.* New York: Random House, 2007.


## Yorktown

Brookhiser, Richard. *George Washington: Founding Father.* New York: Free Press, 1996.

Chernow, Ron. *Alexander Hamilton.* New York: Penguin, 2004.

———. *Washington: A Life.* New York: Penguin, 2010.

Daughan, George C. *If by Sea: The Forging of the American Navy—From the Revolution to the War of 1812.* New York: Basic Books, 2008.

Davis, Burke. *The Campaign That Won America: The Story of Yorktown.* New York: Dial Press, 1970.

Edgar, Walter. *Partisans and Redcoats: The Southern Conflict That Turned the Tide of the American Revolution.* New York: William Morrow, 2001.

Ellis, Joseph E. *His Excellency: George Washington.* New York: Knopf, 2004.

———. *Revolutionary Summer: The Birth of American Independence.* New York: Knopf, 2013.

Fenn, Elizabeth A. *Pox Americana: The Great Smallpox Epidemic of 1775–1782.* New York: Hill & Wang, 2001.

Ferling, John. *Almost a Miracle: The American Victory in the War of Independence.* New York: Oxford University Press, 2007.

———. *The Ascent of George Washington: The Hidden Political Genius of an American Icon.* New York: Bloomsbury, 2009.

Fischer, David Hackett. *Washington's Crossing.* New York: Oxford University Press, 2004.

Fleming, Thomas. *Duel: Alexander Hamilton, Aaron Burr, and the Future of America.* New York: Basic Books, 1999.

# Bibliography

———. *Liberty! The American Revolution.* New York: Viking, 1997.

———. *The Perils of Peace: America's Struggle for Survival After Yorktown.* New York: Smithsonian Books, 2007.

———. *Washington's Secret War: The Hidden History of Valley Forge.* New York: Smithsonian Books, 2005.

Flexner, James Thomas. *Washington: The Indispensable Man.* New York: Little, Brown, 1974. (Single-volume abridgment of Flexner's four-volume Washington biography.)

Hibbert, Christopher. *Redcoats and Rebels: The American Revolution Through British Eyes.* New York: Norton, 2002.

Isaacson, Walter. *Benjamin Franklin: An American Life.* New York: Simon & Schuster, 2003.

Ketchum, Richard M. *Decisive Day: The Battle of Bunker Hill.* New York: Owl Books, 1999.

———. *Saratoga: Turning Point of America's Revolutionary War.* New York: Holt, 1997.

Kranish, Michael. *Flight from Monticello: Thomas Jefferson at War.* New York: Oxford University Press, 2010.

Martin, Joseph Plumb, with introduction by Thomas Fleming. *A Narrative of a Revolutionary Soldier.* New York: New American Library, 2001. (Previously published as *Private Yankee Doodle.*)

McCullough, David. *1776.* New York: Simon & Schuster, 2005.

Nash, Gary B. *The Forgotten Fifth: African Americans in the Age of Revolution.* Cambridge, MA: Harvard University Press, 2006.

———. *The Unknown American Revolution: The Unruly Birth of Democracy and the Struggle to Create America.* New York: Viking Penguin, 2005.

Neimeyer, Charles Patrick. *America Goes to War: A Social History of the Continental Army.* New York: New York University Press, 1996.

Nelson, James L. *Benedict Arnold's Navy: The Ragtag Fleet That Lost the Battle of Lake Champlain but Won the American Revolution.* New York: McGraw-Hill, 2006.

———. *George Washington's Great Gamble and the Sea Battle That Won the American Revolution.* New York: McGraw-Hill, 2010.

———. *George Washington's Secret Navy: How the American Revolution Went to Sea.* New York: McGraw-Hill, 2008.

Palmer, Dave R. *George Washington and Benedict Arnold: A Tale of Two Patriots.* Washington, DC: Regnery, 2006.

# Bibliography

Puls, Mark. *Henry Knox: Visionary General of the American Revolution.* New York: Palgrave, 2008.

Rakove, Jack. *Revolutionaries: A New History of the Invention of America.* New York: Houghton Mifflin, 2010.

Raphael, Ray. *Founders: The People Who Brought You a Nation.* New York: Free Press, 2009.

———. *A People's History of the American Revolution: How Common People Shaped the Fight for Independence.* New York: New Press, 2001.

Royster, Charles. *A Revolutionary People at War: The Continental Army and American Character, 1775–1783.* Chapel Hill: University of North Carolina Press, 1979.

Schama, Simon. *Rough Crossings: The Slaves, the British, and the American Revolution.* New York: HarperCollins, 2006.

Schecter, Barnet. *The Battle for New York: The City at the Heart of the American Revolution.* New York: Walker, 2002.

Seagrave, Ronald Roy. *Jefferson's Isaac: From Monticello to Petersburg.* Denver: Outskirts Press, 2011.

Stephenson, Michael. *Patriot Battles: How the War of Independence Was Fought.* New York: HarperCollins, 2007.

Tonsetic, Robert L. *1781: The Decisive Year of the Revolutionary War.* Philadelphia: Casemate, 2011.

Twohig, Dorothy, ed. *George Washington's Diaries: An Abridgement.* Charlottesville: University of Virginia Press, 1999. (Edited version of six-volume Washington diaries published in 1979.)

Unger, Harlow Giles. *Lafayette.* New York: John Wiley, 2002.

———. *The Unexpected George Washington: His Private Life.* New York: John Wiley, 2006.

Wiencek, Henry. *An Imperfect God: George Washington, His Slaves, and the Creation of America.* New York: Farrar, Straus & Giroux, 2003.

Wilkins, Roger. *Jefferson's Pillow: The Founding Fathers and the Dilemma of Black Patriotism.* Boston: Beacon Press, 2001.

Williams, Glenn F. *Year of the Hangman: George Washington's Campaign Against the Iroquois.* Yardley, PA: Westholme, 2005.

Wood, Gordon S. *The Radicalism of the American Revolution.* New York: Vintage, 1991.

———. *Revolutionary Characters: What Made the Founders Different.* New York: Penguin, 2006.

Wright, Robert K., Jr. *The Continental Army*. Army Lineage Series. Washington, DC: Center of Military History, 1983.


## Petersburg

Bartoletti, Susan Campbell. *They Called Themselves the K.K.K.: The Birth of an American Terrorist Group*. New York: Houghton Mifflin, 2010.

Bearss, Edwin C., with Bryce Suderow. *The Petersburg Campaign*. Vol. 1, *The Eastern Front Battles, June–August 1864*. El Dorado Hills, CA: Savas Beattie, 2012.

Brands, H. W. *The Man Who Saved the Union: Ulysses Grant in War and Peace*. New York: Doubleday, 2012.

Faust, Drew Gilpin. *Mothers of Invention: Women of the Slaveholding South in the American Civil War*. Chapel Hill: University of North Carolina Press, 1996.

Furgurson, Ernest B. *Ashes of Glory: Richmond at War*. New York: Random House, 1996.

———. *Not War but Murder: Cold Harbor 1864*. New York: Knopf, 2000.

Glatthaar, Joseph T. *Forged in Battle: The Civil War Alliance of Black Soldiers and White Officers*. New York: Free Press, 1990.

Goodwin, Doris Kearns. *Team of Rivals: The Political Genius of Abraham Lincoln*. New York: Simon & Schuster, 2005.

Grant, Ulysses S. *Personal Memoirs*. New York: Modern Library, 1999. (Reprint of 1885 edition of *Personal Memoirs of U. S. Grant*.)

Guelzo, Allen C. *Gettysburg: The Last Invasion*. New York: Knopf, 2013.

Jaynes, Gregory, and the editors of Time-Life Books. *The Killing Ground: Wilderness to Cold Harbor*. Alexandria, VA: Time-Life Books, 1986.

Levin, Kevin M. *Remembering the Battle of the Crater: War as Murder*. Lexington: University Press of Kentucky, 2012.

Levine, Bruce. *Confederate Emancipation: Southern Plans to Free and Arm Slaves During the Civil War*. New York: Oxford University Press, 2006.

McPherson, James M. *Battle Cry of Freedom: The Civil War Era*. New York: Oxford University Press, 1988.

———. *The Negro's Civil War: How American Blacks Felt and Acted During the War for Union*. New York: Vintage, 2003.

Newton, A. H. *Out of the Briars: An Autobiography and Sketch of the Twenty-Ninth Regiment, Connecticut Volunteers*. Miami, FL: HardPress, on-demand printing, September 2013.

Oates, Stephen B. *A Woman of Valor: Clara Barton and the Civil War.* New York: Free Press, 1994.

———. *With Malice Toward None: The Life of Abraham Lincoln.* New York: Harper & Row, 1977.

Schultz, Duane. *Over the Earth I Come: The Great Sioux Uprising of 1862.* New York: St. Martin's, 1992.

Smith, Andrew. *Starving the South: How the North Won the Civil War.* New York: St. Martin's, 2011.

Smith, Jean Edward. *Grant.* New York: Simon & Schuster, 2001.

Taylor, Alan. *The Internal Enemy: Slavery and War in Virginia, 1792–1832.* New York: Norton, 2013.

Trudeau, Noah Andre. *The Last Citadel: Petersburg, Virginia, June 1864–April 1865.* New York: Little, Brown, 1991.

Winik, Jay. *April 1865: The Month That Saved America.* New York: HarperCollins, 2001.

Yacovone, Donald, ed. *Freedom's Journey: African American Voices of the Civil War.* Chicago: Lawrence Hill Books/Chicago Review Press, 2004.

## Manila

Arnold, James R. *The Moro War: How America Battled a Muslim Insurgency in the Philippine Jungle, 1902–1913.* New York: Bloomsbury, 2011.

Fulton, Robert A. *Moroland: The History of Uncle Sam and the Moros, 1899–1920.* Bend, OR: Tupelo Creek Press, 2009.

Jones, Gregg. *Honor in the Dust: Theodore Roosevelt, War in the Philippines, and the Rise and Fall of America's Imperial Dream.* New York: New American Library, 2012.

Karnow, Stanley. *In Our Image: America's Empire in the Philippines.* New York: Ballantine, 1989.

Linn, Brian McAllister. *The Philippine War, 1899–1902.* Lawrence: University Press of Kansas, 2000.

Morris, Edmund. *The Rise of Theodore Roosevelt.* New York: Coward, McCann & Geoghegan, 1979.

———. *Theodore Rex.* New York: Random House, 2001.

Silbey, David J. *A War of Frontier and Empire: The Philippine-American War, 1899–1902.* New York: Hill & Wang, 2007.

Thomas, Evan. *The War Lovers: Roosevelt, Hearst, and the Rush to Empire, 1898.* New York: Little, Brown, 2010.

## Berlin

Anonymous. *A Woman in Berlin: Eight Weeks in the Conquered City: A Diary*. New York: Henry Holt, 2006.

Applebaum, Anne. *Iron Curtain: The Crushing of Eastern Europe, 1944–1956*. New York: Doubleday, 2012.

Atkinson, Rick. *An Army at Dawn: The War in North Africa, 1942–1943*. New York: Henry Holt, 2002.

———. *The Day of Battle: The War in Sicily and Italy, 1943–1944*. New York: Henry Holt, 2007.

———. *The Guns at Last Light: The War in Western Europe, 1944–1945*. New York: Henry Holt, 2013.

Beevor, Antony. *The Fall of Berlin 1945*. New York: Viking Penguin, 2002.

———. *The Second World War*. New York: Little, Brown, 2012.

Best, Nicholas. *Five Days That Shocked the World: Eyewitness Accounts from Europe at the End of World War II*. New York: St. Martin's, 2011.

Dobbs, Michael. *Six Months in 1945: From World War to Cold War*. New York: Knopf, 2012.

Eisenhower, Dwight D. *Crusade in Europe*. Baltimore: Johns Hopkins University Press, 1997.

Fullilove, Michael. *Rendezvous with Destiny: How Franklin D. Roosevelt and Five Extraordinary Men Took America into the War and into the World*. New York: Penguin Press, 2013.

Hasegawa, Tsuyoshi. *Racing the Enemy: Stalin, Truman, and the Surrender of Japan*. Cambridge, MA: Belknap/Harvard University Press, 2005.

Hastings, Max. *Inferno: The World at War, 1939–1945*. New York: Knopf, 2011.

Hitchcock, William I. *The Bitter Road to Freedom: A New History of the Liberation of Europe*. New York: Free Press, 2008.

Jones, Vincent C. *Manhattan: The Army and the Atomic Bomb*. Washington, DC: Center of Military History, 1985.

Judt, Tony. *Postwar: A History of Europe Since 1945*. New York: Penguin, 2005.

McCullough, David. *Truman*. New York: Simon & Schuster, 1992.

Ryan, Cornelius. *The Last Battle: The Classic History of the Battle for Berlin*. New York: Simon & Schuster, 1966.

Service, Robert. *Stalin: A Biography*. Cambridge, MA: Belknap/Harvard University Press, 2005.

# Bibliography

Sheinkin, Steve. *Bomb: The Race to Build—and Steal—the World's Most Dangerous Weapon.* New York: Roaring Brook Press, 2012.

Smith, Jean Edward. *Eisenhower: In War and Peace.* New York: Random House, 2012.

Taylor, Frederick. *Dresden: Tuesday, February 13, 1945.* New York: HarperCollins, 2004.

Wicker, Tom. *Dwight D. Eisenhower.* New York: Henry Holt/Times Books, 2005.

## Hué and Vietnam

Anderson, David L. *The Columbia Guide to the Vietnam War.* New York: Columbia University Press, 2002.

Arlen, Michael. *Living-Room War.* New York: Viking, 1969.

Associated Press. *Vietnam: The Real War: A Photographic History.* New York: Abrams, 2013.

Beschloss, Michael, ed. *Reaching for Glory: Lyndon Johnson's Secret White House Tapes, 1964–1965.* New York: Simon & Schuster, 2001.

Brinkley, Douglas. *Cronkite.* New York: HarperCollins, 2012.

Caro, Robert A. *The Passage of Power.* Vol. 4 of *The Years of Lyndon Johnson.* New York: Knopf, 2012.

Dallek, Robert. *Flawed Giant: Lyndon Johnson and His Times, 1961–1973.* New York: Oxford University Press, 1999.

Goodwin, Doris Kearns. *Lyndon Johnson and the American Dream.* New York: St. Martin's Griffin, 1991.

Halberstam, David. *The Best and the Brightest.* New York: Random House, 1972.

———. *Quagmire: America and Vietnam During the Kennedy Era.* Rev. ed. Lanham, MD: Rowman & Littlefield, 2008.

Hammel, Eric. *Fire in the Streets: The Battle for Hue, Tet 1968.* Pacifica, CA: Pacifica Military History, 1991.

Herr, Michael. *Dispatches.* New York: Knopf, 1977.

Karnow, Stanley. *Vietnam: A History.* New York: Penguin, 1997.

Kurlansky, Mark. *1968: The Year That Rocked the World.* New York: Random House, 2005.

Laurence, John. *The Cat from Hué: A Vietnam War Story.* New York: PublicAffairs, 2002.

Lawrence, Mark Atwood. *The Vietnam War: A Concise International History.* New York: Oxford University Press, 2008.

Moore, Harold, and Joseph L. Galloway. *We Were Soldiers Once... and Young: Ia Drang—The Battle That Changed the War in Vietnam.* New York: Random House, 1992.

Oberdorfer, Don. *Tet! The Turning Point in the Vietnam War.* Baltimore: Johns Hopkins University Press, 2001.

Robbins, James S. *This Time We Win: Revisiting the Tet Offensive.* New York: Encounter Books, 2012.

Sheehan, Neil. *A Bright Shining Lie: John Paul Vann and America in Vietnam.* New York: Random House, 1988.

Smith, George W. *The Siege at Hué.* Boulder, CO: Lynne Rienner, 1999.

Truong, Nhu Tang. *A Vietcong Memoir: An Inside Account of the Vietnam War and Its Aftermath.* New York: Vintage, 1986.

Turse, Nick. *Kill Anything That Moves: The Real American War in Vietnam.* New York: Henry Holt/Metropolitan Books, 2013.

Willbanks, James H. *The Tet Offensive: A Concise History.* New York: Columbia University Press, 2007.

**Fallujah**

Atkinson, Rick. *In the Company of Soldiers: A Chronicle of Combat.* New York: Henry Holt, 2005.

Baker, Peter. *Days of Fire: Bush and Cheney in the White House.* New York: Doubleday, 2013.

Bergen, Peter L. *Manhunt: The Ten-Year Search for Bin Laden from 9/11 to Abbottabad.* New York: Crown, 2012.

Coll, Steve. *Ghost Wars: The Secret History of the CIA, Afghanistan, and Bin Laden, from the Soviet Invasion to September 10, 2001.* New York: Penguin, 2005.

Eichenwald, Kurt. *500 Days: Secrets and Lies in the Terror Wars.* New York: Simon & Schuster, 2012.

Gates, Robert M. *Duty: Memoirs of a Secretary at War.* New York: Knopf, 2014.

Gordon, Michael R., and General Bernard Trainor. *The Endgame: The Inside Story of the Struggle for Iraq, from George W. Bush to Barack Obama.* New York: Pantheon, 2012.

Hersh, Seymour M. *Chain of Command: The Road from 9/11 to Abu Ghraib.* New York: HarperCollins, 2004.

Junger, Sebastian. *War.* New York: Twelve, 2010.

Kaplan, Robert D. *Imperial Grunts: The American Military on the Ground.* New York: Random House, 2005.

# Bibliography

Kean, Thomas H., and Lee Hamilton. *The 9/11 Commission Report: The National Commission on Terrorist Attacks upon the United States. With Reporting and Analysis by The New York Times.* New York: St. Martin's, 2004.

Mayer, Jane. *The Dark Side: The Inside Story of How the War on Terror Turned into a War on American Ideals.* New York: Doubleday, 2008.

Mazzetti, Mark. *The Way of the Knife: The CIA, a Secret Army, and a War at the Ends of the Earth.* New York: Penguin, 2013.

McChrystal, Stanley. *My Share of the Task: A Memoir.* New York: Penguin, 2013.

Packer, George. *The Assassins' Gate: America in Iraq.* New York: Farrar, Straus & Giroux, 2005.

Parnell, Sean. *Outlaw Platoon: Heroes, Renegades, Infidels, and the Brotherhood of War in Afghanistan.* New York: William Morrow, 2012.

Ricks, Thomas E. *Fiasco: The American Military Adventure in Iraq.* New York: Penguin, 2006.

———. *The Gamble: General David Petraeus and the American Military Adventure in Iraq, 2006–2008.* New York: Penguin Press, 2009.

Sanger, David E. *Confront and Conceal: Obama's Secret Wars and Surprising Uses of American Power.* New York: Crown, 2012.

Scahill, Jeremy. *Blackwater: The Rise of the World's Most Powerful Mercenary Army.* New York: Nation Books, 2008.

———. *Dirty Wars: The World Is a Battlefield.* New York: Nation Books, 2013.

Schmitt, Eric, and Thom Shanker. *Counterstrike: The Untold Story of America's Secret Campaign Against Al Qaeda.* New York: Times Books/Henry Holt, 2011.

West, Bing. *No True Glory: A Frontline Account of the Battle for Fallujah.* New York: Bantam Dell, 2005.

Woodward, Bob. *The Commanders.* New York: Simon & Schuster, 1991.

———. *Obama's Wars.* New York: Simon & Schuster, 2010.

———. *Plan of Attack.* New York: Simon & Schuster, 2004.

———. *The War Within: A Secret White House History, 2006–2008.* New York: Simon & Schuster, 2008.

# Notes

## Introduction

1. Karl von Clausewitz, *On War*, cited in *Bartlett's Familiar Quotations*, 16th ed., p. 393.

2. Walt Whitman, *Whitman: Poetry and Prose* (New York: Library of America, 1982), p. 778.

3. Renata Adler, review of *The Green Berets*, *New York Times*, June 20, 1968, http://movies.nytimes.com/movie/review?res=990ce1d8163ae134bc4851dfb0668383679ede.

4. John Kifner, "A Case Study in Disaster for Tomorrow's Generals," *New York Times*, April 28, 2000, http://www.nytimes.com/2000/04/28/world/a-case-study-in-disaster-for-tomorrow-s-generals.html?pagewanted=print&src=pm.

5. Cited in Karl W. Eikenberry and David M. Kennedy, "Americans and Their Military, Drifting Apart," *New York Times*, May 26, 2013, http://www.samuel-adams-heritage.com/documents/samuel-adams-to-james-warren-1776.html.

6. Noah Andre Trudeau, *The Last Citadel*, p. xi.

7. Madison cited in Christopher Collier and James Lincoln Collier, *Decision in Philadelphia* (New York: Random House, 1986), p. 316.

8. Elbridge Gerry cited in Walter Isaacson, *Benjamin Franklin: An American Life*, p. 456; and in Collier and Collier, *Decision in Philadelphia*, p. 324.

9. Text transcript of the Bill of Rights, National Archives, Washington, D.C., http://www.archives.gov/exhibits/charters/bill_of_rights_transcript.html, accessed March 26, 2014.

10. George Washington, "First Annual Message to Congress," January 8, 1790, Avalon Project, Yale Law School, http://avalon.law.yale.edu/18th_century/washs01.asp, accessed January 14, 2014.

11. Barbara W. Tuchman, *The March of Folly*, p. 7.

12. Ta-Nehisi Coates, "The Unromantic Slaughter of the Civil War," *Atlantic*, June 20, 2013, http://www.theatlantic.com/national/archive/2013/06/the-unromantic-slaughter-of-the-civil-war/277051/, accessed January 14, 2014.

# Notes

## Chapter One. Washington's Men

1. Joseph Plumb Martin, *A Narrative of a Revolutionary Soldier*, p. 199.

2. Ronald Roy Seagrave, *Jefferson's Isaac*, p. 41.

3. Washington and Olney cited in Ron Chernow, *Washington*, p. 415.

4. Rochambeau cited in Burke Davis, *The Campaign That Won America*, p. 226.

5. Martin, *A Narrative*, p. 202.

6. Davis, *The Campaign That Won America*, pp. 225–27.

7. Thomas Fleming, *The Perils of Peace*, pp. 14–15.

8. Charles Royster, *A Revolutionary People at War*, p. 220.

9. Martin, *A Narrative*, p. 203.

10. Davis, *Campaign*, p. 232; Chernow, *Washington*, p. 415.

11. Cited in Harlow Giles Unger, *Lafayette*, pp. 156–57.

12. Cited in Davis, *Campaign*, p. 232.

13. Christopher Hibbert, *Redcoats and Rebels*, p. 328.

14. Lafayette letter cited in Fleming, *Perils of Peace*, p. 16; Unger, *Lafayette*, p. 159.

15. Chernow, *Washington*, p. 390.

16. Cited in Hibbert, *Redcoats and Rebels*, p. 322.

17. Cited in ibid.

18. Walter Edgar, *Partisans and Redcoats*, p. 51.

19. Diary of Lieutenant Anthony Allaire of Ferguson's Corps, in Lyman C. Draper, *King's Mountain and Its Heroes* (Cincinnati: Peter G. Thomson, 1881), p. 494, cited in "The Colleton Family in South Carolina," http://archive.org/stream/jstor-27574930/27574930_djvu.txt, accessed March 26, 2014.

20. Edgar, *Partisans and Redcoats*, p. 57.

21. Fleming, *Perils of Peace*, p. 7.

22. Gary B. Nash, *The Forgotten Fifth*, p. 39.

23. Barbara A. Mitchell, "Bankrolling the Battle of Yorktown," *Military History Quarterly* 19, no. 3 (Spring 2007), published online, November 28, 2012, http://www.historynet.com/bankrolling-the-battle-of-yorktown.htm.

24. Ibid.

25. Ibid.

26. Davis, *Campaign*, p. 61.

27. Mitchell, "Bankrolling the Battle of Yorktown."

28. Martin, *A Narrative*, p. 198.

29. Davis, *Campaign*, p. 223.

30. Ibid., p. 235.

31. Unger, *Lafayette*, p. 159.

32. Martin, *A Narrative*, p. 207.

33. Brendan Morrissey, *Yorktown 1781: The World Turned Upside Down* (London: Osprey, 1997), p. 77.

34. Davis, *Campaign*, p. 273.

35. Henry Wiencek, *An Imperfect God*, p. 247.

36. George C. Daughan, *If by Sea*, p. 234.

37. Ian W. Toll, *Six Frigates*, p. 16.

38. James Kirby Martin and Mark Edward Lender, *A Respectable Army: The Military Origins of the Republic, 1763–1789*, 2nd ed. (Wheeling, IL: Harland Davidson, 2006).

39. Royster, *A Revolutionary People at War*, p. 46.

40. Cited in Eikenberry and Kennedy, "Americans and Their Military, Drifting Apart."

41. Fleming, introduction to *A Narrative of a Revolutionary Soldier*, p. xiv.

42. Michael Kranish, *Flight from Monticello*, p. 130.

43. Thomas Jefferson, "Notes on Virginia: Query XXII: The Public Income and Expenses?," in *The Life and Selected Writings of Thomas Jefferson* (New York: Modern Library, 1944), p. 262.

44. Knox cited in Stephen E. Ambrose, *Duty, Honor, Country*, p. 8.

45. Charles Patrick Neimeyer, *America Goes to War*, pp. xii–xiv.

46. Martin, *A Narrative*, p. 249.

47. Ray Raphael, *A People's History of the American Revolution*, p. 118.

48. Kranish, *Flight*, p. 127.

49. Gary B. Nash, *The Unknown American Revolution*, p. 344.

50. Elizabeth A. Fenn, *Pox Americana*, p. 129.

51. Cited in Nash, *The Forgotten Fifth*, p. 37.

52. Martin, *A Narrative*, p. 207.

53. Ibid.

54. Wiencek, *Imperfect God*, p. 251.

55. Chernow, *Washington*, p. 419.

56. Seagrave, *Jefferson's Isaac*, p. 40.

57. Ibid., p. 41.

58. Ibid.

59. Wiencek, *Imperfect God*, p. 253.

60. Cited in Chernow, *Washington*, p. 415.

61. Chernow, *Alexander Hamilton*, p. 95.

62. Nash, *The Forgotten Fifth*, p. 13.

63. Ibid., p. 11.

64. Simon Schama, *Rough Crossings*, p. 67.

65. Nash, *The Forgotten Fifth*, pp. 12–13.

66. Chernow, *Hamilton*, pp. 85–86.

67. Hamilton cited in ibid., p. 163.

68. Unger, *Lafayette*, p. 15.

69. Davis, *Campaign*, p. 113.

70. Nash, *The Forgotten Fifth*, p. 39.

71. Schama, *Rough Crossings*, p. 11.

72. Cited in Gail Buckley, *American Patriots*, p. 34.

73. Fleming, *Perils of Peace*, p. 3.

74. Mark Puls, *Henry Knox*, pp. 176–77.

75. Chernow, *Washington*, p. 434.

76. "The Newburgh Conspiracy, December 1782–March 1783," http://www.loc.gov/teachers/classroommaterials/presentationsandactivities/presentations/timeline/amrev/peace/newburgh.html, accessed January 27, 2014.

77. Chernow, *Washington*, p. 436.

78. "Rochambeau," http://www.mountvernon.org/educational-resources/encyclopedia/rochambeau, accessed October 7, 2013.

79. "Lafayette's Plan for Slavery," http://www.mountvernon.org/educational-resources/encyclopedia/lafayettes-plan-slavery#note1, accessed October 7, 2013.

80. Wiencek, *Imperfect God*, p. 262.

81. Ibid., pp. 274–75.

82. Unger, *Lafayette*, p. 328.

83. Ibid., p. 354.

84. Fleming, *Perils of Peace*, p. 207.

85. Hamilton cited in Chernow, *Hamilton*, p. 172.

86. Hamilton cited in ibid.

87. Ibid., pp. 180–81.

88. Allan R. Millett and Peter Maslowski, *For the Common Defense*, p. 90.

89. Stephen E. Ambrose, *Duty, Honor, Country*, p. 9.

90. Patrick Henry cited in Daughan, *If by Sea*, p. 245.

91. Millett and Maslowski, *For the Common Defense*, p. 95.

92. Ibid.

93. Ibid., p. 156.

# Notes

## Chapter Two. The Battle of the Old Men and the Young Boys

1. Cited in Ron Field, *Petersburg 1864–1865* (Oxford: Osprey, 2009), p. 5.

2. Alexander H. Newton, *Out of the Briars*, cited in Donald Yacovone, ed., *Freedom's Journey*, p. 363.

3. Percy H. Epler, *The Life of Clara Barton*, cited in Stephen B. Oates, *A Woman of Valor*, frontispiece.

4. Waddell cited in Noah Andre Trudeau, *The Last Citadel*, p. 8.

5. Ibid., p. 4.

6. Jean Edward Smith, *Grant*, p. 365.

7. M. P. Gabriel, "Battle of Old Men and Young Boys," *Encyclopedia Virginia*, Virginia Foundation for the Humanities, http://www.encyclopediavirginia.org/Old_Men _and_Young_Boys_Battle_of_June_9_1864, accessed January 20, 2014.

8. Ibid.

9. Trudeau, *The Last Citadel*, p. 9.

10. Waddell cited in ibid.

11. Edwin Bearss, *The Petersburg Campaign*, Kindle ed., loc. 510.

12. Christopher M. Calkins and the *Dictionary of Virginia Biography*, "Fletcher H. Archer (1817–1902)," *Encyclopedia Virginia*, Virginia Foundation for the Humanities, http://www .encyclopediavirginia.org/Archer_Fletcher_H_1817-1902, accessed August 15, 2013.

13. Gabriel, "Battle of Old Men and Young Boys."

14. Noah Andre Trudeau, *The Siege of Petersburg* ([Conshohocken, PA]: Eastern National Park and Monument Association, 1995), p. 28.

15. Bearss, *Petersburg Campaign*, loc. 597.

16. Ibid., loc. 643.

17. Field, *Petersburg 1864–1865*, p. 20.

18. Gabriel, "Battle of Old Men and Young Boys."

19. Trudeau, *The Last Citadel*, p. 11.

20. Ibid., p. 4.

21. James M. McPherson, *Battle Cry of Freedom*, p. 328.

22. Oates, *A Woman of Valor*, p. 248.

23. Newton, *Out of the Briars*, cited in Yacovone, ed., *Freedom's Journey*, p. 363.

24. Butler letter cited in Oates, *A Woman of Valor*, p. 235.

25. Ibid., p. 242.

26. Grant cited in H. W. Brands, *The Man Who Saved the Union*, p. 303.

27. Ernest B. Furgurson, *Not War but Murder*, p. 278.

28. Ulysses S. Grant, *Personal Memoirs*, p. 462.

29. Cited in Oates, *With Malice Toward None*, p. 420.

30. McPherson, *Battle Cry of Freedom*, p. 742.

31. Kevin M. Levin, *Remembering the Battle of the Crater*, p. 9.

32. Field, *Petersburg 1864–1865*, p. 22.

33. Lincoln letter to Grant cited in Brands, *The Man Who Saved the Union*, p. 310.

34. Oates, *A Woman of Valor*, p. 259.

35. Trudeau, *The Siege of Petersburg*, p. 6.

36. Henry M. Turner, "A Very Important Letter from Chaplain Turner," *Christian Recorder*, July 9, 1864, cited in "United States Colored Troops in the Opening Assault on Petersburg," National Park Service, http://www.nps.gov/pete/historyculture/upload/United-States-Colored-Troops-in-the-Opening-Assault-on-Petersburg.pdf, accessed April 1, 2014.

37. Joseph T. Glatthaar, *Forged in Battle*, p. 157.

38. Ibid., p. 158.

39. James M. McPherson, *The Negro's Civil War*, p. 229.

40. Trudeau, *The Last Citadel*, p. 54.

41. Ibid., p. 7.

42. Grant, *Memoirs*, p. 474.

43. Trudeau, *The Last Citadel*, p. 30.

44. Furgurson, *Not War but Murder*, p. 256.

45. Cited in Oates, *With Malice Toward None*, p. 424.

46. McPherson, *Battle Cry of Freedom*, pp. 634–35.

47. McPherson, *Forged in Battle*, p. 184.

48. Cited in Geoffrey C. Ward, *The Civil War: An Illustrated History* (New York: Knopf, 1990), p. 309.

49. Cited in ibid., p. 310.

50. Levin, *Remembering the Battle of the Crater*, p. 14.

51. Ibid., pp. 11–12.

52. Ibid., p. 12.

53. Account of General Ledlie in Ward, *Civil War*, p. 314; Levin, *Remembering the Battle of the Crater*, p. 15.

54. Ward, *Civil War*, p. 315.

55. Levin, *Remembering the Battle of the Crater*, p. 27.

56. Ibid., p. 47.

57. Stewart Sifakis, *Who Was Who in the Civil War* (New York: Facts on File , 1988), p. 428.

58. Oates, *Woman of Valor,* p. 262.

59. Ibid., p. 263.

60. Levin, *Remembering the Battle of the Crater,* pp. 7–8.

61. Heidi Campbell-Shoaf, "Siege of Petersburg: The City and the Citizens Were Impacted from the Start," *Civil War Times,* August 2004, http://www.historynet .com/siege-of-petersburg-the-city-and-citizens-were-impacted-from-the-start .htm, accessed November 12, 2013.

62. Ibid.

63. Ibid.

64. Andrew F. Smith, *Starving the South,* pp. 161–62.

65. Trudeau, *The Last Citadel,* p. 258.

66. Ibid.

67. Ibid., p. 259.

68. Ibid., p. 280.

69. Smith, *Starving the South,* p. 196.

70. Oates, *With Malice Toward None,* p. 456.

71. Ibid., pp. 456–57.

72. Ibid.

73. Kevin M. Levin, "Meet William Mahone, the Ex-Confederate General Who Built His Political Career on the Black Vote," History News Network, September 30, 2013; http://hnn.us/article/153423, accessed February 5, 2014.

74. "General Orders No. 11," Grand Army of the Republic, May 5, 1868, http://www .usmemorialday.org/order11.html, accessed April 4, 2014.

75. Jay Winik, *April 1865,* p. 360.

76. Millett and Maslowski, *For the Common Defense,* p. 248.

77. Ibid., pp. 248–49.

78. Julia Keller, *Mr. Gatling's Terrible Marvel* (New York: Viking, 2008), p. 7.

79. "Brady's Photographs: Pictures of the Dead at Antietam," *New York Times,* October 20, 1862, http://www.nytimes.com/1862/10/20/news/brady-s-photographs -pictures-of-the-dead-at-antietam.html, accessed December 19, 2013.

80. Millett and Maslowski, *For the Common Defense,* p. 249.

81. Buckley, *American Patriots,* p. 113.

82. Millett and Maslowski, *For the Common Defense,* p. 276.

## Chapter Three. The Water Cure

1.  http://highered.mcgraw-hill.com/sites/dl/free/0072424362/40804/chap20 elem1.htm, accessed January 21, 2014.

2.  *Soldier's Letters*, pamphlet, Anti-Imperialist League, 1899, reprinted in Philip S. Foner and Richard Winchester, *The Anti-Imperialist Reader: A Documentary History of Anti-Imperialism in the United States*, vol. 1 (New York: Holmes & Meier, 1984), pp. 316–23.

3.  Smith quoted in Gregg Jones, *Honor in the Dust*, p. 242.

4.  Brian McAllister Linn, *The Philippine War, 1899–1902*, p. 312.

5.  Jones, *Honor in the Dust*, p. 232.

6.  Linn, *The Philippine War*, p. 311.

7.  Ibid., p. 312.

8.  Jones, *Honor in the Dust*, p. 234.

9.  Linn, *The Philippine War*, p. 311.

10. Stanley Karnow, *In Our Image*, p. 191.

11. Ibid., p. 190.

12. Ibid., p. 313.

13. Jones, *Honor in the Dust*, p. 237; Karnow, *In Our Image*, p. 191.

14. Jones, *Honor in the Dust*, p. 237.

15. Ibid.

16. Linn, *The Philippine War*, p. 312.

17. Jones, *Honor in the Dust*, p. 238.

18. Ibid., p. 239.

19. Max Boot, *The Savage Wars of Peace*, p. 127.

20. Philip Zimbardo, *The Lucifer Effect*, "Overview," http://www.lucifereffect.com/about_synopsis.htm, accessed January 21, 2014.

21. Edward Tick, *War and the Soul: Healing Our Nation's Veterans from Post-Traumatic Stress Disorder*, cited in Kevin Sites, *The Things They Cannot Say*, p. xxiii.

22. Linn, *The Philippine War*, p. 223.

23. Ibid., p. 314.

24. Cited in Jones, *Honor in the Dust*, p. 242.

25. Linn, *The Philippine War*, p. 316.

26. Ibid., p. 317.

27. Stephen Kinzer, *Overthrow*, p. 53.

28. "The Destruction of the U.S.S. Maine," Department of the Navy, Naval History and Heritage Command, http://www.history.navy.mil/faqs/faq71-1.htm, accessed October 13, 2013.

29. Ibid.

30. Evan Thomas, *The War Lovers*, p. 60.

31. Edmund Morris, *The Rise of Theodore Roosevelt*, pp. 582–83.

32. Jones, *Honor in the Dust*, p. 12.

33. H. W. Brands, *American Colossus* (New York: Doubleday, 2010), p. 517.

34. McKinley cited in Morris, *The Rise of Theodore Roosevelt*, p. 627.

35. Thomas, *War Lovers*, pp. 336–37.

36. Buckley, *American Patriots*, p. 145.

37. Davis cited in Brands, *American Colossus*, p. 521.

38. Brands, *American Colossus*, p. 521.

39. Thomas, *War Lovers*, p. 337.

40. Buckley, *American Patriots*, p. 152.

41. Cited in Millett and Maslowski, *For the Common Defense*, p. 296.

42. Thomas, *War Lovers*, p. 343.

43. Brands, *American Colossus*, p. 522.

44. Cited in Karnow, *In Our Image*, p. 163.

45. Buckley, *American Patriots*, p. 140.

46. Morris, *The Rise of Theodore Roosevelt*, p. 592.

47. Ibid., p. 603.

48. Roosevelt cable cited in Brands, *American Colossus*, pp. 515–16.

49. Jones, *Honor in the Dust*, p. 42.

50. Linn, *The Philippine War*, p. 15.

51. "The Battle of Manila Bay, 1898," http://www.eyewitnesstohistory.com/manilabay
    .htm, accessed October 13, 1013.

52. Paul K. Davis, *100 Decisive Battles*, p. 342.

53. Cited in Karnow, *In Our Image*, p. 104.

54. Linn, *The Philippine War*, p. 19.

55. Ibid.

56. Karnow, *In Our Image*, p. 185.

57. William Safire, "Language: You Break It, You Own It, You Fix It," *New York
    Times*, October 18, 2004, http://www.nytimes.com/2004/10/17/arts/17iht-safi8
    .html, accessed December 31, 2013.

58. Millett and Maslowski, *For the Common Defense*, p. 298.

59. Karnow, *In Our Image*, p. 124.

60. Ibid., p. 174.

61. "William Howard Taft: Life Before the Presidency," Miller Center, University of Virginia, http://millercenter.org/academic/americanpresident/taft/essays/biography/2.

62. Karnow, *In Our Image*, p. 170.

63. Linn, *The Philippine War*, p. 215.

64. "Aguinaldo, 94, Dies; Led Filipino Revolts," *New York Times*, February 6, 1964, http://select.nytimes.com/gst/abstract.html?res=F40D14F83E5415738DDDAF0894DA405B848AF1D3, accessed January 24, 2014.

65. Kinzer, *Overthrow*, p. 55.

66. *New York Post*, cited in ibid., p. 54.

67. Senator Tillman cited in Edmund Morris, *Theodore Rex*, p. 55.

68. Morris, *Theodore Rex*, p. 79.

69. Ibid.

70. Taft testimony cited in Jones, *Honor in the Dust*, p. 273.

71. Karnow, *In Our Image*, p. 193.

72. James R. Arnold, *The Moro War*, p. 242.

73. Floyd Whaley, "Philippine Rebel Group Agrees to Peace Accord to End Violence in South," *New York Times*, October 7, 2012, http://www.nytimes.com/2012/10/08/world/asia/manila-and-rebel-group-take-step-toward-peace-plan.html, accessed January 24, 2014.

74. Floyd Whaley, "Rebel Rifts on Island Confound Philippines, *New York Times*, September 15, 2013, http://www.nytimes.com/2013/09/16/world/asia/rebel-rifts-on-island-confound-philippines.html, accessed January 24, 2014.

75. James Brooke, "U.S.-Philippine History Entwined in War Booty," *New York Times*, December 1, 1997.

76. Roosevelt cited in Millett and Maslowski, *For the Common Defense*, p. 316.

77. Buckley, *American Patriots*, p. 159.

78. "Black Sailors in the Great White Fleet, 1907–1909," Naval History Blog, U.S. Naval Institute, Naval History and Heritage Command, http://www.navalhistory.org/2011/02/01/black-sailors-in-the-great-white-fleet-1907-1909, accessed October 19, 2013.

79. Millett and Maslowski, *For the Common Defense*, pp. 341–42.

80. "The Great Pandemic: The United States in 1918–1919," United States Department of Health and Human Services, http://www.flu.gov/pandemic/history/1918/the_pandemic/index.html, accessed April 5, 2014.

81. Millett and Maslowski, *For the Common Defense*, pp. 375–76.

82. Franklin D. Roosevelt, "Pearl Harbor Speech," December 8, 1941, *FDR, American Experience*, PBS, http://www.pbs.org/wgbh/americanexperience/features/primary-resources/fdr-harbor/, accessed February 5, 2014.

## Chapter Four. Berlin Stories

1. Cited in Antony Beevor, *The Fall of Berlin 1945*, p. 146.
2. Dorothea von Schwanenfluegel Lawson, *Laughter Wasn't Rationed* (1999), cited in "The Battle of Berlin, 1945," http://www.eyewitnesstohistory.com/berlin.htm, accessed February 5, 2014.
3. General Whitelaw letter, cited in Michael Dobbs, *Six Months in 1945*, p. 347.
4. Dwight D. Eisenhower, speech, Ottawa, Canada, January 10, 1946, cited in Leonard Roy Frank, *Random House Webster's Quotationary* (New York: Random House, 1998), p. 913.
5. Andrew Roberts, *The Storm of War* (New York: Harper, 2011), p. 172.
6. Beevor, *The Fall of Berlin 1945*, p. 224.
7. Cited in Max Hastings, *Inferno*, p. 593.
8. Ibid., p. 601.
9. Beevor, *The Fall of Berlin 1945*, p. 224.
10. Anonymous, *A Woman in Berlin*, p. 20.
11. "The Bombing of Germany: Timeline of the Air War, 1939–1945," *American Experience*, PBS, http://www.pbs.org/wgbh/americanexperience/features/timeline/bombing/.
12. Anonymous, *A Woman in Berlin*, p. 17.
13. Cornelius Ryan, *The Last Battle*, pp. 417–18.
14. Frederick Taylor, *Dresden: Tuesday, February 13, 1945*, Appendix B: Counting the Dead; "Death Toll Debate: How Many Died in the Bombing of Dresden?," *Spiegel Online*, October 2, 2008, http://www.spiegel.de/international/germany/death-toll-debate-how-many-died-in-the-bombing-of-dresden-a-581992.html, accessed January 23, 2014.
15. Anonymous, *A Woman in Berlin*, p. 23.
16. Ibid., pp. 34–35.
17. Beevor, *The Fall of Berlin 1945*, p. 274.
18. Ibid., p. 285.
19. Hastings, *Inferno*, p. 530.
20. Ibid., p. 596.
21. Beevor, *The Fall of Berlin 1945*, p. 285.
22. Ibid., p. 336.

# Notes

23. Nicholas Best, *Five Days That Shocked the World: Eyewitness Accounts from Europe at the End of World War II* (New York: Thomas Dunne, 2011), p. 249.

24. Ibid., p. 17.

25. Antony Beevor, introduction to *A Woman in Berlin*, p. 2.

26. Hildegard Knef, *The Gift Horse* (1980), cited in Best, *Five Days That Shocked the World*, p. 16.

27. Erik Larson, *In the Garden of Beasts*, p. 56.

28. Hastings, *Inferno*, pp. 473–74.

29. Karl Deutmann, cited in Hastings, *Inferno*, pp. 476–77.

30. Beevor, *The Fall of Berlin 1945*, p. 23.

31. Hastings, *Inferno*, p. 472.

32. Anonymous, *A Woman in Berlin*, p. 73.

33. William L. Hitchcock, *The Bitter Road to Freedom*, p. 187.

34. Roberts, *The Storm of War*, p. 445.

35. Ibid., p. 194.

36. Hastings, *Inferno*, p. 468.

37. Roberts, *The Storm of War*, p. 432.

38. Rommel cited in ibid., p. 289.

39. Hastings, *Inferno*, p. 471.

40. Ryan, *The Last Battle*, pp. 15–16.

41. Best, *Five Days That Shocked the World*, p. 71.

42. Hastings, *Inferno*, pp. 488–89, 494–95.

43. Ibid., p. 152.

44. Antony Beevor, "They Raped Every German Female from Eight to 80," *Guardian*, April 30, 2002. Beevor also addresses this subject in *The Fall of Berlin 1945*.

45. Ibid.

46. "Fallen Hero: Charles Lindbergh in the 1940s," *American Experience*, PBS, http://www.pbs.org/wgbh/amex/lindbergh/sfeature/fallen.html, accessed April 5, 2014.

47. Franklin D. Roosevelt: "Campaign Address at Boston, Massachusetts," October 30, 1940, American Presidency Project, http://www.presidency.ucsb.edu/ws/?pid=15887, accessed April 5, 2014.

48. "Official Declarations of War by Congress," http://www.senate.gov/pagelayout/history/h_multi_sections_and_teasers/WarDeclarationsbyCongress.htm, accessed October 18, 2013.

49. For Eisenhower's views of the war plan, see Thomas E. Ricks, *The Generals*, p. 48.

50. "Scarred by History: The Rape of Nanjing," http://news.bbc.co.uk/2/hi/223038.stm, accessed February 4, 2014.

51. Roberts, *The Storm of War*, p. 275.
52. Ibid., p. 280.
53. Millett and Maslowski, *For the Common Defense*, p. 433.
54. Jean Edward Smith, *Eisenhower in War and Peace*, pp. 417–18.
55. Cited in Robert Service, *Stalin*, p. 473.
56. Ibid.
57. Smith, *Eisenhower in War and Peace*, p. 450.
58. Beevor, *The Fall of Berlin 1945*, p. 324.
59. John Keegan, *Intelligence in War*, p. 294.
60. Dobbs, *Six Months in 1945*, p. 241.
61. Ibid., p. 247.
62. Hitchcock, *The Bitter Road to Freedom*, p. 347.
63. Dobbs, *Six Months in 1945*, pp. 346–48.
64. Mary Louise Roberts, *What Soldiers Do: Sex and the American GI in World War II France* (Chicago: University of Chicago Press, 2013), p. 10.
65. Cited in Hitchcock, *The Bitter Road to Freedom*, p. 194.
66. Ibid., pp. 51–55.
67. Hastings, *Inferno*, p. 590.
68. Anonymous, *A Woman in Berlin*, pp. 307–8.
69. John Lewis Gaddis, *The Cold War*, p. 63.
70. Ibid., p. 65.
71. Dwight D. Eisenhower: "Address 'The Chance for Peace' Delivered Before the American Society of Newspaper Editors," April 16, 1953, American Presidency Project, http://www.presidency.ucsb.edu/ws/?pid=9819, accessed February 5, 2014.
72. Millett and Maslowski, *For the Common Defense*, pp. 494–95.
73. Fred Anderson and Andrew Cayton, *The Dominion of War*, p. 396.
74. Anthony Judt, *Postwar*, p. 91.
75. Morris J. MacGregor Jr., "Integration of the Armed Forces, 1940–1965," Defense Studies Series, Center of Military History, U.S. Army, Washington, D.C., 1985, http://www.history.army.mil/books/integration/IAF-FM.htm, accessed October 24, 2013.
76. "Military-Industrial Complex Speech, Dwight D. Eisenhower, 1961," http://avalon.law.yale.edu/20th_century/eisenhower001.asp.
77. Tim Weiner, *Legacy of Ashes*, p. 13.
78. Ibid., pp. 28–29.

79. Graham Allison, "The Cuban Missile Crisis at 50," *Foreign Affairs*, July/August 2012, http://www.foreignaffairs.com/articles/137679/graham-allison/the-cuban-missile -crisis-at-50, accessed April 6, 2014.

80. Ibid.

## Chapter Five. The "Living-Room War"

1. Cited in Millett and Maslowski, *For the Common Defense*, p. 570.

2. Michael Arlen, *Living-Room War*, p. 7.

3. Palmer cited in Ricks, *The Generals*, p. 218.

4. Albin Krebs, "Maxwell D. Taylor, Soldier and Envoy, Dies," *New York Times*, April 21, 1987, http://www.nytimes.com/1987/04/21/obituaries/maxwell-d-taylor-soldier -and-envoy-dies.html, accessed January 30, 2014.

5. George W. Smith, *The Siege at Hué*, p. 34.

6. Cited in ibid., p. 37.

7. Don Oberdorfer, *Tet!*, p. 198.

8. Ibid., p. 200.

9. Ibid., p. 202.

10. John Laurence, *The Cat from Hué*, p. 5.

11. Neil Sheehan, *A Bright Shining Lie*, pp. 717–18.

12. Oberdorfer, *Tet!*, p. 159; also cited in Douglas Brinkley, *Cronkite*, p. 367.

13. James S. Robbins, *This Time We Win*, p. 188.

14. Ernest C. Cheatham cited in ibid., p. 190.

15. Michael Herr, *Dispatches*, p. 73.

16. Ibid., p. 83.

17. Ibid., p. 81.

18. Nick Turse, *Kill Anything That Moves*, pp. 103–4.

19. Arlen, *Living-Room War*, p. 8.

20. Brinkley, *Cronkite*, p. 367.

21. Ricks, *The Generals*, p. 232.

22. Stanley Karnow, *Vietnam*, p. 361.

23. James H. Willbanks, "Winning the Battle, Losing the War," *New York Times*, March 5, 2008, http://www.nytimes.com/2008/03/05/opinion/05willbanks.html?_r=0, accessed October 25, 2013.

24. Westmoreland cited in Karnow, *Vietnam*, p. 527.

25. Ibid., pp. 525–26.

26. LeMay cited in ibid., p. 415; "Gen. Curtis LeMay, an Architect of Strategic Air Power, Dies at 83," *New York Times*, October 2, 1990, http://www.nytimes.com/1990/10/02/obituaries/gen-curtis-lemay-an-architect-of-strategic-air-power-dies-at-83.html, accessed January 30, 2014.

27. Brinkley, *Cronkite*, p. 372.

28. James Mueller, "Tet Offensive: Battle for Hué," *Vietnam*, February 1997, http://www.historynet.com/tet-offensive-battle-for-hue.htm, accessed October 25, 2013.

29. Sheehan, *A Bright Shining Lie*, p. 719.

30. Smith, *The Siege at Hué*, p. ix.

31. Karnow, *Vietnam*, p. 543.

32. Turse, *Kill Anything That Moves*, p. 102.

33. Sheehan, *A Bright Shining Lie*, p. 720.

34. Robbins, *This Time We Win*, p. 196.

35. Laurence, *The Cat from Hué*, p. 28.

36. Brinkley, *Cronkite*, p. 372.

37. Laurence, *The Cat from Hué*, p. 41.

38. Cited in Robbins, *This Time We Win*, p. 194.

39. Ho Chi Minh telegram to President Truman, February 28, 1946, National Archives, http://media.nara.gov/media/images/37/6/37-0573a.gif, accessed January 24, 2014.

40. Ricks, *The Generals*, p. 222.

41. Eisenhower cited in Smith, *Eisenhower in War and Peace*, pp. 614–15.

42. Ricks, *The Generals*, p. 223.

43. Karnow, *Vietnam*, p. 255.

44. Ibid., p. 464.

45. Ibid.

46. Ibid., p. 294.

47. Weiner, *Legacy of Ashes*, p. 242.

48. Ibid., p. 243.

49. Karnow, *Vietnam*, pp. 464, 390.

50. Weiner, *Legacy of Ashes*, pp. 279–80.

51. Ibid., p. 280.

52. Karnow, *Vietnam*, pp. 464, 392.

53. Ibid., pp. 464, 390.

54. Brinkley, *Cronkite*, p. 377.

55. Ibid., pp. 377–78.

56. Ibid., pp. 379–80.

57. Robert Dallek, *Flawed Giant*, p. 506.

58. Tim Weiner, "Robert S. McNamara, Architect of a Futile War, Dies at 93," *New York Times*, July 6, 2009, http://www.nytimes.com/2009/07/07/us/07mcnamara .html?pagewanted=1&ref=robertsmcnamara, accessed January 4, 2014.

59. Dallek, *Flawed Giant*, p. 523.

60. Boot, *Savage Wars of Peace*, pp. 308–9.

61. Truong Nhu Tang, *A Viet Cong Memoir*, p. 192.

62. Weiner, *Legacy of Ashes*, p. 332.

63. "Tet Offensive: Turning Point in Vietnam War," *New York Times*, January 31, 1988, http://www.nytimes.com/1988/01/31/world/tet-offensive-turning-point-in-vietnam -war.html, accessed October 25, 2013.

64. Karnow, *Vietnam*, pp. 464, 558.

65. Neil Sheehan interview with C-SPAN, cited in Brinkley, *Cronkite*, p. 381.

66. James H. Willbanks, *The Tet Offensive*, p. 117.

67. Turse, *Kill Anything That Moves*, p. 104.

68. Truong Nhu Tang, *Memoirs*, p. 154.

69. Willbanks, *The Tet Offensive*, p. 103.

70. Dallek, *Flawed Giant*, p. 586.

71. Ibid., p. 591.

72. Flora Lewis, "Tho Rejects Nobel Prize," *New York Times*, October 24, 1973.

73. Weiner, *Legacy of Ashes*, p. 386.

74. Millett and Maslowski, *For the Common Defense*, p. 616.

75. Ibid., p. 608.

76. Weiner, *Legacy of Ashes*, pp. 454–55.

77. Vincent Canby, review of *Heartbreak Ridge*, *New York Times*, December 5, 1986, http:// www.nytimes.com/movie/review?res=9a0de4db113af936a35751c1a960948260, accessed April 7, 2014.

78. John H. Cushman Jr., "Pentagon Study Faults Planning on Grenada," *New York Times*, July 12, 1986, http://www.nytimes.com/1986/07/12/world/pentagon-study -faults-planning-on-grenada.html, accessed April 7, 2014.

79. "Terrorist Attacks on Americans, 1979–1988," "Target America," *Frontline*, PBS, October 4, 2001, http://www.pbs.org/wgbh/pages/frontline/shows/target/etc/ cron.html, accessed April 7, 2014.

80. Weiner, *Legacy of Ashes*, p. 465.

# Notes

## Chapter Six. The Bridge over the River Euphrates

1. Abdulrazzaq al-Saiedi, "The Bridge," *New York Times Magazine*, March 17, 2013.
2. Willy Wold interview, cited in Kevin Sites, *The Things They Cannot Say*, p. 37.
3. Ivey quoted in *Washington Post*, cited in Thomas E. Ricks, *The Gamble*, p. 10.
4. Cited in Jeremy Scahill, *Blackwater*, p. 18.
5. Ibid., p. 48.
6. Richard A. Oppel Jr., "Fallujah's Fall Stuns Marines Who Fought There," *New York Times*, January 9, 2014.
7. George Packer, *The Assassins' Gate*, p. 190.
8. Sean Flynn, "The Day the War Turned," *GQ*, October 2006, http://www.gq.com/news-politics/big-issues/200610/fallujah-private-contractors-lawsuit, accessed December 2, 2013.
9. Scahill, *Blackwater*, pp. 182–85.
10. Thomas Ricks, *Fiasco*, p. 331.
11. Bing West, *No True Glory*, p. 6.
12. Ibid., p. 167.
13. Flynn, "The Day the War Turned."
14. Peter Baker, *Days of Fire*, p. 321.
15. West, *No True Glory*, p. 6.
16. Scahill, *Blackwater*, p. 168.
17. al-Saiedi, "The Bridge."
18. Flynn, "The Day the War Turned."
19. Ibid.
20. Robert D. Kaplan, *Imperial Grunts*, p. 355.
21. Ricks, *Fiasco*, p. 332.
22. Flynn, "The Day the War Turned."
23. Baker, *Days of Fire*, p. 321.
24. Kaplan, *Imperial Grunts*, p. 354.
25. Ricks, *Fiasco*, pp. 338–39.
26. Ibid., pp. 340–41.
27. White House news release, March 31, 2004, cited in Scahill, *Blackwater*, p. 170.
28. Colin Powell, "U.S. Forces: Challenges Ahead," *Foreign Affairs*, Winter 1992/93, http://www.cfr.org/world/us-forces-challenges-ahead/p7508, accessed April 8, 2014.
29. Brent Scowcroft and George H. W. Bush, *A World Transformed* (New York: Knopf, 1998), p. 489.

30. Gideon Rose, *How Wars End*, p. 235.

31. "The Gulf War: How Many Iraqis Died?," *Frontline*, PBS, January 9, 1995, http://www.pbs.org/wgbh/pages/frontline/gulf/appendix/death.html, accessed January 7, 2014.

32. Jeremy Scahill, *Dirty Wars*, pp. 14–15.

33. Ricks, *The Generals*, p. 398.

34. Peter L. Bergen, *Manhunt*, pp. 48–49.

35. Kurt Eichenwald, *500 Days*, p. 184.

36. General Franks cited in Bergen, *Manhunt*, p. 49.

37. Ibid., p. 48.

38. Summary of National Security Strategy on the United States, http://georgewbush-whitehouse.archives.gov/nsc/nss/2006/print/sectionV.html, accessed April 8, 2014.

39. Colin S. Gray, "The Implications of Preemptive and Preventive War Doctrines: A Reconsideration," Strategic Studies Institute, July 2007, http://www.strategicstudiesinstitute.army.mil/, accessed April 8, 2014.

40. "The Bush Doctrine," editorial, *New York Times*, September 22, 2002, http://www.nytimes.com/2002/09/22/opinion/the-bush-doctrine.html, accessed April 8, 2014.

41. Phillip Knightley, *The First Casualty*, p. 532.

42. Eric Schmitt, "Pentagon Contradicts General on Iraq Occupation's Force Size," *New York Times*, February 28, 2003, http://www.nytimes.com/2003/02/28/us/threats-responses-military-spending-pentagon-contradicts-general-iraq-occupation.html, accessed January 25, 2014.

43. Baker, *Days of Fire*, pp. 248–49.

44. Ricks, *The Generals*, p. 403.

45. Packer, *The Assassins' Gate*, pp. 140–41.

46. Bob Woodward, *Plan of Attack*, p. 433.

47. Tim Arango, "Early Backer of War, Finally Within Grasp of Power," *New York Times*, March 19, 2010, http://www.nytimes.com/2010/03/20/world/middleeast/20chalabi.html; James Risen and David Johnston, "Chalabi Reportedly Told Iran That U.S. Had Code," *New York Times*, June 2, 2004, http://www.nytimes.com/2004/06/02/world/the-reach-of-war-the-offense-chalabi-reportedly-told-iran-that-us-had-code.html, accessed April 8, 2014.

48. Laura Miller, "'Arrows of the Night': The Man Behind the Iraq War," *Salon*, December 4, 2011, http://www.salon.com/2011/12/05/arrows_of_the_night_the_man_behind_the_iraq_war/, accessed April 8, 2014.

49. Ricks, *Fiasco*, p. 154.

50. Packer, *The Assassins' Gate*, p. 147.

51. Paul Krugman, What Went Wrong?," *New York Times*, April 23, 2004, http://www.nytimes.com/2004/04/23/opinion/what-went-wrong.html, accessed January 7, 2014.

52. Bush cited in Packer, *The Assassins' Gate*, p. 145.

53. Kinzer, *Overthrow*, p. 311.

54. Ricks, *The Generals*, p. 411.

55. Packer, *The Assassins' Gate*, p. 222.

56. Michael R. Gordon and Bernard E. Trainor, *Endgame*, p. 23.

57. James Mattis cited in ibid., p. 61.

58. Kaplan, *Imperial Grunts*, p. 361.

59. Baker, *Days of Fire*, p. 322.

60. Kaplan, *Imperial Grunts*, pp. 368–69.

61. Baker, *Days of Fire*, p. 322.

62. Ibid., p. 320.

63. Dan Senor cited in Ricks, *Fiasco*, p. 335.

64. General Stanley McChrystal, *My Share of the Task*, p. 131.

65. Sites, *The Things They Cannot Say*, p. 26.

66. Packer, *The Assassins' Gate*, p. 298.

67. Sites, *The Things They Cannot Say*, p. 28.

68. Ibid., p. 9ff.

69. Alex Chadwick, "No Court-Martial for Marine Taped Killing Unarmed Iraqi," National Public Radio, May 10, 2005, http://www.npr.org/templates/story/story.php?storyId=4646406, accessed February 1, 2014; "U.S. Probes Shooting at Fallujah Mosque," NBCnews.com, Updated 11/6/2004, http://www.nbcnews.com/id/6496898/#.U86Bi1b_Reh; David Hancock, "No Charges in Fallujah Shooting," CBSNews.com, May 4, 2005, http://www.cbsnews.com/news/no-charges-in-fallujah-shooting/.

70. Scahill, *Blackwater*, p. 286.

71. Ibid.

72. Ricks, *The Gamble*, pp. 8–9.

73. Bob Woodward, "Why Did Violence Plummet? It Wasn't Just the Surge," *Washington Post*, September 8, 2008, http://www.washingtonpost.com/wp-dyn/content/article/2008/09/07/AR2008090701847.html; also detailed in Bob Woodward, *The War Within*.

74. Andrew Bacevich, "Avoiding Defeat," *New York Times*, February 8, 2013, http://www
.nytimes.com/2013/02/10/books/review/the-endgame-and-my-share-of-the-task
.html?ref=stanleyamcchrystal, accessed January 7, 2014.

75. Joseph Neff and Jay Price, "Fallujah Ambush Report Is Harsh," *Raleigh News and
Observer*, September 28, 2007, http://www.newsobserver.com/2007/09/28/33752/
fallujah-ambush-report-is-harsh.html, accessed February 4, 2014.

76. James Risen, "Blackwater Chief at Nexus of Military and Business," *New York
Times*, October 8, 2007, http://www.nytimes.com/2007/10/08/washington/08prince
.html, accessed January 30, 2014.

77. Andrew Bacevich, *Breach of Trust*, p. 127.

78. "'Way of the Knife' Explains CIA Shift from Spying to Killing," National Public Radio, April 9, 2013, http://www.npr.org/2013/04/09/176172590/way-of-the
-knife-explains-cia-shift-from-spying-to-killing, accessed February 1, 2014.

79. Mark Mazzetti, *The Way of the Knife*, pp. 122–23.

80. Scahill, *Blackwater*, p. 46.

81. Bacevich, *Breach of Trust*, p. 127.

82. "Executive Summary of Private Military Contractors in Iraq: An Examination
of Blackwater's Actions in Fallujah," http://oversight-archive.waxman.house.gov/
documents/20070927104643.pdf.

83. Neff and Price, "Fallujah Ambush Report Is Harsh."

84. John M. Broder, "Report Says Firm Sought to Cover Up Iraq Shootings," *New
York Times*, October 2, 2007, http://www.nytimes.com/2007/10/02/washington/
02blackwater.html?pagewanted=1&ref=washington, accessed February 4, 2014.

85. John M. Broder, "Chief of Blackwater Defends His Employees," *New York Times*,
October 3, 2007, http://www.nytimes.com/2007/10/02/washington/02blackwater
.html?pagewanted=1&ref=washington, accessed February 4, 2014.

86. Ricks, *Fiasco*, p. 115.

87. Tuchman, *The March of Folly*, p. 7.

88. Asjylyn Loder, "Chuck E. Cheese Enlists Gen. Franks," *Tampa Bay Times*, April
2, 2008, http://www.tampabay.com/news/business/chuck-e-cheese-enlists-gen
-franks/440862, accessed February 5, 2014.

89. Baker, *Days of Fire*, p. 369.

90. Uwe E. Reinhardt, "How Efficient Is Private Charity?," *New York Times*, January
14, 2011, http://economix.blogs.nytimes.com/2011/01/14/how-efficient-is-private
-charity/, accessed February 5, 2014; Philip Rucker, "Chief of Veterans Charities
Grilled on Groups' Giving," *Washington Post*, January 18, 2008, http://www.washington

post.com/wp-dyn/content/article/2008/01/17/AR2008011703620.html, accessed February 5, 2014.

91. Mark Mazzetti, "KKR Hires Petraeus to Lead Institute," *New York Times*, May 30, 2013, http://dealbook.nytimes.com/2013/05/30/k-k-r-hires-petraeus/?ref=davidhpetraeus, accessed January 7, 2014.

92. Michael Hastings, "The Runaway General," *Rolling Stone*, June 22, 2010, http://www.rollingstone.com/politics/news/the-runaway-general-20100622, accessed December 3, 2013.

93. "President Obama on Afghanistan, General McChrystal & General Petraeus," The White House blog, June 23, 2010, http://www.whitehouse.gov/blog/2010/06/23/president-obama-afghanistan-general-mcchrystal-general-petraeus, accessed February 5, 2014.

94. McChrystal, *My Share of the Task*, p. 390.

95. Stanley McChrystal, "Why America Needs National Service," *Newsweek*, January 23, 2011, http://www.newsweek.com/mcchrystal-why-america-needs-national-service-66925, accessed April 8, 2014.

96. Mark Mazzetti and Emily B. Hager, "Secret Desert Force Set Up by Blackwater's Founder," *New York Times*, May 14, 2011, http://www.nytimes.com/2011/05/15/world/middleeast/15prince.html?pagewanted=all, accessed January 30, 2014.

97. al-Saiedi, "The Bridge."

98. Sites, *The Things They Cannot Say*, pp. 52–54.

99. Duraid Adnan, "Attacks Across Iraq Kill Dozens," *New York Times*, November 13, 2013.

100. Yasir Ghazi and Tim Arango, "Qaeda-Linked Militants in Iraq Secure Nearly Full Control of Fallujah," *New York Times*, January 3, 2014; "Iraq Fighters, Qaeda Allies Claim Fallujah as New State," *New York Times*, January 4, 2014.

101. Oppel, "Fallujah's Fall Stuns Marines Who Fought There."

102. Ibid.

## Afterword

1. Gates cited in Thom Shanker, "After Years at War, the Army Adapts to Garrison Life," *New York Times*, January 18, 2014, http://www.nytimes.com/2014/01/19/us/after-years-at-war-the-army-adapts-to-garrison-life.html, accessed February 6, 2014.

2. Mazzetti, *The Way of the Knife*, p. 5.

3. President Barack Obama, "State of the Union Address," January 28, 2014, http://swampland.time.com/2014/01/28/full-text-of-obamas-2014-state-of-the-union/#ixzz2rw3hVjIR, accessed February 6, 2014.

4. "Transcript of Final 2012 Presidential Debate," CBS News, October 23, 2012, http://www.cbsnews.com/news/transcript-of-final-2012-presidential-debate/5/, accessed February 11, 2014.

5. Denise Chow, "Military's 'Iron Man' Suit to Be Ready to Test This Summer," CBS News, http://www.cbsnews.com/news/militarys-iron-man-suit-may-be-ready-to-test-this-summer/, accessed February 20, 2014.

6. Elisabeth Bumiller and Thom Shanker, "Pentagon Is Set to Lift Combat Ban for Women," *New York Times*, January 23, 2013.

7. Shanker, "After Years at War, the Army Adapts to Garrison Life."

8. Thom Shanker, "Waging War on a Shoestring," *New York Times*, November 19, 2013, http://atwar.blogs.nytimes.com/2013/11/19/waging-war-on-a-shoestring/, accessed February 6, 2014.

9. H. R. McMaster, "The Pipe Dream of Easy War," *New York Times*, July 20, 2013.

10. Thom Shanker, "Pentagon Releases Strategy for Arctic," *New York Times*, November 22, 2013, http://www.nytimes.com/2013/11/23/world/pentagon-releases-strategy-for-arctic.html, accessed February 6, 2014.

11. James Dao and Andrew W. Lehren, "Baffling Rise in Suicides Plagues the U.S. Military," *New York Times*, May 15, 2013, http://www.nytimes.com/2013/05/16/us/baffling-rise-in-suicides-plagues-us-military.html?pagewanted=all, accessed February 6, 2014.

12. "Veteran Homelessness," U.S. Department of Veterans Affairs, Office of Public and Intergovernmental Affairs, http://www.va.gov/opa/issues/Homelessness.asp, accessed February 6, 2014.

13. Jennifer Steinhauer, "Reports of Military Sexual Assault Rise Sharply," *New York Times*, November 7, 2013, http://www.nytimes.com/2013/11/07/us/reports-of-military-sexual-assault-rise-sharply.html, accessed February 6, 2014.

14. Bacevich, *Breach of Trust*, p. 14.

15. Karl Marlantes, *What It Is Like to Go to War*, p. 256.

16. John Stuart Mill, "The Contest in America," *Fraser's Magazine*, February 1862, reprinted in *Dissertations and Discussions*, vol. 1 (Boston: Little, Brown, 1862), p. 31, http://books.google.com/books?id=Bi4s1I2QGycC&q=war+is+an+ugly+thing#v=onepage&q&f=false, accessed January 9, 2014.

# Index

# Index

in Vietnam, 251, 273, 276, 283
  waterboarding, 153n
Chaffee, Adna Romanza, 150–51
Chalabi, Ahmad, 325–26
Charles III of Spain, 42
Charleston, Battle of, 64–65
Cheatham, Ernest C., 260, 269–70
Cheney, Dick, 315, 323, 339
Chennault, Anna, 287–88
Chennault, Claire Lee, 287
Chernow, Ron, 58, 62n, 66, 72, 73, 80
Cheyenne Indians, 134, 135
Chickamauga, Battle of, 178
China, 198, 272
  Boxer Rebellion, 142, 150, 154, 178
  Cold War and, 237, 238, 239
  Nanking Massacre, 222
  USS Panay incident, 222
Cholera, 146
Church, Frank, 290
Churchill, Winston
  on atomic weapons, 238
  on the Iron Curtain, 236
  Japan and, 221–22, 223–24
  Potsdam Conference, 198, 228–29, 231
  Yalta Conference, 198, 226, 227–28, 234,
    235–36
"Citizen-soldiers," 16, 33. See also Militias
City Point, Virginia, 112–13
Civil rights movement, 244
Civil War. See American Civil War
Claiborne, Herbert, 125
Clark, Al, 339–40
Cleveland, Grover, 137, 151, 158
Clifford, Clark, 253
Climate change, 354
Clinton, Bill, 295, 296
Clinton, Henry, 32, 34–37, 39, 41, 44, 48–49,
    63–64, 75
Cmuda, Hannelore von, 214
Coalition to Support America's Heroes, 343–44
Coates, Ta-Nehisi, 20
Cobb, David, 31
Cold Harbor, Battle of, 91, 94, 104, 110–11, 115–16
Cold War, 231–43, 246–47, 291–94, 313–14
Colleton, John, 37–38
Collins, James, Jr., 244
Colonial America, militia service in, 14–15
Colored Troops, U.S. (USCT), 93, 98–99, 104–5,
    113–14, 117–20, 127–28
Colston, Raleigh, 99–100
Common Sense (Paine), 61, 65
Concentration camps, 158, 215
Concord, Battle of, 23, 26
Conein, Lucien, 276
Confiscation Act of 1862, 90, 105

Connell, Thomas, 145–49
Conscription, 51, 53, 90, 220
Conscription Act of 1863, 90
Constitution, U.S., 15–16, 16n, 71, 82–84, 289
Constitutional Convention, 17, 71
Continental Army, 15, 61–62, 64–65
  Battle of Yorktown, 25–33
  battles in New York, 23–24, 34–36
  Washington assumes control, 33–34, 52–53, 54
Continental Congress, 23, 33, 41, 60–61, 80–81
Continental Navy, 16, 74
Contrabands, 105
Cornwallis, Charles, 36–40, 68
  Battle of Yorktown, 24, 32, 40, 44, 46–49,
    57–58
Cowpens, Battle of, 24
Crandall, Tom, 139–40
Crater, Battle of the, 118–23
Cristóbal Colón (Spanish cruiser), 164–65
Cronkite (Brinkley), 267, 270, 280, 281
Cronkite, Walter, 5, 263, 266–67, 270, 279–81,
    284–85
"Cross of Iron" speech, 238
Crusade in Europe (Eisenhower), 229n
Cuba
  American Revolution and, 42–43
  Bay of Pigs Invasion, 246, 264
  Spanish-American War and, 151, 161–65
Cuban Missile Crisis (1962), 246–47
Cuban War of Independence, 156–60, 186
Cushman, John H., Jr., 294–95
Custer, George Armstrong, 131–32, 135, 149–50
Custis, Daniel Parke, 69–70
Custis, John Parke ("Jackie"), 69–70
Czechoslovakia, 195, 218–19

Dade, Francis, 149n
Daimler-Benz, 201
Dallek, Robert, 281, 282, 287–88
Da Nang, Vietnam, 252
Danzig, Poland, 219
Daughan, George C., 50
Davis, Benjamin O., Jr., 201, 201n
Davis, Burke, 67–68
Davis, Jefferson, 91, 102, 103–4, 128
Davis, Richard Harding, 162
D-Day invasion (1944), 197, 213n, 215
Declaration of Independence, 23, 53
Defense Department (Pentagon), 242–45
  budget sequestration of 2013, 353–54
De Grasse, François Joseph Paul, Comte, 36, 40,
    41–43
Demandowsky, Ewald von, 202–3, 207–8
Democratic National Convention (1968), 5, 287
Democratic Republic of Vietnam (DRV), 272
Denmark, 219, 241, 354

# Index

# Index

# Index

# Index

# Index